Twelfth Night

This volume in the Shakespeare Criticism series offers a range of approaches to *Twelfth Night*, including its critical reception, performance history, and relation to early modern culture.

James Schiffer's extensive introduction surveys the play's critical reception and performance history, while individual essays explore a variety of topics relevant to a full appreciation of the play: early modern notions of love, friendship, sexuality, madness, festive ritual, exoticism, social mobility, and detection. The contributors approach these topics from a variety of perspectives, such as new critical, new historicist, cultural materialist, feminist and queer theory, and performance criticism, occasionally combining several approaches within a single essay.

The new essays from leading figures in the field explore and extend the key debates surrounding *Twelfth Night*, creating the ideal book for readers approaching this text for the first time or wishing to further their knowledge of this stimulating, much loved play.

Contributors: Christa Jansohn, Ivo Kamps, Marcela Kostihová, Cynthia Lewis, Catherine Lisak, Laurie E. Osborne, Patricia Parker, Elizabeth Pentland, Alan W. Powers, Nathalie Rivère de Carles, David Schalkwyk, James Schiffer, Bruce R. Smith, Goran V. Stanivuković, Jennifer C. Vaught.

James Schiffer is Professor of English and Dean of the College of Liberal Arts and Sciences at the State University of New York, New Paltz.

Shakespeare Criticism
Philip C. Kolin, *General Editor*

Romeo and Juliet
Critical Essays
Edited by John F. Andrews

Coriolanus
Critical Essays
Edited by David Wheeler

Titus Andronicus
Critical Essays
Edited by Philip C. Kolin

Love's Labour's Lost
Critical Essays
Edited by Felicia Hardison Londré

The Winter's Tale
Critical Essays
Edited by Maurice Hunt

Two Gentlemen of Verona
Critical Essays
Edited by June Schlueter

Venus and Adonis
Critical Essays
Edited by Philip C. Kolin

As You Like It: from 1600 to the Present
Critical Essays
Edited by Edward Tomarken

The Comedy of Errors
Critical Essays
Edited by Robert S. Miola

A Midsummer Night's Dream
Critical Essays
Edited by Dorothea Kehler

Shakespeare's Sonnets
Critical Essays
Edited by James Schiffer

Henry VI
Critical Essays
Edited by Thomas A. Pendleton

The Tempest
Critical Essays
Edited by Patrick M. Murphy

Pericles
Critical Essays
Edited by David Skeele

The Taming of the Shrew
Critical Essays
Edited by Dana E. Aspinall

The Merchant of Venice
New Critical Essays
Edited by John W. Mahon and Ellen Macleod Mahon

Hamlet
New Critical Essays
Edited by Arthur F. Kinney

Othello
New Critical Essays
Edited by Philip C. Kolin

Julius Caesar
New Critical Essays
Edited by Horst Zander

Antony and Cleopatra
New Critical Essays
Edited by Sara M. Deats

All's Well, That Ends Well
New Critical Essays
Edited by Gary Waller

Macbeth
New Critical Essays
Edited by Nick Moschovakis

King Lear
New Critical Essays
Edited by Jeffrey Kahan

Twelfth Night
New Critical Essays
Edited by James Schiffer

Twelfth Night

New Critical Essays

Edited by James Schiffer

Shakespeare Criticism Volume 34

LONDON AND NEW YORK

First published 2011
by Routledge
2 Park Square, Milton Park, Abingdon, OX14 4RN

Simultaneously published in the USA and Canada
by Routledge
270 Madison Ave, New York, NY 10016

Routledge is an imprint of the Taylor & Francis Group, an informa business

Typeset in Times New Roman by
The Running Head Limited, Cambridge, www.therunninghead.com
Printed and bound in Great Britain by
CPI Rowe, Chippenham, Wiltshire

British Library Cataloguing in Publication Data
A catalogue record for this book is available from the British Library

Library of Congress Cataloging in Publication Data
Twelfth night: new critical essays / edited by James Schiffer. — 1st ed.
p. cm. — (Shakespeare criticism)
Includes bibliographical references and index.
1. Shakespeare, William, 1564–1616. Twelfth night. I. Schiffer, James.
PR2837.T95 2011
822.3'3—dc22

2010030386

ISBN: 978–0–415–97335–9 (hbk)

For Pamela

Contents

Figures

Acknowledgments

We live in a great age for the study and performance of Shakespeare's works. His plays, translated into countless languages, are performed in growing numbers on amateur and professional stages around the world. Scholarly articles and books proliferate at a remarkable pace. Certainly *Twelfth Night* has had its share of critical and theatrical attention in recent times, and in writing my introduction I have profited greatly from a number of earlier surveyors of the play's history in criticism and in the theatre. Most of these debts are acknowledged as they arise in the pages that follow; however, here I would like to recognize a more general debt to the following scholars for their outstanding work on *Twelfth Night*: J. M. Lothian and T. W. Craik, Roger Warren and Stanley Wells, Lois Potter, Penny Gay, Ralph Berry, Karen Greif, Anne Barton, John R. Ford, Paul Edmondson, Michael Billington, and Keir Elam. I am also deeply indebted to earlier studies on *Twelfth Night* by several contributors to this volume, especially Laurie E. Osborne's *The Trick of Singularity*, Bruce R. Smith's *Twelfth Night: Texts and Contexts*, Cynthia Lewis's *Particular Saints*, and David Schalkwyk's *Speech and Performance in Shakespeare's Sonnets and Plays* and *Shakespeare, Love and Service*. It is an honor to have these distinguished scholars represented in these pages. To all my contributors I owe a tremendous debt for their wonderfully erudite, perceptive essays and their timely responses to my email queries and requests. Despite their slow-moving editor, they have been Patience on a monument, and I hope now that all of them are smiling with relief.

I began this project while serving as Head of the English Department at Northern Michigan University, and I am grateful to my colleagues there, especially to Terry Seethoff, former Dean of the College of Arts and Sciences, for his steady support of my scholarship through the years. I am also grateful for a summer fellowship at the Folger Shakespeare Library in 2006. The library staff there, as always, was helpful and gracious in every way. Since coming to the State University of New York at New Paltz in 2008, I have profited from many conversations Shakespearean with Tom Olsen, Cyrus Mulready, Frank Kraat, Tom Festa, and Frank Trezza. To my editors at Routledge/Taylor & Francis I also owe great thanks for their patience and professionalism. Commissioning Editor Polly Dodson and Senior Editorial

Assistant Emma Nugent have been my primary contacts in recent years; their good natured persistence and careful attention to detail have been invaluable. I am grateful as well to Carole Drummond of The Running Head Limited for her careful shepherding of the manuscript through the production process. Series editor Philip Kolin has offered generous support at every step of the way. I am in awe of his inexhaustible energy and many scholarly accomplishments. I owe a debt as well to Shakespearean colleagues Laury Magnus, Anthony DiMatteo, Marvin Hunt, David Bevington, Richard Strier, Valerie Wayne, Joe Wagner, Susan Baker, Joyce Sutphen, Walter Cannon, Kate Narveson, Michael Schoenfeldt, Valerie Traub, and the late Mark Taylor for their warm support and encouragement through the years. To long-time friend Dorothea Kehler, I owe great thanks for her help with this collection and for her inspiration. Finally, I am grateful to many friends – especially to Debbie Morris, Steve Shapiro, Matt Shapiro, Richard Stern, Alane Rolllins, Lizzie and Robby Ross, Genevive DiChellis, and Sam Kelly, as well as to my daughter, Tanja, my son, Toby (Sir Toby), and my grandchildren, Addison and Sam. Their love and encouragement have long sustained me through the wind and the rain.

Contributors

Christa Jansohn is Professor of British Culture and Director of the Centre for British Studies at the University of Bamberg, Germany. She completed her PhD and Habilitation at Bonn University. Since then she has spent semesters at the Humboldt University, Berlin and Cambridge, as well as at the Folger Shakespeare Library, Washington, DC, and the Harry Ransom Center, Austin, Texas.

Ivo Kamps is Professor of English at the University of Mississippi. He is the author of *Historiography and Ideology in Stuart Drama* (1996), and the editor of several collections and editions. He is the Early Modern Cultural Studies series co-editor with Jean Howard for Palgrave, and co-editor of *Early Modern Ecostudies* (2008).

Marcela Kostihová is an Associate Professor of English and co-director of Collaborative Research at Hamline University, Minnesota. She researches the intersections between post-communist appropriations of Shakespeare and national identity construction in Eastern Europe, particularly the Czech Republic.

Cynthia Lewis, Charles A. Dana Professor of English at Davidson College, North Carolina, has published many articles on Shakespeare's plays, particularly the comedies, and a book, *Particular Saints: Shakespeare's Four Antonios, Their Contexts, and Their Plays*. She is currently writing a book on sports and Shakespeare, and she publishes both personal and reported essays, often on American culture and sometimes on crime.

Catherine Lisak is a full Professor at the University of Bordeaux III. Her thesis was on "Treason in Shakespeare's Histories" (1999, University of Paris VII – Charles V). She has written many articles on Shakespeare, is the editor of *Richard II* for the Internet Shakespeare Editions, and is currently working on George Puttenham, characterization in early modern drama, and the staging of animality.

Laurie E. Osborne is the NEH/Class of 1940 Distinguished Professor of the Humanities at Colby College, Maine. She has published *The Trick of*

Singularity: Twelfth Night and the Performance Editions (1996) and several articles on Shakespearean performance, most recently "Speculations on Shakespearean Cinematic Liveness" (*Shakespeare Bulletin*, 2006), and "A Local Habitation and a Name: Television and Shakespeare" (*Shakespeare Survey* 62).

Patricia Parker is Margery Bailey Professor of English at Stanford University, author most recently of *Shakespeare from the Margins* and co-editor of anthologies including *Women, "Race," and Writing in the Early Modern Period*. She is editor of the new five-volume *Shakespeare Encyclopedia* and at work on several new books as well as Norton Critical Editions of *Twelfth Night* and *Much Ado About Nothing*.

Elizabeth Pentland is Assistant Professor of English at York University in Toronto. She is co-author, with Patricia Parker, of the "Introduction to Illyria" for the Norton Critical Edition of *Twelfth Night*. Her essay on Jacobean representations of Elizabeth I appeared in *Resurrecting Elizabeth I in the Seventeenth Century*, and her current book project examines Elizabethan and Jacobean writing about France.

Alan W. Powers, an Emeritus Professor at Bristol Community College in Massachusetts, has written two books on science and literature, *Birdtalk* (2004) and *The Worlds of Giordano Bruno* (2010). His Shakespeare articles, particularly on law and oral culture, have grown out of a dozen national fellowships and grants, eight from the National Endowment for the Humanities.

Nathalie Rivère de Carles is a Junior Lecturer in Renaissance Studies at the University of Toulouse II Le Mirail. Her current work focuses on the semiotics of props and theatre history as well as the expression and the impact of suffering in early modern culture. She has published articles in *Cahiers Elisabéthains* and *Anglophonia* and in various collections of essays.

David Schalkwyk is Director of Research at the Folger Shakespeare Library, and editor of *Shakespeare Quarterly*. He also holds a position as Professor of English at the University of Cape Town. His books include *Speech and Performance in Shakespeare's Sonnets and Plays* (2002), *Literature and the Touch of the Real* (2004), and *Shakespeare, Love and Service* (2008).

James Schiffer is Dean of the College of Liberal Arts and Sciences at the State University of New York at New Paltz. In addition to publishing essays on various Shakespearean plays and poems, he is the editor of *Shakespeare's Sonnets: Critical Essays* (1999). He is also the creator/director of *Sonnet Variations*, distributed by Films for the Humanities and Sciences.

Bruce R. Smith is Dean's Professor of English at the University of Southern California. A former president of the Shakespeare Association of

America, he is the author of five books on Shakespeare and early modern culture, most recently *The Key of Green* (2009) and *Phenomenal Shakespeare* (2010), and is general editor of the Cambridge World Shakespeare project.

Goran V. Stanivuković is an Associate Professor of English at Saint Mary's University, Canada. He has published a critical edition of Emanuel Forde's *Ornatus and Artesia* (2003), and edited volumes, *Ovid and the Renaissance Body* (2001), *Prose Fiction and Early Modern Sexualities* (with Constance C. Relihan, 2003), and *Remapping the Mediterranean World in Early Modern English Writings* (2006).

Jennifer C. Vaught is Jean-Jacques and Aurore Labbé Fournet Associate Professor of English at the University of Louisiana at Lafayette. She is the author of *Masculinity and Emotion in Early Modern English Literature* (2008) and has edited and introduced the collections *Grief and Gender: 700–1700* (2003) and *Rhetorics of Bodily Disease and Health in Medieval and Early Modern England* (2010).

General Editor's introduction

The continuing goal of the Shakespeare Criticism series is to provide the most significant and original contemporary interpretations of Shakespeare's works. Each volume in the series is devoted to a Shakespeare play or poem (e.g., the sonnets, *Venus and Adonis*, *Othello*) and contains 15 to 25 new essays exploring the text from a variety of critical perspectives.

A major feature of each volume in the series is the editor's introduction. Each volume editor provides a substantial essay identifying the main critical issues and problems the play (or poem) has raised, charting the critical trends in looking at the work over the centuries, and assessing the critical discourse that has linked the play or poem to various ideological concerns. In addition to examining the critical commentary in light of important historical and theatrical events, each introduction functions as a discursive bibliographic essay citing and evaluating significant critical works – books, journal articles, theater documents, reviews, and interviews – giving readers a guide to the vast amounts of research on a particular play or poem.

Each volume showcases the work of leading Shakespeare scholars who participate in and extend the critical discourse on the text. Reflecting the most recent approaches in Shakespeare studies, these essays approach the play from a host of critical positions, including but not limited to feminist, Marxist, new historical, semiotic, mythic, performance/staging, cultural, and/or a combination of these and other methodologies. Some volumes in the series include bibliographic analyses of a Shakespeare text to shed light on its critical history and interpretation. Interviews with directors and/or actors are also part of some volumes in the series.

At least one, sometimes as many as two or three, of the essays in each volume is devoted to a play in performance, beginning with the earliest and most significant productions and proceeding to the most recent. These essays, which ultimately provide a theater history of the play, should not be regarded as different from or rigidly isolated from the critical work on the script. Over the last 30 years or so Shakespeare criticism has understandably been labeled the "Age of Performance." Readers will find information in these essays on non-English-speaking productions of Shakespeare's plays as well as landmark performances in English. Editors and contributors also include photographs from productions across the world to help readers see and further appreciate the ways a Shakespeare play has taken shape in the theater.

Ultimately, each volume in the Shakespeare Criticism series strives to give readers a balanced, representative collection of the most engaging and thoroughly researched criticism on the given Shakespeare text. Each volume provides a careful survey of essential materials in the history of the criticism for a Shakespeare play or poem as well as cutting-edge essays that extend and enliven our understanding of the work in its critical context. In offering readers innovative and fulfilling new essays, volume editors have made invaluable contributions to the literary and theatrical criticism of Shakespeare's greatest legacy, his work.

Philip C. Kolin
University of Southern Mississippi

1 Introduction: taking the long view

Twelfth Night criticism and performance

James Schiffer

> Now the melancholy god protect thee, and the tailor make thy doublet of changeable taffeta, for thy mind is a very opal.
>
> *Twelfth Night*, 2.4.73–75[1]

Twelfth Night has long enjoyed a reputation as one of Shakespeare's greatest comedies. Written and first performed at the mid-point of his career, probably in 1601, the play seems to have been popular in its own time up to the closing of the theatres in 1642. When the theatres reopened during the Restoration, *Twelfth Night* was revived briefly, but it was not until Charles Macklin's London production in 1741 that it became a mainstay of Shakespeare's theatrical repertoire, one of his most often performed plays. Since the late eighteenth century to the present day, it has been hailed by critics and directors as the culmination of Shakespeare's festive comedies, as well as a precursor to the darker problem plays, tragedies, and romances that follow. While not one of his most controversial plays, it has proven to be very elusive, difficult to interpret and to stage. Nevertheless, the play "rarely fails to afford pleasure," according to Michael Billington. "But equally, it is difficult to achieve . . . its ambivalent darkness and resonant comedy" (1990, xxx). After stating that there have been many lively discussions of *Much Ado About Nothing*, M. M. Mahood notes that there have been "comparatively few of *Twelfth Night*." Critics, she claims "[s]ometimes . . . overwhelm it in a highly schematic attempt to relate it to all that has gone before . . . and at other times they retreat unabashed before its elusive grace" (1979, 7). In more recent times, to the dismay of some formalists, the play has become a rich site for cultural critics who have explored the play's relation to early modern ideas about sexuality and the body, gender, identity, festive misrule, religion, and social class and hierarchy.

Despite almost universal praise for *Twelfth Night*, what is emphasized and admired in the play has often varied from one age to the next, and even from critic to critic within each age. To account for this fact, we must look not only to changing cultural and historical factors that shape different audience responses at different times but also to the richness of the play itself, the complexity of its genre and effects, its multiple themes and characters and the subtlety with which they are rendered. Like the mind of the love-obsessed Duke Orsino, *Twelfth Night* has proven over time to be "a very opal," and the different lights of different ages and the various perspectives of interpreters have brought out a multitude of facets in this Shakespearean gem.

Twins

Much of the complexity of *Twelfth Night* resides in the play's intricate structure, particularly its double plot, each with its own set of varied and interesting characters and themes, its own kinds of brilliant language. A play that features male and female twins, *Twelfth Night* is split between two lines of action that reflect one another in various ways, even as they often differ in emotional tones. This doubleness extends even to the level of the pun and raises profound issues regarding the instability of language and identity. One line of action is the romantic plot of Viola, Duke (or Count) Orsino, Countess Olivia, Sebastian, and Antonio, involving a shipwreck and the separation and eventual reunion of twins, cross-dressed disguise, same-sex and heterosexual attraction, unrequited and reciprocated love. Intertwined with the story of romance is the satiric or comic plot, often called the "subplot," of Malvolio, Sir Toby Belch, Sir Andrew Aguecheek, Maria, Fabian, and Feste (who actually moves between the households of Olivia and Orsino and helps unify the play), involving holiday excess, Puritan restraint, and comic revenge. The nomenclature does matter. The terms "romantic" and "comic" or "satiric" can mislead. It is more accurate to say that both plots are comic, one veering in Northrop Frye's terms in *Anatomy of Criticism* toward the summer of romance and ending in the promise of marriage and the reuniting of separated twins, the other toward the winter of realism, irony, satire, and the "expulsion" of Malvolio. Moments in both plots provoke laughter, though the sources of laughter differ, and a strain of sadness, attributable in part to Feste's songs, hovers over the entire play. Characters, actions, and themes in each plot have been subject to various and often mutually exclusive interpretations and have provoked a great range of emotional responses, especially over the last 200 years. There is no unanimous critical agreement about the genre of the work as a whole or about how the two separate strands of action affect and reflect one another.

The two plots are materially connected in only a few scenes, as when in act 3 scene 4 the disguised Viola is drawn into a duel with Sir Andrew and soon after is rescued by Antonio, and the final scene when Sebastian makes his miraculous appearance, and then Malvolio enters and exits soon after with his cry of vengeance. Yet the two plots complement and complicate each other in both obvious and subtle ways. In the "changeable taffeta" of the play's interpretation over the last 400 years, one plot or the other has often been emphasized at the expense of the other. One of the greatest contributions of mid-twentieth-century criticism and performance has been to find in the play a brilliant artistic unity of the whole, a powerful blending of romantic, satiric, and melancholy tones. More recently, since the 1980s, the critical emphasis (and sometimes the theatrical emphasis, especially on the European continent) has been on the play's disquieting variety, its disharmonies, its unresolved issues and emotions.

In the sections that follow, after discussing such issues as text, date of composition and first staging, and the play's sources, I shall trace some of the main issues of criticism and performance that have emerged over the last four centuries. To an unusual degree even for a Shakespearean play, issues of criticism and performance have been intertwined, each at times having a significant effect on the other. The earliest comments about the play are responses to performances; in its long history, theatrical practice has often shaped as well as been shaped by criticism, and today some of the finest interpretations come from actors and directors of the play. In fact, Lois Potter maintains that the play's "theatrical history is often more illuminating than its criticism" (1985, 14). Performance always involves, and ultimately always is, interpretation. Each performance of *Twelfth Night* inevitably realizes some potentialities resident in the text at the expense of others. Capturing the play in its totality of potential meanings and effects is an almost impossible task, the work of ages. The longer this play's history, the more we discover about it and about the complexity of each age that responds to it. Of course, no age is monolithic, and the danger of surveys is that they sometimes over-generalize, simplifying for the sake of clear contrast between one period and another. Like interpreters of the play itself, those who approach the play's reception must do so with humility and caution. After all, this is among other things a play about the perils of misinterpretation. The temptation to "crush things a little," as Malvolio does with the contrived letter, is ever present.

The text

The first known printed edition of *Twelfth Night* appeared in the First Folio (1623), produced by fellow actors John Heminge and Henry Condell seven years after Shakespeare's death. The play was entered into The Stationers' Register on November 8, 1623, along with 15 other previously unpublished plays by Shakespeare. *Twelfth Night* is the next-to-last comedy in the First Folio, following *Measure for Measure* and preceding *The Winter's Tale*. Charleton Hinman has found evidence that there was some delay in printing these last two plays, perhaps because of a delay in obtaining the complete manuscripts. The great majority of scholars have long regarded the Folio text of *Twelfth Night* as "unusually clean" and relatively unproblematical (Lothian and Craik 1975, xvii). There are nevertheless inconsistencies that continue to lure the attention of textual scholars. For example, Orsino is referred to in the play as both a Duke and a Count. In the second scene of the play Viola mentions her singing voice and her intention to disguise herself as "an eunuch," yet she has no songs assigned to her later in the play, and no mention of her posing as a eunuch is made after the scene; Olivia clearly would not wish to marry a eunuch, nor would Orsino encourage Cesario to choose to marry a younger woman if the Duke thought Cesario was less than adequately equipped. Other critics have pointed to Fabian's late entry into the play, possibly to keep Feste less involved in the plot against Malvolio, and to the "double time" of *Twelfth Night*, the fact that there are references to the events of the play occurring over the course of both three days (1.4.3) and three months (5.1.90, 95).

Based on some of these and other inconsistencies, John Dover Wilson has argued that the Folio text shows signs of revision, perhaps in response to changing theatrical circumstances. However, Dover Wilson's theory has been challenged in separate works by R. K. Turner and S. L. Bethell, and most would agree that such changes as Viola's not singing are "as likely to reflect a change of mind in the process of composition as subsequent revision, and so is the apparent uncertainty about whether Orsino is 'duke' or 'count'" (Warren and Wells 1994, 75). Another textual question is the manuscript upon which the Folio text is based. Dover Wilson believes the text was set from a prompt book because it contains phrases like "at several doors," yet Roger Warren and Stanley Wells observe that "such standard theatrical terminology could just as easily have originated with the dramatist himself" (1994, 74). R. K. Turner has more persuasively argued that the source of the Folio text was a scribal copy; Craik concludes that "[t]he probability is that the printer's copy was a transcript of Shakespeare's foul papers, that he [Shakespeare] gave the text of the play as it was originally written, and that nothing was added with the exception of what may be called editorial decoration, namely the inscribing of the act-endings and of the headings of acts and scenes" (Lothian and Craik 1975, xxv). The truth here is that we will probably never know with certainty how far removed the text we have is from Shakespeare's original, how much it may have been unintentionally modified by the printer or typesetter, or deliberately changed during the course of composition, or in rehearsal – the result of collaboration with his fellow actors, or altered to suit specific audiences or acting venues or changes in the acting company. In postmodern editing circles, the idea of recovering – or even getting nearest to – an originary Shakespearean text has been largely abandoned. After noting that some critics claim the Folio text of *Twelfth Night* is "uniquely authoritative," Laurie E. Osborne reminds readers that the First Folio is "an edited copy as well" (1996, 17). In her view, "the material existence of texts within history means that there is no singular text which establishes the playwright's initial or final intentions" (1996, 18). The "real" *Twelfth Night* for Osborne is the sum of its many versions in print and performance on stage over the last 400 years.

Discussion of textual matters, of course, continues to the present day. Patricia Parker's essay in this collection argues for the restoration of a number of First Folio words, phrases, and entire lines altered by various editors, beginning in the eighteenth century. In her essay, Cynthia Lewis discusses some of the inconsistencies mentioned above, speculating that such "imperfections" are part of the design and fabric of the play. As scholarship on *Twelfth Night* evolves, proposed solutions to many of these puzzling issues will no doubt continue to emerge.

Date of composition, first performance, and title

In the late eighteenth century, at a time when the first efforts were being made to create a biography of Shakespeare and a chronology for his works, Edmond Malone speculated that *Twelfth Night* was written in 1614, after Shakespeare had retired from the stage and returned to Stratford. Malone's theory, which he credited to a Thomas Tyrwhitt, made *Twelfth Night* Shakespeare's final play "his farewell to theatre" (Osborne 1996, xv). This notion prevailed for 50 years until John P. Collier's discovery of John Manningham's 1602 diary entry, which clearly refers to the play. Manningham, a law student at the Middle Temple of the Inns of Court in London, records seeing a performance on Candlemas, February 2, 1602:[2]

> At our feast wee had a play called ~~Mid~~ 'Twelve night, or what you will'; much like the commedy of errores, or Menechmi in Plautus, but most like and neere to that in Italian called Inganni.
>
> A good practise in it to make the steward beleeve his Lady widowe was in Love with him, by counterfayting a letter, as from his Lady, in generall termes, telling him what shee liked best in him, and prescribing his gesture in smiling, his apparraile, &c., and then when he came to practise, making him beleeve they tooke him to be mad.
>
> (Elam 2008, 3–4)

Manningham's entry, as we shall see, is fascinating for a number of reasons. Its discovery led critics to revise their notion of *Twelfth Night*'s place in the Shakespearean canon. No longer his final play, it now became his final "happy" comedy, written at approximately the same time that he was writing the satiric *Troilus and Cressida* and tragic *Hamlet*.

Manningham's comments have provoked theories about the play's first performance and Shakespeare's relationship with both the royal court and the Inns of Court. Most notable of these is Leslie Hotson's *The First Night of Twelfth Night* (1954), which puts forth the theory that the play was written "in ten or eleven days" at the request of Queen Elizabeth and was first performed at Whitehall on January 6, 1601, to entertain a visiting Italian dignitary named Virginio Orsini, Duke of Bracciano (Hotson incorrectly renames him "Orsino").[3] Hotson contends that the character of Olivia represents the young Elizabeth and Orsino the visiting guest of honor, while Malvolio is a thinly veiled portrayal of the Comptroller of her Majesty's Household, Sir William Knollys, Earl of Banbury (1954, 99). Hotson's most important conjectures have not fared well with most scholars, who doubt the real Duke Orsini would be flattered by any resemblance to Shakespeare's Orsino or that Queen Elizabeth would discover herself in the humbled, love-plagued Olivia. Scholars have also questioned whether Shakespeare could (or would) whip up a play so quickly on royal command. Nevertheless, Hotson's book is filled with fascinating information about both life at Court and royal Twelfth Night festivities. In his Arden edition of *Twelfth Night*, Keir Elam agrees with Hotson that there are a number of "striking coincidences"; Elam also finds some of the arguments other scholars have made against Hotson's theory "rather weak," although Elam does not necessarily endorse all of the theory himself (2008, 94).

Another hypothesis, proposed by John Dover Wilson, is that the first performance of the play was the one Manningham witnessed at the Middle Temple on February 2, 1602. This theory has recently gained the support of Anthony Arlidge, who in *Shakespeare and the Prince of Love: The Feast of Misrule in the Middle Temple* contends that the play parodies well-known Inns of Court figures. Though Arlidge's study is rich in detail about entertainments at the Middle Temple, the argument is speculative at best. Before Arlidge published his study, Lois Potter wrote that it is tempting to think Fabian's part was written for a law student for the Middle Temple performance, but then adds, "tempting, but pointless" (1985, 34). Most editors and scholars seem to be in agreement with the earlier conclusion of Craik that there is little reason to think the first performance occurred at the Middle Temple (Lothian and Craik 1975, xxvii). Craik also maintains that topical references suggest Shakespeare began writing the play "by the middle of the year" 1601 and that he completed it "before year's end, with the approach of the Christmas holiday period perhaps suggesting, but not dictating, its title" (xxxiv–v). The first performance, he speculates, would also have taken place in 1601. Critics are uncertain about whether *Twelfth Night* precedes or follows the writing and first performance of *Hamlet*. Lois Potter, for instance, thinks it is likely Richard Burbage played Malvolio as well as Hamlet. The steward's first entrance, she notes, is "remarkably like Hamlet's." While she admits that we do not know which play came first, "if the comedy were later than the tragedy, it could have been an opportunity for Burbage to parody his own performance" (1985, 35).[4] Summarizing the various theories, Elam writes that there are "four possible first nights for *Twelfth Night*: at Whitehall on January 6, 1601; at the Middle Temple on February 2, 1602; at the public theatre – the Globe – rather than a private venue, presumably at some time in 1601; or on January 6, 1602 in some other private performance space, prior to its appearance at the Middle Temple, and then on the public stage. This last hypothesis is probably the most plausible, but in the lack of new evidence the jury is likely to be out for a long time to come" (1985, 96).

While the title *Twelfth Night* may simply reflect the time of year when the play was first performed, several scholars over the last two centuries have related the title to religious themes in the play and to seasonal rituals like the Feast of Epiphany and the Feast of Fools. Lois Potter believes the title "implies that revelry must come to an end" (1985, 36), an idea taken up in several recent productions. The second part of the title has also provoked speculation. R. K. Turner suggests that *What You Will* may have been Shakespeare's original name for the play, but that John Marston published a play with this title early in 1601: "it is very possible that Shakespeare retained the original title in order to make it absolutely clear to his audience that the new title *Twelfth Night* bore no more significance than had the casual titles of his two previous comedies, *Much Ado About Nothing* and *As You Like It*" (quoted in Lothian and Craik 1975, xxxiii). Others have found meaning in "What You Will" as a reference to the multiple and often conflicting desires of the characters in the play, as well as to the multitudinous desires of the audience. Thus, Paul Edmondson writes, Shakespeare's "alternative title invites its audiences to position (or to find) themselves in relation to the play, to interpret it in their own image: such is the desire of every critical act" (2005, 78).

Sources

There is a rich body of commentary on possible sources that Shakespeare drew on for the romance plot in *Twelfth Night*; scholars have identified "at least twelve versions of the source story, in no fewer than five languages" of a female twin disguised as a male, yet there is little certainty about which of them he actually read or used (Pentland 2007). None of these sources is all in all sufficient, and none affords a close earlier version of the Malvolio subplot. The Viola/Sebastian story, it seems, was "in the air" and, as Warren and Wells observe, one "cannot prove debts that are unprovable" (1994, 15). Manningham was on track in pointing in the directions he did: to Plautus's *Menaechmi*, to a mid-sixteenth-century Italian play, Nicolo Secchi's *Gl'Inganni*, and to Shakespeare's own *The Comedy of Errors*. Modern scholars have both confirmed and added to these likely influences. For example, Keir Elam has shown the relation of *Twelfth Night* (and especially its eunuch theme) to Terence's *Eunuchus* as well as to comedies by Plautus (especially his love of the comic confusion caused by twins), while others have traced the play's Italian roots back to an earlier version than *Gl'Inganni*, a play titled *Gl'Ingannati*, first performed in 1531 in Siena by the Accademia degli Intronati ("The Thunderstruck by Love").[5] This work, it seems, is the ultimate source not just for *Gl'Inganni* but for an Italian prose narrative by Matteo Bandello that was later translated into French by François de Belleforest and finally adapted into English by Barnabe Riche in "Of Apolonius and Silla" in *Riche his Farewell to Military Profession* (1581), Shakespeare's most immediate source. Another English source that Shakespeare probably drew upon was a version of the story found in Emanuel Forde's prose romance *Parismus the Renowned Knight of Bohemia* (1598).

These works share with *Twelfth Night* a similarity of plot, particularly the male and female twins, with the female twin disguised as a male, but Shakespeare invariably chastens his more ribald sources. The female disguised as male creates opportunities for sexual adventure in the Italian versions not found in *Twelfth Night*; *Gl'Ingannati* has episodes that consist of "titillating, salacious flirting with the disguise situation" (Warren and Wells 1994, 15); Riche's tone is "closer to the bawdiness of the Italian than Shakespeare's" – the sea captain in Riche attempts to rape Silla, the young heroine, and later, at the moment of crisis, Silla-as-Silvio shows Julina "his breastes and pretie teates" to prove it was not she (Silla) who impregnated her (Warren and Wells 1994, 17). As Salingar observes, Viola "is a more romantic heroine than the rest, and the only one to fall in love *after* assuming her disguise" (1986, 196); later he adds, "Shakespeare is alone in making the heroine reveal herself *after* her brother's marriage with the second heroine, as a consequence of it" (204). In the opinion of Warren and Wells, Shakespeare's tone "in some respects" is closer to Forde's: "While the situation is not exactly the same as in *Twelfth Night*, since Pollipus's constant resolution is to Violetta herself rather than to another woman, and Violetta, unlike Viola, only gradually falls in love, the image of a disguised heroine attending and ultimately curing her beloved's love-sickness, while their relationship matures without the man being aware of it, is very likely to have had its effect on the genesis of *Twelfth Night*. And both Forde and Shakespeare share a quality notably absent from Riche and the Italian plays: tenderness" (1994, 17–18). Another link between *Parismus* and *Twelfth Night*, of course, are names. The heroine's name is Violetta, and a Princess Olivia falls in love with her. Goran V. Stanivuković's essay later in this collection explores yet another connection to Forde's romance: the depiction of various forms of masculinity. Shakespeare's play reflects and at times also parodies such representations in Forde.

Shakespeare's earlier comedies, as Manningham observed in his reference to *The Comedy of Errors*, are yet another important source for both plots in *Twelfth Night*. *The Comedy of Errors* shares with the later play a shipwreck and separated twins – in fact, *The Comedy of Errors* has two sets of twins, though neither set is male–female (Shakespeare, it should be noted, was father to male and female twins, Hamnet and Judith). Both plays also depict a character falsely presumed to be mad who is accordingly subjected to a "cure" (Malvolio the dark house with catechism from Feste disguised as Sir Topas, Antipholus of Ephesus an exorcism with Dr. Pinch in *The Comedy of Errors*). Warren and Wells observe that the treatment of the twins is "one measure of the difference between the two plays." *The Comedy of Errors* is "basically a comedy of situation with psychological touches," while *Twelfth Night* is "a comedy of character built upon a comedy of situation" (1994, 22). *A Midsummer Night's Dream* offers another parallel in its depiction of youthful characters "following them that fly from us" (as Barnaby Riche writes in "Apolonius and Silla"). Parallels have also been drawn with *Love's Labor's Lost* with its emphasis on idealistic young men coming of age, on love and mortality. Both plays have wonderful eavesdropping scenes. In *Love's Labor's Lost* (4.3) various aristocratic men – each thinking he is alone when in fact he is being observed and overheard – recite their love poems; the scene looks forward to the moment when Malvolio finds and reads the forged letter, all the while observed by Toby, Andrew, and Fabian. Other Shakespearean precursors include the three comedies with women disguised as males: *Two Gentlemen of Verona*, *The Merchant of Venice*, and *As You Like It*. In the first of these, Julia serves the man she loves, Proteus, even as he loves another woman; *As You Like It*, like *Twelfth Night*, offers a female protagonist (Rosalind) disguised as a male who teaches the man she loves (Orlando) how to love while another female character (Phebe) falls in love with her. The parallels with *The Merchant of Venice* extend beyond that between Portia and Viola to those between the two killjoy figures, Shylock and Malvolio, though the two also differ in important ways; the danger Shylock poses to Antonio is far greater than anything Malvolio threatens in *Twelfth Night*. Some critics also point to a resemblance between Falstaff of the *Henry IV* plays and Sir Toby Belch and the general theme of misrule; all agree, however, that Sir Toby lacks Falstaff's imaginative brilliance even as he shares Falstaff's love of wine.

While no direct source has been found for the Malvolio plot, most scholars recognize a more general kind of debt to the "humours" comedies of Ben Jonson, with their emphasis on the "explosion" and expulsion of "blocking characters." Yet, Shakespeare tempers Jonsonian satire, incorporates it into a larger, more humane vision. Thus, J. M. Gregson writes that "In Shakespeare's steward the Puritanism is one part of a larger whole: Malvolio, gnawed by his self-love, is not against any institution or practice in particular but against life itself" (1980, 12). Shakespeare's comedy is "in direct contrast to Jonson's clear-sighted attack upon specific targets" (12). Yet, as was noted before, Hotson, Dover Wilson, and Arlidge all speculate that Malvolio is modeled upon a real person, either at Whitehall or the Inns of Court. It is doubtful that this issue will ever have any more of a definitive answer than will issues of date of composition or first performance.

Early responses: 1602–1741

Evidence suggests that the play's first audiences loved the gulling of Malvolio. The first testimony, Manningham's diary, singles out for praise the

Malvolio subplot but makes no mention of the romantic plot, except in speculating about its sources. The next records we have of the play are of a performance in 1618, and another in 1623; of the latter production, Master of the Revels Sir Henry Herbert wrote: "At Candlemas *Malvolio* was acted at Court by the King's Servants." The change in title clearly indicates the prominence given to Olivia's steward. In his copy of the Second Folio (1632), King Charles I wrote marginal notes alongside the titles of various plays; by *Twelfth Night* he wrote "Malvolio." In yet another indication of the steward's popularity, Leonard Digges writes the following lines in his poem in praise of Shakespeare's dramatic works in the 1640 edition of Shakespeare's *Poems*:

> The Cockpit Galleries, Boxes, all are full
> To heare Malvolio that crosse garter'd Gull.

Elam offers a likely explanation of the delight early audiences seemed to take in the steward's humiliation: "If the comedy is taken to re-enact the century-long struggle between old 'Merry England,' with its vestiges of Christianized pagan ritual, and the reformation of English customs and manners, then the punishment of the 'Puritan' Malvolio looks like revenge comedy of a particular historical and cultural kind. The play's comic plot becomes the expression of nostalgia for a pre-Reformation world" (2008, 20–21). Alan W. Powers and Ivo Kamps elaborate on this insight later in this volume. Kamps observes that Malvolio's cry of revenge at the end of the play is prophetic of the civil war and Puritan triumph to come just a few decades later.

In fact, it was only two years after Digges's homage was published that the Puritans closed the London theatres. When they reopened in 1660 with the Restoration, William Davenant revived a number of Shakespeare's plays, including *Twelfth Night*, with Thomas Betterton cast as Sir Toby, perhaps another indication of the primacy of the satiric plot at this time; not only is Sir Toby's role the one with the most lines, but Sir Toby drives the attack on Malvolio's dignity. Despite Betterton's performances, the play as a whole seemed not to be as popular as it had been or would one day again become. Samuel Pepys saw *Twelfth Night* three times (in 1661, 1663, and 1669) and disliked it each time. On the first occasion, he called it a "silly" play "not related at all to the name or day"; after he saw it a third time, he wrote that it was "one of the weakest plays that ever I saw on the stage" (Spencer 1940, 175). After the 1669 production, *Twelfth Night* disappeared from the stage for 72 years. During this quietus, there was one theatrical adaptation, a play by Charles Burnaby titled *Love Betray'd: or, the Agreeable Disappointment*, which borrowed some elements of the plot and approximately 60 lines from Shakespeare's play; there were only two known performances, one in 1703, the other in 1705, before it faded into theatrical obscurity.

Aside from Burnaby's adaptation, there are few traces of the play during the early eighteenth century except for occasional critical commentary, most of it focused on Malvolio. Shakespearean editor Nicholas Rowe (1709), for example, finds "something singularly Ridiculous and Pleasant in the fantastical Steward *Malvolio*," and Richard Steele shows a similar interest when he writes in 1711 that Malvolio "has Wit, Learning, and Discernment, but temper'd with an allay of Envy, Self-Love, and Detraction. *Malvolio* turns pale at the Mirth and good Humour of the Company if it center not in his Person" (Harris 1984, 540). One other source of appeal, however, would play an important part in the revival of *Twelfth Night* later in the eighteenth century. From 1660 and onward, women were for the first time permitted to perform on the public stage; the term "breeches parts" would eventually be applied to roles like Viola's in which females portrayed girls or women in disguise as boys or men. A great appeal for audiences, evidently, was the opportunity to see the legs of the actresses bared or with little covering.

1741–1901: Macklin to Beerbohm Tree – Johnson to Swinburne

The disappearance of *Twelfth Night* and most other Shakespearean comedies from the English Stage for some 70 years reflected a preference during this time for Shakespearean tragedy over comedy, and when it came to comedy, for authors like Jonson, Dryden, and Wycherley over Shakespeare. The great revival of Shakespeare's plays in general can largely be attributed to one person, David Garrick, who in the mid-to-late eighteenth century did much not only to stage all of Shakespeare's plays, but also to do so for most of the plays in a way that removed many editorial alterations and restored Shakespeare's language. A signal event in Garrick's revival of the Shakespearean canon was the production of *Twelfth Night* at the Drury Lane Theatre in London on January 15, 1741, with Charles Macklin starring as Malvolio. According to John R. Ford, "Macklin's casting of himself as Malvolio began a long tradition of actors and actor managers choosing that role" (2006, 138–39). Since that time *Twelfth Night* has remained one of the most frequently staged and best regarded of Shakespeare's comedies. In many ways, however, it had become a different play from the one that Manningham reported seeing in the early seventeenth century. As Penny Gay notes, "Since the play's revival in 1740–41 . . . the interest that the play engenders has shifted to its exploration of romantic love and desire, and it is read within the paradign of romantic comedy, where the ending always envisages marriage" (1985, 36). The explanation for this shift, Gay continues, resides to a great degree in the fact that women now consistently performed the female parts: "The roles of Viola and Olivia – exemplifying two favorite qualities of the mid-eighteenth century, wit and sensibility – soon became vehicles for star actresses of the eighteenth century such as Dora Jordan and Elizabeth Farren. Viola's pathos was even evoked beyond the play in an onset setting by Haydn of 'She never told her love' (Canzonets, 1795)" (37). This did not mean, of course, that

Malvolio's role or the plot that featured him was forgotten or always downplayed, but rather that his role and the satiric subplot and how they were presented and received were subtly transformed. Such changes were part of the shifting tastes and sensibilities of late eighteenth-century – and then nineteenth-century – audiences.

One can trace such changes not just on stage but in the criticism. Stanley Wells has written that "except for notices of performances . . . there is little lasting criticism of the comedy before the present [twentieth] century" (1986, x). In the main, this seems a fair assessment in regard to the quantity of commentary. Nevertheless, it overlooks the work of critics in the eighteenth and nineteenth centuries who wrote intelligently about the play and who actually anticipated many of the issues that continue to occupy us today. One of the earliest commentators to focus on the romantic plot was Charlotte Lennox, though what she wrote in 1753 was more in the way of disapproval than of praise. After noting that no reason is ever given for why Sebastian and Viola go to sea in the first place, she writes of Viola's "unaccountable resolution" to serve Orsino: "A very natural Scheme this for a beautiful and virtuous young Lady to throw off all at once the Modesty and Reservedness of her sex, mix among men, herself disguised like one; and, prest by no Necessity, influenced by no Passion, expose herself to all the dangerous Consequences of so unworthy and shameful a Situation" (Harris 1984, 541). Lennox would not be the last to raise questions of this kind about Viola's disguise. Of Olivia's passion for Viola, she states that it "is attended with Circumstances that make it appear highly improbable and ridiculous" (541). Lennox also questions the actions of the final act, finding Orsino's proposal to Viola too improbable: "why should the Duke, a sovereign Prince who so passionately adored Olivia, all at once take a Resolution to marry Viola, a Stranger whom he had never seen in her proper Garb, because she had served him in Disguise; 'tis absurd to suppose he could in a Moment pass from the most extravagant passion imaginable for Olivia, to one no less extravagant, for a Person, whom till then he had always believed to be a Boy; and, 'tis also highly improbable that a great Prince would so suddenly resolve to marry a Girl, who had no other Title to his Favour than an imprudent Passion, which had carried her greatly beyond the Bounds of Decency" (542).

Samuel Johnson's 1765 edition of Shakespeare's plays provides the first extended commentary and annotation for *Twelfth Night*. While Johnson shared some of Lennox's misgivings about Viola's character (he called her "a cunning schemer, never at a loss") and about the play's resolution, he appreciated the play's blending of tones, declaring that *Twelfth Night* "is in the graver part elegant and easy, and in some of the lighter scenes exquisitely humorous." Johnson singles out for praise the depiction of Malvolio, noting that "[t]he soliloquy of *Malvolio* is truly comick; he is betrayed to ridicule merely by his pride" (Harris 1984, 542). While Johnson's comments on Malvolio seem to reflect a continuation of audience pleasure in the steward's comic humiliation, there is no trace of political or religious animus towards him as a Puritan, as there probably was for audiences in earlier times; Johnson sees him as a generalized character type whose humiliation is the appropriate punishment for his pride. Johnson's criticism of the rendering of Sir Andrew follows from the same principle of poetic justice; Sir Andrew's punishment is undeserved because he has no choice in being the way he is: "*Ague-cheek* is drawn with great propriety, but his character is in a great measure that of natural fatuity, and is therefore not the proper prey of a satirist" (542). Like Lennox, furthermore, Johnson is critical of the play's resolution because of what he considers its lack of probability, decorum, and moral instruction: "The marriage of *Olivia* and the succeeding perplexity, though well enough contrived to divert on stage, wants credibility, and fails to produce the proper instruction required in the drama, as it exhibits no just picture of life" (542). The objections in regard to "credibility" raised by both Lennox and Johnson in regard to the play's resolution continue to be voiced by many recent commentators as well, though not everyone finds the play's resolution in two marriages problematical or disappointing.

Over the next few decades, neoclassical standards gradually began to give way to a more Romantic sensibility, one that appreciated the depiction of individual characters more than generalized types. Thus, Ford notes that during the sixteenth and seventeenth centuries, audiences were relatively detached from characters, but later eighteenth-century audiences, influenced by the rise of the novel as a form of entertainment, began "to look more into the interior life of characters," and this tendency was "reinforced by a more star-driven interest in major actors and in their ability to create life-like characters" (2006, 140). The comments of William Hazlitt in 1817 offer a marked contrast to those of Johnson and Lennox. In fact, Hazlitt seems to be responding to Johnson's criticism of the "satire" against Sir Andrew when he notes that the play "is full of sweetness and pleasantry. It is perhaps too good-natured for comedy. It has little satire, and no spleen . . . It aims at the ludicrous rather than the ridiculous . . . Shakespeare's comedy is of a pastoral and poetical cast. Folly is indigenous to the soil, and shoots out with native, happy, unchecked luxuriance. Absurdity has every encouragement afforded it; and nonsense has room to flourish in" (Harris 1984, 544). For Hazlitt, as for many of the nineteenth-century critics that followed him, "the great and secret charm of *Twelfth Night* is Viola," particularly "Viola's confession of her love" (544). To some degree the idealization of Viola in Hazlitt and others in the nineteenth century may have been compensation, conscious or not, for a different source of her appeal for theatre-goers – the bared legs of the actresses who played her part. Citing Leigh Hunt's description of an actress's leg and ankle in 1820, Lois Potter writes that "The stress on purity and melancholy seems an over-reaction to the embarrassment caused by her disguise" (1985, 39).

Hazlitt's comments about Malvolio stand in marked contrast to Johnson's and usher in a trend that continues to this day: "we feel a regard for Malvolio, and sympathize with his gravity, his smiles, his cross-garters, his yellow stockings, and imprisonment in the stocks" (Harris 1984, 544). Later in the same essay he acknowledges that "poor Malvolio's treatment afterwards is a little hard," though not so hard as to disrupt the audience's delight in the play's romantic resolution (545). Writing just a few years later, Charles Lamb would echo Hazlitt's comments, but Lamb would take Hazlitt's sympathy for Malvolio even farther. Recalling a performance by actor Robert Bensley that he had seen two decades earlier (and perhaps inaccurately – or at least embellished by memory, according to Sylvan Barnet [1954]), he writes that Bensley "threw over the part an air of Spanish loftiness. He looked, spake, and moved like an old Castillian" (Lamb 1986, 53). Comparing Malvolio to Don Quixote, Lamb adds, "I confess that I never saw the catastrophe of this character, while Bensley played it, without a kind of tragic interest" (54). Lamb's comments about Malvolio would later inspire Henry Irving's portrayal in 1884. As Lois Potter notes, "The interpretation of Malvolio offers an interesting example of the interdependence of literary and theatrical criticism" (1985, 40). Irving's production, which also starred Ellen Terry as Viola, was apparently not well received; nevertheless, "[n]o director or critic since Irving has been able to ignore the disturbing implications of this part of the plot" (1985, 42).

Viola, Olivia, Sir Andrew, and Malvolio were not the only characters to draw the attention of nineteenth-century critics, of course. For example, G. G. Gervinus in 1850 seems to have been the first to pronounce Orsino to be "'more in love with his love, than with his mistress' . . . and he pressed the charge to the point of deducing that this was why Olivia refused the Duke" (Lothian and Craik 1975, lii); this criticism of Orsino has been repeated countless times since. Many other critics followed Johnson in admiring the play's artistry. George Steevens, writing as "HIC et UBIQUE" in 1772, praises the variety of *Twelfth Night* and Shakespeare's construction of the plot:

> surely when we consider the Variety and proper Contrast of Characters, the many uncommon Situations to unfold and bring forth several Humors, Passions, and Peculiarities of the *Dramatis Personae*, there is no performance of five short Acts which contains such Matter for Mirth . . . All the Parts being thus well and easily connected with the whole commands Attention, mixed with Pleasure, which real Criticks acknowledge to be the best Proof of Genius of a Comic Writer.
>
> (Harris 1984, 542)

Steevens's praise is echoed in 1811 by A. W. Schlegel, who notes that the play "treats love more as an affair of the imagination than of the heart," and observes that the "ideal follies" of the main plot are provided with a contrast in the "undisguised absurdities" of the wholly comic characters arising "in like manner under pretense of love" (Harris 1984, 543). This strategy of finding thematic connections between the two plots culminates in many fine New Critical analyses of the play in the mid-twentieth century. Even the focus on festivity and misrule, recognized to be so important to the play's structure and meaning by C. L. Barber and others in the twentieth century, is first observed in the nineteenth century by E. Montégut (1867), who "stressed the element of masquerade, festival, topsyturveydom, and ambiguity" (Lothian and Craik 1975, lii).

Despite Henry Irving's 1884 experiment with playing Malvolio as a tragic figure, the tendency through most of the nineteenth century was to render *Twelfth Night* as a happy play, filled with sunshine and song. Thus, H. J. Ruggles (1870) writes that "Besides the air of elegance it possesses, it is filled to the brim and overflowing with the spirit that seeks to enjoy this world without one thought or aspiration beyond. It jumps the hereafter entirely. Every scene of it glows with the warmth and sunshine of physical enjoyment" (quoted in Lothian and Craik 1975, lii). Swinburne offers similar praise in 1880 for *Twelfth Night*'s "sunny identity of spirit," a trait which he thinks it shares with *As You Like It* (Lothian and Craik 1975, lii). "Even when (as by F. J. Furnivall, 1877) attention was drawn to its elements of pathos and danger, and to the absence of Beatrice's or Rosalind's vivacity from Viola's part," observes Craik, it was "still one of the comedies of Shakespeare's bright, sweet time" (lii; Furness 1901, 385). To achieve this happy effect in pre-twentieth-century productions, the actor manager modified or cut some of the more disturbing elements of the play. Feste's part was usually pared. Penny Gay notes that actresses of *ingénue* roles were expected to sing in the eighteenth century, and Feste's songs were usually cut in favor of songs for Viola and Olivia (1985, 38). This tendency to turn the play into song reached a crescendo in 1820 when Frederick Reynolds and composer Henry Bishop created a musical version of the play at Covent Garden with "Songs, Glees, and Choruses, the Poetry selected *entirely* from the Plays, Poems, and Sonnets of Shakespeare" with a masque from *The Tempest* added for good measure (Warren and Wells 1994, 3). In some productions, the dark room scene was also cut, and a number of promptbooks dating back to the eighteenth century and forward through the nineteenth century add an invented pardon of Antonio in Orsino's final speech. Laurie E. Osborne concludes that "[t]he invention of a pardon for Antonio in the late eighteenth century and its use throughout the nineteenth are most important because they mark the initial awareness that Antonio's place at the end of the play is a problem" (1994, 113). Towards the end of the nineteenth century, the "happy" *Twelfth Night* remained the dominant model. Augustin Daly cut Malvolio entirely from the final act in his very popular production in 1894; Feste's reference to the "whirligig of time" bringing in "his revenges" was also excised. Ralph Berry notes that in other productions during the Victorian period "it was customary to interpolate these lines for the Duke (after Malvolio's exit): 'And now after twelve nights of tastes and pleasures, / Let me commend you in your dancing measures.' A dance followed." Thus, he concludes,

> the old model took every opportunity to play up the farcical and comic elements; it softened the asperities of Malvolio's humiliation; it projected, finally, an apotheosis of romance, good-humour and social accord. But it strained somewhat at the text to achieve these effects.
> (Berry 1981a, 111–12)

Another prominent feature of productions from the late eighteenth century through the nineteenth was the emphasis on spectacle, on sets that were increasingly, lavishly realistic. This development, which coincided with the advent of the proscenium stage, reached heights of ever-growing splendor in the Victorian period. The problem was that the more elaborate sets could not easily be changed, resulting in one of three possibilities – long delays between scenes; a reordering of scenes to make the action in the same locale consecutive (for example, reversing act 1 scene 1 and act 1 scene 2 – a change still followed to this day in many productions); or using the same setting for scenes obviously meant to be staged in other locations. Herbert Beerbohm Tree's 1901 London production was "the last major production in the high Victorian style" (Warren and Wells 1994, 4). The set for Olivia's estate, designed by Hawes Craven, featured a beautifully terraced Italian garden with fountains, real grass, and trees. The spectacle made its impression on George O'Dell, who wrote, "I never saw anything approaching it for beauty and *vraisemblance*," but "once put up, this scene could not be easily removed, and it was perforce used for many of the Shakespearian episodes for which it was entirely inappropriate" (Gay 1985, 38). Tree starred in the production, playing a much admired Malvolio as an absurdly haughty, pretentious figure (see the cover illustration to this volume). In case the audience failed to recognize the steward was being played mainly for laughter, Tree's Malvolio was "attended by four smaller Malvolios, who aped the great chamberlain in dress, in manners, in deportment" (Sprague 1986, 40).

Twentieth-century revolutions

Even before the turn of the century and Hawes Craven's magnificent set for Beerbohm Tree's production, revolutionary changes were brewing, changes that would affect how *Twelfth Night* was staged and how characters were portrayed; these changes often had a profound effect on the tone of the play and, consequently, on how audiences were affected. In 1895 William Poel and his semi-professional Elizabethan Stage Society performed a two-hour version of *Twelfth Night* at Burlington Hall, using a platform stage without scenery, but with Elizabethan costumes; Poel staged *Twelfth Night* again in 1897 at the Middle Temple, and the production was revived once more in 1903. His aim was to return to Elizabethan simplicity, away from elaborate sets and a focus on visual splendor. According to Edward M. Moore, Poel "became convinced that Elizabethan drama was primarily a spoken drama . . . His researches led Poel to a thoroughgoing rejection of all scenery and scenic embellishments, except costume, and a consequent rejection of the picture-frame stage in favor of the platform, making an 'intimacy' between actors and audience that was impossible from behind the proscenium arch and footlights" (1972, 25). He also tried to speed up the delivery of the verse. To stage the play in just two hours, Poel felt compelled to cut the dark room scene. The production had numerous detractors, especially Max Beerbohm and William Archer. Archer "suggested that the program for the performance should read 'Staged (more or less) after the manner of the Sixteenth Century; acted after the manner of the Nineteenth Century Amateur'" (Moore 1972, 28). On the other hand, George Bernard Shaw was impressed by the possibilities of the empty stage and absence of footlights, even as he was aware of the shortcomings in the acting (Moore 1972, 31).

Poel's experiment had a profound impact on Harley Granville-Barker, who in 1912 staged *Twelfth Night* at the Savoy Theatre in London. This greatly admired production was to influence generations of directors and scholars. Granville-Barker used a minimalist set that abandoned any attempt at realistic splendor. In place of real trees were brightly colored cone-like shapes. According to John R. Ford, Granville-Barker "succeeded in recovering the theatrical energies Poel saw in Elizabethan conditions of performance without falling into a strictly historical literalism" (2006, 151). Granville-Barker, like Poel, was also one of the first directors, as that term is understood today. Most eighteenth- and nineteenth-century productions were under the control of stage manager/actors like David Garrick, Henry Irving, Augustin Daly, and Herbert Beerbohm Tree; their productions tended to focus on one or at most two stars. Unlike the manager/actors, directors were better able to see *Twelfth Night* in its entirety as a play with a number of interesting characters.

One of Granville-Barker's most important and lasting innovations was the prominence he gave to Feste, a character whose part was reduced and de-emphasized in most earlier productions. In Herbert Beerbohm Tree's 1901 staging, Feste remained on stage for the entire production as the "presiding genius"; nevertheless, he "remained an uncomplicated figure, a waggish Lord of Misrule overseeing the holiday fun" (Greif 1988, 63). It was not until Granville-Barker's production that Feste was anointed "as the spokesman for the comedy's bittersweet undertones" (Greif 1988, 63). C. Hayden Coffin was a performer of musical comedies whom Granville-Barker chose for the role. Clearly, Coffin's singing voice was a factor, but so was the fact that Coffin was no longer in his prime. Thus, Granville-Barker writes in his "Preface" to the acting edition of the play, "Feste, I feel, is not a young man either [the other older character, according to Granville-Barker, is Fabian]. There runs through all he says and does that vein of irony by which we may so often mark one of life's self-acknowledged failures" (1974, 30). Several later directors would emphasize "the fool's ironic, faintly cynical detachment from his companions; his poignant, almost melancholy awareness of time's passage; and his use of wit as a shield against despair" (Greif 1988, 63). The rise of Feste has had the profound effect in many modern productions of complicating – and darkening – the mood of the play. "We are intrigued by ambiguities, obsessed with ironies, and bewitched by paradoxes," writes Karen Greif. "Just as the Romantics found near-tragic pathos in Malvolio's misadventures, or as the Victorians transformed Viola into a model of womanly devotion, we have searched for our own answers in the play's mirror; and the image cast back has been that of a wryly smiling, somewhat weary jester, one of life's privileged spies into the mystery of things" (1988, 61).

After Granville-Barker's landmark production, there were many others of note, which featured most of the important Shakespearean actors of the twentieth century. In Paris at the Théâtre du Vieux-Colombier in 1914, Jacques Copeau directed the play and also played the part of Malvolio, while Louis Jouvet designed the set and also acted as Sir Andrew Aguecheek, and Suzanne Bing played Viola. In 1931, John Gielgud's Malvolio paired with Ralph Richardson's Sir Toby at Sadler's Wells, while in 1932 at a production at the Old Vic and at Sadler's Wells, Harcourt Williams directed Richardson as Sir Toby, Robert Speaight as Malvolio, and Edith Evans as Viola. That same year at the Chicago Drama Festival, Orson Welles directed the play and starred as Malvolio; a film version of this production was made in 1933. In 1937 Tyrone Guthrie directed *Twelfth Night* at the Old Vic, with Alec Guinness as Sir Andrew, Laurence Olivier as Sir Toby, and Jessica Tandy as Viola/Sebastian. The first post-World War II production was staged in Stratford, England, on Shakespeare's birthday, April 23, 1947, with Jack Hylton directing, Paul Scofield as Sir Andrew, Walter Hudd as Malvolio, Daphne Slater as Olivia, and Beatrix Lehmann as Viola. In 1954 at the Old Vic Denis Carey directed Paul Daneman as Feste, Michael Hordern as Malvolio, John Neville as Orsino, Richard Burton as Sir Toby, and Claire Bloom as Viola. At Stratford, England, in 1955, John Gielgud directed Vivien Leigh as Viola and Laurence Olivier as Malvolio. According to Craik, most Malvolios of the twentieth century "may be roughly classified into the old kill-joys and the young upstarts"; Olivier's Malvolio was of the latter variety. His "speech suggested his origin by an affected, lisping veneer that flaked away suddenly to reveal the barrow-boy vowels" (Lothian and Craik 1975, xcii). Maurice Evans had also played him with a Cockney accent in 1939, and others have followed this lead after Olivier, for example, Ian Holm in 1966 (Lothian and Craik 1975, xcii).[6]

According to numerous theatre historians, two of the most memorable productions of the modern age came at the midpoint of the twentieth century, and both were direct descendents of the revolution begun by Poel and

Granville-Barker. Both, that is, were productions that held the two plots and their romantic and satiric elements in balance instead of repressing the bitter and melancholy elements in favor of the festive. The first was Peter Hall's RSC production at the Memorial Theatre in Stratford in 1958. Hall began the practice "of producing the play emphasizing a specifically 'autumnal' or fin-de-siècle quality"; the set design by Lila de Nobili created "a romantic Caroline world to be seen through a filter of gauze curtains" (Gay 1985, 41). Set right before the outbreak of the English Civil War, the Cavalier costumes offered the ultimate contrast to Malvolio's sober Puritan garb and provide a historical context to the hostilities that upset Olivia's household (Billington 1990, 12). According to Karen Greif, Hall saw the play as "complex, ambiguous, and heartbreakingly funny," a play situated between the earlier comedies, on the one hand, and the problem comedies and tragedies on the other; for him "the comedy is rich, because there is darkness and disturbance" (1988, 66). Like Granville-Barker, Hall identified Feste as the key to the play's tone and therefore cast older actors to play the part, first Cyril Luckham and later, and more famously, Max Adrian in 1960. As directed by Hall, "Feste was unusually astringent," a "dry fool . . . behind the jokes and the imposture an idealist embittered by experience" (Greif 1988, 67). Trevor Nunn, Hall's successor at the Royal Shakespeare Company, felt Hall "had touched a Chekhov-like centre of the play" (Berry 1981a, 113). Hall cast a young actress, Geraldine McEwan, to play Olivia: "her *poseuse* Olivia, complete with giggles and squeaks, undercut the Romantic tradition. Olivia's used to be played in the country matron manner. For the rest, Sir Toby (Patrick Wymark) was a gentleman. (To take Sir Toby seriously is a sign of a modern production.) Malvolio (Eric Porter) was a recognizable human being" (Berry 1981a, 113). His Orsino, however, verged on the satiric; the lightness provided by Olivia and Orsino helped to balance the dominant, melancholic performance by Adrian as Feste.

The second landmark production, also with the Royal Shakespeare Company, was directed some ten years later (1969, and revived at the Aldwych in 1970) by John Barton. Inspired by Hall's vision of the play, Barton directed what many still regard as the best production of *Twelfth Night* ever mounted. Like Hall, Barton worked against the tradition of the play as "an unequivocal call to revelry"; he saw in the title "a central dualism: a feast, an end to feasting. And, astonishingly, Barton illustrates the point through Maria to this end" (Berry 1981a, 114). His Maria was an "elderly spinster" (played by Elizabeth Spriggs) who sees Sir Toby as her "last chance," writes Berry. "So there's an elegiac quality at the heart of even the comic action" (113–14). Barton's goal was to realize the play's complex variety, "to sound all the notes that are there" (Ford 2006, 153). He recognized the need for a strong ensemble production, with no character dominating at the expense of the others; he was aided by several outstanding performances. According to Lois Potter, he took all the characters seriously as people "and had them take each other seriously as well" (1985, 56). Judi Dench as Viola greatly impressed critics: "Deeply touching in her moments of emotional vulnerability, yet sprightly and witty when necessary (and particularly athletically hilarious in the duel scene), Dench's performance lives on for those who saw it as definitive – not because the role of Viola cannot be played any other way, but because Dench's art convinced the audience of the character's complex reality" (Gay 1985, 41).

Like Hall, Barton cast a young actress, Lisa Harrow, to play Olivia. Emrys James played "a wryly compassionate fool, whose experience had earned him wisdom but not bitterness"; unlike more astringent Festes, this one was on good terms with Viola (Greif 1988, 73). Donald Sinden's Malvolio was "extremely funny in his bravura scenes"; he "brought a striking note of pathos both to the 'dark house' scene and to his final exit" (Gay 1985, 41). Sinden has written that Malvolio leaves the stage with the intention of killing himself (1985, 66). Richard Pascoe played a young, passionate, dangerous Orsino (the name means "little bear"); the production opens with his listening for several minutes to strains of music. Barton's attention to sound is noted by numerous commentators. Music not only opens and closes the play (the only play by Shakespeare to do so), but Barton had characters unexpectedly humming snippets of the songs that Feste sings, and he used the sound of the sea to underscore moments of emotional power. Furthermore, Stanley Wells writes that the production illustrated "one of John Barton's greatest skills as a director; that is, the capacity to train his actors to deliver verse with a sensitivity to its full potential range of meaning, both intellectual and emotional" (1977, 46). The set, designed by Christopher Morley, was a receding, slatted gauze tunnel which was back-lit "not only to suggest magic and the sea and the world outside they'd come from, but also to intensify moments that were at once mysterious and intensely human" (Billington 1990, 12–13). Stanley Wells praised the production for its "beauty of communication, of sympathy, understanding, and compassion. It had a Chekhovian quality" (1977, 62). "Shot through with sadness though the production was," Wells continues, "its ultimate effect was a happy one" (62).

Criticism through much of the twentieth century mirrored developments on stage at least as much as if not more than literary criticism influenced performance. As with theatrical productions, there was an ever-increasing recognition of the play's more serious themes and the notes of sadness that had been for so long overlooked or given scant attention. According to Craik, the awareness of the play's "elements of pathos and danger has pressed more and more heavily upon *Twelfth Night* [in the twentieth century]: it is Shakespeare's 'Farewell to Comedy' (A. T. Quiller-Couch, 1930), it has 'a silvery undertone of sadness' (J. Middleton Murry, 1936), its poetry is of 'an almost elegiac quality' (T. M. Parrot, 1949)" (Lothian and Craik 1975, lii–liii). While some critics like W. H. Auden (1962) and Jan Kott (1966) "regard *Twelfth Night* not merely as a farewell to comedy but as a positive rejection of mirth and romance" (Lothian and Craik 1975, liii), others sought to argue for the play's complex balance of conflicting parts, its trick of harmonizing various kinds of music, mingling prose and verse, the sweet and the stinging, in almost equal proportions.[7]

For much of the twentieth century, the dominant mode of literary analysis was "close reading," as practiced by the New Critics, who tended to treat literary works as self-contained artifacts, fictional worlds that could and should be understood and appreciated apart from consideration of authors' biographies or the political, economic, or social concerns of the times when they were written, and without reference to when the works are read or the responses of the people who read them at different times and in different places. Some New Critical studies examine the play's language and imagery, or both. Of the latter, Carolyn Spurgeon and G. Wilson Knight were early forerunners in exploring the ways imagery unifies the play, while Elizabeth Yearling's essay "Language, Theme, and Character in *Twelfth Night*" (1982) contrasts the speech patterns of individual characters. Of course, older forms of criticism continued as well. Source studies by Geoffrey Bullough, Kenneth Muir, Robert C. Melzi, and L. G. Salingar added greatly to our understanding of the play's literary roots. In addition, there were historical studies, for example, Leslie Hotson's *The First Night of* Twelfth Night (1954), which imagines a first performance of the play at Whitehall, and John Draper's *The "Twelfth Night" of Shakespeare's Audience* (1950), a sociological study of Olivia's household, which maintains that the play is about "social security" through marriage rather than about romance. In other words, although New Criticism was the dominant mode, older forms of analysis persisted, and avatars of newer, so-called "postmodern" approaches began to appear.

Of the efforts to find unity, most take the form of thematic readings. Obviously, the theme of love is prominent in several studies – love's power, love's folly, self-love and selfless love, narcissism and love of God. Alexander Leggatt explores the theme of unrequited love; H. B. Charlton also finds the play to be mostly concerned with romantic love. In his view, the moral center of *As You Like It* and *Twelfth Night* resides in their heroines, Rosalind and Viola: "It was in women that Shakespeare found this equipoise, this balance which makes personality in action a sort of ordered interplay of the major components of human nature. In his women, hand and heart and brain are fused in a vital and practicable union" (1938, 279). Harold Jenkins takes a similar line in maintaining that the theme of *Twelfth Night* is "the education of a man or woman"; in his view, "Orsino and Olivia come to their happy ending when they have learnt a new attitude to others and themselves" (1959, 21). Viola is the primary agent of change: "In the emotional pattern of the play Viola represents a genuineness of feeling against which the illusory can be measured" (30). Others have focused on the theme of self-love and self-deception. Joseph Summers connects the many forms of disguise in the play to instances of self-deception, a topic sounded early in the twentieth century by E. K. Chambers. Summers also sees Viola as the center of the play, able to see behind the masks of others while maintaining her own disguise. Bertrand Evans explores the importance of dramatic irony to the play, examining the audience's knowledge at various points as a crucial ingredient in the experience of the comedy. Others, like Morris Tilley, explore the contrast between indulgence and restraint as an important organizing principle of the play. Looking back to the nineteenth-century French critic Montégut and forward to C. L. Barber, Enid Welsford explores the Saturnalian elements in the play and finds Feste as Lord of Misrule is central to the play's structure. Meanwhile Barbara Lewalski and John Hollander connect the holiday theme to the Christian theme of epiphany. Later critics like Cynthia Lewis, who is represented in this collection, and Yu Jin Ko continue this investigation of religious themes in the play.

As is clear even in a brief survey of thematic criticism, character studies persisted throughout the twentieth century and often figure in discussions of the play's thematic unity and coherence. A. C. Bradley's 1916 essay on Feste would at first seem a continuation of nineteenth-century concern with characters as real people, as much of Bradley's work epitomizes that approach. Yet, his essay, influenced by Granville-Barker's 1912 Savoy Theatre production, was as much concerned with Feste's unifying role in the play, and thus with the play's overall structure, as it was with thinking of Feste as a real person with a history before the play began. In a marvelous essay, "A Star is Born," Karen Greif traces Feste's rise from relative obscurity in the eighteenth and nineteenth centuries to centrality in the twentieth. As we have also observed, numerous commentators maintain that Viola is the play's most important figure, the key to its elusive themes, the embodiment of whatever ideal is thought to be central to the play – for example, selfless love or self-awareness or insight into other characters. Even greater attention has fallen on the treatment of Malvolio, which has been an issue much debated in the wake of Henry Irving's "tragic" rendition of the part in 1884. Twentieth-century critics as diverse as Cedric Watts and Ralph Berry believe the punishment Malvolio endures is cruel and excessive, horrendously unfair; rather than merely enjoy Malvolio's suffering, Berry contends, audiences experience a growing unease as they watch the last three acts unfold; the "ultimate effect . . . is to make the audience ashamed of itself" (1981b, 119). We are party to a prank that has gotten out of control. "I would we were well rid of this knavery," states Sir Toby (4.2.66–67), and the audience agrees. On the other side, critics like C. L. Barber and Harry Levin show little sympathy for the steward, who plays kill-joy to the revelers, Alazon to Feste's Eiron, scapegoat to the gods of comedy. He is a threat to festivity and to life, according to this line of thinking. "It is . . . fitting that he be plunged into literal darkness," Levin writes. "[W]e should be glad to get rid of Malvolio" (1986, 168). Barber acknowledges the pathos of Malvolio's being "so utterly cut off from everyone else by his anxious self-love," and he also recognizes that the "contest of revelers with intruder does not lead to neglecting ironies about those who are on the side of pleasure" (1959, 256, 249). Nevertheless, for being "hostile to holiday," Malvolio becomes one of "Shakespeare's two greatest comic butts," Shylock being the other (256).

The final act of *Twelfth Night* has drawn commentary from both directors and scholars. Granville-Barker complained that it is a "scandalously ill-arranged and ill-written last scene, the despair of any stage manager" (1974, 28), while in her study of *Twelfth Night* Lois Potter carefully examines the artistry of the long final scene before describing how it is staged in four separate productions. A main issue is the question of the play's genre. Throughout the twentieth century, *Twelfth Night* has edged further and further from being seen as simply a happy celebration of cakes and ale or a romance fulfilled when Sebastian and Viola are reunited and the Duke recognizes and returns Viola's love. Philip Edwards writes that in *Twelfth Night*, Shakespeare seems "detached from romance," while Julien Markels has explored the relation of Feste to the Fool in *Lear* and some of the darker themes the two plays share.

If not a happy comedy, what kind of play is *Twelfth Night*? While most commentators are moved by the reunion of Sebastian and Viola, many have noted that Malvolio's vengeful exit upsets whatever short-term happiness is achieved. Also less than comic is Sir Toby's nasty rejection of Sir Andrew: "Will you help? An ass-head and a coxcomb and a knave, a thin-faced knave, a gull?" (5.1.202–3), and Orsino's earlier threat against Viola – to "sacrifice the lamb that I do love" (5.1.126) – also leaves an unpleasant taste. Others have complained that the romantic pairings at the end seem perfunctory, though much depends, no doubt, on how these relationships (especially between Viola-as-Cesario and Orsino) are rendered earlier in the play.

Perhaps the most perceptive analysis of the final act and how it determines the play's genre is by Anne Barton in her 1972 essay, "*As You Like It* and *Twelfth Night*: Shakespeare's sense of an ending."[8] Barton notes that the first four acts of the play take place in a heightened, festive world. As members of the audience, we make "common cause" with Toby, Maria, and Feste against Malvolio "because we do not want him to spoil the fun which in a sense is ours as well as that of characters actually on the stage. By means of laughter, we too cast Malvolio out" (106). But the final scene "displays a marked harshening of tone" (106). Furthermore, she notes, Shakespeare "treats [the] joining of hands summarily, and turns away at once to the very different issue of Malvolio" (109). In her opinion, the final scene of the play "fights a kind of desperate rearguard action against the cold light of day. It survives only in part, and then by insisting upon an exclusiveness that is poles apart from the various and crowded dance at the end of *As You Like It*" (109). For Viola, Orsino, Sebastian, and Olivia, "this heightened world perpetuates itself. For them, there will be no return from holiday, no need to leave Illyria" (109). Their world is a fiction. Maria, Sir Toby, Sir Andrew, and Malvolio, however, do not partake of the harmony of the play's final lines. For them, "the dream is over and the moment of awakening bitter." Only Feste, writes Barton,

> can restore some sense of unity . . . mediating between the world of the romantic lovers and our own world . . . he has kept us continually aware of the realities of death and time: that "pleasure must be paid, one time or another" (2.4.70–71), that "beauty's a flower" (1.5.52), and "youth's a stuff will not endure" (2.3.52) . . . Two contradictory kinds of time have run parallel through the comedy, diverging only at its end. One is the time of holiday and of fiction, measureless and essentially beneficent, to which Viola trusts when she remains passive and permits the happy ending to work itself out with no positive assistance from her (2.2.40–41). The other time is remorseless and strictly counted.
>
> (Barton 1972, 110)

Later she concludes, "Only with *Twelfth Night* did Shakespeare, apparently, lose faith in endings of this kind" (that is, happy, romantic endings). Instead, in *Twelfth Night* "realism collides painfully with romance" (112).

At the midpoint of the twentieth century, two studies were published that have had a monumental influence on the analysis of Shakespearean comedy; both go well beyond the usual boundaries of formalist criticism. Published in 1957, Northrop Frye's *The Anatomy of Criticism* describes the structure of comedy by relating it to the universal myth of the waste land and its renewal.[9] Following Frye, C. L. Barber's *Shakespeare's Festive Comedy* (1959) examines Shakespeare's comedies in relation to English folk customs and rituals. For Frye, comedy is a *social* genre grounded in universal myths and rituals, which depicts "the movement from one kind of society to another. At the beginning of the play the obstructing characters are in charge of the play's society, and the audience recognizes that they are usurpers. At the end of the play the device in the plot that brings hero and heroine together causes a new society to crystallize around the hero" (163). Equally important is his description of "the drama of the green world" often found in Shakespeare's romantic comedies, "its plot being assimilated to the ritual theme of the triumph of life and love over the waste land . . . Thus the action of the comedy begins in a world represented as a normal world, moves into the green world, goes into a metamorphosis there in which comic resolution is achieved, and returns to the normal world" (182). In *Twelfth Night*, he notes, the "entire action takes place in the second world" (185), a heightened world. The "workaday world," as Anne Barton observes, influenced by Frye and Barber, lies outside the gates of Illyria. It is the world of wind and rain Feste sings of in his final song.[10]

Barber's book has as its subtitle "A Study of Dramatic Form and Its Relation to Social Custom"; his formula for folk rituals like the Feast of Fools (with its attendant Lord of Misrule) – "from release to clarification" – parallels Frye's transformative comedy of the green world (1959, 6). The festive (mis)behavior associated with seasonal rituals leads to festive release (and often to excess), which in turn leads to a new perspective and a more contented return to the everyday social order. While Frye's approach is anthropological in its understanding of mythic patterns, Barber's is both anthropological and psychological. As M. M. Mahood notes, "[l]ike Frye, Barber views Shakespearean comedy as the fruit of the union between classical comedy and the 'folk' element, but for him the all-important aspect of the Saturnalian tradition is its communal character. The audience does not merely witness the archetypal progress 'through release to clarification.' Because the play's context is traditional revelry, it experiences this archetypal progress for itself" (1979, 3). It should further be noted that Frye's work is ahistorical, "universal." Society for him is "society in general," be it ancient Athens or Shakespeare's London or Toronto in 1957. Barber's work is more grounded in the customs of Shakespeare's age, yet by the historicist standards of recent decades, his study might be regarded by some as deficient in this regard. The important point with both Frye and Barber, however, is that they moved literary criticism well beyond the exclusive focus on the text that is the hallmark of the New Criticism. Barber goes beyond the limits of New Criticism in exploring the psychosocial function of drama and ritual. His theory posits that most rituals have a conservative function; holiday celebrations and the excesses of misrule tend to contain discontent and maintain the status quo. Of the confusions caused by Viola's disguise as a male, he writes, "The most fundamental distinction the play brings home to us is the difference between men and women . . . the disguising of a girl as a boy in *Twelfth Night* is exploited so as to renew in a special way our sense of the difference. Just as a saturnalian reversal of social roles need not threaten the social structure, but can serve instead to consolidate it, so a temporary, playful reversal of sexual roles can renew the meaning of a normal relation" (1959, 245). Even though several later critics would disagree with Barber on this and other issues, few would fail to credit him with opening many new areas of critical exploration.

Postmodern dissonance

In speaking of the postmodern critical trends of recent decades, one needs to recognize the lack of a strict boundary or momentous event or publication that separates modern (or even just New Critical) from postmodern. Some approaches in the big tent of the "postmodern," like the psychoanalytic, have been around for many decades. For example, in an essay published in 1973, Helene Moglen draws on Freud's theories of "normal" (i.e., heterosexual) psychosexual development to account for the "brief" homoerotic attachments in the play between Viola/Cesario and Orsino and Viola/Cesario and Olivia, as well as that between Antonio and Sebastian. Her conclusions about sex and gender are in many respects similar to those expressed by C. L. Barber in his landmark study. More recently, Richard P. Wheeler sees in *Twelfth Night* "a situation structurally analogous to the death of [his twin son] Hamnet and the survival of [his twin daughter] Judith in the Shakespeare family. And that action will bring the dead son and brother back" (2000, 147). Critics like Joel Fineman and Barbara Freedman rely on the complex theories of René Girard and Jacques Lacan respectively to read the play's themes of doubling, narcissism, and mourning. Long before the term "deconstruction" was in the vernacular, close readers like William Empson and Norman Rabkin sought variety and ambiguity and potential conflict of meanings rather than the stable, definitive meanings characteristically sought by most New Critics. Readings of Shakespearean texts by Empson especially "had the unexpected effect not of confirming the unity of a text but of destabilizing it, showing a text that restlessly argues with itself" (Ford 2006, 115). More recently, Geoffrey Hartman locates the dramatic action of the play in "the effect of language on character" (1985, 38), while Stephen Booth has explored "the manifestations of a phenomenon whereby listeners and readers casually and effortlessly perceive sense in texts that . . . 'contain' the sense they deliver but that can be demonstrated to be nonsense" (1998, 149). As his chapter title, "*Twelfth Night* 1.1: The Audience as Malvolio," suggests, Booth demonstrates that like the deceived steward, audiences assume they understand much more about the play than they actually do. "Postmodern" is often synonymous with subversive, resistant reading, with the habit of "reading against the grain" of surface meanings (what used to be called "obvious authorial intention") or traditional interpretations.

Another characteristic of many postmodern approaches is that they require the critic to "historicize," to view the literary work as part of and in relation to the cultural and historical milieu in which it was produced. For most New Critics of the mid-twentieth century, by contrast, the literary text is timeless and self-contained. It can be understood without extensive reference to history or the cultural context in which the work was first performed; its meaning is stable regardless of time or place. In his essay on *Twelfth Night*, "Fiction and Friction," Stephen Greenblatt illustrates this important difference between New Critics and the more recent New Historicists. His "Shakespearean" topic is how sex and gender are represented in *Twelfth Night*; to answer this he needs to go beyond the world of the play to understand "the curve of gender" depicted in the play (his metaphor comes from the game of bowls): "I propose that we examine the bowl more carefully, search out the off-center weight implanted in it, analyze why it follows the curve of gender. To do so we must historicize Shakespearean sexual nature, restoring it to its relation of negotiation and exchange with other social discourses of the body. For this task it is essential to break away from the textual isolation that is the primary principle of formalism and to move outside the charmed circle of a particular story and its variants" (1988, 72–73).

Over the last three decades *Twelfth Night* has drawn scores of scholars who explore early modern ideas in the play about gender, sexuality, and the body, as well as issues related to early modern social class and economy.

Viola's disguise as Cesario, its cultural and psychological implications, has been discussed from a variety of postmodern perspectives. Some have theorized that her disguise is an attempt to give herself time to grieve and to suspend her participation in courtship, or perhaps it is even an unconscious attempt to keep her brother alive. Viola's disguise as Cesario has proven to be an especially rich mine for feminist critics, and they have reached a great variety of conclusions. For example, in the first wave of contemporary feminism, Juliet Dusinberre writes that "Rosalind, Portia, even Viola, whose minds travel easily between the world of men and the world of women, extend rather than endanger their sense of self when they assume a man's dress . . . A man's attire, like a man's education, allows them to be more complete and fully developed women" (1975, 264–65). In her 1982 study of gender and genre in Shakespeare, Linda Bamber contrasts Shakespeare's comic and tragic women, and finds the former more confident and resourceful. Later feminists, meanwhile, have seen in the disguise confirmation of Judith Butler's theory in *Gender Trouble* that gender is a culturally-constructed performance rather than a natural and essential set of traits, different for males and females. Regarding the degree to which Viola's disguise is subversive, not all feminists agree. Catherine Belsey suggests "that Shakespearean comedy can be read as disrupting sexual difference, calling in question that set of relations between terms which proposes as inevitable an antithesis between masculine and feminine, men and women" (1985, 171). In discussing the exchange between Viola and Orsino in act 2 scene 4, Belsey asks who it is that tells "the blank history of Viola's father's pining daughter? The answer is neither Viola nor Cesario, but a speaker who at this moment occupies a place which is not precisely masculine or feminine, where the notion of identity itself is disrupted to display a difference within subjectivity, and the singularity which resides in this difference" (192). Jean Howard, by contrast, claims Viola is not truly a threat to the "gender hierarchical system" because her female subjectivity is never in question. The real threat is Olivia, Howard claims; the countess is "punished, comically but unmistakably, by being made to fall in love with the cross-dressed Viola . . . The good woman, Viola, thus becomes the vehicle for humiliating the unruly woman in the eyes of the audience" (1988, 432). Christina Malcolmson explores the gendered differences between Malvolio's fate and Viola's. Both servants aspire to wed above their social rank. Viola thrives while Malvolio is punished. Lisa Jardine also focuses on issues of class, maintaining that "'eroticism,' in the early modern period, is not gender specific, is not grounded in the sex of the possibly 'submissive' partner, but is an expectation of that very submissiveness. As twentieth-century readers we recognize the eroticism of gender *confusion*, and reintroduce that confusion as a feature of the dramatic narrative. Whereas, for the Elizabethan theatre audience, it may be the very clarity of the mistakenness – the very indifference to gendering – which is designed to elicit the pleasurable response from the audience" (1992, 34). John Kerrigan and David Schalkwyk also take up issues related to social class and service in the play. Kerrigan looks at "secrecy and gossip" in the play, while Schalkwyk finds many parallels between *Twelfth Night* and Shakespeare's sonnets.

Yet another line of exploration provoked by Viola's disguise is the issue of same-sex desire. Many critics today would disagree with the "hetero-normative" interpretations of sexual development and desire offered to earlier generations by C. L. Barber and Helene Moglen (Edmondson 2005, 80–81). In an essay published in 1992, Joseph Pequigney contends that the Antonio–Sebastian relationship is indisputably homosexual, and would have been perceived that way by Shakespeare's original audience, an opinion also expressed by Stephen Orgel when he writes, "I think it is also to the point that *Twelfth Night* includes the only overtly homosexual couple in Shakespeare except for Achilles and Patroclus" (1996, 51). Jessica Tvordi, meanwhile, finds that the female bond between Maria and Olivia "challenge[s] and refigure[s] the play's heterosexual imperatives" (1999, 115); "The friendship of Celia and Rosalind [in *As You Like It*] suggests ways to read the domestic alliance of Maria and Olivia, an alliance heretofore unexamined for its homoerotic potential in a notably queered play" (116). In her study of early modern desire, Valerie Traub writes that "the homoeroticism of *Twelfth Night* . . . is anxious and strained. This text explores a diversity of desire, proceeding with erotic plurality as far as it can; then, in the face of anxiety generated by this exploration, it fixes the homoerotic interest onto a marginalized figure [Antonio] . . . The homoerotic energies of Viola, Olivia, and Orsino are displaced onto Antonio, whose relation to Sebastian is finally sacrificed for the maintenance of institutionalized heterosexuality and generational continuity" (1992, 123).

Viola's disguise has also led to lively discussion of the significance of the transvestite theatre in early modern England. In his essay "Fiction and Friction," Stephen Greenblatt assumes the general acceptance during Shakespeare's time of Galen's single-sex model of human anatomy. In this model, male and female were thought to be points along a single continuum, with male as the superior of the two. The genitalia of men and women were thought to be homologous, the female's the male's turned inside out. The female also had the potential through sufficient heat to become male, and Greenblatt notes there were contemporary accounts of such remarkable transformations recorded by Montaigne and others. Greenblatt argues that "a conception of gender that is teleologically male and insists upon a verifiable sign that confirms nature's final cause finds its supreme literary expression in a transvestite theatre" (1988, 88). Furthermore, he writes, "Shakespeare realized that if sexual chafing [necessary for both arousal and conception] could not be presented literally onstage, it could be represented figuratively: friction could be fictionalized, chafing chastened and hence made fit for the stage, by transforming it into the witty, erotically charged sparring that is at the heart of the lovers' experience" (89). Greenblatt's essay has drawn some sharp responses, particularly from Janet Adelman and Lorna Hutson. Adelman objects for two reasons: "First, because the model may not in fact be entirely historically accurate, or not accurate in quite the hegemonic way its proponents suppose. And second, because elevation of the one-sex model to hegemonic status – as the single prototype that determined the way that early modern people thought about anatomical sexual difference – sometimes turns out to be only the most recent way of reinforcing lack, made respectable by its apparent claim to historical accuracy" (1999, 25). Hutson sets out to "challenge the operation of a certain kind of 'body history' within recent Shakespeare criticism" (1996, 140). The real subject of *Twelfth Night*, in her opinion, is the obtaining of "social credit." She faults Greenblatt and others for ignoring "the way in which, in sixteenth-century society, a woman's sexual behavior was perceived to affect the honor and therefore the credit and economic power of her kinsmen. Nor do they consider the way in which such traditional conceptions of sexual honor, credit, and wealth were themselves being rapidly transformed by the technology of persuasion – or 'credit' – that such dramatic texts as Shakespeare's represented" (146).

This brief review of recent developments in *Twelfth Night* criticism is by no means meant to be exhaustive. It fails to mention until now recent work in performance criticism and in reception history – for example, Laurie E. Osborne's study of the performance editions of *Twelfth Night*, or her analyses of Trevor Nunn's film version of the play. Nor have I mentioned the important work of Michael Bristol and François Laroque in extending C. L. Barber's insights into early modern rituals, their relevance to Shakespeare's plays, and their likely effect on and meaning for the play's first audiences. Some readers trained as New Critics have complained that in these recent postmodern times the relation between literature and history in literary criticism has tilted too much toward history and to the analysis of early modern ideology and power relations. Artistry and pleasure, some protest, are slighted, and literature's formal beauties are ignored; today's critics read plays, novels, and poems only to learn about early modern intellectual and material culture, or at least that is the charge that is sometimes made. Yet another claim against some recent approaches is that their authors have obvious political agendas that distort their "objective" analysis of the evidence. This accusation has been leveled at times against critical "schools" that promote identity politics such as feminism and queer theory. Then, too, there are complaints about the opacity of some kinds of theory, especially concepts borrowed from the social scientists and continental philosophers. Elizabeth Donno speaks for some who lament postmodern developments and the decline of literary formalism. In reviewing essays on *Twelfth Night* published during the last two decades of the twentieth century, she asks, "What is the predominant characteristic of these twenty-odd pieces written, in general, over the last fifteen years? I suppose that the most apt term would be 'tendentious' because of their deriving, or imposing, ideological concepts from or on to the text." She notes "the scant concern" given to "artistic" and "dramatic" elements in the play; then speculates that this scant concern "indicates either that these have received sufficient earlier discussion, or that other factors have more current appeal" (1999, 327). I think Donno is correct in noting the abandonment of New Critical concerns, but I believe she is wrong to think a detailed and thoughtful understanding of history and culture has little or no relevance to aesthetic appreciation and analysis. Ideally, as I hope the essays later in this volume will demonstrate, understanding the culture from which a literary work like *Twelfth Night* emerges adds greatly to our ability to understand the play and to appreciate its artistry.

Postmodern staging

On stage there have been many bitter-sweet, autumnal renditions of *Twelfth Night* since the early 1970s in the Hall-and-Barton Chekhovian mode of naturalism. These productions attempt to create a harmony of contrasting tones, to find a unity while at the same time celebrating the play's variety. Sam Mendes's Donmar Warehouse production in 2002 is a recent example in the Barton tradition; according to Penny Gay, in repertoire with *Uncle Vanya*, Mendes's production "demonstrated again the fin-de-siècle or 'end of the old order' feeling that can be located in the play if it is viewed through Chekhovian spectacles. On the tiny Donmar stage, the production strove for psychological rather than visual realism" (1985, 45). Trevor Nunn's 1996 film version, set at the end of the nineteenth century, also evokes Chekhovian tones of sadness and laughter and recalls the work of Nunn's RSC predecessors. Some directors, like Terry Hands (RSC 1979) and Kenneth Branagh (Renaissance Theatre Company 1987), "took the elegiac mood of *Twelfth Night* even further, and set the play in its titular season, winter" (Gay 1985, 41), while Bill Alexander (RSC 1987) set the play in summer in an Adriatic fishing village. The locale for Declan Donnellan's 1986 Cheek by Jowl production was Chekhov's Russia, while his 2003 version, first performed in Moscow, was spoken entirely in Russian.

Other productions, like Peter Gill's (RSC 1974), emphasized particular themes, and here the influence of postmodern theory on the staging of the play has been evident. Gill's production drew on psychoanalysis, with an emphasis on erotic self-love; the set was "dominated by a painted panel showing Narcissus gazing into a pool" and two lines from the sonnets written on walls: 'O learn to read what silent love hath writ' (23) and 'O, know, sweet love, I always write of you' (76)" (Potter 1985, 49). Gill also played up the sexual confusion with lots of physical contact between the various characters. In fact, Olivia's (Mary Rutherford) tendency to touch Malvolio (Nicol Williamson) seemed to encourage his romantic designs on her. His Orsino, played by John Price, seemed bisexual to many reviewers, while

Jane Lapotaire played a boyish Viola. No doubt influenced by postmodern explorations of early modern gender and sexuality, many productions play up instances of same-sex attraction in the play. It is not unusual in contemporary productions to have Viola-disguised-as-Cesario kissed by both Orsino and Olivia, and it has become the theatrical norm for Antonio and Sebastian to be played as a homosexual couple. In Donnellan's 1986–87 production at the RSC's Swan Theatre in Stratford, Orsino almost walks off with Sebastian at the end of the play, and a gay Feste makes a pass at Antonio.

In other kinds of experiment, the Shenandoah Shakespeare Express of the late 1990s recalled the work of William Poel slightly more than 100 years ago. The Virginia-based company directed by Ralph Alan Cohen performed Shakespeare's plays on thrust stages, with minimal sets and natural lighting and lots of interaction with the audience. Like Poel's company, SSE sought to perform the plays within two hours, which at times made for fast-paced, if not madcap speed of delivery. Even more daring was the all-male production by the Globe Theatre Company. The play was directed by Tim Carroll at the Middle Temple and later at the new Globe Theatre; Mark Rylance is said to have performed Olivia to perfection. To find the most daring productions of *Twelfth Night*, one must look to the European continent. According to Penny Gay, "At the end of the twentieth century it seemed that productions not in England, or not in English, were finding more varied meanings in the play. Continental European theatre, with a long history of experiment, is less reverential towards the Shakespearean text . . . Eclectic, anti-historical costumes and sets emphasized psychological and even political possibilities that strongly reflected the cultural fashions of the time and place of production" (1985, 46). Essays in this collection by Nathalie Rivère de Carles, Christa Jansohn, and Marcela Kostihová describe some of the most interesting productions by Ariane Mnouchkine and many others in France, Italy, Germany, and the Czech Republic.

Writing over a half a century ago, John Russell Brown noted that the "opportunities for swinging a production round into line with a chosen mood – to make it 'what they will,' to reverse roles as in a 'Twelfth Night' revel – have encouraged directors to tackle *Twelfth Night* and to experiment widely in the search for original interpretations" (1986, 30). Nevertheless, he claims, these different theatrical interpretations of the play

> are not finally irreconcilable . . . each new revelation reflects on earlier ones and, in the mind, a single view of the play is continually growing in complexity and range, and in understanding. We may believe that a single production might, one day, represent to the full our single, growing awareness . . . Our knowledge of *Twelfth Night* and of human behaviour may assure us that an Olivia is both mature and immature, according to which side of her personality is in view; a Sir Toby energetic *and* melancholy, vulgar *and* well-schooled; and a Viola lyrical *and* practical, *and*

> helpless. The world of the play is gay, quiet, strained, solemn, dignified, elegant, easy, complicated, precarious, hearty, homely; the conclusion close to laughter, song, awe *and* simplicity. And this is an understanding which begs not to be hid, but to be realized on stage.
>
> (Brown 1986, 30)

Brown suggests that a five-year study of successive productions under changing conditions, for different audiences, "might make possible a production which would be original, not by one-sidedness, but by answering more fully than before to Shakespeare's text and combining the excitement of many interpretations" (31). Perhaps Brown is correct in his speculation, but it may be more likely that it is impossible to see all angles of this rare theatrical gem in a single production, or even in five years of productions combined. The play will continue to change and evolve as we change and evolve. That is the lesson learned when one takes the long view.

Twelfth Night: New Critical Essays

The essays in this collection contribute to many of the on-going discussions described in the earlier sections of this introduction, while some also open new lines of investigation. These original works of criticism are essentially of two kinds: those that attempt to recover early modern meanings that have been partially obscured or entirely lost to readers and audiences today, and those essays, like much of this introduction, that describe and analyze how the play has been received – that is, understood and performed – at different times over the last 400 years, particularly in recent times, not just in Great Britain, Canada, and the United States, but on the European continent as well. Essays of the first kind are deeply historicist, while those that concern theatre history often reveal how *Twelfth Night* has been appropriated to serve various ideological causes at various historical moments. Rather than segregate the essays on performance, I have chosen to intermingle them with the others – in part because of the close connection over the centuries between criticism and performance, and in part because of other kinds of thematic links between the two kinds of essay.

Patricia Parker's contribution is a model of textual recovery and in that regard serves as a prelude to many of the historicist essays that follow. As editor of the forthcoming Norton edition of *Twelfth Night*, she "foregrounds cases in which the ambiguous, portmanteau, or polysemous quality of the play that appeared in the Folio of 1623 has been (in one sense or the other) obscured" by editors in later incarnations of the play. Thus, she writes, "the text we get to see in modern editions differs repeatedly from it [the First Folio] in ways that suggest editorial 'interference.'" A second line of exploration in her essay suggests a meaning of the word "eunuch" never before applied by scholars to Viola's plan in act 1 scene 2 to disguise herself. Parker's theory represents an important contribution to the many attempts to solve this riddle, most recently by Keir Elam.

The next four essays – by Bruce R. Smith, David Schalkwyk, Laurie E. Osborne, and Goran V. Stanivuković – explore early modern notions of love, friendship, and masculinity. Drawing on Renaissance medical and scholastic psychological texts, Smith explores the role of "fancy" and its relation to imagination, love, and sexuality. While most twenty-first-century readers think of "fancy" as another word for "imagination, with a pun on sexual desire or falling in love," Smith explains that in Shakespeare's time "fancy" was also "a creative capacity that was engaged every single time they saw, heard, smelled, tasted and/or touched anything – or anyone, for that matter." While Queer Theory "is concerned with what comes *after* words," early modern psychology "is concerned with what comes *before* words." In analyzing the opening speech of the play, Smith argues that "Orsino's language . . . is so sense laden that any separation of 'sense' from 'speech' seems wildly misleading. Putting sensation back into sexuality enables us to understand the sexuality of Shakespeare and his contemporaries on *their* terms, not *ours*."

David Schalkwyk, meanwhile, discusses competing early modern notions of love – one represented by Orsino as spokesman for Galen's misogynistic humoral distinctions between men and women, the other demonstrated by Viola's all-but-silent example. Hers, Schalkwyk argues, is love "in deed" – love as selfless action: "Insofar as love as passion is at stake in *Twelfth Night*, we might thus say that it is displayed through dedicated behavior and action rather than the causal interiority of bodily heat or humour. Viola as Cesario calls into question the very basis for distinguishing between men and women on the basis of an intrinsic difference in humoural fluids and temperatures." Love, he concludes, is not an emotion or a passion, but is rather "a force that begins with God and infuses human life with its coherence and meaning." Laurie E. Osborne's essay also focuses on Viola/Cesario's relationship with Orsino. In having Viola seek and achieve "amity" with her master while in disguise as Cesario, Shakespeare offers an implicit challenge to Montaigne's claim that women were incapable of participating in amity, the highest form of friendship between men. "Through this sleight of gender," Osborne contends, "Shakespeare maintains the non-erotic idealism of amity while also underscoring erotic desire." Amity prepares the way for the happy comic resolution, for Orsino's turn in act 5 from Olivia to Viola. "In *Twelfth Night*," concludes Osborne, "the best male friend is a woman and the most desirable wife is the loving male friend."

Goran V. Stanivuković's essay is concerned with the ways masculinity is represented in the play; his thesis is that the play's instability of gender categories owes much to romance literature, particularly to Emanuel Forde's *Parismus*, almost certainly one of Shakespeare's sources for *Twelfth Night*. Shakespeare's plot, he writes, "registers, through Forde, the cultural shift from chivalric to romantic masculinity" in the late sixteenth and early seventeenth centuries. The play "opposes heroic masculinity" of the kind depicted in *Parismus* "by parodying it, and promotes and mocks forms of romantic masculinity in a variety of plot situations, such as courtship, seduction, marriage, or queer bonding." Despite the focus in the play on the "cross-dressed body and its sexual signification," the play is "in fact more interested in social status than sex, because the culture has started to define masculinity more according to parentage and social rank and less according to heroic achievements."

Marcela Kostihová's essay offers a break from efforts to recover early modern meanings as it is the first in the volume to discuss performance issues, in this case, recent stagings in the post-communist Czech Republic, yet it follows Stanivuković's contribution because like that essay hers recognizes that "[t]he text of *Twelfth Night* lends itself particularly well to the explorations of various forms of masculinity." She focuses on the ways recent Czech productions portray the Antonio–Sebastian relationship, "two characters who simultaneously exhibit the most traditional masculine traits and affection for each other, presenting contemporary directors with the challenge of representing a complex and socially acceptable Renaissance bond to a subtly and subversively homophobic audience likely to read the characters' desires, if their speech is unedited, as evidence of emasculating homosexuality." Later in her essay she states that "any interpretation of Antonio's and Sebastian's relationship is in a contemporary production political"; this is especially so in a nation that is in the process of constructing a new "western" identity; given that fact, the productions she describes "speak volumes about current tensions between traditional and re-defined views on what makes or breaks a 'true man.'"

Elizabeth Pentland's contribution offers a revision of claims by various scholars that Illyria represented for Shakespeare's contemporaries an unfamiliar, exotic locale – one that, in Kenneth Muir's words, was "conveniently obscure." In fact, she contends, Shakespeare's choice of Illyria was "not motivated by a desire for mystery or romantic dislocation, but had everything to do with the region's concrete historical and geographic associations." The setting was well known both as a "locus of classical antiguity" and as a "modern" Adriatic region famous for trade and piracy; in addition, it was a place associated with independent women and female rule with obvious parallels to Elizabethan England. "Shakespeare and his contemporaries," she asserts, "knew far more about Illyria (or Sclavonia) than most readers and playgoers do today." Following Pentland's essay, and in some ways reflecting more traditional ideas about Elizabethan lack of familiarity with Illyria, is Catherine Lisak's exploration of the themes of foreignness and strangeness in *Twelfth Night*. Lisak observes that "Viola may begin her career in Illyria as an outsider and an intruder, but . . . swiftly shifts the spotlight of strangeness onto Illyria." By placing the setting in a foreign land, Shakespeare in *Twelfth Night* "emancipates foreignness from strangeness. Foreignness no longer systematically carries with it the idea of strangeness any more than strangeness systematically implies foreignness . . . As this last of the romantic and festive comedies unfolds, its spectators are made to feel foreign, estranged, or strange, for the play continually challenges their sense of what it means to be human."

Like Lisak, and unlike Pentland, Nathalie Rivère de Carles emphasizes the exotic in her account of important European stagings of *Twelfth Night* (particularly on the continent) over the last 125 years. The "geographical indeterminacy of the play's setting," she states, "is an essential feature of both the plot and the staging. Indeed, this special license enables Shakespeare to superimpose English and non-English influences within the action but also allows a complete scenographical flexibility." In tracing productions over the last century in France and Italy (and Declan Donnellan's production first in Russia and then later in England), Rivère de Carles notes that directors have had to make major alterations of the script for contemporary audiences, substituting the "indeterminacy of the oneiric world" for Shakespeare's "spaciotemporal ambiguity." Antonio Latella (Italy in 2004), she notes, "shows no respect for time, place and persons," while Declan Donnellan transplants the play to Chekhov's Russia. The ultimate form of exoticism, she notes, is metatheatricality: "The gap between the spectators' expectations and the actual performance suffices to create the distancing effect that enables the exotic to develop." In the final essay in this collection focused on theatrical performance, Christa Jansohn traces German productions of the play from the late nineteenth century to the present, paying particular attention to "the changing conceptions of the stage design, the age of the main characters and the costuming." While she relates some of these changes to socio-political forces at work in Germany during various epochs, she avoids the "risk of stereotyping and/or simplifying the reception of *Twelfth Night* in the German theatre."

With Alan W. Powers's essay on popular ceremonies, particularly the exchange of rings, in *Twelfth Night*, we return again to the recovery of early modern meanings of which only vestiges remain. A great many people in Shakespeare's original audience, Powers reminds us, were illiterate; in an oral culture like Shakespeare's, rituals, ceremonies, and tokens took on great significance which is all but lost to us today. In the case of rings, he observes, "their vestigial use in our modern culture abrades their original significance." The gifting of tokens by Olivia and Orsino "raises the tone of *Twelfth Night* from everyday gifts such as those bought at fairs, or 'fayings.' These tokens contribute to the overall poetic tone of the play, while grounding it securely in the popular culture of the day." In the course of his discussion Powers notes in passing that Malvolio is a Brownist, one of the Puritan sects responsible for closing the theatres in 1642, a fact that may explain his harsh treatment in the play. Through his Puritan identity, he is to "any American inheritor of Brownist Protestant culture . . . recognizably one of a very few upward-mobile 'Americans' in Shakespeare." For attempting to marry not the boss's daughter "but the boss herself," Malvolio is regarded by characters in the play and by Shakespeare's audience as mad. Similar thoughts about Malvolio, politics, upward mobility, and madness are sounded in the essay by Ivo Kamps that follows Powers'. According to Kamps, "Shakespeare playfully explores the dynamics of madness, diagnosis, and cure in the Toby-Maria-Malvolio plot of *Twelfth Night*." In tricking Malvolio into performing an identity "unrecognizable to members of Olivia's household," Maria and the others expose Malvolio's secret fantasy of marrying Olivia as a form of insanity; "what could be more fitting," Kamps remarks, "than to have him act out his desire and be declared insane for it." Like Powers, however, Kamps observes that the last word, if not the last laugh, may be Malvolio's as representative of Puritan social mobility: "The battle to preserve an absolute difference between commoner and aristocrat may . . . already be lost."

Implicit in the readings of both Powers and Kamps is an awareness of the conservative politics and nostalgia for a more rigid, unchanging social hierarchy that underlie the Malvolio subplot. Jennifer C. Vaught's essay applies this insight to more recent American rituals – the Louisiana traditions of Twelfth Night and Mardi Gras: "Both Shakespeare's *Twelfth Night*, a play about aristocratic reactions to the rising middle ranks, and the Twelfth Night Revelers [of New Orleans] . . . expose the potentially conservative and violent underbelly of literary and cultural celebrations of the Feast of the Epiphany." In examining both the Malvolio subplot, in which an upstart is punished for aspiring to climb the social ladder, and the racist agenda of the New Orleans Twelfth Night Revelers, she "reveals the extent to which popular, festival customs can be appropriated by elite groups for conservative, repressive purposes."

If Patricia Parker's essay serves as prologue to the essays that follow, Cynthia Lewis's contribution stands as epilogue. Her focus is on the unsolved mysteries of the play, which range from questions about Viola's eunuch disguise to the ultimate fates of Antonio, Malvolio, and the sea captain who has preserved Viola's female attire. The play, she writes, "would seem to include too many examples of unresolved plot elements to be construed as accidental." One fact she notes is how many of the play's characters are involved in acts of detection, and what is true of characters in the play is even more true of members of the audience. This is a play about interpretation. In leaving so many issues unresolved, Shakespeare achieves a kind of "slice-of-life realism" in which the play "cracks a window on the disordered world just beyond its boundaries." Nevertheless, she concludes, "[t]he absence of such total concordance need not signify postmodern chaos." In noting the efforts of some critics to decipher the riddle of "*M. O. A. I.*," Lewis offers a strong caution to us all to avoid falling into the trap that dooms Malvolio. In pointing to the play's multiple possibilities of interpretation, Lewis reminds us – as do all the essays in this collection – that no single critical interpretation or theatrical performance will probably ever stand as the final word on *Twelfth Night*.

Notes

1. Unless contained within quotations of other critics, all quotations and citations are from Keir Elam's 2008 Arden 3 edition.
2. Elam states that "[t]he year 1601 in the old Julian calendar corresponds to 1602 in the reformed Gregorian calendar introduced in 1582 but not adopted in England until 1752. In Shakespeare's day the New Year began on 25 March" (3, note 1).
3. German critic Gregor Sarrazin was the first to mention the visit of Duke Orsini in relation to Shakespeare's comedy; J. W. Draper later takes up this "Italian connection," which Hotson then turns into a full-length study (Elam 2008, 93).
4. It is here worth noting that M. C. Bradbrook (1969) has convincingly argued that the role of Feste was played by Robert Armin, who replaced Will Kempe in 1599.
5. *Gl'Ingannati* a play by the "Accademia degli Intronati di Siena, written as an apology to the ladies for a sketch performed the previous evening, which was Twelfth Night, 1531" (Hutson 1996, 151).
6. I am grateful to Keir Elam's list of 120 performances of *Twelfth Night* in the Arden 3 edition (146–53).
7. Jan Kott links *Twelfth Night* to the Sonnets when he observes that "[e]very character here has something of the fair youth and the Dark Lady. Every character has been endowed with a bitter knowledge about love. Love in Illyria is violent and impatient; it cannot be gratified or reciprocated." Illyria, Kott surmises, "is a country of erotic madness" (1966, 311). Later in the chapter he states that *Twelfth Night* "is a very bitter comedy about the Elizabethan *dolce vita*, or, at any rate, about the *dolce vita* at all levels and wings of Southampton" (334).
8. Scholar Anne Barton, formerly Anne Righter, married RSC director John Barton in 1968. In fact, she wrote a program note on the play for his 1969 RSC production of *Twelfth Night*, and many of the ideas expressed there are in the 1972 essay as well. The degree to which her views influenced her husband's direction, or his production influenced her literary interpretation, is probably impossible to untangle. It is yet another example of what Lois Potter calls "the interdependence of literary and theatrical criticism"of *Twelfth Night*.
9. Frye's third chapter, "Theory of Myths" especially its subsection "The Mythos of Spring: Comedy," contains material first presented in "The Argument of Comedy," which he published in English Institute Essays in 1948.
10. Barton begins her essay by noting the important contributions of Frye and Barber: "Critics, aware now of the 'social' nature of the comedies, of their complex structure of silently juxtaposed scenes, tend to take this form more seriously than they once did." She credits Frye and Barber for arguing "the essential unity of Shakespearean comedy" as "plays concerned primarily with transformation, with the clarification and renewal attained, paradoxically, through a submission to some kind of disorder, whether festive or not. We have learned to notice as typically Shakespearean the way characters move between two contrasted locales – one of them heightened and more spacious than the other – and we regard that 'new society' which makes its way back to the normal world at the end of the play as a subtler and more consequential achievement than older critics did" (1994, 92).

Works cited

Adelman, Janet. "Making Defect Perfection: Shakespeare and the One-Sex Model." In *Enacting Gender on the English Renaissance Stage*. Ed. Viviana Comensoli and Anne Russell. Urbana and Chicago: University of Illinois Press, 1999: 23–52.

Arlidge, Anthony. *Shakespeare and the Prince of Love: The Feast of Misrule in the Middle Temple*. London: Giles de la Mare, 2000.

Auden, W. H. "Music in Shakespeare." In *The Dyer's Hand*. New York: Random House, 1962: 500–527.

Bamber, Linda. *Comic Women, Tragic Men: A Study of Gender and Genre in Shakespeare*. Stanford, CA: Stanford University Press, 1982.

Barber, C. L. *Shakespeare's Festive Comedy: A Study of Dramatic Form and Its Relation to Social Custom*. New York: Meridian Books, 1959.

Barnet, Sylvan. "Charles Lamb and the Tragic Malvolio." *Philological Quarterly* 23 (1954): 178–88.

Barton, Anne. "*As You Like It* and *Twelfth Night*: Shakespeare's Sense of an Ending." In *Shakespearean Comedy*. Ed. J. R. Brown and Bernard Harris. Stratford-upon-Avon Studies, 14. London: Edward Arnold, 1972. Reprinted in *Essays, Mainly Shakespearean*. Cambridge: Cambridge University Press, 1994: 91–112.

Belsey, Catherine. "Disrupting Sexual Difference: Meaning and Gender in the Comedies." In *Alternative Shakespeares*. Ed. John Drakakis. London and New York: Methuen, 1985: 166–90.

Berry, Ralph. "The Season of *Twelfth Night*." In *Changing Styles in Shakespeare*. London: George Allen & Unwin, 1981a: 109–18.

——. "*Twelfth Night*: The Experience of the Audience." *Shakespeare Survey* 34 (1981b): 111–19.

Bethell, S. L. *Shakespeare and the Popular Tradition*. London: King and Staples, 1944.

Billington, Michael. *Directors' Shakespeare: Approaches to Twelfth Night*. London: Nick Hern Books, 1990.

Booth, Stephen. *Precious Nonsense: The Gettysburg Address, Ben Jonson's Epitaphs on His Children, and* Twelfth Night. Berkeley: University of California Press, 1998.

Bradbrook, M. C. "The New Clown: *Twelfth Night*." *Shakespeare the Craftsman*. New York: Barnes and Noble, 1969: 49–74.

Bradley, A. C. "Feste the Jester." In Twelfth Night*: Critical Essays*. Ed. Stanley Wells. New York: Garland, 1986: 17–22.

Bristol, Michael D. *Carnival and Theater: Plebian Culture and the Structure of Authority in Renaissance England*. New York: Methuen, 1985.

Brown, John Russell. "Directions for *Twelfth Night*." In Twelfth Night*: Critical Essays*. Ed. Stanley Wells. New York: Garland, 1986: 25–37.

Bullough, Geoffrey. *Narrative and Dramatic Sources of Shakespeare*. Vol. II: *The Comedies, 1597–1603*. London: Routledge and Kegan Paul, 1968.

Butler, Judith. *Gender Trouble: Feminism and the Subversion of Identity*. New York: Routledge, 1999.

Charlton, H. B. *Shakespearian Comedy*. London: Methuen, 1938.

Donno, Elizabeth Story. "*Twelfth Night*." In *International Shakespearean Yearbook* 1. Ed. W. R. Elton and John M. Mucciolo. London: Ashgate, 1999: 322–28.

Draper, John W. *The "Twelfth Night" of Shakespeare's Audience*. Stanford, CA: Stanford University Press, 1950.

Dusinberre, Juliet. *Shakespeare and the Nature of Women*. Basingstoke and London: Macmillan, 1975.

Edmondson, Paul. Twelfth Night*: A Guide to the Text and Its Theatrical Background*. The Shakespeare Handbooks. Basingstoke: Palgrave Macmillan, 2005.

Elam, Keir, ed. *Twelfth Night*. By William Shakespeare. The Arden Shakespeare, series 3. London: Cengage Learning, 2008.

Empson, William. *Seven Types of Ambiguity*. London: Chatto and Windus, 1930.

Evans, Bertrand. *Shakespeare's Comedies*. Oxford: Oxford University Press, 1960.

Fineman, Joel. "Fratricide and Cuckoldry: Shakespeare's Doubles." In *Representing Shakespeare. New Psychoanalytic Essays*. Ed. Murray Schwartz and Coppélia Kahn. Baltimore, MD, and London: Johns Hopkins University Press, 1980: 70–105.

Ford, John R. Twelfth Night*: A Guide to the Play*. Westport, CT: Greenwood Press, 2006.

Forde, Emanuel. *The First Part of Parismus the Renowmed Prince of Bohemia*. London: Thomas Creede, 1598.

Freedman, Barbara. "Naming Loss: Mourning and Representation in *Twelfth Night*." In *Staging the Gaze: Postmodernism, Psychoanalysis, and Shakespearean Comedy.* Ithaca, NY: Cornell University Press, 1991: 192–235.

Frye, Northrop. *The Anatomy of Criticism: Four Essays*. Princeton, NJ: Princeton University Press, 1957.

Furness, Horace Howard, ed. *Twelfth Night, or What You Will*. By William Shakespeare. Philadelphia: J. B. Lippincott, 1901.

Gay, Penny. "Introduction." In *Twelfth Night*. Ed. Elizabeth Story Donno. Cambridge: Cambridge University Press, 1985: 1–53.

Granville-Barker, Harley. "Preface to *Twelfth Night*." In *More Prefaces to Shakespeare*. Ed. E. M. Moore. Princeton, NJ: Princeton University Press, 1974: 26–32.

Gregson, J. M. *Shakespeare:* Twelfth Night. London: Edward Arnold, 1980.

Greenblatt, Stephen. "Fiction and Friction." In *Shakespearean Negotiations: The Circulation of Social Energy in Renaissance England*. Berkeley: University of California Press, 1988: 66–93.

Greif, Karen. "A Star Is Born: Feste on the Modern Stage." *Shakespeare Quarterly* 39 (1988): 61–78.

Harris, Laurie Lanzen, ed. *Twelfth Night*. *Shakespeare Criticism*. Vol. 1. Detroit: Gale, 1984: 537–667.

Hartman, Geoffrey H. "Shakespeare's Poetical Character in *Twelfth Night*." In *Shakespeare and the Question of Theory*. Ed. Patricia Parker and Geoffrey H. Hartman. New York and London: Routledge, 1985: 37–53.

Hollander, John. "*Twelfth Night* and the Morality of Indulgence." *Sewanee Review* 68 (1959): 220–38.

Hotson, Leslie. *The First Night of* Twelfth Night. New York: Macmillan, 1954.

Howard, Jean. "Crossdressing, the Theatre, and Gender Struggle in Early Modern England." *Shakespeare Quarterly* 39 (1988): 418–40.

Hutson, Lorna. "On Not Being Deceived: Rhetoric and the Body in *Twelfth Night*." *Texas Studies in Literature and Language* 38 (1996): 140–74.

Jardine, Lisa. "Twins and Travesties: Gender, Dependency, and Sexual Availability in *Twelfth Night*." In *Erotic Politics: Desire on the Renaissance Stage*. Ed. Susan Zimmerman. New York and London: Routledge, 1992: 27–38.

Jenkins, Harold. "Shakespeare's *Twelfth Night*." *The Rice Institute Pamphlet* 45 (1959): 19–42.

Kerrigan, John. "Secrecy and Gossip in *Twelfth Night*." *Shakespeare Survey* 50 (1997): 65–80.

Knight, G. Wilson. *The Shakespearean Tempest*. London: Oxford University Press, 1932.

Ko, Yu Jin. "The Comic Closure of *Twelfth Knight* and Viola's *Noli me tangere*." *Shakespeare Quarterly* 48 (1997): 391–405.

Kott, Jan. *Shakespeare Our Contemporary*. Trans. Boleslaw Taborski. New York: Anchor, 1966.

Lamb, Charles. "On Some of the Old Actors." In Twelfth Night*: Critical Essays*. Ed. Stanley Wells. New York: Garland, 1986: 49–56.

Laroque, François. *Shakespeare's Festive World: Elizabethan Seasonal Entertainment and the Professional Stage*. Trans. Janet Lloyd. Cambridge: Cambridge University Press, 1991.

Leggatt, Alexander. *Shakespeare's Comedy of Love*. London and New York: Methuen, 1974.

Levin, Harry. "The Underplot of *Twelfth Night*." In Twelfth Night *Critical Essays*. Ed. Stanley Wells. New York: Garland, 1986: 161–69.

Lewalski, Barbara. "Thematic Patterns in *Twelfth Night*." *Shakespeare Studies* 1 (1965): 168–81.

Lewis, Cynthia: *Particular Saints: Shakespeare's Four Antonios, Their Contexts, and Their Plays*. Newark: University of Delaware Press, 1997.

——. "Soft Touch: On the Renaissance Staging and Meaning of the 'Noli me tangere' Icon." *Comparative Drama* 36 (2002): 53–73.

Lothian, J. M., and T. W. Craik, eds. *Twelfth Night*. By William Shakespeare. The Arden Shakespeare, series 2. London: Methuen, 1975.

Mahood, M. M. "Shakespeare's Middle Comedies: A Generation of Criticism." *Shakespeare Survey* 32 (1979): 1–13.

——, ed. *Twelfth Night, or What You Will*. By William Shakespeare. New Penguin Shakespeare. Harmondsworth: Penguin, 1968.

Malcolmson, Christina. "'What You Will': Social Mobility and Gender in *Twelfth Night*." In *New Casebooks: Twelfth Night*. Ed. R. S. White. New York: St. Martin's Press, 1996: 160–93.

Markels, Julian. "Shakespeare's Confluence of Tragedy and Comedy: *Twelfth Night* and *King Lear*." *Shakespeare Quarterly* 15 (1964): 75–88.

Melzi, Robert C. "From Leila to Viola." *Renaissance Drama* 9 (1966): 67–81.

Moglen, Helene. "Disguise and Development: The Self and Society in *Twelfth Night*." *Literature and Psychology* 23 (1973): 13–20.

Moore, Edward M. "William Poel." *Shakespeare Quarterly* 23 (1972): 21–36.

Muir, Kenneth, ed. *Shakespeare: The Comedies*. Englewood Cliffs, NJ: Prentice Hall, 1965.

——. *The Sources of Shakespeare's Plays*. London: Methuen, 1977.

Orgel, Stephen. *Impersonations: The Performance of Gender in Shakespeare's England*. Cambridge: Cambridge University Press, 1996.

Osborne, Laurie E. "Antonio's Pardon." *Shakespeare Quarterly* 45 (1994): 108–14.

——. *The Trick of Singularity:* Twelfth Night *and the Performance Editions*. Iowa City: University of Iowa Press, 1996.

——. "Editing Frailty in *Twelfth Night*: 'Where lies your text?'" In *Reading Readings: Essays on Shakespeare Editing in the Eighteenth Century*. Ed. Joanna Gondris. London: Associated University Presses, 1998: 209–23.

——. "Cutting up Characters in Trevor Nunn's *Twelfth Night*." In *Spectacular Shakespeare: Critical Theory and Popular Cinema*. Ed. Courtney Lehmann and Lisa Starks. Cranbury, NJ: Associated University Presses, 2002: 89–109.

Pentland, Elizabeth. "Reading around in Belleforest." Unpublished paper for Shakespeare Association of America Seminar on *Twelfth Night*, San Diego, 2007.

Pequigney, Joseph. "The Two Antonios and Same-Sex Love in *Twelfth Night* and *The Merchant of Venice*." *English Literary Renaissance* 22 (1992): 201–21.

Potter, Lois. Twelfth Night*: Text and Performance*. Basingstoke: Macmillan, 1985.

Quiller-Couch, Sir Arthur, and John Dover Wilson, eds. *The New Shakespeare*. Cambridge: Cambridge University Press, 1930.

Rabkin, Norman. *Shakespeare and the Problem of Meaning*. Chicago, University of Chicago Press, 1981.

Riche, Barnabe. "Apolonius and Silla." In *Riche his Farewell to Military Profession*. Ed. Donald Beecher. Ottawa and Binghamton, NY: Dovehouse Editions and Medieval and Renaissance Texts and Studies, 1992: 180–201.

Salingar, L. G. "The Design of *Twelfth Night*." In Twelfth Night*: Critical Essays*. Ed. Stanley Wells. New York: Garland, 1986: 191–213.

Schalkwyk, David. "Love and Service in *Twelfth Night* and the Sonnets." *Shakespeare Quarterly* 56 (2005): 76–100

Shakespeare, William. *Twelfth Night, or What You Will.* Ed. Keir Elam. The Arden Shakespeare, series 3. London: Cengage Learning, 2008.

Sinden, Donald. "Malvolio in *Twelfth Night*." In *Players of Shakespeare 1. Essays in Shakespearean Performance by Twelve Players with the Royal Shakespeare Company*. Ed. Philip Brockbank. Cambridge: Cambridge University Press, 1985: 41–66.

Spencer, Hazelton. "Mr. Pepys Is Not Amused." *ELH* 7 (1940): 163–76.

Sprague, Arthur Colby. "*Twelfth Night*." Ed. Stanley Wells. *Twelfth Night: Critical Essays*. NY: Garland, 1986: 38–48.

Spurgeon, Caroline F. E. *Shakespeare's Imagery and What It Tells Us*. Cambridge: Cambridge University Press, 1935.

Tilley, Morris P. "The Organic Unity of *Twelfth Night*." *PMLA* 29 (1914): 550–66.

Traub, Valerie. *Desire and Anxiety: Circulations of Sexuality in Shakespearean Drama*. London: Routledge, 1992.

Turner, Robert K. "The Text of *Twelfth Night*." *Shakespeare Quarterly* 26 (1975): 128–38.

Tvordi, Jessica. "Female Alliance and the Construction of Homoeroticism in *As You Like It* and *Twelfth Night*." In *Maids and Mistresses, Cousins and Queens: Women's Alliances in Early Modern England.* Ed. Susan Frye and Karen Robertson. New York and Oxford: Oxford University Press, 1999: 114–30.

Warren, Roger, and Stanley Wells, eds. "Introduction to *Twelfth Night*." In *Twelfth Night, or What You Will.* By William Shakespeare. Oxford: Clarendon Press, 1994: 1–76.

Watts, Cedric. "The Problem of Malvolio." In *Critical Essays on* Twelfth Night. Ed. Linda Cookson and Bryan Loughrey. Harlow: Longman, 1990: 19–26.

Wells, Stanley. *Royal Shakespeare. Studies of Four Major Productions at the Royal Shakespeare Theatre, Stratford-upon-Avon.* Manchester: Manchester University Press, 1977.

——, ed. Twelfth Night*: Critical Essays*. New York: Garland, 1986.

Welsford, Enid. *The Fool: His Social and Literary History*. New York: Farrar and Rinehart, 1935.

Wheeler, Richard P. "Deaths in the Family: The Loss of a Son and the Rise of Shakespearean Comedy." *Shakespeare Quarterly* 51 (2000): 127–53.

Yearling, Elizabeth M. "Language, Theme, and Character in *Twelfth Night*." *Shakespeare Survey* 35 (1982): 79–86.

Works consulted

Appelbaum, Robert. *Aguecheek's Beef, Belch's Hiccup, and Other Gastronomic Interjections: Literature, Culture, and Food among the Early Moderns*. Chicago: University of Chicago Press, 2006.

Astington, John. "Malvolio and the Eunuchs: Texts and Revels in *Twelfth Night*." *Shakespeare Survey* 46 (1993): 23–34.

Belsey, Catherine. "*Twelfth Night*: A Modern Perspective." In *Twelfth Night*. Ed. Barbara Mowat and Paul Werstine. New York: Washington Square Press, 1993: 197–207.

Berry, Ralph. *Shakespearean Comedies: Explorations in Form*. Princeton, NJ: Princeton University Press, 1972.

Billings, Timothy. "Caterwauling Cataians: The Genealogy of a Gloss." *Shakespeare Quarterly* 54 (2003): 1–28.

Brown, John Russell. "The Interpretation of Shakespeare's Comedies: 1900–1953." *Shakespeare Survey* 8 (1955): 1–13.

Cahill, Edward. "The Problem of Malvolio." *College Literature* 23 (1996): 62–82.

Callahan, Dympna. "'And All Is Semblative a Woman's Part': Body Politics and *Twelfth Night*." *Textual Practice* 7 (1993): 428–52.

Carnegie, David. "'Maluolio Within': Performance Perspectives on the Dark House." *Shakespeare Quarterly* 52 (2001): 393–414.

Casey, Charles. "Gender Trouble in *Twelfth Night*." *Theatre Journal* 49.2 (1997): 121–41.

Coddon, Karin S. "'Slander in an Allow'd Fool: *Twelfth Night*'s Crisis of the Aristocracy." *SEL* 33 (1993): 309–25.

Cox, Lee Sheridan. "The Riddle in *Twelfth Night*." *Shakespeare Quarterly* 13 (1962): 360.

Crewe, Jonathan. "In the Field of Dreams: Transvestism in *Twelfth Night* and *The Crying Game*." *Representations* 50 (1995): 101–21.

Dash, Irene G. *Women's Worlds in Shakespeare's Plays*. Newark and London: Associated University Presses, 1997.

DiGangi, Mario. *The Homoerotics of Early Modern Drama*. Cambridge: Cambridge University Press, 1997.

Dollimore, Jonathan. *Sexual Dissidence: Augustine to Wilde, Freud to Foucault*. Oxford: Clarendon Press, 1991.

Donno, Elizabeth Story, ed. *Twelfth Night or What You Will*. By William Shakespeare. Cambridge: Cambridge University Press, 1985.

Duffin, Ross W. *Shakespeare's Songbook*. New York and London: W. W. Norton & Company, 2004.

Eagleton, Terence. "Language and Reality in *Twelfth Night*." *Critical Quarterly* 9 (1967): 217–28.

Edwards, Philip. *Shakespeare and the Confines of Art*. London: Methuen, 1968.

Elam, Keir. "The Fertile Eunuch: *Twelfth Night*, Early Modern Intercourse, and the Fruits of Castration." *Shakespeare Quarterly* 47 (1996): 1–36.

Everett, Barbara. "Or What You Will." *Essays in Criticism* 35 (1985): 294–314.

Fowler, Alistair. "Maria's Riddle." *Connotations* 23 (1992): 269–70.

Gash, Anthony. "Bidding Farewell to Carnival: The Politics of *Twelfth Night*." *Q/W/E/R/T/Y* 5 (1995): 11–19.

Goldberg, Jonathan. "Textual Properties." *Shakespeare Quarterly* 37 (1986): 213–17.

——. *Sodometries: Renaissance Texts, Modern Sexualities*. Stanford, CA: Stanford University Press, 1992.

Grady, Hugh. "Shakespeare Criticism, 1600–1900." In *The Cambridge Companion to Shakespeare*. Ed. Stanley Wells and Margreta de Grazia. Cambridge: Cambridge University Press, 1986: 265–78.

Greenblatt, Stephen, et al., eds. *The Norton Shakespeare*. New York: Norton, 1997.

Greif, Karen. "Plays and Playing in *Twelfth Night*." *Shakespeare Survey* 34 (1981): 121–30. Reprinted in Twelfth Night*: Critical Essays*. Ed. Stanley Wells. New York: Garland, 1986: 261–77.

Hammond, Paul. *Figuring Sex between Men from Shakespeare to Rochester*. Oxford: Clarendon Press, 2002.

Hartwig, Joan. "Feste's 'Whirligig' and the Comic Providence of *Twelfth Night*." *English Literary History* 40 (1973): 501–13.

Hassel, R. Chris. "The Riddle in *Twelfth Night* Simplified." *Shakespeare Quarterly* 25 (1974): 356.

Hunt, Maurice. "Malvolio, Viola, and the Question of Instrumentality: Defining Providence in *Twelfth Night*." *Studies in Philology* 90 (1993): 277–97.

Hunter, G. K. "Elizabethans and Foreigners." *Shakespeare Survey 17* (1964): 37–52.

Hurworth, Angela. "Gulls, Cony-Catchers and Cozeners: *Twelfth Night* and the Elizabethan Underworld." *Shakespeare Survey* 52 (1999): 120–32.

Jensen, Ejner J. *Shakespeare and the Ends of Comedy*. Bloomington: Indiana University Press, 1991.

King, Walter N., ed. *Twentieth Century Interpretations of* Twelfth Night. Englewood Cliffs, NJ: Prentice Hall, 1968.

Laqueur, Thomas. *Making Sex: Body and Gender from the Greeks to Freud*. Cambridge, MA: Harvard University Press, 1990.

Levin, Richard A. *Love and Society in Shakespearean Comedy: A Study of Dramatic Form and Content*. Newark: University of Delaware Press, 1985.

Palmer, D. J. "*Twelfth Night* and the Myth of Echo and Narcissus." *Shakespeare Survey* 32 (1979): 73–79.

Parker, Patricia. "Altering the Letter of *Twelfth Night*: 'Some are born great' and the Missing Signature." *Shakespeare Survey* 59 (2006): 49–62.

——. "Was Illyria as Mysterious and Foreign as We Think?" In *The Mysterious and the Foreign in Early Modern England*. Ed. Helen Ostovich, Mary Silcox, and Graham Roebuck. Newark: University of Delaware Press, 2008: 209–33.

Pennington, Michael. Twelfth Night*: A User's Guide*. London: Nick Hern, 2000.

Relihan, Constance C. "Erasing the East from *Twelfth Night*." In *Race, Ethnicity, and*

Power in the Renaissance. Ed. Joyce Green MacDonald. Madison, NJ: Fairleigh Dickinson Press, 1997: 80–94.

Scragg, Leah. "'Her C's, Her U's, and Her T's: Why That?' A New Reply for Sir Andrew Aguecheek." *The Review of English Studies* n.s. 42 (1991): 1–16.

Shannon, Laurie. "Nature's Bias: Renaissance Homonormativity and Elizabethan Comic Likeness." *Modern Philology* 98 (2000–2001): 183–210.

Siegel, Paul N. "Malvolio: Comic Puritan Automaton." In *Shakespearean Comedy*. Ed. Maurice Charney. New York: New York Literary Forum, 1980: 217–30.

Smith, Bruce R. *Shakespeare and Masculinity*. Oxford: Oxford University Press, 2000.

——, ed. *Twelfth Night or What You Will: Texts and Contexts*. Boston and New York: Bedford/St. Martin's, 2001.

——. "Ragging *Twelfth Night*: 1602, 1996, 2002–3." In *A Companion to Shakespeare and Performance*. Ed. Barbara Hodgdon and W. B. Worthen. London: Blackwell Publishing, 2005: 57–78.

Smith, Peter J. "M.O.A.I. 'What Should that Alphabetical Position Portend?' An Answer to the Metamorphic Malvolio." *Renaissance Quarterly* 51 (1998): 1199–224.

Stanivuković, Goran V. "'What Country, Friends, Is This?': The Geographies of Illyria in Early Modern England." *Litteraria Pragensia* 12 (2002): 5–20.

——. "Illyria Revisited: Shakespeare and the Eastern Adriatic." In *Shakespeare and the Mediterranean*. Ed. Tom Clayton, Susan Brock, and Vicente Fores. Newark: University of Delaware Press, 2004: 400–415.

Styan, J. L. "Stage Space and the Shakespeare Experience." In *Shakespeare in Performance*. Ed. Robert Shaughnessy. Basingstoke: Macmillan, 2000: 24–41.

Ungerer, Gustav. "'My Lady's a *Catayan*, We Are Politicians, Malvolio's a Peg-a-Ramsie.'" *Shakespeare Survey* 32 (1979): 85–104.

——. "The Viol da Gamba as a Sexual Metaphor in Elizabethan Music and Literature." *Renaissance and Reformation/Renaissance et Réforme* n.s. 7.2 (1984): 79–90.

Wanamaker, Zoë. "Viola in *Twelfth Night*." In *Players of Shakespeare 2. Further Essays in Shakespearean Performance by Players of the Royal Shakespeare Company*. Ed. Russell Jackson and Robert Smallwood. Cambridge: Cambridge University Press, 1988: 81–91.

White, R. S. "Shakespeare Criticism in the Twentieth Century." In *The Cambridge Companion to Shakespeare*. Ed. Stanley Wells and Margreta de Grazia. Cambridge: Cambridge University Press, 1986: 265–78.

——, ed. Twelfth Night*: New Casebooks*. New York: St. Martin's Press, 1996.

2 *Twelfth Night*

Editing puzzles and eunuchs of all kinds

Patricia Parker

Wherefore are these things hid?

Twelfth Night, 1.3.125

Plays such as *Hamlet* and *King Lear* have long been subject to studies that stress their textual problems, including divergences between folio and quarto versions. But the text of *Twelfth Night* has not been subject to such scrutiny, largely because "the excellence of the Folio text of this play ought to give pause to any interference with it" (Sisson 1956, 1: 186). Yet despite the almost universally agreed excellence of the First Folio here, the text we get to see in modern editions differs repeatedly from it in ways that may indeed suggest editorial "interference." In at least one quite spectacular example, the lines we find most familiar from *Twelfth Night* appear nowhere in the Folio passage. One of the most striking discoveries that awaits, then, if we return to the Folio is that the famous formula "Some are born great, some achieve greatness, and some have greatness thrust upon them" does not appear in the Letter Scene itself but only in Malvolio's cross-gartered version before a surprised Olivia in act 3 – creating the oddity that when we quote from these familiar lines, we are quoting not the letter but Malvolio, that avowed crusher of "letters" so that they might "bow" to him (2.5.140–41).[1]

Returning to the Folio likewise makes clear that even particular Folio spellings can suggest much that has been effaced by editorial alterations. In the first scene in which the play's revelers appear, for example, Sir Toby (1.3.26) describes Sir Andrew as able to play the "Viol-de-gamboys" (TLN, 142–43), a spelling for the viola-de-gamba that persists (as "gamboys" or "gamboyes") through all four Folio texts. In the eighteenth century – beginning with Rowe (1709) – it was frequently changed to "Viol-de-Gambo," a spelling that evokes the legs between which this instrument was played (from *gamba* in Italian: see Ungerer 1984, 79–90) but completely effaces the "boys" or "boyes," though that ending is arguably much more suggestive for a play where "Viola" (originally played by a boy actor) is dressed and addressed as a "boy" throughout most of the play, including in the final scene's pairing with Orsino.[2] Such a playing on the sound of "boys" is shared not only by Chapman's *Bussy d'Ambois*, where Bussy's name is alternately spelled "D'Amboys," but also by *As You Like It*, where the name of de Boys similarly combines "boys" and "bois" (DiGangi 1997, 55), in a play that features a "Ganymede" or boy lover. So even if *gamba* retains the obscene sense of between the legs and "gambo" approximates the "correct" term for the instrument Sir Andrew is described as playing, it is far from being the most suggestive choice for the text itself.

If the "Viol-de-gamboys" has been restored in modern editions, another suggestive Folio spelling has not been so lucky, with the result that attention has frequently been focused on finding a presumed external referent when the key might reside within the play itself. The same scene that introduces the night revelers ends with a curious reference to a curtained "picture" that editors (following Rowe) routinely make of "Mistress Mall," when Toby responds (to Andrew's vaunted prowess in the "caper" and "back-trick") "Wherefore are these things hid? Wherefore have these gifts a curtain before 'em? Are they like to take dust, like Mistress Mall's picture?" (1.3.125–27), though the Folio has "mistris *Mals* picture" (F2–4: "Mistris *Mals* picture") instead. Why should this matter, in an exchange in which Toby goes on to ask "Is it a world to hide virtues in?" (131–32) and Andrew alternatively proposes "some revels" (136)? Rowe's 1709 altering of the Folio to "Mistress *Malls* Picture" makes a connection to the name "Mary" or "Mall" which has been frequently assumed to refer to a historical person, from Moll Cutpurse (or Mary Frith) and Mary Ambrée who fought at the Siege of Ghent in 1584 to "Mary Fitton, one of Elizabeth I's maids of honour, disgraced for bearing the Earl of Pembroke's child in 1601" (Warren and Wells, Oxford, 99; see also Lothian and Craik, Arden 2, 17; Elam, Arden 3, 179). When commentators have rejected or gone beyond the assumption of an external referent, it has been to identify "Mall" as another name for "Maria," though she is never called by that name in the play and it is unclear why Toby should allude to her "picture" (Donno, New Cambridge, 55; Furness 1901, 48–50; Elam, Arden 3, 179). But there is another character in the play – Olivia, or the "Mistris" of the house (3.1.41: TLN, 1252–53) – who is directly aligned with this curtained picture when, unveiling later in this same first act, she says to Cesario, "we will draw the curtain, and show you the picture" (1.5.233). The Folio's spelling of "mistris *Mal*" – which sounds the syllable of "Mal" or "ill" heard in "*Mal*volio" and in repeated references to the "*Ill*yria" of Olivia's cloistered mourning – may thus be suggestive of the larger transition within the play itself, from the melancholy of which Sir Toby complains ("What a plague meanes my Neece to take the death of her brother thus? I am sure care's an enemie to life,"1.3; TLN, 119–21) to the eventual unveiling of the curtained picture herself,[3] as Olivia brings that mourning to an end – though she may catch a different kind of malaise ("Even so quickly may one catch the plague?," [1.5.295]), when she unveils for Orsino's attractive young messenger.

Other editorial corrections of the Folio that may appear to be "interference" include the time-honored tradition of correcting the language of Sir Toby, despite the characteristic malapropisms of this character who mishears Olivia's "lethargy" as "lechery" (1.5.124–25) and refers to Sir Andrew's "substractors" (1.3.34–35) rather than "detractors." Boswell once observed of such editorial labors, "It is surely rather ludicrous to see four sober commentators gravely endeavouring to ascertain the correct meaning of what Sir Toby says when he is drunk" (quoted in Furness 1901, 296). Yet much editorial effort has gone into ascertaining the correct form of words Sir Toby may be confusing or slurring together. In the same scene as "mistris *Mals* picture," Toby says to Andrew, "Why dost thou not goe to Church in a Galliard, and come home in a Carranto? My verie walke should be a Iigge: I would not so much as make water but in a Sinke-a-pace" (TLN, 235–38). With very few exceptions, editors do not change "Sinke-a-pace" to "cinquepace," or the proper name for that dance. But (following Rowe's 1714 edition) editors have routinely changed "carranto" to "coranto" as this dance's correct name, though it obliterates the slurring in Toby's speech of "corranto" and "car," the term used later in the Letter Scene ("Though our silence be drawne from vs with cars," TLN, 1078). The Folio's portmanteau "Carranto" manages to suggest not only the coranto as a (literally) "running" dance but the "car" that is elsewhere foregrounded as a means of transport.[4] Why, then, we might ask, alter *its* spelling when the unaltered "sink-a-pace" is already recognized as combining so many meanings that would be lost if *cinquepace* replaced it?

Other such changes began not in the eighteenth century but with the Second Folio, which introduced its own readings of the First Folio's ambiguous lines. In the First Folio version of the final scene (5.1.190–201), Sir Toby enters "halting" and "in drinke" (TLN, 2355–56) and pronounces of "Dicke Surgeon," who is similarly "drunke" (TLN, 2360–61), that he is not only "a drunken rogue" but also "a passy measures panyn" (TLN, 2363–64). In the Second Folio this was changed to "a passy measures Pavin," an alteration retained in the subsequent Folios and taken by editors to be the name of a stately dance known as the "pavan" (most recently in Keir Elam's Arden 3 edition). But other editors (following F1) have assumed its "panyn" to be a form of "paynim" or pagan, so that Toby is calling this "rogue" not the name of a dance but rather a "passing-measure [or past measure] paynim."[5] There is no way of trusting absolutely that the Second Folio's alteration is "right": in the same line, for example, it prints "he's a Rogue after a passy measures Pavin," an "after" editors routinely reject in favor of the First Folio's "and." Toby's "panyn" in F1 may even be a drunken *conflation* of "paynim" with the "pavin" or pavan, simultaneously brought to his mind by "passy measures," a phrase that evokes both the name of a dance and the sense of something past measure. It may, in other words, not be a matter of trying to figure out what Toby was "correctly" saying (with the assumption of a compositorial error) but a hopelessly confused formulation of Toby himself that has indeed reduced editors to trying to ascertain the correct meaning of what he says "when he is drunk."

In virtually all modern editions, readers of the Letter Scene similarly find Malvolio compared to a "staniel" (kestrel or hawk), as Fabian and Toby comment on his engagement with Maria's letter ("*Fab*. What dish a' poison has she dress'd him! / *Sir To*. And with what wing the [staniel] checks at it!," 2.5.112–14), although the Folio has "with what wing the stallion checkes at it?" (TLN, 1123). "Stallion" here persisted through all four Folio texts of the play and appears not to have bothered Rowe, Pope, or Theobald, who did not hesitate to make other changes. It was not until Hanmer decided to change "stallion" to "stanyel" (1743–44, 458) that it became what Furness subsequently pronounced to be "an *emendatio certissima*" because of the mention of "wings" and "checking" (Furness 1901, 169). But (like "check," which *OED* cites in senses compatible with "stallion") "wings" could also belong with the Folios' "stallion" (as in the winged stallion Pegasus, emblem of the very flights of fancy and upwardly mobile presumption that Malvolio is exhibiting here). Whether or not the *OED* (on *staniel*, *stannel*) is justified in its hypothesis that the Folio's "stallion" here may have been "a corrupt or dialectal variant of *staniel*" (Elam, Arden 3, 244), editorially changing Toby's "stallion" to Hanmer's "stanyel" once again loses the portmanteau nature of the phrase itself, which is capable of suggesting not only a bird (in ways consistent with the earlier comparison of Malvolio to a "woodcock" and "turkey-cock") but also the sexual senses of "stallion" for the steward who has just pictured himself as coming "from a day-bed, where I have left Olivia sleeping" (2.5.48–49).[6] In a play that elsewhere refers to a gelding called "cut" (2.3.187), "stallion" (as an uncastrated male horse) nicely anticipates the irony of the incipient gelding of Malvolio as a result of the letter and its C-U-T (Goldberg 1986, 217; Astington 1993, 24–26; Callaghan 2000, 44). Effacing Toby's "stallion" and replacing it with Hanmer's "stanyel" thus not only corrects what Toby may have confused but reduces the line to just one of its possible resonances. Even if "with what wing the stallion checks at it!" were to be the "nonsense" commentators have frequently condemned it as, nonsense is precisely what the audience who has already heard his "lechery" for "lethargy" and other verbal misprisions would expect from Olivia's malapropping kinsman.

Other editorial alterations – of such long standing that they are assumed to be part of the original wit of the play itself – have effaced elements in the Folio that would support more contemporary criticism of the play in relation to gender. In act 1 scene 3, audiences and readers encounter the following exchange between Andrew and Toby, as a result of an influential change made by Theobald in 1733:

Sir To. *Pourquoi*, my dear knight?
Sir And. What is '*pourquoi*'? Do, or not do? I would I had bestow'd that time in the tongues that I have in fencing, dancing, and bear-baiting. O had I but follow'd the arts!
Sir To. Then hadst thou had an excellent head of hair.
Sir And. Why, would that have mended my hair?
Sir To. Past question, for thou seest it will not [curl by] nature.
Sir And. But it becomes [me] well enough, does't not?
Sir To. Excellent, it hangs like flax on a distaff, and I hope to see a huswife take thee between her legs, and spin it off.

(1.3.90–104)

In addition to correcting the Folio's "*Pur-quoy*" (TLN, 204) in Toby's first line (which may suggest that he is mispronouncing the French word, despite Andrew's assumption that he is more versed in the "tongues"), editors have continued to reprint "curl by nature," which was first printed by Theobald and compounded by subsequent suggestions of a pun on "tongues" and curling "tongs" here. But apart from the fact that there is no evidence that curling tongs were part of the vocabulary of Shakespeare's day – a potential problem acknowledged by one scholar who proposed the pun on "tongs" and "tongues," though it seems to have dropped out of editions that cite it without question – Theobald's alteration of the Folio text may yield an interpretively less pertinent line.[7] What the Folio has is *not* "thou seest it will not curl by nature" but rather "thou seest it will not coole my nature" (TLN, 211), a "cool(e)" that remained through all four Folios, Rowe, and Pope before it was altered by Theobald and one whose reference to cooling (or effeminating) a male "nature" suggests the calorics of gender and reversal of the traditional progression from (cooler) female to (hotter) male that critics have seen as crucial to the play as a whole (Greenblatt 1988, 66–93; Laqueur 1990, 25–62; Paster 2004, 77–134 and 212–13).[8]

Another striking example of the tendency of editions to continue printing certain centuries-old textual alterations despite more recent arguments advanced by critics is the continuing editorial reproduction of particular emended lines in the soliloquy delivered by Viola (disguised as Cesario) after her first meeting with Olivia. When Malvolio, the "churlish messenger," has returned to "Cesario" the ring never given to Olivia, the soliloquy in the Folio proceeds as follows (2.2.17–41; TLN, 673–97):

I left no Ring with her: what meanes this Lady?
Fortune forbid my out-side haue not charm'd her:
She made good view of me, indeed so much,
That me thought her eyes had lost her tongue,
For she did speake in starts distractedly.
She loues me sure, the cunning of her passion

Inuites me in this churlish messenger:
None of my Lords Ring? Why he sent her none;
I am the man, if it be so, as tis,
Poore Lady, she were better loue a dreame:
Disguise, I see thou art a wickednesse,
Wherein the pregnant enemie does much.
How easie is it, for the proper false
In womens waxen hearts to set their formes:
Alas, O frailtie is the cause, not wee,
For such as we are made, if such we bee:
[EMENDED TEXT: "Alas, our frailty is the cause, not we,
For such as we are made of, such we be."]
How will this fadge? My master loues her deerely.
And I (poore monster) fond asmuch on him:
And she (mistaken) seemes to dote on me:
What will become of this? As I am man,
My state is desperate for my maisters loue:
As I am woman (now alas the day)
What thriftlesse sighes shall poore *Oliuia* breath?
O time, thou must vntangle this, not I,
It is too hard a knot for me t'vnty.

The Folio's "O frailtie" leaves the gendering of "frailty" uncertain, while its "such as we are made, *if* such we bee" (my italics) imports into these lines the "much virtue in If" already underscored in the gender uncertainties of *As You Like It* (5.4.103). But despite the suggestiveness of the Folio text here, pointed out by critics over the past 20 years (Levin 1985, 127–28; Osborne 1998, 209–23), editors have continued to print the time-honored emendations – the Second Folio's substitution of "Alas, our frailty is the cause" (which appears to identify the Folio's "O frailtie" with the frailty of women in particular) and the late-eighteenth-century change of punctuation and removal of the crucial "if" (which is in all four Folios of the play) by the substituted line "such as we are made of, such we be" that is still found in even the most recent editions.[9] This continually reproduced eighteenth-century emendation thus further effaces the indeterminacy of gender stressed elsewhere in the disguised Viola's speech (in "As I am man . . . As I am woman" and its androgynous "monster") and the transvestite ambiguities of "disguise" itself (including that of the boy player who says earlier "I am not that I play" [1.5.184]), which permeate not only the soliloquy but the play as a whole.

Editorial changes of punctuation – often treated as an insignificant "accidental" – can also alter the way an entire exchange might be performed and what might be concluded from it.[10] In act 1 scene 3, modern editions have Sir Andrew assuming that Maria's name is "Mistress Mary Accost," as a result of his mistaking the verb "accost" for a proper name:

Sir And. Bless you, fair shrew.
Mar. And you too, sir.
Sir To. Accost, Sir Andrew, accost.
Sir And. What's that?
Sir To. My niece's chambermaid.
[*Sir And.*] Good Mistress Accost, I desire better acquaintance.
Mar. My name is Mary, sir.
Sir And. Good Mistress Mary Accost —
Sir To. You mistake, knight. 'Accost' is front her, board her, woo her, assail her.
Sir And. By my troth, I would not undertake her in this company. Is that the meaning of 'accost'?

(1.3.47–59)[11]

But in the Folio this exchange is punctuated very differently, with no confirmation that the "accost" in Andrew's "Good Mistris accost" and "Good mistris *Mary*, accost" are understood by him as names at all:

Enter Sir *Andrew*.
And. **Sir *Toby Belch*. How now ſir *Toby Belch*?**
To. **Sweet ſir *Andrew*.**
And. **Bleſſe you faire Shrew.**
Mar. **And you too ſir.**
Tob. **Accoſt Sir *Andrew*, accoſt.**
And. **What's that?**
To. **My Neeces Chamber-maid.**
Ma.**Good Miſtris accoſt, I deſire better acquaintauce**
Ma. **My name is *Mary* ſir.**
And. **Good miſtris *Mary*, accoſt.**
To, **You miſtake knight: Accoſt, is front her, boord her, woe her, aſſayle her.**
And. **By my troth I would not vndertake her in this company. Is that the meaning of Accoſt?**

It was not until Rowe in the eighteenth century that the "accost" that appears as a verb in this Folio passage was enshrined as a name. Rowe's 1709 edition prints "Good Mistress Accost" and "Good Mistress *Mary* accost," omitting the comma between "Mary" and "accost" that appeared in all four Folio texts; and in 1714 Rowe fully capitalized "Good Mistress *Accost*" and "Good Mistress Mary *Accost*," the form encountered in modern editions. With Rowe's almost universally followed alteration, the joke becomes one simply at Andrew's expense. But what the Folio punctuation makes possible is a very different take on these lines, where the confusions are more general, in a way more suggestive for *Twelfth Night* as a whole.

In the Folio, when Sir Toby first says "Accost Sir *Andrew*, accost" (TLN, 165), the line might as easily be addressed to Maria as to Andrew, since the absence of a comma *before* his name leaves uncertain whether he is the subject or object of the accosting, or who is being asked to accost whom.[12] When Andrew responds "What's that?" (TLN, 166), the confusions become even more bewildering, since it is unclear what "that" even refers to – the meaning of "accost" or, as Toby responds, either deliberately or sharing in the confusion, "My Neeces Chamber-maid" (TLN, 167).[13] When Andrew then says "Good Mistris accost,"editors (perhaps like Maria herself, caught in the confusion and the impossibility in *sound* of hearing the difference) assume that he is giving her this name (which is thus editorially capitalized as "Mistress Accost"). But Andrew's "Good Mistris accost, I desire better acquaintance" (TLN, 168) does not necessarily assume at all that "accost" is part of her name. Since "accost" has been used up to this point as a *verb*, he may simply be asking *her* to approach *him* (if that is what the word means), because he desires "better acquaintance" – a sense of *accost* (as something *she* is being asked to *do*) that is then continued in the Folio lines that follow, in Andrew's "Good mistris *Mary*, accost" (TLN, 170). When Toby responds "You mistake knight: Accost, is front her, boord her, woe her, assayle her" (TLN, 171–72), it not only clarifies the direction the accosting is to take, since he is asking Andrew to accost *her*, but comes with a meaning that Andrew says he "would not vndertake . . . in this company" (TLN, 173–74: see Lothian and Craik, Arden 2, 14; Evans, Riverside, 444; Elam, Arden 3, 174).

The crucial Folio comma that appears in all four Folio texts – producing Andrew's "Good mistris *Mary*, accost" (F1–2), "Good Mistresse *Mary*, accost" (F3), and "Good Mistress *Mary*, accost" (F4) – does *not* therefore (as in Rowe and modern editions) create the mistake of "Mistress Mary Accost" as her name. Ironically, what has been assumed to be *Andrew*'s error is a phantom creation of the editorial tradition itself. What emerges much more suggestively from the Folio text are confusions in which not just Andrew but potentially Toby and Maria become involved as the exchange proceeds; and an accosting where it is unclear (in relation to gender) who is the expected accoster, with implications not just for Maria (later called a "Penthesilea" or Amazon [2.3.177]) but for the broader Olivia plot, where the woman is more than half the wooer.[14] Even editors are confused – uncertain whether Toby's response to the ambiguous "What's that?" is deliberately misleading or part of his own misunderstanding. The bewilderments of this early Folio exchange – far from being a joke exclusively at Andrew's expense – thus take us into the comedy of errors, confusions, and "misprision" (1.5.55) that is Illyria, and *Twelfth Night*, itself.

Not only variants in text and punctuation but also added editorial stage directions may affect both what we read and what we imagine should be performed. Editors of *Twelfth Night* frequently add stage directions to help keep the reader from becoming confused, a pedagogically benign motive but one problematic at moments where confusion itself may be the point. In the Recognition Scene, for example, when the final appearance of both twins on stage creates the bewilderment registered in Olivia's "Most wonderful!" (5.1.225), Antonio's "An apple, cleft in two, is not more twin" (5.1.223), and Orsino's "One face, one voice, one habit, and two persons" (5.1.216), editors following Rowe frequently add "[*To Viola*]" when Orsino says, "Boy, thou hast said to me a thousand times / Thou never shouldst love woman like to me" (5.1.267–68) and "Your master quits you; and for your service done him, / . . . / . . . you shall from this time be / Your master's mistress" (5.1.320–26). But in modern productions that include all-male stagings of this scene (where Viola/Cesario, originally played by a boy actor, is still in male "habit" or clothing, as is Sebastian her twin brother), Orsino has addressed the wrong twin instead, successfully exploiting an ambiguity that such added editorial stage directions would remove.

On a different front, adding stage directions to indicate that particular lines should be sung (as editors routinely do) may also interfere with a striking combination central to this play. Viola's curious reference to the fact that she can "sing / And speak" in "many sorts of music" (1.2.57–58) opens up the possibility that lines now assumed to be *sung*, as a result of the long-standing editorial practice of adding such stage directions, might be spoken instead, creating a combination of both "sorts of music" throughout. By the nineteenth century, the play had developed into what we might call "Twelfth Night the Musical," with even speeches such as "Patience on a monument" (2.4.114) arranged as songs. In contrast – though this does not necessarily indicate the *absence* of music – such musical stage directions in the Folio are much more sparse. It has "*Musicke playes*" (TLN, 898) after Orsino says "play the tune the while" (TLN, 897) and both "*Musicke*" (TLN, 939) and "*The Song*" (TLN, 940) before "*Come away, come away death*"; the explicit direction "*Clowne sings*" (TLN, 2559) before Feste's final song and "*O Mistris mine where are you roming?*" (TLN, 738–39); and "*Catch sung*" (TLN, 769) for what Maria ironically describes as the "catterwalling" (TLN, 771) of "*Hold thy peace*." But there are no other such Folio directions even in this traditionally most musical of caterwauling scenes, making it unclear what is sung and what is (however drunkenly) spoken. Since *O Mistris mine* and *Come away death* are all in italics in the Folio, this graphic marker might be expected to provide a clue: but if that were the case, Feste's "Hey Robin" and "I am gone sir" (4.2: TLN, 2057, 2105) – which have neither italics nor any "sings" direction in the Folio – would be spoken rather than sung.[15]

Most modern editors similarly assume that "Farewell deere heart" (TLN, 798) – whose lines are adapted to make fun of Malvolio in the night-reveling scene (2.3.102–12) – must *entirely* be sung, perhaps because it was based on a recent popular song.[16] But even in our contemporary experience, snatches of popular songs readily become part of the spoken language of everyday culture; and in this case the Folio provides no direction for singing and italicizes only some of its lines, leaving open the possibility that it too might be a combination of both "sorts of music," speaking and singing.[17] In contrast to modernized editions that routinely add "Sings" or "Music playing," in other words, the absence of such directions in the Folio leaves radically uncertain what kind of "music" is being heard; and adding them affects at the most basic level how *Twelfth Night* might be sounded throughout.

Most radically, it is not even clear from the Folio whether music is actually playing at the play's beginning, while Orsino utters his famous opening speech. Editors following Capell in 1767–68 have added "Musicians attending" (or simply "Music") to the Folio's "*Enter Orsino Duke of Illyria, Curio, and other Lords*," and frequently an additional "Music ceases" direction after Orsino's "Enough, no more" (1.1.7). But eighteenth-century editions before Capell do not add anything to the Folio entry indicating that music is playing or musicians are present, although they do add numerous "Singing" directions to the scene of night revelry in 2.3 and the "Hey Robin" and "I am gone, sir" of act 4. This absence of any clear Folio direction leaves open the question of whether music at this opening should simply be assumed – though, as David Lindley observes (2006, 203), it remains uncertain where it begins and ends – or whether the entire speech summons a music that is only in (and directed by) Orsino's "fancie" (TLN, 18), as part of what he himself calls the "high fantasticall" (TLN, 19), just as his final spoken line in the play (with "Cesario" still in male clothes) is about "his fancies Queene" (TLN, 2558). My own guess is that music may well have been playing here, given what we know about Elizabethan stage practices. But in this case, what might be more appropriate for a twenty-first-century edition than automatically reproducing Capell's added "Musicians" or the "Music" that often appears without brackets to signal that it even *is* an editorial addition would be a note that gets the reader thinking – right from the play's beginning – about the problem itself and the multiple possibilities for performance (and interpretation) it raises.

* * *

> Thou shalt present me as an eunuch to him . . .
>
> Viola, *Twelfth Night*, 1.2.56

> an instrument without a true voice of its own, but through which the voice of another could make itself heard . . .
>
> E. W. Naylor, *The Poets and Music* (98)

In the second scene of *Twelfth Night*, Viola – shipwrecked off the coast of Illyria – tells the Captain of her intention to become a "eunuch" for Orsino, in the same lines in which she announces that she can "speak" as well as "sing": "Thou shalt present me as an eunuch to him, / It may be worth thy pains; for I can sing / And speak to him in many sorts of music / That will allow me very worth his service" (1.2.56–59). To her request for his "silence" (61) with regard to her plan, the Captain responds: "Be you his eunuch, and your mute I'll be; / When my tongue blabs, then let mine eyes not see" (62–63). Editors have been more or less unanimous in relating the Captain's "eunuch" and "mute" directly or indirectly to the play's Eastern setting and the contemporary association of both with the Ottoman Turk (e.g., Lothian and Craik, Arden 2, 11; Donno, New Cambridge, 50; Warren and Wells, Oxford, 93; Smith, 125–28; Elam, Arden 3, 72, 170). This assumption makes sense not only because of "send them to th' Turk to make eunuchs of" in *All's Well That Ends Well* (2.3.87–88) or the "Turkish mute" of *Henry V* (1.2.232) but also because of evidence that Illyria itself in the period was repeatedly linked with the Turk (Parker 2008, 209–33). In a play where the transformed Malvolio is termed a "renegado" (3.2.70) after the Letter Scene and its "C-U-T" and other Eastern references include the Persian "Sophy" (3.4.279), this resonance of "eunuch" thus signals a well-known cultural geography of which Illyria was a part.

The lines in which Viola announces her intention to become Orsino's "eunuch" have presented, by contrast, one of the greatest puzzles to editors, who observe (supposing an inconsistency here) that she does not literally become Orsino's "eunuch" in the castrated sense as the play proceeds. Arden 2 editors Lothian and Craik comment on the association of eunuchs as singers with Eastern Mediterranean courts (citing the Athenian eunuch of *A Midsummer Night's Dream* and the Egyptian Mardian of *Antony and Cleopatra*), but note, for example, that "After this scene no further reference is made to this part of the plan" and that "The Duke's attitude to Cesario" in act 2 scene 4 "shows that Viola has not entered his service in this character but as a page" (Lothian and Craik, Arden 2, 10). Though the revision theory has by now been discredited, the apparent inconsistency in Viola's plan to become Orsino's "eunuch," together with the fact that it is not Cesario but Feste who sings for Orsino in act 2, even contributed to the argument that the play itself had been revised (Lothian and Craik, Arden 2, xxii–xxiii, 10; Donno, New Cambridge, 16, 49; Warren and Wells, Oxford, 75–76).

The revision theory rested on a particular kind of literalism, including the assumption that Viola would have to become an actual (or detectable) anatomical gelding. In a more general sense, however, overtones of eunuchry or castration pervade the entire play (Orgel 1996, 53–57; Elam 1996, 32; Arden 3, 14, 17, 57–62), from Viola's choice of the name "Cesario" (from *caesus*, cut) and her "little thing . . . I lack of a man" (3.4.302–3) to the multiple "cuts" that sound within it: in Andrew's "cut a caper" (and Toby's response "I can cut the mutton to't" [1.3.121–22]), in Toby's "if thou hast her not i' th' end, call me cut" (2.3.186–87) – another potential reference to a gelding – and in the "C-U-T" of the Letter Scene itself, which figures (in ways compounded by the description of Malvolio as a "renegado") the threat of gelding or phallic incision as well as the female "cut" or "C-U-N-T" (Goldberg 1986, 217; Astington 1993, 24–26; Paster 1993, 30–34; Callaghan 2000, 36–47; Taylor 2000, 114, 151).

Clearly, as commentators have suggested, the association of Viola's "eunuch" with singing evokes the *castrato* or boy singer.[18] But – I want to add here – in the lines that simultaneously (and curiously) announce that she can "speak" as well as "sing" in "many sorts of music," there is a striking contemporary resonance to her becoming a "eunuch" in Orsino's "service" (1.2.56–59) that has not yet been (critically or editorially) heard, though it appears prominently in both phallic and musical senses in another Shakespeare play. In *Coriolanus*, when Coriolanus is counseled to seek the love of the rabble he despises, he expresses his distaste for the transformation this will involve in lines whose "eunuch" evokes simultaneously an effeminating reversal of gender (or regression to the status of a boy) and the "eunuch" that was a well-known musical instrument in the period: "My throat of war be turn'd / . . . into a pipe / Small as an eunuch, or the virgin voice / That babies lull asleep" (3.2.112–15). Critics and editors of *Coriolanus* have glossed the "eunuch" of these lines not just as an actual or imagined sexual "castrate" but also as this musical instrument, a small pipe that famously had no voice or sound of its own. As long ago as 1928, Naylor's *Poets and Music*, commenting on the changing of Coriolanus's "throat of war" into "a gentle treble voice, as of a boy or woman," correctly noted that this Shakespearean "allusion is to the 'eunuch' flute," a slender pipe with a vibrating "thin membrane," an "instrument without a true voice of its own, but through which the voice of another could make itself heard, an artificial voice, not natural to the speaker": this "eunuch" – having "no proper sound of its own" – was thus only the passive instrument through which the voice of another was sounded.[19] In 1986, an article focused exclusively on describing and illustrating this instrument invoked in *Coriolanus* along with the eunuch's sexual or genital senses, concluded that for the effeminization and subjection that Coriolanus envisages, "the image of the eunuch-flute, which alone of musical instruments is unable to generate any sound of its own, is the most powerful that Shakespeare could have devised" (Crookes 1986, 161).

With regard to *Twelfth Night*, however, as often happens in the history of editorial commentary where the focus is on a single play, this "eunuch" that transmits the voice of another has not been applied to the notoriously puzzling lines where Viola announces her intention to become Orsino's "eunuch," even though editors of *Coriolanus* (while not citing Viola's "eunuch") have compared Coriolanus's "virgin voice" and "pipe" to Cesario's "small pipe," described by Orsino as high-pitched like "the maiden's organ, shrill and sound" (1.4.32–33), so "all is semblative a woman's part' (1.4.32–34).[20] In the exchange that envisages his unmanning, in subjection to the rabble that would make him their "eunuch" instrument, Coriolanus further compares this transformation to the soft effeminate state (or "unbarb'd sconce") of the beardless boy (3.2.99), a beardlessness (shared by boy, woman, and eunuch) that is highlighted in the case of "Cesario" as well (3.1.45).

It is crucially important that this early modern resonance – of an instrumental "eunuch" that transmits the voice of another outside it – be heard in relation to *Twelfth Night*, not only because of Viola's intention to become a "eunuch" that can "speak" as well as "sing" in Orsino's "service" (1.2.56–59) but also because of its added "charm," even as it functions as an apparently passive transmitter. Marin Mersenne's *Harmonie Universelle* (1635) says of this slender "pipe" called a "Eunuch" that

> it has no other tone than that of the mouth or the tongue which speaks, whose force and resonance it augments by means of its length and capacity and by a small piece of thin skin, as thin as an onion peel, in which the top is wrapped . . . so that the wind and the voice pushed through the hole . . . goes to strike this peel like a small tambourine, which gives a new charm to the voice through its small vibrations.
>
> (298–99)

The description goes on to say that this "Eunuch" is able like no other instrument to "imitate the human voice" (299), while amplifying it and adding something "new."

The combination of genital and musical in the speech of Coriolanus suggests the transformation from male to female (or boy) and the simultaneously phallic and vocal small "pipe" that would make him a "eunuch," both in the sense of castration or gelding and as an instrument subjected to the voice (and power) of another. But Mersenne's description of the instrumental "eunuch" simultaneously attributes to it this added "charm." In his study of the many sorts of music in *Twelfth Night*, including spoken words, John Hollander (1961, 159–60) does not register an awareness of this contemporary (and Shakespearean) "eunuch"; but he stresses that Viola/Cesario becomes Orsino's "instrument" in the other punning sense of the term, as Orsino's "nuntio" (1.4.28) or message-bearer.[21] Within the play as it unfolds, Cesario not only serves as Orsino's more passive "instrument," delivering the Duke's voice or message as the sounder of his "speech" (1.5.181) or "text" (1.5.220), but also charms or enchants the ears of Olivia (3.1.108–12) and of Orsino himself. The resonances of this overdetermined "instrument" in Viola's intention to become Orsino's "eunuch" thus introduce not just what Viola might "lack of a man," or the high-pitched "treble" voice of the *castrato* or boy singer, or the overtones of castration as well as cross-dressing from the influential legacy of Terence's *Eunuch*, but in addition the larger issue of whether Viola as "Cesario" (a name that suggests not only "cut" but another form of "delivery," or new birth) is the merely passive transmitter of Orsino's "message" (1.5.191), simply serving his "will" (in a play whose Folio title was

Twelfe Night, Or what you will), or adds a new "charm" that makes all of the difference, providing yet another (and different) perspective on the question of whether she does finally become his "eunuch."

The puzzles examined here involve many sorts of cases: in the first, aspects of the Folio that have been altered by editors and continue to affect the text we read; in the second, a "eunuch" assumed to be a sign of inconsistency or error, or restricted in its implications for the plot unless we hear the multiple resonances of its early modern meanings. Taken together, they foreground cases in which the ambiguous, portmanteau, or polysemous quality of the play that appeared in the Folio of 1623 has been (in one sense or the other) obscured. Returning to the Folio is not to proceed in the illusion of reconstructing an "authentic Shakespeare," beyond the "veil of print." But it is to participate in an enterprise that is paradoxically both "radical" and "conservative," seeking to conserve but also to foreground (rather than to hide from readers) such early printed texts, as part of a commitment to historicizing that will be sabotaged if we continue to quote exclusively from "modern, emended, reformatted, modernized, repunctuated editions" (Masten 1996, 158, 154). Returning in a different sense to the multiple resonances of the plays' and period's copious terms is, in a parallel but ultimately related way, to become learners of a language that never ceases to surprise.

Notes

1. Unless otherwise noted, the modern edition used for parenthetical references to *Twelfth Night* throughout this essay is Evans, Riverside. TLN (Through Line Number) references throughout are to the line numbers provided for the Folio (F1) in Hinman (1996). On the absence of "born great" in the Letter Scene (in all four Folios) and the subsequent editorial changes introduced into that scene, see Parker (2006, 49–62). Though claiming fidelity to the Folio, Andrews, Everyman (95) does not in fact accurately reflect the Folio's "are become great" in the Letter Scene and prints the "Fortunate Unhappy" signature for the letter, which was editorially created in the eighteenth century. I am grateful to audiences and readers who have responded to work in progress toward my new Norton Critical Edition of *Twelfth Night*, including Tom Berger, Alan Dessen, Andrew Gurr, Jonathan Hope, Mariko Ichikawa, M. J. Kidnie, the late Scott McMillin, Lois Potter, Eric Rasmussen, Bradley Ryner, Sanford Robbins, Michael Warren, and Paul Werstine.
2. Lothian and Craik, Arden 2, xxiii–iv, n. 3, includes a reminder that "a theatre audience never learns Viola's real name till less than two hundred lines from the end of the last scene." Work on boy actors, homoeroticism, and transvestite theatre has stressed that even in this final scene, after being named on stage, "Viola" still remains in male clothing and is called "boy" by Orsino: see, for example, Orgel (1996, 104); DiGangi (1997, 41–42); and Smith (2001, 14–18, 202, 213, 239, 273–74).
3. Andrews, Everyman – which also changes F1's "*Mals*" to "Mall's" – comments (22) that "*Mall* was a diminutive of 'Mary'. Sir Toby may also be thinking of a 'Moll', a less respectable 'Mistress.'" Musgrove (1969, 90) observes that "The

dialogue at I.v.200 suggests that 'Mal' might mean 'Ol-ivia': but I can find no authority for this abbreviation." However, such syllabic correspondence is unnecessary when "Mal" already means "Ill," and there are numerous parallels between Malvolio and Olivia in the play (Astington 1993, 26–27; Callaghan 2000, 33–45).

4. On "car" as cart or chariot, see Lothian and Craik, Arden 2 (66) with Warren and Wells, Oxford (145) and Evans, Riverside (455). Andrews, Everyman – printing "Carranto" – comments that "Toby is probably punning on 'car', chariot" (22); but slurring or malapropping may be more likely than deliberate punning here.
5. *OED* "paynim" also notes that its variant spellings included "painen," "paynen," "paynon," "paynyn," and "paynynne." If modernized to "paynim," Toby's F1 "panyn" would lose the additional homophonic "pain in." The "Pavin" of F2–4 was printed in Rowe (1709, 881), while Pope (1723) printed "a past-measure *Painim*" (542). Editors since have gone back and forth between "pavin" or "pavan" and "paynim" (Furness 1901, 295–98). Clark et al., Cambridge (1863–66, 302) printed F1 ("a passy measures panyn"), as did the Clark and Wright, Globe (1864, 301), but most modern editions have "pavin" or "pavan." See Lothian and Craik, Arden 2 (141), Donno, New Cambridge (141), Elam, Arden 3 (337). Warren and Wells, Oxford (210), while printing "pavan" and glossing it as the dance, also acknowledges the possible "paynim" in F1's "panyn."
6. Lothian and Craik, Arden 2 (68) puzzlingly concludes that "a quibble on 'stallion' (*OED*, 2.b. = a man of lascivious life) . . . would not be in Sir Toby's style," when Toby has already responded "Fire and brimstone" (50) to the idea of the steward coming from Olivia's bed. Warren and Wells, Oxford (147) notes: "if, as *OED* claims, stallion is a corrupt or dialect form of staniel, perhaps it is used here for its additional slang sense 'prostitute'. This would match the comparisons of Malvolio to Jezebel (l. 38) and Peg-o'-Ramsey (2.3.72)." For sexual senses of "stallion," including Q2 *Hamlet* "stallyon" and "stallion trade" as "male whoring," see Williams (1994, 3: 1304–5). Musgrove prints F1's "stallion," noting that it "keeps the sexual implications" (45), as does Andrews, Everyman (92), citing both *Hamlet* and Pegasus.
7. Furness (1901, 43–44) notes that Theobald first "proposed his emendation in 1729, in a letter to Warburton," where he says that "*curl by* nature" means "no more, I think, than, if Sir Andrew had art enough in him to tie up his hair, it had not hung so lank as it did by Nature," and that Rann's edition may have been the first to note a pun on "tongs," but also records it from Otto Gildemeister's "Notes to his translation of *Twelfth Night*, in 1869" (who acknowledges "I know not if, in the 16th century, *tongs* were used for curling hair") and from Joseph Crosby in *The American Bibliopolist* (June 1875), 143. There are no pre-eighteenth-century curling instruments under *OED* "tongs" or "crisping" (i.e. curling).
8. Andrews, Everyman (20–21), idiosyncratically printing "cool my Nature" with a capitalization not in F1 and commenting that "Toby probably plays on 'Tongues' (line 93) to refer to 'tongs' for the curling of hair," notes that "following 'the Arts' (being expert in all the skills of a Renaissance man, including those that make me attractive to women) will not turn my hair straight and limp (symbolic of a 'cool' nature: bloodless, impotent, and cowardly)."
9. See most recently Elam's Arden 3 edition (210). Lothian and Craik, Arden 2 (42) and Warren and Wells, Oxford (122) date the editorial change from "made, if" to "made of" to Rann's edition (from conjectures independently made by Thirlby and Tyrwhitt). See Furness (1901, 104–5) for the larger editorial history, including some resistance to this emendation (which has otherwise been followed by most editors). Modern exceptions here – in addition to Laurie Osborne's Folio-based edition of *Twelfe Night* (1995, 57) – include Mahood, New Penguin (1968,

69), which prints the F2 emendation ("our frailty") but keeps the Folio's "if" in the next line; and Andrews, Everyman (59), which once again, however, uses capitals not in F1.

10. Though there is not space to examine these here, there are also other instances where widely accepted editorial re-punctuation has altered what the Folio text suggests.
11. Evans, Riverside's square brackets *[Sir And.]* signal F2's correction of F1 speech prefix (*Ma.*) for this line.
12. F2 has the same punctuation for this entire exchange as F1. F3–4 add a comma in Sir Toby's first mention of "accost," rendering it not as F1–2's "Accost Sir *Andrew*, accost" but as "Accost, Sir *Andrew*, accost" (F3–F4), the punctuation used in Rowe's 1709 edition and subsequent editions. However, both F3 and F4 keep the F1–2 comma in "Good mistris *Mary*, accost" that Rowe removes to produce "Mistress Mary Accost" or the name assumed in modern editions and criticism reliant on them.
13. Lothian and Craik, Arden 2 (14) assumes that Toby's "My niece's chambermaid" is "intended by Sir Toby as the object of his imperative verb" (i.e., "accost") but "misunderstood by Sir Andrew as a reply to his question." Donno, New Cambridge (52) comments of "My niece's chambermaid" that "Sir Toby wilfully misunderstands in order to jest at Maria's expense; a gentlewoman attending the countess, she is later to become Lady Belch." Warren and Wells, Oxford (95) comments that "Sir Andrew is asking what 'accost' means, but Sir Toby (deliberately?) takes him to mean 'Who is that woman?', hence his reply, and Sir Andrew's subsequent misunderstandings of *accost* as a name." Elam's Arden 3 edition (174) reproduces the familiar longstanding eighteenth-century emendation, printing the same text as Warren and Wells, Oxford (95) for this exchange (with the small difference of not putting a comma after "By my troth").
14. More narrowly, Andrews, Everyman (16–17) restricts the import of F1's punctuation to Andrew's confusion, commenting that "the Folio rendering of the passage, preserved here, suggests that Sir Andrew is unsure of what *accost* means" and that "Mary, accost" suggests "that Sir Andrew is instructing Maria to 'accost' (and thereby give him a hint about what *accost* signifies)." As with its often unreliable claims that it preserves the Folio, Andrews's Everyman prints "Accost, Sir Andrew, accost" (not in F1 or F2, but rather the F3–4 punctuation also used by Rowe).
15. Duffin (2004, 207) notes of "I am gone sir": "It is not entirely clear that this is a song rather than spoken verse, but the text is separated like other songs in the First Folio and is assigned to Feste who sings elsewhere in the play."
16. See Duffin (2004, 139) on Robert Jones's "Farewel dear loue" from his *First Booke of Songes* (1600). Greer notes that "there is a minor puzzle: how much of it was actually sung?" (1990, 223), but this "puzzle" is rarely foregrounded in modern editions.
17. Alan Dessen has pointed out to me that speaking a song occurs in *Cymbeline* (4.2): Arviragus proposes the singing of a song earlier sung for their mother ("though now our voices, / Have got the mannish crack," 4.2.235–36), but when Guiderius responds "I cannot sing. I'll weep, and word it with thee" (240), answers "We'll speak it then" (242).
18. See Donno, New Cambridge (49), Warren and Wells, Oxford (92), Orgel (1996, 53–56) on *castrati*, "Caesar," caesarian delivery, and "*caesus*, cut," and Elam's "Fertile Eunuch" (1996, 34–36) and Elam, Arden 3 edition (2008, 57–62), which also trace the tradition from Terence's *Eunuchus*, as does Hutson (1996, 151–65, with endnotes, particularly 172, nn. 45–46).

19. Naylor (1928, 97–98). *OED* "eunuch" cites not only meaning 1.a. ("A castrated person of the male sex; also, such a person employed as a harem attendant, or in Oriental courts and under the Roman emperors, charged with important affairs of state.") and 1.b. ("A male singer, castrated in boyhood, so as to retain an alto or soprano voice," or castrato), but also the musical instrument identified by Naylor in *Coriolanus*, as meaning 2 ("eunuch flute, a type of mirliton"), citing both his 1928 book and the "Eunuque" described by Mersenne in 1635, quoted below.
20. Brockbank (1976, 225) does not cite Naylor's 1928 discussion for Coriolanus's "eunuch" (or Viola's) but does compare Coriolanus's "pipe" to Viola/Cesario's "small pipe" (with *As You Like It* 2.7.161–63: "his big manly voice, / Turning again toward childish treble, pipes / And whistles in his sound"). R. B. Parker's edition of *Coriolanus* (1994, 273) notes (citing Crookes 1986) that Coriolanus's "eunuch" is the "musical instrument" and "possibly also an adjective bridging to 'virgin': the image is of a reverse voice-change from maturity back to adolescence." Although for Coriolanus's "eunuch" it cites *Twelfth Night* 1.4.32–33 on Viola/Cesario's high-pitched voice ("thy small pipe / Is as the maiden's organ, shrill and sound"), it also does not cite Viola's "eunuch" lines. Iselin (1984, 215–16 and 1991, 167–68) connects Coriolanus's "eunuch" to the musical instrument described by Mersenne, but does not mention Viola's "eunuch." Elam's Arden 3 edition of *Twelfth Night* (2008, 183) cites the lines from *Coriolanus* as a gloss for Viola/Cesario's "small pipe" but does not make the link with the musical instrument.
21. As Alan Dessen has suggested to me, another such punningly double-functioning "instrument" might be the "recorder" in *Hamlet*. See Parker (2009, 359) on the "recorder" in *A Midsummer Night's Dream* (5.1.123) and Hamlet's response (in the scene involving "recorders") to Rosencrantz and Guildenstern's attempts to "govern" his "stops" (*Hamlet* 3.2.357–60), which continues with "you would sound me from my lowest note to [the top of] my compass" (3.2.366–67) and "'Sblood, do you think I am easier to be play'd on than a pipe? Call me what instrument you will, though you fret me [yet] you cannot play upon me" (3.2.369–72).

Works cited

Andrews, John F., ed. *Twelfth Night*. By William Shakespeare. London: J. M. Dent, 1994. ["Everyman"]

Astington, John. "Malvolio and the Eunuchs: Texts and Revels in *Twelfth Night*." *Shakespeare Survey* 46 (1993): 23–34.

Brockbank, Philip, ed. *Coriolanus*. By William Shakespeare. London and New York: Methuen, 1976.

Callaghan, Dympna. *Shakespeare without Women: Representing Gender and Race on the Renaissance Stage*. London and New York: Routledge, 2000.

Capell, Edward, ed. *Mr William Shakespeare, his Comedies, Histories, and Tragedies*. 10 vols. Vol. 4 (1767–68).

Clark, William George [John Glover,] and William Aldis Wright, eds. *The Works of William Shakespeare*. 9 vols. Vol. 3. Cambridge Shakespeare, 1863–66. ["Cambridge"]

Clark, W. G., and W. A. Wright, eds. *Works of Shakespeare*. London: Globe Shakespeare, 1864. ["Globe"]

Crookes, David Z. "'Small as a Eunuch': A Problem in 'Coriolanus', Act III Scene 2." *Music and Letters* 67.2 (April 1986): 159–61.

DiGangi, Mario. *The Homoerotics of Early Modern Drama*. Cambridge: Cambridge University Press, 1997.

Donno, Elizabeth Story, ed. *Twelfth Night or What You Will*. By William Shakespeare. Cambridge: Cambridge University Press, 1985. ["New Cambridge"]

Duffin, Ross W. *Shakespeare's Songbook*. New York and London: W. W. Norton & Company, 2004.

Elam, Keir. "The Fertile Eunuch: *Twelfth Night*, Early Modern Intercourse, and the Fruits of Castration." *Shakespeare Quarterly* 47.1 (1996): 1–36.

——, ed. *Twelfth Night, or What You Will*. By William Shakespeare. London: Cengage Learning, 2008. ["Arden 3"]

Evans, G. Blakemore, et al., eds. *The Riverside Shakespeare*. Boston: Houghton Mifflin, 1974. Second edn., 1997. ["Riverside"]

Furness, Horace Howard, ed. *Twelfe Night, or What You Will*. By William Shakespeare. Philadelphia: J. B. Lippincott Company, 1901.

Goldberg, Jonathan. "Textual Properties." *Shakespeare Quarterly* 37.2 (Summer 1986): 213–17.

Greenblatt, Stephen. *Shakespearean Negotiations: The Circulation of Social Energy in Renaissance England*. Berkeley: University of California Press, 1988.

Greer, David. "Five Variations on 'Farewel dear loue.'" In *The Well-Enchanting Skill: Music, Poetry, and Drama in the Culture of the Renaissance: Essays in Honour of Frederick W. Sternfeld*. Ed. John Caldwell, Edward Olleson, and Susan Wollenberg. Oxford: Clarendon Press, 1990: 213–29.

Hanmer, Thomas, ed. *The Works of Shakespear*. 6 vols. Vol. 2. Oxford, 1743–44.

Hinman, Charlton (comp.). *The First Folio of Shakespeare. Based on the Folios in the Folger Shakespeare Library Collection*. The Norton Facsimile. Prepared by Charlton Hinman. Second edn. With a new introduction by Peter W. M. Blayney. New York and London: W. W. Norton & Company, 1996. ["TLN"]

Hollander, John. *The Untuning of the Sky: Ideas of Music in English Poetry 1500–1700*. Princeton, NJ: Princeton University Press, 1961.

Hutson, Lorna. "On Not Being Deceived: Rhetoric and the Body in *Twelfth Night*." *Texas Studies in Literature and Language* 38.2 (1996): 140–74.

Iselin, Pierre. "Les références musicales dans l'oeuvre dramatique de Shakespeare." Unpublished PhD dissertation, University of Limoges, France, 1984: 215–16.

——. "De l'analogie à l'anamorphose: visions du corps musical dans le drame shakespearien." In *Shakespeare et le Corps à la Renaissance*. Ed. M. T. Jones-Davies. Paris: Les Belles Lettres, 1991: 153–74.

Laqueur, Thomas. *Making Sex: Body and Gender from the Greeks to Freud*. Cambridge MA: Harvard University Press, 1990.

Levin, Richard A. *Love and Society in Shakespearean Comedy: A Study of Dramatic Form and Content*. Newark: University of Delaware Press, 1985.

Lindley, David. *Shakespeare and Music*. London: Thomson Learning, 2006.

Lothian, J. M., and T. W. Craik, eds. *Twelfth Night*. By William Shakespeare. London: Methuen, 1975. London: Thomson Learning/Arden Shakespeare, 2003. ["Arden 2"]

Mahood, M. M., ed. *Twelfth Night*. By William Shakespeare. New Penguin Shakespeare. Harmondsworth: Penguin, 1968.

Masten, Jeffrey. "Textual Deviance: Ganymede's Hand in *As You Like It*." In *Field Work: Sites in Literary and Cultural Studies*. Ed. Marjorie Garber, Paul B. Franklin, and Rebecca L. Walkowitz. New York and London: Routledge, 1996: 153–63.

Mersenne, Marin. *Harmonicorum Libri* (Paris, 1635). Trans. Roger E. Chapman in *Harmonie Universelle: The Books on Instruments*. The Hague: Martinus Nijhoff, 1957.

Mr. William Shakespeares Comedies, Histories, & Tragedies. Published according to the True Originall Copies. London: Printed by Isaac Iaggard, and E. Blount [at the charges of W. Iaggard, Ed. Blount, I. Smithweeke, and W. Aspley], 1623. ["Folio or First Folio/F1"]

Mr. William Shakespeares Comedies, Histories, and Tragedies . . . The second Impression. London, 1632. ["Second Folio or F2"]

Mr. William Shakespear's Comedies, Histories, and Tragedies . . . The third Impression. London, 1663–64. ["Third Folio or F3"]

Mr. William Shakespear's Comedies, Histories, and Tragedies . . . The Fourth Edition. London, 1685. ["Fourth Folio or F4"]

Musgrove, S., ed. *Twelfth Night or What You Will*. Edinburgh: Oliver and Boyd Ltd., 1968; Berkeley and Los Angeles: University of California Press, 1969.

Naylor, Edward W. *The Poets and Music.* London and Toronto: J. M. Dent, 1928.

Orgel, Stephen. *Impersonations: The Performance of Gender in Shakespeare's England.* Cambridge: Cambridge University Press, 1996.

Osborne, Laurie E., ed. *Twelfe Night, or What You Will*. By William Shakespeare. Hemel Hempstead: Prentice Hall, 1995.

——. "Editing Frailty in *Twelfth Night*: 'Where lies your Text?'" In *Reading Readings: Essays on Shakespeare Editing in the Eighteenth Century*. Ed. Joanna Gondris. London: Associated University Presses, 1998: 209–23.

Parker, Patricia. "Altering the Letter of *Twelfth Night*: 'Some are born great' and the Missing Signature." *Shakespeare Survey* 59 (2006): 49–62.

——. "Was Illyria as Mysterious and Foreign as We Think?" In *The Mysterious and the Foreign in Early Modern England*. Ed. Helen Ostovich, Mary V. Silcox, and Graham Roebuck. Newark: University of Delaware Press, 2008: 209–33.

——. "Shakespeare's Sound Government: Sound Defects, Polyglot Sounds, and Sounding Out." *Oral Tradition* 24.2 (2009): 359–72. http://journal.oraltradition.org/

Parker, R. B., ed. *Coriolanus*. By William Shakespeare. Oxford and New York: Oxford University Press, 1994.

Paster, Gail Kern. *The Body Embarrassed: Drama and the Disciplines of Shame in Early Modern England.* Ithaca, NY: Cornell University Press, 1993.

——. *Humoring the Body: Emotions and the Shakespearean Stage*. Chicago: University of Chicago Press, 2004.

Pope, Alexander, ed. *The Works of Shakespear*. 6 vols. Vol. 2. London, 1723–25.

Rann, Joseph. *The Dramatic Works of Shakespeare*. 6 vols. Vol. 2. Oxford, 1786–[94].

Rowe, Nicholas, ed. *The Works of Mr. William Shakespear*. 6 vols. Vol. 2. London, 1709.

——, ed. *The Works of Mr. William Shakespear*. 3rd edn. 8 vols. Vol. 2. London, 1714.

Sisson, C. J. *New Readings in Shakespeare*. 2 vols. Vol. 1. Cambridge: Cambridge University Press, 1956.

Smith, Bruce R., ed. *William Shakespeare, Twelfth Night or What You Will: Texts and Contexts*. Boston and New York: Bedford/St. Martin's Press, 2001. ["Smith"]

Taylor, Gary. *Castration: An Abbreviated History of Western Manhood*. New York and London: Routledge, 2000.

Theobald, Lewis, ed. *The Works of Shakespeare*. 7 vols. Vol. 2. London, 1733.

Ungerer, Gustav. "The Viol da Gamba as a Sexual Metaphor in Elizabethan Music and Literature." *Renaissance and Reformation/Renaissance et Réforme* n.s. 8.2 (1984): 79–90.

Warren, Roger, and Stanley Wells, eds. *Twelfth Night, or What You Will*. By William Shakespeare. Oxford: Clarendon Press, 1994. Oxford World's Classics edition, 1995. ["Oxford"]

Williams, Gordon. *A Dictionary of Sexual Language and Imagery in Shakespearean and Stuart Literature*. 3 vols. London: Athlone Press, 1994.

3 "His fancy's queen"

Sensing sexual strangeness in *Twelfth Night*

Bruce R. Smith

"So full of shapes is fancy / That it alone is high fantastical": the climax to Orsino's opening speech in *Twelfth Night* metamorphoses the poly-sensuous into the polysemous. Love is imagined as food that can be tasted; sound, as a breath that touches the ears and carries odor to the nostrils; the "spirit of love," as something "quick and fresh" (the violets on the bank? motion that can be seen? motion that can be felt like a breeze? motion that can be touched?), then as the sea, receiving and confounding waters of varying "validity and pitch," waters that in turn become marketplace commodities with falling prices (*TN* 1.1.9, 12, 14–15, in Shakespeare 1997). What is "fancy" that it should have such powers to conflate the five senses and to undo the fixity of words? Glosses of the term in current editions of *Twelfth Night* fail to explain these metamorphic and deconstructive powers. The editors of *Twelfth Night* in the Arden Shakespeare, series 2 and 3, do connect fancy with image-formation, but they are content to define "fancy" as "love" and to paraphrase "high fantastical" as "imaginative in the highest degree' (Shakespeare 1975, 6). The Norton edition lets "fancy" pass without comment and modernizes "high fantastical" as "uniquely imaginative." My own edition of the play, which incorporates text and notes from David Bevington's fourth Riverside edition, limits "fancy" to "love" and paraphrases the last line as "it surpasses everything else in imaginative power." Given these cues, Shakespeare's twenty-first-century readers and listeners are apt to conclude that "fancy" is just another word for "imagination," with a pun on sexual desire or falling in love.

On the tongues and in the ears of Shakespeare and his contemporaries /faencɪ/ was both of these things, but only because in their heads Shakespeare and his contemporaries understood *fancy*, *fansy*, *phancy*, *phansy*, *fantasy*, *fantosy*, *phantsie*, *feintasy*, etc., to be a creative capacity that was engaged every single time they saw, heard, smelled, tasted, and/or touched anything – or anyone, for that matter. Fancy was a "faculty," in the root sense of that term as power, ability, opportunity (*OED* "faculty" etymology, Connor 2005, 321). As such, it was a factor in early modern psychology, in the story that early modern men and women told themselves about what was happening inside them as they perceived something and spoke, to themselves or to others, about what they were perceiving. Fancy in *Twelfth Night* invites us as post-modern readers to question modern assumptions about the relationship of sense experience to speech. Instructed by Saussure's *General Course in Linguistics* (French text 1916, English translations 1959, 1966, 1983), we have come to regard speech as a self-contained system of arbitrary difference-marking. What speech may have to do with sense experience is beyond Saussure's frame of reference – and that of most practitioners of deconstruction, who all start from Saussure's premiss. Saussure's move is a radical version of what Thomas Hobbes was already doing in the mid-seventeenth century. In *Humane Nature* (1650), Hobbes distinguishes two kinds of knowledge, sense and science. "Both of these sorts are but *Experience*; the former being the experience of the effects of things that work upon us from *without*, and [the latter] the experience men have from the proper use of *names* in Language" (D6). Only the latter, Hobbes argues, has any claims to true knowledge. As for sense experience, it has been abstracted from the human body and located "without," not "in here." What's "in here," Hobbes assumes, is language. Criticism since "the linguistic turn" of the 1960s has followed Hobbes's lead – with a vengeance. But *Twelfth Night* predates Hobbes by nearly 50 years and Saussure by more than 300. Changing ideas about gender and sexuality turn on these paradigm-shifts about sensation and speech. Gender and sexuality, we have been telling ourselves for 40 years, are performances that are dictated by language. Orsino's language, however, is so sense-laden that any separation of "sense" from "speech" seems wildly misleading. Putting sensation back into sexuality enables us to understand the sexuality of Shakespeare and his contemporaries on *their* terms, not *ours*.

In *Twelfth Night*, as in other Shakespeare plays, fancy carries meanings that extend beyond imagination and love-longing. Sebastian, mistaken for Cesario by Olivia and invited into her house, exclaims, "Let fancy still my sense in Lethe steep. / If this be dream, still let me sleep" (4.1.58–59). Incredulity is what Sebastian expresses here, using the word "fancy" to suggest illusion or delusion (*OED* "fancy" *n.* and *a.* A.2, 3), just as the Lord does in setting up Christopher Sly in *The Taming of the Shrew*. Scented clothes, rings on his fingers, a banquet by his bed, attendants awaiting his commands: these feints will seem strange to the drunken Sly when he wakes up, "Even as a flatt'ring dream or worthless fancy" (Ind.1.40). With Sebastian, as with Sly, "fancy" edges into "feintasy." It is not delusion but caprice or whim (*OED* A.7.a) that Orsino has in mind when he counsels Cesario about the differences between men and women. Compared with women, he says, "Our fancies are more giddy and unfirm" (2.4.32). Caprice becomes visible, audible, and risible in affectations of clothing, speech, and gesture (*OED* A.7.b), as when the King in *Love's Labor's Lost* makes fun of "This child of fancy, that Armado hight" (1.1.168). With respect to apparel Polonius counsels Laertes, "Costly thy habit as thy purse can buy, / But not expressed in fancy; rich not gaudy" (*Ham* 1.3.70–71). Don Armado's counterpart in *Twelfth Night* is Malvolio in his yellow stockings and crossed garters. Fancy as amorous inclination (*OED* A.8.a) figures not only in Orsino's first speech but in Malvolio's self-flattery when he is being duped by Maria and company. Maria once told him, he reflects, that Olivia "did affect me, and I have heard herself come thus near, that should she fancy it should be one of my complexion" (2.5.21–22). Fancy in the sense of erotic desire runs riot in *A Midsummer Night's Dream*, where it is associated with a specifically female "complexion," as when Oberon tells Robin how to recognize Helena: "All fancy-sick she is, and pale of cheer, / With sighs of love that costs the fresh blood dear" (3.2.96–97).

Delusion, whim, affectation, love-longing: use of the same word to denominate these diverse experiences is informed by "fancy" or "fantasy" as a faculty of mind in scholastic psychology (*OED* "fancy" A.1). For Shakespeare and his contemporaries the Aristotelian axiom "There is nothing in the intellect that was not first in the senses" gave sense experience an epistemological importance that modern science, with its protocols of objective proof, has attempted to compensate for if not deny (Park 1988, 470). The five external senses (sight, hearing, smell, taste, and touch) were imagined to have their counterparts in five internal senses. In the forepart of the brain, close to the external sense organs, were situated two faculties, common sense, which received and compared sense data, and imagination, which held as images or *species* the data that had been collated by common sense. The process of perception continued in the central part of the brain, where two more faculties did their work: fantasy combined sense data to produce new images or *phantasmata*, and estimation determined whether the perceiver's reaction should be attraction or avoidance. Finally, memory, at the rear of the brain, stored sense data, *phantasmata*, and the perceiver's reaction (Park 1988, 470–71).

There was, however, some controversy over just where in the body "estimation" took place. To encourage her chooser-of-choice to choose the correct casket, Portia in *The Merchent of Venice* arranges for a song to be sung "*the whilst* BASSANIO *comments on the caskets to himself*" (SD before 3.2.63). The word "comments" ("to remark mentally; to meditate; ponder" [*OED* "comment" *v.* II.5]) in this stage direction from the 1623 folio text suggests that the actor playing Bassanio does something to indicate that his faculties of fantasy and estimation are at work. The song, sung according to the 1619 quarto text, by "ONE FROM PORTIA'S TRAIN," gives Bassanio his cues for cogitation:

> Tell me where is fancy bred,
> Or in the heart, or in the head?
> How begot, how nourishèd?
> (3.2.63–65)

Whereupon, according to the 1619 text, everyone sings, "Reply, reply" (3.2.66). But no word yet from Bassanio. The single singer continues:

> It is engendered in the eyes,
> With gazing fed, and fancy dies
> In the cradle where it lies.
> Let us all ring fancy's knell.
> I'll begin it: ding, dong, bell.
> (3.2.67–71)

Whence all join in: "Ding, dong, bell" (3.2.72). This time, Bassanio does reply, perhaps in a "comment" or aside to himself, as the Norton text suggests: "So may the outward shows be least themselves" (3.2.64–73). He has picked up on Portia's hint *not* to trust his eyes and fancy the gold and the silver caskets. The fancy that makes him choose the leaden casket is engendered, not in the head, but in the heart.

That is just where Thomas Wright places the power of estimation in *The Passions of the Mind in General* (1604, 1630). As soon as sensation has registered in the imagination, "presently the purer spirits, flocke from the brayne, by certaine secret channels to the heart, where they pitch at the dore, signifying what an obiect was presented, conuenient or disconuenient for it" (D7). The heart's response is immediate. If the object in prospect is desirable, the heart dilates. If it is dangerous or displeasing, it contracts. Then the heart, "better to effect that affection, draweth other humours to helpe him" (D7). So "pure spirits" induce pleasure, "melancholy blood" pain and sadness, "blood and choler" ire (D7). Passion, in this model, is inescapably part of perception. When Orsino refers to the "spirit" of love, he is thinking in quite physical terms of an aerated fluid that he imagines to be welling up in his heart, circulating throughout his body, and coloring his understanding. Hence those images of rivers and the sea. In *The Merchant of Venice*, Bassanio's choice may be rational ("The world is still deceived with ornament" [3.2.74]), but the result is a welling up of passion on both Portia's part and his. "How all the other passions fleet to air," Portia exclaims when Bassanio has rejected the gold and silver caskets and is about to open the leaden one. Doubt, despair, fear, "green-eyed jealousy" give way to an "ecstasy," an "excess," a "blessing," a "surfeit" of love (3.2.108–14). Bassanio's body is no less overwhelmed by passion: "Madam, you have bereft me of words," he tells Portia. "Only my blood speaks to you in my veins, / And there is such a confusion in my powers" that everything "being blent together / Turns to a wild of nothing save of joy, / Expressed and not expressed" (3.2.175–77, 181–83).

A Jesuit writing under the influence of Augustine, Wright assumes that passions like these work at cross purposes to the soul's faculty of understanding. The soul without passions may be compared, he says, "to a calme sea, with sweet, pleasant, and crispling streames: but the passionate, to the raging gulfe, swelling with waues, surging by tempests, minacing the stony rockes, and endeauouring to ouerthrow Mountaines" (E6). Orsino's soul, needless to say, is in the second state. His love for Olivia, he tells Cesario, "is all as hungry as the sea, / And can digest as much" (2.4.98–99). A more sanguine estimate of the passions, something closer to Portia's, Bassanio's, and Orsino's exclamations, is entertained by Edward Reynolds in *A Treatise of the Passions and Faculties of the Soul of Man*. Written in the 1620s, the treatise was not published until 1640 at the behest of James I's granddaughter Elizabeth, Princess Palatine, ten years after Reynolds had succeeded John Donne as preacher at Lincoln's Inn. In 1660 he became Bishop of Norwich. Reynolds acknowledges the disasters that ensue when passions anticipate reason rather than serve under reason's direction, but at the same time he recognizes the usefulness of passions "for adding spirit and edge to all good undertakings" (G3). In these enterprises "Fancie" plays a major role, as it assists the understanding and stimulates the will. With respect to the understanding, fancy has a "double prerogative": in the form of *phantasmata* it captures the "quicknesse and volubilitie" of thoughts, even as it fixes objects for meditation by the understanding. By "thoughts" Reynolds means "those springings and glances of the heart, grounded on the sudden representation of sundry different objects" (D3v). Reynolds's model of perception, like Wright's, accommodates the heart as well as the brain, passion as well as reason, but Reynolds gives much more scope to how thought *feels*. "Though the Act of Apprehending be the proper worke of the Vnderstanding," Reynolds writes, "yet the forme and qualitie of that Act . . . namely, the lightnesse, volubilitie, and suddennesse thereof, proceeds from the immediate restlesnesse of the Imagination" (D4–D4v). We can almost hear Orsino in Reynolds's summary statement: "the Imagination is a Facultie boundlesse, and impatient of any imposed limits, save those which it selfe maketh" (D4v).

Reynolds's attention to the sensuous qualities of apprehension, to its quickness and simultaneity, stands in the sharpest possible contrast to Descartes's emphasis on clarity and distinctness as criteria for knowledge. In *Principles of Philosophy* (published in Latin 1644) Descartes gives these terms precise definition: "A perception which can serve as the basis for a certain and indubitable judgement needs to be not merely clear but also distinct. I call a perception 'clear' when it is present and accessible to the attentive mind . . . I call a perception 'distinct' if, as well as being clear, it is so sharply separated from all other perceptions that it contains within itself only what is clear" (1988, 174–75). Clearness and distinctness, I submit, are not necessarily the qualities of perception for which audiences paid a penny in 1602. The number of books on the passions that were published in the 1640s and 1650s – Reynolds's *Treatise* in 1640 (with new editions in 1651, 1656, and 1658), Marin Cureau de la Chambre's *The Character of the Passions* (in five volumes 1640–62, English translation of volume one 1650, of volume two 1661), Descartes's *The Passions of the Soul* (1649, with an English translation the very next year) – suggest that the mid-seventeenth century witnessed a crisis of sorts with respect to understandings of human perception. Reynolds and La Chambre speak for the older view that has its origins in Aristotle; Descartes, for the newer view that still manifests itself in developments like cognitive theory. Orsino, needless to say, is situated on the *far* side of that epistemological divide.

According to the older theory, the imagination is a place where things are perpetually in a state of becoming. The tower of Spenser's Castle of Alma comprises three chambers, one devoted to things future, one to things present, and one to things past. The first chamber, assigned to a figure named Phantastes, is "dispainted all within, / With sundry colours, in the which were writ / Infinite shapes of things dispersed thin," including things "such as in the world were neuer yit," as well as things "daily seene, and knowen by their names, / Such as in idle fantasies doe flit" (*The Faerie Queene* 2.9.50.1–7 in Spenser 1978, 324). Sounds as well as images fill the room: "And all the chamber filled was with flyes, / Which buzzed all about, and made such sound, / That they encombred all mens eares and eyes" (2.9.51.1–3). In the second chamber, presided over by "a man of ripe and perfect age" (2.9.54.2), the colors and shapes become "gestes" of wise men and "picturals" of social institutions (2.9.53.3, 4), while, implicitly among the picturals, the buzzing sounds become words in the form of laws, judgments, decrees, arts, science, and philosophy. In the third chamber gestes, picturals, and words are committed to the keeping of memory in the form of books and parchment scrolls. There is a teleological progression here – "idle" fantasies in the first room become "memorable gestes" in the second and written records in the third – but Spenser, like Reynolds, is exquisitely sensitive to the colors, the thinly dispersed images, the buzzing sounds that have not yet become characters, deeds, and words.

About fancy, we have to conclude, Shakespeare and his contemporaries were ambivalent. Wright is cautious. Reynolds is enthusiastic. Spenser is both. We can catch that ambivalence on the verge between night and day, between woods and city, in *A Midsummer Night's Dream* 5.1. "Strange" is Hippolyta's non-judgmental description of what the lovers have reported about events in the forest. "More strange than true," Theseus fires back.

> I never may believe
> These antique fables, nor these fairy toys.
> Lovers and madmen have such seething brains,
> Such shaping fantasies, that apprehend
> More than cool reason ever comprehends.
> (5.1.1–6)

To lovers and lunatics Theseus quickly adds poets and goes on to ridicule the over-active imaginations of all three types. Hippolyta, on her side, remains firm: all that the lovers have said "More witnesseth than fancy's images"

(5.1.25). The male–female divide in this stand-off between "cool reason" and "shaping fantasies" perhaps reflects the notion that *phantasmata* provide the "matter" for engendering thought in the same way that women were believed to provide the "matter" on which male-produced "forms" were stamped in the engendering of children (Wallace 1988, 202, Laqueur 1990, 29–30). Fancy, in this scheme, takes on specifically sexual qualities.

That erotic valence can be witnessed in the early modern spaces where sexual relations took place. Mendoza in John Marston's tragicomedy *The Malcontent*, acted by the King's Men a year or two after *Twelfth Night*'s first performance in 1601 or 1602, sets the scene for wanton sex: "sweet sheets, wax lights, antique bedposts, cambric smocks, villainous curtains, arras pictures, oil'd hinges, and all the tongue-tied lascivious witnesses of great creatures' wantonness" (1.7.38–41 in Marston 1964, 37). The bedposts are "antic" because they are carved with what Edward Phillips in *The New World of English Words* (1658) defines as "a disorderly mixture of divers shapes of men, birds, flow'rs, *&c.*" (C2). Hence Theseus's "antique fables." The bed head made for Henry VIII and Anne of Cleves, preserved today in the Burrell Collection, Glasgow (inventory 14/236), features, on Henry's side of the bed, a carved male figure opening his doublet while a nude male counterpart in the spandrel above grabs his penis and, on Anne's side of the bed, a female figure pulling up her skirts while a nude female counterpart thrusts forward her vulva (illustrated in Thurley 1993, 237).

The bed curtains strike Mendoza as "villainous" probably because they are woven with sexual escapades out of Ovid's *Metamorphoses.* Three such panels dating from the sixteenth and early seventeenth centuries are usually on display in the British Galleries of the Victoria and Albert Museum, London: one showing the story of Venus and Adonis (inventory T.879-1904), one the story of Myrrha (T.879A-1904), and one the story of Lucrece (T.125-1913). Another, depicting Europa and the Bull, is on display at Blickling Hall, Norfolk (illustrated in Clabburn 1988, 29). Still another, woven with the story of Philomel (its present location unknown) is illustrated in Remington 1945, figure 34. "Villainous" in a more literal sense is a bed valence in the Victoria and Albert Museum (T.117-1934) that shows folk disporting themselves in a landscape, including two couples who embrace while a bagpiper shrills and a male figure dances. (See detail in Figure 3.1, overleaf.) Grotesque masks and outsized foliage, flowers, and birds in the panels above suggest how erotic desire was insinuated into the antic work catalogued by Phillips and dismissed by cooly reasonable Theseus. John Donne's celebratory poem for the marriage of King James's daughter Elizabeth to the Count Palatine in 1613 is altogether typical of epithalamia in situating the poem's readers and listeners within the bridal suite, right outside the bed curtains. Donne seems to be taking his cue from the weavings when he addresses the bedded Princess Elizabeth and Count Palatine and describes how he and the other wedding guests "As Satyres watch the Sunnes uprise, will stay / Waiting, when

Figure 3.1 Tapestry valence for a bed, English, Sheldon workshops, 1590–1620. © V&A Images, Victoria and Albert Museum, London.

your eyes opened, let out day" (R1v). Donne and his satyr-companions take their place among the antic players in the bed curtains. (Among the children eventually engendered by the Count and Princess was the Princess Elizabeth who asked Edward Reynolds to publish his *Passions and Faculties of the Soul of Man*.) In two extensive inventories of beds and curtains, one devoted to actual furniture in upper-class houses and one to stage properties in plays like *Romeo and Juliet* and *Othello*, Sasha Roberts traces the intricate connections among curtained beds, sexual imaginings, and moveable goods that signify social status (Roberts 1995, 325–57 with numerous illustrations, Roberts 2002, 153–74). The carvings on early modern bedposts and the woven subjects in early modern bed curtains were products of fancy, just as were the sexual acts that took place within them.

And so were events dramatized on London's public and private stages. About the design of the arras, curtain, or hangings that concealed the space "within" at the Globe and in the Blackfriars no definitive evidence exists, but the prominence of "antic work" in bed curtains and in the wall hangings, cushion covers, and book covers produced by the Sheldon workshops in Warwickshire and Worcestershire between 1590 and 1620 suggests that Orsino and other protagonists played out their scenes of passion against a backdrop of plant forms and perhaps creatures that were part human, part animal, even part plant (Wells-Cole 1997, 220–34; Bardnard and Wace 1928, 392–40; Humphreys 1928, *passim*). The contract for the Fortune Theatre specifies that the columns of the theatre's "fframe and Stadge forward" shall be made "palasterwise, with carved proportions called Satiers to be placed & sett on the topp of every of the same postes" (Shakespeare 1997, 3331). The satyr-carved posts of the Globe's *scenae frons* shape up in this description as being not unlike the antic bed posts excoriated by Marston's satiric Malevole. Taken together, this evidence suggests that visual perception in the playhouse involved the same mobile play of imagination that Reynolds celebrates in his treatise on the passions. We are invited to imagine a visual matrix alive with motion, suffused with erotic desire, out of which figures emerge with quickness and volubility, before they are fixed for contemplation by the understanding. The stage of the Globe functioned as the sort of space Spenser might have called "The House of Fancy."

An aural equivalent to this visual experience of fancy can be heard in the sound effects of speeches like Orsino's. "If music be the food of love": the ensuing lines are full of [s] sounds in "excess," "surfeiting," "sicken," "strain," "sweet sound," violets," "stealing," "sweet," "spirit," "notwithstanding," "capacity," "receiveth," "sea," "so," "price," "so," "shapes," "fancy," "fantastical" (1.1.1–15). Post-eighteenth-century poetics would prompt us to think of these alliterations as decorations applied to the words; early modern notions of fancy invite us to hear them as buzzings, as abstract sounds out of which the individual words emerge. The effect is enhanced by the fact that music is playing when Orsino speaks. The [u:] sounds in Orsino's first line –"music," "food," and (in early modern pronunciation) "loove"– are of a piece with the music that inspires them. Most modern linguists would stress the phonemes, the frequency peaks, that an Anglophone listener picks as meaningful amid the continuous stream of sound. Reynolds, with his sensitivity to quickness, volubility, suddenness, and variety, would appreciate the non-verbal sensuousness of [o:], [s], [ʃ], and [u:], the sounds that are not yet words (Smith 2003, 147–68). Early modern explanations of perception left much more room than we do for the margins, for the physical and temporal space in which sense experiences become objects of reason.

After Orsino's opening speech, *Twelfth Night* is replete with moments in which visual sensations and sounds hover between sensuous numinousness and semantic specificity. That is to say, *Twelfth Night* is replete with moments in which fancy holds sway. Maria's trick on Malvolio depends on the colors, dispersed images, and buzzings of fancy. The plan as she first announces it is to drop a letter that will contain visual clues to the secret object of Lady Olivia's passion, "the color of his beard, the shape of his leg, the manner of his gait, the expressure of his eye, forehead and complexion," wherein Malvolio "shall find himself most feelingly personated" (2.3.140–41). In the event, she excites Malvolio's fancy, not with images, but with sounds: "M.O.A.I. doth sway my life" (2.5.97). Volubility is the essence of Malvolio's response. "O peace," Fabian commands the hidden onlookers, "now he's deeply in. Look how imagination blows him" (2.5.37–38). Combining and recombining the sounds of [m], [o:], [a], [i], Malvolio is as sure as ever that he is proceeding according the dictates of reason, even as he falls into fancy as deeply as Orsino: "I do not fool myself," he tells the audience, "to let imagination jade me; for every reason excites to this, that my lady loves me" (2.5.144–45).

As it happens, what Olivia comes to fancy is the person named Cesario. As does Orsino. The primary focus of fancy in the play is indeed the part-man-part-woman part-child-part-adult part-eunuch-part-sexual-partner whom the other characters attempt to fix with various names: "Cesario," "Sebastian," "Viola." In itself, this figure would be at home in Spenser's chamber of Phantastes, among the sundry colors and infinite shapes of things dispersèd thin. In his description of Phantastes's chamber Spenser provides a catalogue of these shapes, a catalogue that begins with witches, proceeds through creatures out of antic work, and ends with just the kind of figure that Viola/Cesario/Sebastian cuts in the world: "Infernall Hags, *Centaurs*, feendes, *Hippodames*, / Apes, Lions, Aegles, Owles, fooles, louers, children, Dames" (2.9.50.8–9). The encounters of other characters with this figure of fancy point up the limitations of words in fixing the image. Orsino struggles with the enigmas of gender, age, and sexual availability when he encounters Cesario for the first time: "they shall yet belie thy happy years / That say thou art a man. Diana's lip / Is not more smooth and rubious . . ." (1.4.29–31). The reference to Diana's chastity, via the tactility and color of her lips, is especially piquant. In sound, too, Cesario lacks the clarity and distinctness that Descartes would require: "thy small pipe / Is as the maiden's organ, shrill and sound" (31–32). Malvolio, for his part, describes Cesario in plant images out of a Sheldon tapestry. To Olivia's question about the "personage and years" of the caller at her gate Malvolio replies, "Not old enough for a man, nor young enough for a boy; as a squash is before 'tis a peascod, or a codling when 'tis almost an apple. 'Tis with him in standing water between boy and man" (1.5.139–42). Sebastian works on Antonio the same androgynous charm that Cesario works on Orsino and Olivia. His sister, Sebastian tells Antonio, "though it was said she much resembled me, was yet of many accounted beautiful" (2.1.21–22). Antonio's reckless devotion confirms the resemblance. Orsino may say of men, "Our fancies are more giddy and unfirm" (2.4.34), but confronted with Viola/Cesario/Sebastian, Olivia's fancy proves just as susceptible.

Viola and Sebastian are not just objects of other people's imagination; they indulge imagination themselves. When Antonio mistakes Viola for Sebastian, she exclaims, "Prove true, imagination, O, prove true, / That I, dear brother, be now ta'en for you" (3.4.340–41). Sebastian, in turn, hopes that Olivia's mistaking him for Cesario will never end: "Let fancy still my sense in Lethe steep" (4.1.66). Here, as so often in this play, fancy finds its natural habitat in images of water and the sea. Malvolio's reference to Cesario as being "in standing water," at the point of tide-turn, between boy and man recalls the emergence of Viola/Cesario/Sebastian from the sea in the play's opening scenes. The Captain tells Viola that her brother appeared on the sea's surface "like Arion on the dolphin's back" (1.2.14). The script never makes the connection explicit, but the sea is the domain of Proteus, the god of infinitely changing shapes. Ovid's account in Book 8 of *Metamorphoses* includes stones, plants, water, and fire in Proteus's repertory of shapes:

> Others have powre themselves, at will, to change;
> As thou blew *Protëus*, that in seas do'st range.
> Who now a Man, a Lyon now appeares;
> Now, a fell Bore: a Serpents shape now beares.
> A Bull, with threatning hornes, now seem'st to be:
> Now, like a Stone; now, like a spreading Tree.
> And sometimes like a gentle River flowes:
> Sometimes like Fire, averse to Water, shows.
> (8.730–36 in Ovid 1970, 374)

Viola/Cesario/Sebastian are subject to the same transformations of fancy as Ferdinand's father in Ariel's song: "Nothing of him that doth fade / But doth suffer a sea-change / Into something rich and strange" (*Tem* 1.2.403–5). In these watery metamorphoses we can feel the cross-currents with Orsino's pouring "the spirit of love" into the sea, with Wright's "raging gulf" of the passions, with Reynolds's association of fancy with quickness, lightness, volubility, suddenness, and variety.

> Cesario, come–
> For so you shall be while you are a man;
> But when in other habits you are seen,
> Orsino's mistress, and his fancy's queen.
> (5.1.372–75)

Appreciating what early modern men and women told themselves was happening in their heads and hearts when they saw actors onstage and heard actors speaking helps us to frame *Twelfth Night*'s closing lines in historically specific terms. The timing of Orsino's declaration (it is the very last line in the script, before Feste sings and perhaps dances the jig "When that I was and a little tiny boy") serves as a cue to the spectator-listeners that fancy is precisely what is now required from them. In moments like these fancy takes on a sixth meaning, as creative or productive imagination (*OED* A.4). And so it functions in early modern sexuality.

In meta-theatrical moments throughout his career Shakespeare calls on fancy as the faculty that takes the sights, sounds, smells, tastes, and textures of drama in performance and turns them into something that is more than the sum of these parts. The expected sum is "nature." Implicitly it is his listeners' fancy that Enobarbus engages when he describes Cleopatra in her barge, "O'er-picturing that Venus where we see / The fancy outwork nature" (*Ant* 2.2.207–8). The distinction between nature and fancy that Enobarbus assumes casts an unexpected light on the speech in which Sebastian, newly arrived on the scene and conveniently equipped with a penis, reassures Olivia, "So comes it, lady, that you have been mistook. / But nature to her bias drew in that" (5.1.252–53). Despite warnings from Thomas Laqueur, it is hard for twenty-first-century listeners not to hear biological essentialism in Sebastian's statement. Nature trumps. Trumps *what*? Culture, we tell ourselves. Since Rousseau in the early eighteenth century, perhaps even since Hobbes in the mid-seventeenth century, culture has figured as nature's opposite. New historicism and cultural materialism, even as they warn us that "nature" is ideology in another guise, perpetuate that binary (Laqueur 1990, 29–30, Dollimore 1991, 113–16). What happens if, for nature's opposite, we substitute fancy? Sebastian's pronouncement seems much less authoritative and Orsino's final speech, all the more open-ended. The "other habits" in which Orsino anticipates seeing "Cesario" are not necessarily the binary markers of gender that we are apt to assume. Antic-work and fantastic plant motifs in bed curtains could likewise appear on clothing. Although the weight of fabrics might be different, woven furnishings and dress fabrics in early modern England shared similar designs (Rothstein and Levey 2003, 1: 634). The early seventeenth-century embroidered jacket from the Burrell Collection shown in Figure 3.2 suggests how the stuff of fancy could provide a frame for reading a person's face and neck. It would be the whole ensemble that estimation, or in the heart or in the head, would take under consideration. Henslowe's inventory of costumes includes no fewer than nine "anteckes cootes," two with bases or skirts (Foakes 2002, 318–19). These were presumably intended for performers playing clowns, mountebanks, and other ludicrous roles (*OED* "antic" *n.* B.4), but several embroidered costumes in Henslowe's inventory confirm that Cesario could have presented himself/herself to the gazes of Orsino, Olivia, and the paying customers in a garment not unlike the jacket shown in Figure 3.2. The particular characteristics of Cesario that please Orsino's senses are located above the neck line – to wit, his mouth ("Diana's lip / Is not more smooth and rubious") and his voice ("thy small pipe / Is as the maiden's organ, shrill and sound") – although Orsino does conclude his praise with a more general flourish: "And all is semblative a woman's

Figure 3.2 Embroidered jacket, English, 1610–20, Burrell Collection, Glasgow. Reproduced by permission of Culture and Sport Glasgow.

part" (2.4.30–33). To Cesario's face and voice Olivia in the very next scene adds arms, legs, movement, and an elusive something she calls "spirit": "Thy tongue, thy face, thy limbs, actions, and spirit / Do give thee five-fold blazon" (1.5.262–63). "Spirit" perhaps catches common sense's fusion of vision and hearing in Olivia's fancying of Cesario. A similar play of fancy might be directed to other parts of the body. Figuratively in the perceiver's soul if not physically in the performer's costume, antic-work offers a matrix within which penis or vulva or both are waiting to be, literally, *dis*-covered.

Derrida, inaugurating in 1967 the linguistic turn that has dominated criticism for the past 40 years, would prompt us to interpret the last scene of

Twelfth Night in terms of binaries. Male and female, old and young, prepubescent and sexually available: these, along perhaps with aristocrat and commoner, are the primary markers in the 1 | 0 sequence out of which the play's meanings are made. Concerning what happens to these binary possibilities, recent critical opinion has ranged from free play to imposition of the law of the father, from aporia to patriarchy. If we attend, however, to early modern notions of fancy, Orsino's last two words are not about binaries but about the many becoming one. Orsino's fancy has now ceased its flitting and found its governor in "queen." Fancy, so full of shapes that it alone is high fantastical, has at last come to rest on one particular shape. Or has it? In early modern psychology sensations, *phantasmata*, and passions all count as thoughts – even in Descartes (Alanen 2003, 54). Such thoughts get remembered. According to models of cognition inspired by Aristotle, it is not just acts of naming that are lodged in memory but the sensations of fancy and the assessments of estimation that preceded those acts of naming. Nor will fancy ever cease its surging. With respect to other people, as with respect to all objects of sense experience, fancy is always in play: it functions as an essential factor in *every* act of perception, not just whimsy and dreaming. Early modern understandings of perception may end, momentarily, with a clear and distinct image, indeed with the word that gives that image a name, but the sensations and workings of fancy that lead to the moment of clarity and distinctness have a form and quality of their own.

Shakespeare and his contemporaries had a name for that form and quality: "strange." "Strong fantasy tricking up strange delights" is what Malevole in *The Malcontent* imagines happening amid antic bedposts and villainous curtains (3.2.40). "Nature wants stuff / To vie strange forms with fancy," says Cleopatra (*Ant* 5.2.96–97). The bones and eyes of Ferdinand's father "doth suffer a sea-change / Into something rich and strange," sings Ariel (*Tem* 1.2.404–5). The lovers' story "grows to something of great constancy; / But howsoever, strange and admirable," insists Hippolyta (*MND* 5.1.26–27). "I will be strange, stout, in yellow stockings," declares Malvolio (*TN* 2.5.148–49), not catching the irony that acting like a stranger to his fellows will make him look all the stranger to them. "You throw a strange regard upon me," Sebastian says to Olivia when she realizes she has betrothed herself, not to Cesario, but to a perfect stranger (*TN* 5.1.204). Merging into one another in these speeches are multiple meanings of the word "strange": outlandish (*OED* "strange" *a.* I.1.a–b), unknown or unfamiliar (I.1.7), singular or unexampled (I.1.8), perhaps even shades of the "strange woman" or prostitute of the biblical book of Proverbs (I.1.4). The connection between "strange" and "fancy" has most to do, however, with the strange *affect* of fancy: "unfamiliar, abnormal, or exceptional to a degree that excites wonder or astonishment; difficult to take in or account for; queer, surprising, or unaccountable" (I.1.10.a). Hence Hippolyta's conjoining of "strange" with "admirable."

What is unaccountable about sexuality in *Twelfth Night*? What is it about sexuality that cannot be turned into numbers or a story? Queer theory, informed by deconstruction, is concerned with what comes *after* words, with the arbitrariness of language, the failure of words to match the realities they purport to name, even as the speakers of a given language use those words to construct personal identities and outlaw certain forms of sexual behavior. In this account, "nature" in *Twelfth Night* becomes a norm for separating hetero-normativity from homo-deviancy. In early modern psychology, by contrast, the unaccountable is concerned with what comes *before* words, with what Reynolds calls "those springings and glances of the heart, grounded on the sudden representation of sundry different objects" (D3v). In this account, fancy's sinuosities outrun nature's bias. Thanks to Philip Stubbes's obsession with "sodomy" (Ashley 1988, 170) and our own obsession with "discourse," we know much more about the after-words of early modern sexuality than the before-words. Full historical knowledge demands both.

Works cited

Alanen, Lilli. *Descartes's Concept of Mind.* Cambridge, MA: Harvard University Press, 2003.

Arthur, Liz. *Embroidery 1600–1700 at the Burrell Collection*. London: John Murray, 1995.

Ashley, Leonard R. N. *Elizabethan Popular Culture*. Bowling Green, OH: Bowling Green State University Press, 1988.

Bardnard, E. A. B., and Alan J. B. Wace. "The Sheldon Tapestry Weavers and their Work." *Archaeologia* 78 (1928): 255–314.

Clabburn, Pamela. *The National Trust Book of Furnishing Textiles*. London: The National Trust, 1988.

Connor, Steven. "Michel Serres' Five Senses." In *Empire of the Senses: The Sensual Culture Reader*. Ed. David Howes. Oxford: Berg, 2005.

Derrida, Jacques. *De la grammatologie* (1967). Trans. Gayatri Spivak as *Of Grammatology* (1977). Corrected edn. Baltimore, MD: Johns Hopkins University Press, 1998.

Descartes, René. *Selected Philosophical Writings*. Ed. John Cottingham. Cambridge: Cambridge University Press, 1988.

Dollimore, Jonathan. *Sexual Dissidence: Augustine to Wilde, Freud to Foucault*. Oxford: Clarendon Press, 1991.

Donne, John. *Poems by J. D.* London: M. F. for John Marriot, 1633.

Foakes, R. A., ed. *Henslowe's Diary*. 2nd edn. Cambridge: Cambridge University Press, 2002.

Hobbes, Thomas. *Humane Nature: Or, The Fundamental Elements of Policie.* London: T. Newcomb for Francis Bowman, 1650.

Humphreys, John. *Elizabethan Sheldon Tapestries.* Oxford: Oxford University Press, 1928.

Laqueur, Thomas. *Making Sex: Body and Gender from the Greeks to Freud.* Cambridge, MA: Harvard University Press, 1990.

Leavey, Santina M., and Peter K. Thornton. *Of Household Stuff: The 1601 Inventories of Bess of Hardwick*. London: The National Trust, 2001.

Marston, John. *The Malcontent*. Ed. M. L. Wine. Lincoln: University of Nebraska Press, 1964.

Ovid. *Metamorphosis* [*sic*]. Trans. George Sandys. Ed. Karl K. Hulley and Stanley T. Vandersall. Lincoln: University of Nebraska Press, 1970.

Oxford English Dictionary. Electronic edn. Oxford: Oxford University Press, 1989.

Park, Katharine. "The Organic Soul." In *The Cambridge History of Renaissance Philosophy*. Gen. Ed. Charles B. Schmitt. Cambridge: Cambridge University Press, 1988.

Phillips, Edward. *The New World of English Words, or, A general dictionary containing the interpretations of such hard words as are derived from other languages.* London: E. Tyler, 1658.

Remington, Preston. *English Domestic Needlework of the XVI, XVII, and XVIII Centuries*. New York: Metropolitan Museum of Art, 1945.

Reynolds, Edward. *A Treatise of the Passions and Faculties of the Soule of Man*. London: R. H. for Robert Bostock, 1640.

Roberts, Sasha. "Lying among the Classics: Ritual and Motif in Elite Elizabethan and Jacobean Beds." In *Albion's Classicism: The Visual Arts in Britain, 1550–1660*. Ed. Lucy Gent. New Haven, CT: Yale University Press, 1995.

——. "'Let Me the Curtains Draw': The Dramatic and Symbolic Properties of the Bed in Shakespearean Tragedy." In *Staged Properties in Early Modern English Drama*. Ed. Jonathan Gil Harris and Natasha Korda. Cambridge: Cambridge University Press, 2002.

Rothstein, Natalie, and Santina M. Levey. "Furnishings c. 1500–1780." In *The Cambridge History of Western Textiles*. Ed. David Jenkins. 2 vols. Cambridge: Cambridge University Press, 2003.

Shakespeare, William. *The Norton Shakespeare*. Ed. Stephen Greenblatt et al. New York: Norton, 1997.

——. *Twelfth Night*. Ed. J. M. Lothian and T. W. Craik. The Arden Shakespeare, series 2. London: Methuen, 1975.

——. *Twelfth Night*. Ed. Keir Elam. The Arden Shakespeare, series 3. London: Cengage Learning, 2008.

——. *Twelfth Night: Texts and Contexts*. Ed. Bruce R. Smith. Boston: Bedford/St. Martin's, 2001.

Smith, Bruce R. "Hearing Green." In *Reading the Early Modern Passions*. Ed. Gail Paster and Kathryn Rowe. Philadelphia: University of Pennsylvania Press, 2003.

Spenser, Edmund. *The Faerie Queene*. Ed. Thomas P. Roche, Jr. London: Penguin, 1978.

Thurley, Simon. *The Royal Palaces of Tudor England: Architecture and Court Life 1460–1647*. New Haven, CT: Yale University Press, 1993.

Wallace, William A. "Traditional Natural Philosophy." In *The Cambridge History of Renaissance Philosophy*. Gen. Ed. Charles B. Schmitt. Cambridge: Cambridge University Press, 1988.

Wells-Cole, Anthony. *Art and Decoration in Elizabethan and Jacobean England*. New Haven, CT: Yale University Press, 1997.

Wright, Thomas. *The Passions of the Mind in Generall*. London: Valentine Simmes for Walter Burre, 1604.

4 Music, food, and love in the affective landscapes of *Twelfth Night*

David Schalkwyk

The famous opening line of *Twelfth Night* encapsulates its play's ruling concepts and their interaction: "If music be the food of love, play on . . ." The conditional mode of Orsino's utterance is less a claim than a question about the relationships among its governing concepts: "music," "food," and "love." That question is shaped along the contours of the affective landscape of the play: its representation or expression of what we would today call emotion. "Emotion" is patently anachronistic in the early modern context. The *OED* indicates 1660 as its first – figurative – use: a "vehement or excited mental state." 1808 introduces the sense of "a mental feeling or affection" and 1822 a "(physical) moving, stirring, agitation." Early modern writers combine these disparate senses (both cognitively and historically) under the concept of *passion*, which is regarded as an "agitation of the soul." Passions are thus something suffered by the soul rather than moved outward – "emoted" – from within. Scholarship on early modern ideas of the passions reminds us that the "soul" itself combines what post-Cartesian thought splits into the mental and physical aspects of excitation or agitation in the 1808 and 1822 usages recorded by the *OED* (Babb 1941; Paster 2004a; Paster 2004b; Schoenfeldt 1999).

Orsino may thus be referring to music as a kind of food in a more than merely figurative sense: according to theories of the passions derived from Galen, music acts physically upon the senses, which in turn affect bodily organs via the imagination to produce an agitation in the organs. Such agitation occurs through the distribution of one of the four humors that were thought, by infusing the body, to produce affective states and, more generally, determine an individual (or even a nation's) temperament.[1] David Lindley draws attention to the contradiction between different conceptions of the working of music upon the human spirit: the one, neo-Platonic, derived from the work of Marsilio Ficino, holds that music forms a passage which may unite human spirits and that of the cosmic *spiritus mundi*; the other, more mundanely Galenic, warns against the capacity of music to move the soul to baser passions and deeds, effeminizing men and provoking idleness and lust.

Shakespeare, he suggests, follows Thomas Wright along the middle way, in terms of which the effect of music will finally depend not upon the intrinsic character of the music itself, but rather upon the nature of the listener (Lindley 2006, 33).

The tension between physiological explanation and philosophical analysis will become apparent in due course, as I pursue the differences between love as a kind of interior state and a form of action or behavior. Let us first unpack the possible relationships among harmonious sounds, appetite and desire in Orsino's speech:

> If music be the food of love,
> Give me excess of it that, surfeiting,
> The appetite may sicken and so die.
> That strain again, it had a dying fall.
> O, it came o'er my ear like the sweet sound
> That breathes upon a bank of violets,
> Stealing and giving odour. Enough, no more,
> 'Tis not so sweet now as it was before.
> O spirit of love, how quick and fresh art thou
> That, notwithstanding thy capacity
> Receiveth as the sea, naught enters there,
> Of what validity and pitch so e'er,
> But falls into abatement and low price
> Even in a minute! So full of shapes is fancy
> That it alone is high fantastical.
>
> (1.1.1–14)

The opening lines present love as an essentially interior state which nevertheless maintains a peculiar economy of consumption and waste in its relation to the external world. Rather than merely languishing self-indulgently in an excess of emotion, Illyria's duke is seeking some way to assuage his famished passion. He desires a surfeit of music precisely in order to *overcome* his desire. Suffering from erotic bulimia, Orsino wants to ingest too much of this "food of love" so that, "sickened," he will purge himself of love and consequently of the burning void that Petrarch characterized as erotic desire: "Give me excess of it that, surfeiting, / The appetite may sicken and so die." The speech, which begins with an airy call for harmonious strains ends in nausea and evacuation.

Orsino's plan seems to work – if only for a while. Given more love food, he first indulges in its melancholy plaint, calling for an interruption in its natural progression to savor the "dying fall" twice over, but then he turns away in disgust, now sated – but not satisfied. He continues to love; or perhaps, more accurately, he remains affected or sickened by desire. This returns us to the opening conditional, "if music . . ." Perhaps music is not the food of love after all. Or if it is, it does not work like normal food, and love's appetite does not follow the normal ebb and flow of hunger and satiety. The duke acknowledges this different logic in his apostrophe to the "spirit of love," now markedly different from the material nature of food, appetite, and vomiting. Turning away from love's supposed food in disgust, he now claims that its appetite is in fact incapable of nausea. Its oceanic capacity not only encompasses everything without "cloyment," but it is also able to *negate* everything that feeds it. Orsino's vision of love's capacity to devalue contradicts its notorious tendency to impose or project value onto the meanest objects.[2] But perhaps these two aspects of love work together: love's capacity to fill itself with images and shapes is in fact the epitome of a more general, imaginative projection: "it alone is high fantastical." It is either the epitome of the tendency of fantasy to obliterate reality or the highest object of fantasy, or both. Orsino celebrates the imaginative and imaginary aspects of love that were anxiously denigrated by the moralising psychologists of Shakespeare's time.

The nature of love and its relation to desire have exercised philosophers from Plato onwards. Early modern and classical writers offer no united front on the issue, but rather a series of confusions, differences, and evasions. There is little absolute agreement in Renaissance philosophy and its Classical influences, although certain trends are clearly distinguishable. Nicholas Coeffeteau is one of the few writers who *distinguishes* between love and desire, two concepts that since Plato had become virtually inseparable. In Plato's *Symposium*, for example, Socrates defines love by its intrinsic relation to desire and lack or want:

> everyone who desires, desires that which he has not already, and which is future and not present, and which he has not, and is not, and of which he is in want; – these are the sort of things which love and desire seek.
>
> (Coeffeteau 1621, 41)

Coeffeteau, in contrast, insists on a conceptual difference between the love and lack. He bases this on a distinction in our relation to something we possess, on the one hand, and want to have, on the other:

> *Desire* differs from *Loue*, and *Pleasure*, for that *Loue* is the first motion, and the first *Passion* we haue of any good thing, without respect whether it be present or absent; *Desire* is a *Passion* for a good that is absent, and pleasure a contentment we have when wee haue gotten it.
>
> (Coeffeteau 1621, 219)

Leone Ebreo's female interlocutor in *Dialogi d'Amore* is likewise sceptical about the Platonic reduction of love to desire:

> I am satisfied with your account of love and appetite in relation to pleasure. But I feel some doubt concerning your statement: that we love and

> desire those pleasurable things we lack, but cease to do so when we are in possession of them. For this is true about desire only, and not about love: which is born with possession of these things, not of their lack.
>
> (Ebreo 1937, 17)

Sophia's doubt may be related to Coefetteau's similarly non-Platonic definition of love, which is based not upon desire (absence or lack) but rather on goodwill towards someone who is present: "*Loue* then is no other thing, but, *To will good to some one, not for our owne priuate interest, but for the loue of himselfe; procuring with all our power what we think may bee profitable for him, or may giue him content*" (1621, 103–4). Once they have moved past their obligatory introductions to Galenic theory, Edward Reynolds and Thomas Wright also conceive of love as a disinterested affection in the ideal, even if they simultaneously excoriate its concupiscent form as an unstable and dangerous form of obsession. The double-sided aspects of love thus echo those of music, each being potentially good or bad, capable of achieving spiritual and social harmony or instability and destruction.[3]

In their suggestive "dying fall," and Orsino's sudden withdrawal with the injunction, "enough, no more," *Twelfth Night*'s opening lines appear to endorse the Platonic identification of love with desire. The duke's moody vacillations embody desire's cyclical process of longing and satiety, especially in his rhythmical allusion to the dynamics of sexual orgasm in the procession of "surfeit, cloyment, and revolt" that marks the mixture of dissatisfaction and satiety of post-coital depression. The tendency of desire to embroil itself in an eternal return of craving and aversion is the topic of much Renaissance philosophical debate. (It is also the topic of Shakespeare's sonnet 129.) Leone Ebreo's *Dialogi d'Amore* comments on this paradox of desire in the voice of one of its interlocutors: "when we have partaken of it so far as to be sated then no lack remains, and at the same time all desire and love of such pleasure is exhausted, to be succeeded by dislike and disgust. So that desire and love are bound up with the lack of pleasure, not with its enjoyment" (1621, 18). Tullia D'Aragona's *The Infinity of Love* echoes Ebreo's expression in almost identical words: "Those who are moved by this desire and who love in this guise, as soon as they have reached their goal and satisfied their longing, will desist from their motion and will no longer love . . . As a matter of fact . . . they turn their love into hate" (1997, 90). This paradox is central to the Platonic conception of love-as-desire which, precisely because it makes love and desire identical, creates a self-sustaining dynamic that ensures that no mere mundane or carnal satisfaction will assuage desire. The paradox can be resolved only through a dialectical form of idealism: dissatisfaction with the object of *carnal* longing leads to an ever-ascending search for an *ideal* form of beauty in which goodness, virtue, and perfection are ultimately conjoined. A Galenic, materialist focus on the affinity between love and bodily appetite, on the other hand, must rest with the sorry truth that the idealizing rhetoric of Eros is no more than a form of unstable and insatiable concupiscence. Orsino is caught between these two positions. His unsatisfied nausea at being crammed with the food of love threatens the idealizing indulgence of his "high fantastical" desire for the unattainable Olivia.

In staging desire, Shakespeare also provokes it (or at least the "pangs" of it) in his audience. He uses stage music not only as the sign of desire in the fictional world on the stage, but also to provoke and sustain desire within those listening in the real world of the auditorium. The music that Orsino commands, and subjects to critical commentary, works simultaneously, but to different effect, upon the emotions of his broader attendants. It is therefore much more than the mere sign or food of love within the fictional world of the play, limited by or to the affective state of the play's protagonist. For at the point at which the duke stops the music, cloyed by its melancholy sweetness, the audience has its developing emotional engagement with the harmonious strains abruptly curtailed, in a crisis akin to *coitus interruptus*. At the point at which Orsino's erotic history renders the music's sweetness unbearable, its interruption should leave the audience in a state of heightened desire and frustration, and thus affectively receptive to the plangency of the play's emotional landscape.[4]

Following the nature of music as a structured kind of repetition and variation in time, Shakespeare returns to the interlacing of music, food, and love in act 2, the fourth scene of which is a recapitulation of the opening scene. Its opening line, "Give me some music," reflects at once the previous night's musical performance and the recital which opens the play:

> Now good Cesario, but that piece of song,
> That old and antic song we heard last night.
> Methought it did relieve my passion much,
> More than light airs and recollected terms
> Of these most brisk and giddy-pacèd times.
> (2.4.1–6)

Orsino's call for a repeat performance of the "antic" song of the previous night confirms the idea that, whereas music may have the capacity to "relieve passion," its efficacy does not last. Supposed to assuage desire, it merely "provokes and unprovokes," in a bulimic cycle of alternating appetite and revulsion and evacuation. This cycle, taken together with Orsino's rejection of the "light airs and recollected terms / Of these most brisk and giddy-pacèd times," puts the audience in mind of the *other* songs that were played the previous evening: in the "caterwauling" of Toby, Auguecheek, Maria, and the Fool in Olivia's kitchen. Feste's lateness for the present command performance stitches this scene to its precedent, suggesting that events that the theatre is committed to representing serially occur simultaneously in dramatic time as a kind of fugue. Two different kinds of music, two different forms of investment in desire, two different kinds of appetitive indulgence must be imagined to have been played in counterpoint before and "after midnight" leading up to Orsino's "Good morrow, friends."

Orsino's demand for music at the opening of the play is framed by the reiterated performance in act 2 scene 4 which has a proper beginning and end, designed by the duke as both incontrovertible sign of his passion and the means to ease it. But Viola/Cesario's presence, not merely as dutiful servant but also as an appreciative and responsive audience, transfers the repetition of the duke's music into a different affective key. The song, with its plaintive refrain of death as a result of the unrequited love, looks back to the "dying fall" of the opening scene and forward to the climactic moment when Viola, suddenly freed from the burden of being Cesario, can pledge herself wholly to the man she has desired so ardently, in a further echo of the incomplete dialectic between "death" (as orgasm) and "rest" (as satisfaction): "And I, to do you rest, a thousand deaths will die!" (5.1.131). Anticipating the duke's interrogation of Viola's lovesick alter ego – "But died thy sister of her love, my boy?" – the song suggests that love may not be an inner state but rather a mode of action. For Orsino love that does not *enact* the deathly narrative of the antic song cannot be love indeed. But at this point the play drives a wedge between its protagonist as the embodiment of a conception of love as an essentially internal, self-conscious passion and love as a silent form of *active* suffering. This difference is signaled by the use of music as a sign of the duke's emotional state and its significance for a discretely divided set of listeners. Orsino regards himself the true exemplum of the love celebrated (or lamented) in the song:

> If ever thou shalt love,
> In the sweet pangs of it remember me;
> For such as I am, all true lovers are,
> Unstaid and skittish in all motions else
> Save in the constant image of the creature
> That is beloved.[5] How dost thou like this tune?
> (2.4.16–18)

But in contrast to his self-centred indulgence in the music of the opening scene, Orsino's question opens the possibility of genuinely interactive dialogue with a servant/lover whose subjectivity is for once not merely obliterated by his own narcissism, and where the place of music and its relation to player, audience and affective response is potentially contested rather than wholly controlled by the patriarch. However much the duke would like to occupy center stage as the true embodiment of erotic passion, his rhetorical efforts are countered by the satirical intervention of the fool who takes "pleasure" in his "pains," and by the figure of Viola as Cesario, who is pained by the very pleasure that she gains from her intimacy with her beloved "master."

Though he doesn't know it, Orsino is rivalled in love by the very youth who surprises him with her tactful endorsement of his taste in music. The ironies of the scene are therefore delicious, but they are also heart-rending. It is an affective landscape (or perhaps, following Bruce R. Smith, an affective soundscape) in which, like the comedy as a whole, harmony is sweetened with discord.[6]

The question that the scene from *Twelfth Night* raises is, at the simplest level, who embodies love, Orsino or Cesario? And do we need to say *true* love? For without recourse to any of the standard poses of love or the common discourses of desire, Cesario clearly enacts Coeffeteau's first definition of love even as she silently embodies intensely suppressed desire. Orsino is an expert in the misogynist, early modern, Galenic or materialist conceptions of male and female passion. As such he is all bluster and contradiction:

> There is no woman's sides
> Can bide the beating of so strong a passion
> As love doth give my heart; no woman's heart
> So big, to hold so much. They lack retention.
> Alas, their love may be called appetite,
> No motion of the liver, but the palate,
> That suffer surfeit, cloyment, and revolt.[7]
> But mine is all as hungry as the sea,
> And can digest as much. Make no compare
> Between that love a woman can bear me
> And that I owe Olivia.
>
> (2.4.92–102)

Despite having just declared, in his helpfully avuncular way, that Cesario should take a younger lover than himself, because "however we may praise ourselves, / Our fancies are more giddy and unfirm, / More longing, wavering, sooner lost and worn than women's are" (31–34), he now asserts the incapacity of women to love with anything other than mere desire or appetite. In doing so, he enacts the very instability that he despises in women. Orsino is staking his claim to the inherent superiority of his love on the physiological theory that holds that because men have naturally hot and dry complexions (in the bodily sense of the term) as opposed to the cold and moist dispositions of women, they have a greater capacity to withstand the dilations of the heart that accompany love. The crucial term here is "retention": the capacity to hold the fluid (blood) that is not merely the sign but also the very physical condition of love, seated in the liver. This relegation of women's love to the palate aligns it with the lowest appetite: the desire for food and sex that human beings share with beasts. Orsino thus invokes a physiological explanation, derived from Galen, for a *philosophical* problem that puzzled classical and Renaissance theorists of love alike, and which constitutes the opening paradox of the play: the perverse fluctuations of a purely appetitive desire, which "falls into abatement and low price / Even in a minute" (1.1.12–13).

Neither Ebreo nor D'Aragona imputes exclusively to either gender the propensity for appetitive, non-retentive desire, nor do they seek any kind of physiological explanation for it. Their discourse is philosophical or logical: they trace the Platonic contours of desire, offering their own detours or innovative paths, without subscribing to its physiological, Galenic reductions. Orsino's expertise in and his profession of the humoral psychology of the English Renaissance writers allows him to posit his own capacity for love as God-like, and to proscribe the very possibility of comparison between men and women on the basis of their incommensurable physiological capacity to love.[8] But his self-regarding impatience provokes Viola, smarting under the perceived constancy of her own devotion, into a contrary declaration, derived from her own concealed experience:

Viola. Ay, but I know –
Orsino. What dost thou know?
Viola. Too well what love women to men may owe.
In faith, they are as true of heart as we.
(103–6)

Viola-as-Cesario is trapped within her staged body: desperate to reveal or display herself as an exemplum of the truth that women are indeed as capable of enduring love as men are, she lacks the authority to stake the claim either as an actively desiring woman or as an immature, inexperienced, and therefore unreliable, young man. Viola's alter ego – her fictitious sister who "sat like patience on a monument, smiling at grief" – is a combination of love as embodied behavior with a commonly represented humoral affliction. Her "concealment feed[s] on her damask cheek," and she succumbs to the anorexic "green sickness" – "green and yellow melancholy" – peculiar to unhappy virgins (Paster 2004a, chapter 2). But for the aristocratic professor of humoral psychology, patience as an enduring behavioral sign is not sufficient: the suffering woman would need to be interred *within* the monument to constitute a memorial to the capacity of female love. But Viola herself embodies neither the stereotype of the voraciously unstable "appetite" of Orsino's conception of woman, nor the self-sacrificial melancholy of her alter ego. When she proclaims to her master, in an attempt to shore up the fiction of male solidarity that in fact excludes her as woman, that "We men may say more, swear more, but indeed / Our shows are more than will; for still we prove / Much in our vows, but little in our love" (114–16), she is both tracing the contradiction between Orsino's words and his behavior and claiming that love is less an internal condition (psychological or physiological) than a form of action: something that stands the test of time and behavior. This idea brings erotic love into the conceptual ambit of male friendship, from which it is pointedly excluded by Montaigne in his essay "On Friendship." Viola/Cesario's repetition of "indeed" at the end of consecutive lines (the previous line is: "Was this not love indeed?") invites us to move from what may lie hidden *within* the body to what that body *does*: in *deed*. Orsino has embodied the very variability of mood and appetite for which he has denigrated women. If music is the food of love, then he has exemplified through his behavior the disturbing variability of the "surfeited" and "sickened" palate that he denigrates in women. His patronizing desire to give his young courtier some worldly wise advice about the practicalities of choosing a mate – "Then let they love be younger than thyself, / Or thy affection cannot hold the bent" (2.4.35–36) – is overridden moments later by an indulgent self-importance that blinds him to the sacrifice that his servant-lover is making on his behalf.[9] This tendency to think of himself as the incarnation of a humoral psychology that combines a materialist reduction of passion to the workings of digestion and evacuation with an inherited misogyny aligns Orsino with the distinctly humoral characters of Toby Belch, Malvolio, and Aguecheek, rather than Viola and Antonio. As both the exemplum of and spokesman for humoral theory, Illyria's duke is the sign of the excessive, the anachronistic, at a remove from reality.

It is a commonplace to observe that Orsino's love is a no more than a fantasy. The recent revival of humoral theory as an active ingredient in Shakespeare's work helps us to give a greater degree of precision to the endlessly repeated undergraduate cliché that Orsino is not in love, but rather in love with love itself. He is in love with himself as the paradigmatic embodiment of materialist, Galenic psychology. Orsino as spokesman for Galenic doctrine does not speak *ex cathedra*, but merely as a single, contested voice in a play inhabited by a plethora of Bakhtinian accents. He marks himself both by his self-conscious Galenic discourse and his ironic embodiment of such theory as an artificial, perhaps even anachronistic, embodiment of a concept of love that finds very different, competing forms of expression in other characters, not least in his faithful servant and lover.

Insofar as love as passion is at stake in *Twelfth Night*, we might thus say that it is displayed through dedicated behavior and action rather than the causal interiority of bodily heat or humor. Viola as Cesario calls into question the very basis for distinguishing between men and women on the basis of an intrinsic difference in humoral fluids and temperatures. She unmasks the ridiculous misogyny that denies women the "retention" required for constant affection. The same may be said of her counterpart, Antonio, whose devotion to her brother, Sebastian, is conveyed through self-sacrificial action rather than the anatomizing interiority of humoral description. Antonio describes the intensity of his devotion to Sebastian in language that needs little explanation in the terms of humoral psychology: "I do adore thee so / That danger will seem sport, and I will go" (2.1.41–42):

I could not stay behind you. My desire,
More sharp than filèd steel, did spur me forth,
And not all love to see you – though so much
As might have drawn one to a longer voyage –
But jealousy what might befall your travel,
Being skilless in these parts, which to a stranger,
Unguided and unfriended, often prove
Rough and unhospitable. My willing love
The rather by these arguments of fear
Set forth in your pursuit.

(3.3.4–13)

The "spur" of Antonio's desire is illuminated by Bishop Coeffeteau's less materialist accounts of love as the devoted care for the well-being of another, which echoes moments in D'Aragona and Ebreo, where the Platonically inspired conjunction of love and desire are called into question. Antonio's equally intense anger and resentment when he is confronted by what appears to him to be the indifference and ingratitude embodied in the behavior of his friend is signally not informed by physiological theory:

His life I gave him, and did thereto add
My love without retention or restraint,
All his in dedication. For his sake
Did I expose myself, pure for his love,
Into the danger of this adverse town,
Drew to defend him when he was beset,
Where being apprehended, his false cunning –
Not meaning to partake with me in danger –
Taught him to face me out of his acquaintance,
And grew a twenty years' removèd thing
While one would wink, denied me mine own purse,
Which I had recommended to his use
Not half an hour before.

(5.1.76–88)

This, we may say, following Viola, is "love indeed." The answer to the question "Is love an emotion?" may thus be: "no, it is not." Nor, to be historically correct, is it a passion, at least not if emotions or passions are conceived as agitations that exist wholly or essentially *within* the body. One of the most striking aspects of the most well-known tracts of humoral psychology – by Wright, Reynolds, and Coeffeteau – is that their treatment of love as a passion deals very fleetingly, if at all, with Galenic explanations of the humoral nature of love. Each shares the ambivalence (or "polyvalence," to use D'Aragona's term) towards love that marks philosophical accounts from

Plato to the Italian Renaissance. But each of them recognizes love as a force that begins with God and infuses human life with its coherence and meaning. Coeffeteau opens with the claim that "*to banish* Loue *from a ciuille life, and the conuersation of men, were not only to depriue the* year *of her goodliest season, but also as it were to pull the Sunne out of the firmament, and to fill the whole world with horror and confusion*" (1621, 78). More striking still, Wright deals with love in a completely different rhetorical mode from the style adopted in the initial sections of his treatise. The section devoted to love is introduced by a direct appeal to and dedication of himself to God as the source and goal of all love:

> O My God, the soule, and the life of all true loue: these drie discourses of affections, without any cordiall affection, have long detained, & not a little distasted me. Now that I come towards the borders of Loue, give me leaue, O loving God, to vent out and euaporate the effects of the heart, and see if I can incense my soule to loue thee entirely . . . and that all those motiues which stirre up mine affections to loue thee, may be meanes to inflame all their hearts, which read this treatise penned by me.
>
> (Wright 1604, 193)

In Wright's impassioned appeal to the reciprocity of God's love with his own, love is not something that moves the body to want to ingest anything that may be regarded as its "food;" it is rather a "cordiall affection" – an "effect of the heart" that seeks to be "vented out and evaporated" in a divine madness that inflames not only the heart of the lover, but also "catches" the hearts of others in an infectious "contagion."

These two words, "catch" and "contagion," return us to the bass counterpoint of Orsino's musical indulgence in act 2 scene 4:

> *Feste*. (*sings*) O mistress mine, where are you roaming?
> O stay and hear, your true love's coming,
> That can sing both high and low.
> Trip no further, pretty sweeting.
> Journeys end in lovers meeting,
> Every wise man's son doth know.
> *Sir And.* Excellent good, i' faith.
> *Sir To.* Good, good.
> *Feste.* What is love? 'Tis not hereafter,
> Present mirth hath present laughter.
> What's to come is still unsure.
> In delay there lies no plenty,
> Then come kiss me, sweet and twenty.
> Youth's a stuff will not endure.
> *Sir And.* A mellifluous voice, as I am true knight.

Sir To. A contagious breath.
Sir And. Very sweet and contagious, i' faith.
Sir To. To hear by the nose, it is dulcet in contagion.
(2.3.38–55)

In this, the central comic scene of *Twelfth Night* – perhaps the central scene of the play as a whole – the relationship of time to desire, of music to food, of expenditure to holding back is extrapolated in theatrical ways that will reach their apotheosis only in the great quartets of Mozartian and Verdian opera. Keeping time, beating time, losing time: these fundamental demands, and pitfalls, of music-making are self-consciously inflected as the grounding challenges of human life and its desires. The song could be Orsino's; it could be Viola's; it could even be Olivia's, for it speaks to the condition of all of them. But it is sung in the lower chambers – in the bowels, or the fundament – of the aristocratic household, where food is prepared and its scraps discarded and washed away, and wine is surreptitiously, or in this Rabelaisian outburst, brazenly "snatched" and consumed. Is its music the food of love? Trevor Nunn's recent film draws Maria, Andrew, and Toby into an affective moment that is every bit as plangent as the harmonies rehearsed at the duke's court. In their being mutually touched by the "contagion" of Feste's "sweet breath" (and we must recall that he carries this contagion wherever he sings, in the kitchen or Orsino's court), the three figures are marked by their respective relation to time as it slips through their fingers. The music contaminates them all with its bitter-sweet sentiment, which threatens to tip over into sentimentality. That contagion also passes to the broader audience, who are moved by its bitter-sweet accompaniment to desire and loss. After a moment's silence, however, the broken or lost time that the perfectly kept time of Feste's beautiful song enacts proves too much for even the capacious Toby to ingest. Rather than face the unbearable pathos of music, he chooses the comfortable thoughtlessness of action, of *doing* something rather than listening, feeling, and contemplation:

Sir To. To hear by the nose, it is dulcet in contagion. But shall we make the welkin dance indeed? Shall we rouse the night-owl in a catch that will draw three souls out of one weaver? Shall we do that?
Sir And. An you love me, let's do 't. I am dog at a catch.
Feste. By 'r Lady, sir, and some dogs will catch well.
Sir And. Most certain. Let our catch be "Thou knave."
(2.3.55–62)

"Shall we dance indeed?" This is a fugal inversion of Viola's question: "Was not this love indeed?" Toby's excited invocation of the power of music to draw the soul out of its listener deflates the effects of regulated time and melody that the affective soundscape of *Twelfth Night* has playfully been proffering and withdrawing. Dancing "indeed," keeping time in their "catches," is a form of action through which the contagion threatened by the thought that "time's a thing will not endure" can be kept at bay. If song now erupts into a delightfully libidinous process of "giddy-paced" free association, evoking for the audience a series of well-known popular songs less to do with the plangent affects of love than the broken rhythms of carnival excess in the face of Malvolio's "puritan" injunctions, it returns us, when it finally peters out, to the question of food and consumption: "Dost thou think, because thou art virtuous, there shall be no more cakes and ale?" (2.3.96: see also Duffin 2004). "Cakes and ale" is, of course, a metonymy for a way of life that is as "high fantastical" as Orsino's capacious desire, given the social conditions that lie beyond the closed door of Twelfth Night festivity.

This action should be enjoyed for that excess, conveyed in the broken time of the trio's songs. But Toby's "dance indeed" is a form of action taken to evade the costs that are everywhere apparent in the rest of the play. Toby's insistence upon the vitality of "cakes and ale" obscures the hidden costs of this scene, especially in the way in which it cunningly reveals and conceals another relation to food and desire: Toby's remorseless feeding upon Andrew's desire is a perverse exemplum of what Aristotle calls "secondary friendship" in the *Nicomachean Ethics*. We need not adopt Malvolio's disapproval of "cakes and ale" to acknowledge (and mourn) the death that lurks in the play's "song of good life." Sir Andrew's declaration in the heat of carnival revelry – in which the apparent embodiments of "life" and "death" seem to confront each other directly for the first time over "cakes and ale" – "I care not for good life" (2.3.37), is one of *Twelfth Night's* most poignant moments. In the figure of the unconscious fool, Andrew draws our attention to the difference between the "good life" as his enemy-friend Sir Toby conceives it, and the ethical ideal with which Aristotle frames all human aspirations, including friendship. The choice to which Andrew responds – between a "song of love" and a "song of good life" – exemplifies the degree to which what is presented as the "good life" (cakes and ale) obscures its removal from what Aristotle celebrated as love or friendship. For Aristotle, "love" and "good life" are inseparable. And while we may nod indulgently with the Maria, Belch, and Aguecheek, first succumbing to the sentimentality of Feste's song and then refusing to endure the gravity of its thought by drowning it in "riot," the play refuses to let us forget that time is of the essence in friendship. Jacques Derrida makes much of Aristotle's point that while constancy or endurance without change is a defining characteristic of true friendship, that character can only imprint itself through time. Friendship is something that has to be tested; it has to stand the test of time (Derrida 1997, 15). The "time" that Toby and company "keep" in their "snatches" – in their "song of good life" – maintains a kind of friendship through the community of song, but it fails to establish the faith and confidence that Aristotle and Montaigne require of primary friendship. Its time of community ends with the last beat of the song.

This riff on the costs of friendship takes us from the focus on love as desire in the opening of the play to its distinctive embodiment (against the tradition of male friendship from Aristotle, through Cicero and Montaigne), of the possibility that *women* should be capable of a passion reserved entirely for men. It is striking that when Coeffeteau and Wright write of love (rather than passion in general) they focus almost entirely on love as *friendship*. Their discussions of this topic are devoid of the physiological theory of the passions that marks their treatment of other forms of affect or agitation. This is hardly surprising, given Montaigne's insistence that friendship or *philia* differs from *eros* precisely because it is uncontaminated by the vagaries of emotional perturbation.[10] Montaigne's denigration of *eros* in general echoes Orsino's disparagement of women's capacity for erotic devotion, except that Montaigne would doubt the duke's claim regarding the exclusive constancy of his own erotic passion:

> You cannot compare with friendship the passion men feel for women . . . nor can you put them in the same category. I must admit the flames of passion . . . are more active, sharp and keen. But that fire is a rash one, fickle, fluctuating and variable; it is a feverish fire, subject to attacks and lapses, which only gets hold of a corner of us. The love of friends is a general universal warmth, temperate, moreover, and smooth, a warmth which is constant and at rest, all gentleness and evenness, having nothing sharp nor keen . . . women are in truth not normally capable of responding to such familiarity and mutual confidence as sustain that holy bond of friendship, nor do their souls seem firm enough to withstand the clasp of a knot so lasting and so tightly drawn.
>
> (Montaigne 1991, 209–10)

The theatrical possibilities of Shakespeare's stage allow him to contradict Orsino and Montaigne alike by embodying the kind of friendship that Montaigne reserves for males in the body of a woman disguised as a man, and exemplifying constant erotic devotion in the *same* figure. Viola/Cesario transcends the reductive bias of both humoral physiology and the misogynist tradition of Aristotelian philosophy by representing loving friendship as a kind of behavior rather than an immutable physiological condition: s/he exemplifies the constancy of erotic affection and the selflessness of loving friendship in the figure of a *woman*. Viola makes actual the fantastic possibility of which Montaigne merely dreams – that *if* women were capable of friendship, then friendship between a man and a woman would surpass that between men:

> if it were possible to fashion such a relationship, willing and free, in which not only the souls had this full enjoyment but in which bodies too

> shared in the union – where the whole human being was involved – it is certain that the loving-friendship would be more full and more abundant.
> (Montaigne 1991, 210)

She does so only because as a theatrical figure at a particular historical moment she can embody both man and woman, forging the friendship extolled by Montaigne as man while enacting for the audience the kind of erotic devotion that Orsino misrecognizes when he attributes it exclusively to himself.

The affective landscapes of *Twelfth Night*, which I have been able to sketch only cursorily in this paper, show that if early modern humoral psychology of affect is relevant to the play, it is so negatively: as a form of misrecognition. Love is embodied in a different way – not as something that happens physiologically within the body, but rather as a form of behavior – "willing and free" – represented as the *criterion* of loving affection. We tell by what someone does whether they love someone or not, not by their expertise in applying early modern psychological theory to themselves or others. This use of kinds of action as criteria for love is not itself reductive: I am not saying that love is no more than behavior, that there is no inner state or agitation that we would call passion.[11] I am not reiterating the twentieth-century materialist denial that the early moderns had any notion of interiority or concept of privacy. Love may well be an emotion in the sense of a passion. But that is not all there is to it. We tell love by the modes of behavior that we have made into the "outward and visible" criteria of the condition.

This reading of the affective landscape of *Twelfth Night* suggests that love is not an emotion, in the ordinary sense of the word. Tested by the necessity of time, it is rather a motion of the body, the behavior of which each cultural moment selects as forms of criteria that confirm or deny the affect that is supposed to be occurring in the recesses of the heart or liver. Such criteria do not transcend history. Different forms of behavior may be instantiated as criteria differently at different times. The criteria for erotic devotion or friendship – arising from the body as expressive of both cultural relations and inner feelings – at this time or place may be quite different from those that count as such in that time or place. It is clear from Orsino's behavior, rather than what he tells us of the motions of his heart and liver, that he does not love Olivia. It is less clear, but soon fairly evident, from the way he behaves when Cesario is with him, that this is the person he loves. And it is palpable from their largely self-sacrificial devotion – by what they *do* – that Viola and Antonio embody "love indeed."

But whereas *Twelfth Night* does cast doubt upon the notion that love is primarily a "motion of the liver," it does not reduce it to mere action or kinds of behavior. Music is crucial to the play's representation of love because it does its work *within*, through the passions. If love is judged by a set of culturally determined behavioral forms of action, it remains a matter of the heart. The landscape of affect traced by what characters *do* is thus only one aspect of the contrapuntal soundscape of *Twelfth Night*. If his theatrical medium pushes Shakespeare in the direction of action, its capacity to reproduce music, both as a form of expression between characters on stage and a mode of engaging the affect of the audience, offers a complementary and sometimes dissonant countermelody to the focus on Eros and Philia as forms of behavior. Action may at times be a way of avoiding the confrontation with affect that music demands (in the "caterwauling" of Andrew Aguecheek and Maria, for example). Music both stands for and, in its operation on the senses, feeds and manipulates the affective souls of audience and character alike. It joins them in an awareness of a landscape felt within the body that is *inter*subjective, and it either underscores or negates the action by which love is tested with its "contagious sweet breath."

Notes

1. The four humors are black bile, phlegm, blood, and choler. Paster reminds us that for early moderns, humoral theory based on the Greek physician, Galen, psychology and physiology are one: the bodily humors and the emotion that they sustain and move the body to express an action can be lexically distinguished but not functionally separated. For the early moderns, emotions flood the body not metaphorically but literally (Paster 2004a, 14; also Babb 1941, 1020 and 1026). See also David Lindley's discussion of early modern theories of music (2006, chapter 1).
2. See *A Midsummer Night's Dream*: "Love looks not with the eyes, but with the mind, / And therefore is winged Cupid painted blind. / Nor hath love's mind of any judgement taste; / Wings and no eyes figure unheedy haste" (234–37).
3. See Reynolds (1640, 91 and 96): "there is not onely a *Love* of *Delight* in the *fruition*, but *Love* likewise of *Desire*, in the *privation* of a Good; which the more it wanteth, the more it fixeth itself upon it;" also Wright (1604, 213): "Hee that loveth virtuously, esteemeth the beloved worthy of honour, because he reputeth him vertuous, and therefore in affection yieldeth him condigne honour due to Vertue: he serveth him in regard of his great goodnesse, which in his conceit meroteth all servitude and obsequious compliments. Who would not love a virtuous Lover, who consecrateth himselfe, and all hee hath unto the person beloved?" and "O . . . how potent is this bait of pleasure . . . It is beastly . . . in appearance it promiseth rest and quietnesse, but in effect dispoileth the soule of all rest and quietnesse . . . men affected with pleasure are changed and metamorphosed from themselves, vntroubled with such an inordinat passion. It is exceeding dangerous" (201).
4. Lindley suggests that the music that the audience hears and that Orsino commands is in fact the performance that opens the play, and that it "establishes a mood of pleasurable melancholy for the audience; more specifically, the opening exploits the conventional associations of music with love and appetite which are to be central to the play's action" (2006, 204). My argument gives more specificity to Lindley's reference to the conventional relationship between music, love, and appetite by suggesting that the effect of the music in the real time of the play on appetite may work differently for the audience and for the fictional characters, especially Orsino. Music in "real time" and "fictional time" achieves different effects (and affects).

5. Cf. Coeffeteau: "the soules of such as loue, are perpetually attentiue to contemplate the image of that they loue, and haue no other thought nor greater pleasure . . . but this poore soule thus agitated, hath no certaine consistence . . . she goes, she comes, without any stay or rest . . ." (1621, 166 and 172).
6. I am indebted to Bruce R. Smith for his work on the importance of the soundscape of *Twelfth Night* and Shakespeare's time in general in *Twelfth Night* and *Acoustic World.*
7. Cf. Coeffeteau: "the like may be sayd of *Loue*, and that the aboundance of bloud doth not make men more inclined to the *Passions* of *loue*, for that the *Concupiscible* power resides in the liver, which is the place where the blood takes his forme; but for they that are of a sanguine complexion, haue a hot and moist temperature, which is proper to that *passion*" (1621, 25–26).
8. For the notion that God's love is as boundless as the sea, see Wright (1604, 193).
9. Orsino's constant references to his love in terms of the sea recalls Coeffeteau's description of the person who, under the sway of uncontrollable passion, "plungeth himselfe in superfluities as into a gulph, whereas hee findes neither bottom nor banke, and afflicts himselfe with a thousand torments in the pursuite of his vaine desires" (1621, 221–22).
10. The sense that friendship or Philia is free from the intense heat and vacillation of erotic passion contradicts Wright and Coeffeteau's almost exclusive treatment of such friendship under the rubric of love as a *passion*. Recall Coeffeteau's definition: "So wee properly call passions of the soule, those infirmities wherewith she is inflicted and troubled; as pittie, feare, bashfulnesse, or shame, love, hatred, desires, Choler, and the rest" (1621, 18–19).
11. See Wittgenstein (1953, paras. 181ff.). See also Cavell (1979, 1–128) for a discussion of what Wittgenstein means by criteria. For a discussion of the role that fiction plays in revealing criterial relations, see Schalkwyk (2004).

Works cited

Aristotle. *Nichomachean Ethics*. In *The Basic Works of Aristotle*. Ed. and trans. Richard McKeon. New York: Random House, 1941: 935–1126.

Babb, Lawrence. "The Physiological Conception of Love in the Elizabethan and Early Stuart Drama." *PMLA* 56 (1941): 1020–35.

Cavell, Stanley. *The Claim of Reason*. Oxford: Oxford University Press, 1979.

Coeffeteau, N. *A Table of the Passions. With Their Causes and Effects*. Trans. Edward Grimerton. London, 1621.

D'Aragona, Tullia. *Dialogue on the Infinity of Love*. 1547. Ed. and trans. Rinalda Russell and Bruce Merry. Chicago and London: University of Chicago Press, 1997.

Derrida, Jacques. *Politics of Friendship*. Trans. George Collins. London and New York: Verso, 1997.

Duffin, Ross W. *Shakespeare's Songbook*. London and New York: W. W. Norton, 2004.

Ebreo, Leone. *The Philosophy of Love*. 1535. Trans. F. Friedeberg-Seeley and Jean H. Barnes. London: Soncino Press, 1937.

Lindley, David. *Shakespeare and Music*. London: Arden, 2006.

Montaigne, Michel de. "On Affectionate Relationships." In *The Complete Essays*. Trans. M. A. Screech. Harmondsworth: Penguin, 1991: 205–19.

Paster, Gail Kern. *Humoring the Body: Emotions and the Shakespearean Stage*. Cambridge: Cambridge University Press, 2004a.

Paster, Gail Kern, Katherine Rowe, and Mary Floyd-Wilson. *Reading the Early Modern Passions: Essays in the Cultural History of Emotion*. Philadelphia: University of Pennsylvania Press, 2004b.

Plato. *Symposium*. Trans. Benjamin Jowett. Tedington, Middlesex: Echo Books, 2006.

Reynolds, Edward. *A Treatise of the Passions and Faculties of the Soule of Man*. London, 1640.

Schalkwyk, David. *Literature and the Touch of the Real*. Newark: University of Delaware Press, 2004.

Schoenfeldt, Michael. *Bodies and Selves in Early Modern England: Physiology and Inwardness in Spenser, Shakespeare, Herbert and Milton*. Cambridge: Cambridge University Press, 1999.

Shakespeare, William. *Twelfth Night*. Ed. Bruce R. Smith. Bedford Shakespeare series. Boston and New York: Bedford/St. Martin's Press, 2001.

Smith, Bruce R. *The Acoustic World of Early Modern England: Attending to the O-Factor*. Chicago and London: University of Chicago Press, 1999.

Wittgenstein, Ludwig. *Philosophical Investigations*. Ed. and trans. G. E. M. Anscombe. Oxford: Blackwell, 1953.

Wright, Thomas. *The Passions of the Minde in Generall*. London, 1604.

5 "The marriage of true minds"

Amity, twinning, and comic closure in *Twelfth Night*

Laurie E. Osborne

A woman's face with Nature's own hand painted
Hast thou the master-mistress of my passion

Sonnet 20, 1–2

Structures of erotic substitution and homoerotic attraction are crucially important in *Twelfth Night* and in its performance history. However, as analysis of eros has proliferated, the crucial role of amity in the play has received only passing attention. Sir Thomas Elyot, in *The Boke Named the Governour* (1531), argues that "nothing is of more greatter estimation than loue, called in latine *Amor*, wherof *Amicitia* commeth, named in englisshe frendshippe or amitie" (1992, 150). Elyot's influential work and a wide array of early modern plays and poems attest to the influence of impassioned, idealized male friendship and the increasing conflict between male friendships and heterosexual marriage in early modern England. These issues play a vital role in *Twelfth Night*.

Both Shakespeare's sonnets and comedies reveal his deep interest in these complicated negotiations between passionate male friendship and heterosexual unions. Shakespeare's early comedy *Two Gentlemen of Verona* follows the classic Renaissance amity of Valentine and Proteus, concluding with Valentine's disturbing offer to give his fiancée to the friend who has just tried to rape her. Only the timely faint of Julia, Proteus's beloved disguised as a page, disrupts the conventional self-abnegation of amity that Valentine articulates (Sargent 1950). Because Julia's role so obviously prefigures Cesario's position as the disguised page who woos another for her beloved master, the connections between the two plays have centered around Cesario's comparable heterosexual desire. However, *Twelfth Night* offers an even more radical reworking of the relationship between amity and marital love than Ralph Sargent's comparison of Elyot's work and *Two Gentlemen* reveals. The likeness in feature and simultaneity of experience in Viola/Cesario and Sebastian's twinning enable Shakespeare temporarily to resolve the contradictions between amity and heterosexual union that preoccupy him throughout the canon.

Along with the sonnets, Shakespeare's comedies demonstrate that he used various approaches to explore these colliding loves. For example, Steve Patterson (1999) has argued that *The Merchant of Venice* pits Antonio's flawed quest for the passionate devotion of mutual amity with Bassanio against Bassanio's own heterosexual project. While Patterson cites *Two Gentlemen* as one of Shakespeare's early attempts to resolve the contradiction, neither he nor Sargent even mentions *Twelfth Night*'s more unusual representations of friendship in conflict with sexual love. Whereas Portia and Jessica from *Merchant*, like Julia from *Two Gentlemen*, crossdress to pursue their beloveds, Cesario has no prior heterosexual contract to pursue. Moreover, because her disguise and her male name throughout the play occlude her female identity almost from the start, she can only seek friendship with Orsino. Cesario's femaleness derives from asides and double-edged comments throughout the play, and she is not even named Viola until Sebastian invokes his sister in act 5. In Cesario's twinning and unusual status as both male and female, *Twelfth Night* offers an alternative model of the true friend – a hero who is also a heroine, "the yonge man havinge his harte all redy wedded to his frende" (Elyot 1992, 155), who can literally wed his friend.

However, because of Cesario's insistent yet covert femininity, most critical analyses of homoeroticism and amity in *Twelfth Night* address other characters, concentrating on Antonio's homoerotic love for Sebastian or, more recently, Olivia's love for Cesario as female–female eroticism. Joseph Pequigney (1992) has argued that the Antonios in *Merchant* and *Twelfth Night* are engaged in relationships that could be construed as amity, but that Antonio and Sebastian in *Twelfth Night* have an active and continuing homosexual relationship that goes well beyond the bounds of friendship. In my view, on the contrary, Antonio and Sebastian's close relationship is as important because it reflects and reinforces the central pursuit of amity shared by Cesario and Orsino. Critics who do address Cesario concentrate mostly on her appeal to Olivia through likeness. Laurie Shannon (2000–2001) explores these moments in *Twelfth Night* as part of her overall argument for the "homonormativity" of early modern English social allegiances, often invested heavily in the attractions of like to like, even though all social and erotic relationships in the period appear to be rigidly hierarchical. While Viola's heterosexual yearnings have received ample critical attention, Cesario's quest for amity repays closer examination because Cesario both exemplifies the ideals of amity and reveals its potential for eros.

In refocusing our consideration of Cesario's relationship with Orsino, I argue that Cesario seeks amity with his/her lord in complex ways that test the idealization of male friendships. Within the heterosexual subtext of Viola's desires, Cesario articulates a passionate devotion to Orsino; however, Cesario pursues his love in the context of amity, the only passionate relationship that he finds available to him while Orsino courts Olivia. Through this sleight of gender, Shakespeare maintains the non-erotic idealism of amity while also underscoring erotic desire. Cesario's "little thing [that] would make me tell them how much I lack of a man" (3.4.268–69) makes it unlikely that Cesario is Orsino's bedfellow in a sexual sense. Nonetheless, Cesario's private insistence that "myself would be his wife" (1.4.41) invests her impassioned declarations of love for Orsino with sexual desire. At the same time, keeping with Elyot's contention that friends "that be liberall do with holde or hyde nothing from them whom they love, whereby love increaseth" (1992, 152), Orsino acknowledges almost immediately his intimacy with Cesario by announcing, "I have unclasped / To thee the book even of my secret soul" (1.4.12–13). As R. W. Maslen argues, "This free disclosure of secrets demonstrates that despite their social disparity, in Orsino's eyes Cesario has become what Elizabethan manuals on male friendship describe as a 'second self,' 'another I,' a kind of twin of the duke's, as closely bound to him as Viola is to her twin brother" (2006, 136). Cesario's ongoing, multi-leveled pursuit of friendship with Orsino is even more important and collaborates with other relationships in the play, in particular the friendship between Sebastian and Antonio. *Twelfth Night*'s elaboration of amity validates the closing marriage, which has been much decried by later critics, who are familiar with actresses playing Cesario and with different conventions of male–male friendship and sexuality.

By invoking the improbable, exceptional, and even monstrous likeness in male and female twins (see Thijssen 1987), Shakespeare creates a Cesario who can envision men and women with like desires and a Sebastian who proves that likeness to be true. Two features of twinning prove crucial to my exploration of Cesario's pursuit of the male–male love of amity. First, the twinning experienced by Cesario/Viola and Sebastian explicitly recalls the insistence on likeness imbedded in numerous accounts of amity in early modern literature. As Elyot's example of Titus and Gysippus shows, friends may become so close that they even look alike. In Shakespeare's *The Winter's Tale*, Polixenes's close friendship with Leontes, strongly linked to amity by Nora Johnson, is described as twinning: "We were as twinn'd lambs that did frisk i' th' sun, / And bleat the one at th' other" (1.2.69–70). Obviously, Viola and Sebastian are literally twins and definitely not male friends bound by amity. Shannon underscores this difference: "While friendship and twinship discourses alike depend on 'natural' resemblances, what differs most between them is that twinship seems to split or divide a pre-existing single 'nature,' friendship is understood actively to conjoin pre-existing, separate, 'unnaturally' like natures" (2002, 43). Female–male twin pairs, however, already possess "separate, 'unnaturally' like natures." Although Viola and Sebastian do not experience or express amity for each other, Viola's twinning, as well as her brother's active male friendship with Antonio, strongly associates her with the principle of likeness in amity, especially when she is Cesario. Being a twin allows Cesario an implied parallel access to the model of male–male amity.

Second and more important, Viola's participation in "one face, one voice, one habit, and two persons" (5.1.208) anchors Cesario's account of her/himself as both female and male:

As I am man,
My state is desperate for my master's love.
As I am woman, now alas the day,
What thriftless sighs shall poor Olivia breathe!
(2.2.34–37)

Ever since Cesario was first played on stage by an actress in the Restoration, critics have noted the character's investment and constant revelation of her hidden female identity; Kathleen McLuskie argues that, for an early modern audience, the boy-actress beneath such crossdressed Shakespearean roles would be visible and require the "essentializing" of femininity that this character seems to offer in her asides as Cesario (1987, 123–24). Even without the punning and reminders from Cesario that "I am not that I play" (1.5.164), post-early modern audiences, readers, and critics tend to assume that the character occupies a single gender, usually female. From this assumption, we read Cesario's speeches as essentially revealing Viola's femaleness and desires. Many of Cesario's speeches support that assumption, recalling the fact that she is disguised and anticipating her revelation as female at the end. As a result, it is both convenient and logical to take Cesario as female.

However, her soliloquy embraces her identity as *both* genders. In fact, beyond her self-identification as "I, poor monster," which gestures toward her current double gender and potentially toward her twinship, the most explicit announcement of the character's gender is "I am the man!" (2.2.32, 23). Moreover, her/his experience only intermittently allows self-consideration "as I am woman" and more frequently requires the assumption "as I am man" (2.2.36, 34). Cesario must deal with loving Orsino from a male identity.

To take the character's various declarations and veiled self-revelations as *only* the revelations of a hidden female self is to miss the ways in which Cesario, "as man," pursues amity, an idealized state of male–male devotion, with Orsino. Because of the disguise, Cesario can take up a mutual friendship not usually encouraged or even envisioned as possible between men and women. In "On Friendship," Michel de Montaigne suggests that

> Seeing (to speake truly) that the ordinary sufficiency of women, cannot answer this conference and communication, the nurse of this sacred bond: nor seeme their mindes strong enough to endure the pulling of a knot so hard, so fast and durable. And truly [were it not for that], such a genuine and voluntary acquaintance might be contracted, where not only mindes had this entire jouissance, but also bodies, a share of the alliance, and where a man might be wholly engaged. It is certain that friendship would thereby be more compleat and full: But this sex could never by any example attaine unto it.
>
> (Montaigne 2005, 147, De Florio's translation)

In *Twelfth Night*, Cesario becomes such an example as she and Orsino approach their "loving-friendship." Thus, Shakespeare's Cesario draws on the wide circulation of ideas about idealized friendship and tests the boundaries and features of such friendships as Alan Bray and Laurie Shannon describe them.

When we read Cesario "as man" and explore the development of his friendship with Orsino in detail, we discover how "his" pursuit of amity relies upon and coincides in the "hidden revelations" of Cesario "as I am woman" (2.2.36). Several features of Cesario's and Orsino's relationship, from beginning to end, invoke the conventions of amity. Valentine comments on the instant affinity between Cesario and Orsino, apparently questioning the "favours" that Cesario has achieved in just three days. Cesario names this preferential treatment explicitly and wonders whether Valentine "call[s] in question the continuance of his love: is he inconstant, sir, in his favours?" (1.4.6–7). This speech explicitly equates the "favours" that Orsino grants his new gentleman with "love" – love between men, not heterosexual love. Orsino almost immediately bears out Valentine's observation by claiming to have shared "the book even of my secret soul" (1.4.12–14) and assigning Cesario the role of emissary to Olivia. The principal secret that Orsino has apparently revealed, his all-consuming passion for Olivia, effectively blocks Cesario's heterosexual yearning for Orsino. Amity is the most that Cesario can hope for, as he has no means to regain a female identity and acknowledges as much.

Just as significant, the friendship that Cesario develops with Orsino in the first two acts establishes the strongest of ties between the two, even though commentators since the early modern period have questioned the relationship's plausibility. Cesario's unflagging devotion to Orsino and Orsino's romantic volte-face to embrace the newly revealed sister of Sebastian have created difficulties for productions and critics throughout *Twelfth Night*'s performance history. Nineteenth-century admiration for Viola/Cesario's selfless, submissive, and supposedly silent love falters only because of equally widespread critical disdain for Orsino. Stage directors have wrestled with this relationship since the 1800s (Osborne 1996, 89–96). Recent films like Trevor Nunn's *Twelfth Night* and Tim Supple's production of the play often justify the comic union of Viola and Orsino by emphasizing those elements of Orsino's speeches which acknowledge the youthful attractiveness of his Cesario. For example, the directors of these films manipulate shots like close-ups and soft focus or restructure Shakespeare's scenic sequences to create a "realistic" heterosexual love between Cesario and Orsino for contemporary audiences. Nunn's *Twelfth Night* ekes out an extra scene between the two by including Cesario as the musician that Orsino orders to play "That strain again, it had a dying fall" (1.1.4). Nunn also disperses brief sections of the two early private conversations between Orsino and Cesario, in act 1 scene 4 and act 2 scene 4, so that Cesario, in effect, interacts with Orsino throughout the film and within numerous intimate settings (Osborne 2002, 94–96). The culmination of these intimacies involves Feste's song before Orsino, shifted to late in "act 3," and includes a near kiss between the pair. Tim Supple's 2001 TV film of *Twelfth Night* enacts comparable scene-splitting to develop Cesario's love for Orsino and includes an odd cinematic doubling of Orsino – his "soul" apparently rising out of his body to reach for Cesario – as an indication of Orsino's attraction to the boy. These strategies strive to render the heterosexual alliance between Viola and Orsino plausible at the end of the performances.

Such moves and the frequent critical laments concerning Orsino's unworthiness implicitly raise an important question: why did Shakespeare's representational structure for this relationship work for an early modern audience? The answer is that Cesario and Orsino are more than servant and master in their two scenes together. They partake in amity that challenges Orsino's dysfunctional self-isolation at the same time that it provokes Viola's desires.

The structures of loving friendship that *Twelfth Night* explores in Cesario and Orsino are more nuanced, especially in terms of Cesario's "pursuit" of Orsino, than merely the equality of status that Maslen suggests. As Laurie Shannon points out, the true friend will not merely be a twin or mirror to his friend; according to Cicero, Plutarch, and early modern writers, "speech can ultimately be discerned as that of a true friend, intriguingly, by its acidity in a conflict situation" (2002, 49). True friends will challenge each other for their own good, as indeed Cesario does on several occasions. In fact, one of the striking, if little analyzed, features of Cesario's relationship with Orsino is how frequently the supposed servant opposes or questions Orsino's plans (see Charles 1997, 136).

In act 1 scene 4, not only does Cesario challenge Orsino's instructions, but, perhaps more significant, Orsino also takes into account his servant's views. Cesario immediately questions Orsino's first order to "address thy gait unto her" (1.4.15) and suggests the task is futile since, "If she be so abandoned to her sorrow, / As it is spoke, she never will admit me" (1.4.18–19). In response to this mildly phrased objection, Orsino accepts the scenario that Cesario offers and reframes his command: "Be clamorous, and leap all civil bounds, / Rather than make unprofited return" (1.4.20–21). In his turn accepting this exhortation to be more aggressive in pursuing of Orsino's beloved, Cesario raises a more indirect objection, "what then?" (1.4.22). At this moment, Orsino assumes that Cesario can both "unfold the passion" of his love and "act [his] woes' (1.4.23, 25; see Maslen 2006). Cesario's privileged access to Orsino's passion and to his griefs provides both the justification for Orsino's order and the form that the youth's surrogate courtship should take. Their mutuality will guarantee that Cesario's representation of Orsino's case will be accurate and effective.

However, Orsino goes much further in order to encourage a servant whom he could command to do his bidding. He reassures Cesario about his success in the task because "she will attend it better in thy youth" (1.4.26). When

Cesario answers, "I think not so, my lord" (1.4.28), he could be modestly denying the praise of his youthful persuasiveness, or he could be rejecting the entire premise of Orsino's persuasions – the unfolding, the acting, and the success promised by his person. Completing Cesario's line, "Dear lad, believe it" (1.4.28), Orsino apparently reacts only to the modest disclaimer of skill and counters with a series of revealing compliments that locate Cesario's desirability in his lip, his voice "shrill and sound," and the "all [that] is semblative a woman's part" (1.4.34). In this exhortation, Orsino not only identifies Cesario as the beautiful effeminate youth but also promises the mutuality of male friendship: "Prosper well in this, / And thou shalt live as freely as thy lord, / To call his fortunes thine" (1.4.37–39). The youth, as both Cesario and Viola, responds to a rhetoric of amity that Shakespeare also expresses in the sonnets: as Cesario undertakes the task he has been resisting, Viola discovers heterosexual love.

Although this noteworthy resistance may connote Cesario's pre-existing heterosexual love, in fact Cesario only reveals those desires at the very end of the interchange. Like Olivia who falls in love with Cesario because of "his" imagined wooing, Cesario acknowledges his/her love after the scene that includes misdirected but attractive speech. When Orsino ignites Viola's desires by promising "loving friendship," Cesario becomes the first of several to reveal newly kindled desires in an aside, "Whoe'er I woo, / Myself would be his wife" (1.4.41–42). Cesario's reaction foreshadows Olivia's aside about her love and how "quickly may one catch the plague" (1.5.265) and Sebastian's immediate response to Olivia's love, "If it be thus to dream, still let me sleep" (4.1.59). Orsino persuades his male friend and servant into still closer identification with his desires and goals; Cesario responds as a man by agreeing to make Orsino's case and as a woman by wishing her own marriage to Orsino.

Cesario's expression of heterosexual desire, reinforced when a female actress plays the part, has too often masked the other important features in Cesario and Orsino's behavior. Cesario challenges his master's command with three objections. This is curious behavior indeed, if Cesario is merely a servant. Still more surprising, Orsino chooses to persuade his youthful "servant" rather than simply order his obedience as he has capriciously started and stopped the music with abrupt commands in act 1 scene 1. If amity rather than servitude is at stake, both Cesario's eloquent opposition and Orsino's efforts to persuade the youth through compliment rather than direct order make more sense. These features of the scene not only underscore the closeness that Valentine has noticed but also affirm the allied fortunes of the pair.

When the audience and critics alike assume that Cesario acts only as Viola, Cesario's distinctly non-servile relationship to his "master" becomes evidence *only* of her hidden feminine desires. However, when boy-actresses played Cesario on the early modern stage, idealized male amity and, in particular,

Cesario's pursuit of that relationship would have been more visible. Moreover, if Shannon's reading of the important critical function of the idealized friendship is correct, amity at its best enabled mutual critique, based in total identification with the friend's best interests. The objections that Cesario offers and the way that resistance distracts Orsino from his self-absorbed view of the courtship are the measures of the closeness and classic strength of the amity that Cesario seeks to achieve – and that the play later tests.

The second scene between Orsino and Cesario elaborates their amity at a crucial juncture: after Antonio and Sebastian appear to enact an equally passionate yet unambiguously gendered amity, after Cesario's status as "gentleman" receives the support of his father's name, and after Cesario fully recognizes that "I am the man" (2.2.23). Act 2, scene 4 extends the amity developing between Cesario and Orsino, despite an opening which apparently signals Orsino's continuing emotional stasis. Once again, Orsino calls for music: "Now, good Cesario, but that piece of song, / That old and antic song we heard last night" (2.4.2–3). In act 1 Orsino himself interrupts the music to request "that strain again, it had a dying fall" (1.1.4); in act 2, the particular singer needed, Feste, is missing. As a result, the second scene is structured around the doubling of this song, first in the context of "the tune the while" (2.4.13) and then in the wake of the actual song, with lyrics. Thus the scene invokes and then manipulates the doubled impulses in Orsino's all-male household: toward homosocial bonds and toward heterosexual union.

Whereas Nunn's film, for example, disperses sections of this scene into a series of private conversations over cards, at billiards, and at Orsino's bath-side, Shakespeare's play sets up the interchange between Cesario and Orsino continuously. He frames their relationship as both public and private while grounding it in repetition and likeness. Orsino indulges in both public declamation of his powerful love (again) and private conference with his friend. The tune alone prompts Orsino to acclaim the quality of his love in ways that echo his opening speeches in the play, with one crucial difference. Now he offers himself as the measure of true love for Cesario:

> If ever thou shalt love,
> In the sweet pangs of it remember me;
> For such as I am, all true lovers are,
> Unstaid and skittish in all motions else,
> Save in the constant image of the creature
> That is beloved.
>
> (2.4.14–19)

Although Orsino's "creature / That is beloved" (2.4.18–19) is presumably Olivia, his definition of "true lovers" and willingness to imagine Cesario in love inspire his later questions concerning other possible true lovers.

At this point, Orsino both assumes Cesario's allegiance and – for the first time – inquires directly about someone else's feelings. Cesario's response to Orsino's question about how "dost thou like this tune?" (2.4.19), in turn, leads Orsino to recognize love in Cesario and – more important – to explore his friend's apparent love for a woman of Orsino's favor, complexion, and years. The ready availability of Viola's veiled acknowledgment of her heterosexual passion generates much of the scene's humor. Cesario's indirect efforts to "hyde nothing" from his friend have distracted critics from closely considering Orsino's advice, except insofar as his efforts to correct Cesario's amorous goal result in the first spectacular reversal in his opinions about male and female love. However, the greater inconstancy in love that Orsino now claims for men is only one facet of his counsel. When Orsino insists that his friend should love a woman younger than himself, "so wears she to him" (2.4.29), he simultaneously encourages Cesario to pursue love as he himself does and argues that the love between men and women is necessarily based in inequality. To be sure, Olivia does not fit the model of malleability that Orsino imagines. However, neither is Cesario quite the peer that Orsino urges him to be. As Cesario resisted Orsino's orders in their first scene together, in this scene Orsino challenges Cesario's supposed choice of beloved. All in his friend's best interests, Orsino seeks to persuade his friend to give up an older beloved, resembling Orsino in years and "complexion" (2.4.25), in favor of loving the same way he does himself. Moreover, while Cesario pursues the amity of equals between himself and Orsino by echoing Orsino's views, he/she also recognizes the futility of her heterosexual love since men's – or at least Orsino's – "fancies" for women "are more giddy and unfirm, / More longing, wavering, sooner lost and worn, / Than women's are" (2.4.32–34).

The doubling and mirroring within the interactions between Cesario and Orsino become still more obvious when the scene apparently starts again; after Feste's arrival, Orsino repeats his command for "the song we had last night" (2.4.41). The duplication of the song and the ensuing argument between Orsino and Cesario suggest that the lyrics are important. The singer laments his own death at the hand of a "fair, cruel maid," representing the fatal consequences of unrequited love. The topic seems ideally suited to Orsino's love melancholy as well as predictive of his future failure with Olivia. Nunn's *Twelfth Night* draws on the intensity of these lyrics and uses this song as the background for the near-kiss between Cesario and Orsino. However, the lyrics also imagine "My part of death, no one so true / Did share it" (2.4.56–57). The other important dimension of this unrequited lover's solitude is the absence of a friend: "Not a friend, not a friend greet / My poor corpse" (2.4.60–61). Both beloved and friend are implicated in the song, as they are in the scene itself. The song's extravagant lover, imagining his lonely death and burial, speaks to Cesario's situation as much as to Orsino's. As the lyrics recall Viola's recent loss of a brother, whose grave is also nowhere to be found, the song's account of solitude and loss occasioned by unrequited love resonates with the futility of Viola's love given Orsino's proffered amity and with her initial agreement that women "die even when they to perfection grow" (2.4.40).

After this song, Cesario challenges Orsino even more forcefully than he resists Orsino's pursuit of love in act 1: "But, if she cannot love you, sir" (2.4.85). When Orsino flatly rejects this answer to his love, Cesario offers an ostensibly hypothetical argument:

> Sooth, but you must.
> Say that some lady, as perhaps there is,
> Hath for your love as great a pang of heart
> As you have for Olivia. You cannot love her.
> You tell her so. Must she not then be answer'd?
> (2.4.89–93)

Since the audience knows that Cesario is this imagined lady, the argument seems most important as a veiled revelation of her love, of Viola herself as "some lady." However, the entire interchange, including Orsino's second reversal of opinion about male and female love, occurs also within the loving-friendship between two men. Cesario's covert expression of love represents a woman whose passionate devotion equals Orsino's, but Orsino rejects utterly the idea that a "woman's sides / Can bide the beating of so strong a passion / As love doth give my heart" (2.4.91–93). Although Cesario's love can be "masterly" (2.4.21), Orsino finds "no woman's heart / So big, to hold so much. They lack retention" (2.4.93–94). More than willing to compare Cesario's love with his own, Orsino insists that his friend "make no compare / Between that love a woman can bear me / And that I owe Olivia" (2.4.99–101). This denial leaves only a man's love – Cesario's love – to match Orsino's passion.

In response to Orsino's vehemence, Cesario reframes his next challenge in context of their mutual male friendship and answers that he knows

> Too well what love women to men may owe,
> In faith, they are as true of heart as we.
> My father had a daughter loved a man
> As it might be, perhaps, were I a woman,
> I should your lordship.
> (2.4.104–8)

Adopting Orsino's language to insist that women are "as true of heart as we" and can "owe" rather than just "bear" love, Cesario also likens the daughter's love to his own love for Orsino, not to Orsino's love. This invocation of a woman's love, now linked to Cesario as brother and friend, provokes interest rather than instant rejection. Moreover, Cesario's veiled self-description as "patience on a monument" emphasizes the gender difference in the daughter's silent mourning but closes with an explicit renewal of the male–male tie between Cesario and Orsino: "We men may say more, swear more: but indeed / Our shows are more than will; for still we prove / Much in our vows, but little in our love" (2.4.115–17). In the latter half of this conversation, once Cesario shifts the grounds for his claim about women's love, Orsino cedes control over the interchange. In fact, he evinces enough belief in the comparable love of Cesario's "sister" that he asks whether she died of her love, thus tying her fate into the song which doubly frames the whole scene.

Once again, Cesario asserts a dual gender. As an explicit revelation of femaleness, Cesario's statement that "I am all the daughters of my father's house" (2.4.119) ranks with his sworn assertion to Olivia that "I have one heart, one bosom, and one truth, / And that no woman has, nor never none / Shall mistress be of it, save I alone" (3.1.149–51). However, in response to Orsino, Cesario lays claim to *both* genders, as "all the daughters of my father's house, / And all the brothers too" (2.4.119–20). As a daughter, Cesario is doubly implicated in the gender hierarchy, submissive to paternal power and subsequently to a husband's rule; as brother, however, Cesario invokes both family ties and the closeness of male friendship, frequently configured as the equality of brothers. Although my students often lament Orsino's stupidity in failing to grasp the blatant allusions to Cesario's "true" female gender in act 2 scene 4, what Cesario actually does is hint at his passionate, possibly erotic love for Orsino and affirm his incorporation of both male and female. By claiming both genders, Cesario makes a crucial move toward resolving Orsino's doubled and therefore static loves – for his friend and for a woman. In addition, Cesario's closing offer to return to Olivia and subsequent insistence that she give "Nothing but this: your true love to my master" doubles the typical self-sacrifice of amity (3.4.189), since this support of his friend's courtship threatens both Cesario's amity and Viola's marital desires.

Through this complex interplay between difference/mutual critique and likeness/mutual identification, Shakespeare's play represents an increasing intimacy in the amity between Cesario and Orsino by the end of act 2. Moreover, the "echo" of that mutual friendship in Antonio and Sebastian sustains the image of their intense alliance. Whereas Antonio espouses the kind of passionate self-sacrifice that Cesario offers to Orsino throughout the play, Sebastian, like Orsino, reciprocates by sharing his "secret soul" and accepting Antonio's devoted service. When he catches up to Sebastian in act 3 scene 3, Antonio's language is quite direct and impassioned:

> I could not stay behind you. My desire,
> More sharp than filèd steel, did spur me forth;
> . . . my willing love,
> The rather by these arguments of fear,
> Set forth in your pursuit.
>
> (3.3.4–5, 11–13)

Moreover, Sebastian accepts Antonio's declaration with his own, less effusive response: "My kind Antonio, / I can no other answer make but thanks, / And thanks" (3.3.13–15). Antonio's passion provokes gratitude and Sebastian's assurance that "were my worth as is my conscience firm, / You should find better dealing" (3.3.17–18). The terms of Antonio's devotion as well as their mutual but differing expressions of their friendship recall and contextualize the intimacy that Cesario has achieved with Orsino.

Furthermore, Antonio's rescue of "Sebastian" and subsequent disappointment at his friend's apparent rejection demonstrate the fragility of that mutuality when one rejects or betrays or loves less than the other. As Sargent notes, "the one essential quality of friendship to which Elyot returns again and again is *constancy*" (1950, 1171). Antonio's vehement accusations against that "ingrateful boy" and claims about the betrayal of their ongoing mutual friendship in act 3 scene 4 and later in act 5 scene 1 prefigure Orsino's violent disappointment in his friend Cesario. Orsino's threat in act 5 to "sacrifice the lamb that I do love / To spite a raven's heart within a dove" (5.1.126–27) reveals that he actually cares less about Olivia than for Cesario, about whom his "thoughts are ripe in mischief" (5.1.125). Orsino's jealousy gives Cesario the unusual opportunity that R. W. Maslen notes, "No woman but Viola in Shakespeare's plays gets such an opportunity to achieve, as a man, the ultimate consummation of an Elizabethan man's love for another man, which is to lay down his life for his friend" (2006, 136). Erotic death and literal self-sacrifice coincide when Cesario, "most jocund, apt, and willingly, / To do [Orsino] rest, a thousand deaths would die" (5.1.128–29). The devoted male friend Cesario, sacrificing both his life and his interest in the woman, coincides with Viola, disguised and declaring her love.

The denouement publicly represents the amity between Orsino and Cesario when Cesario declares the depth of his emotional allegiance to Orsino after Olivia's query about his departure:

> After him I love
> More than I love these eyes, more than my life,
> More, by all mores, than e'er I shall love wife.
> If I do feign, you witnesses above
> Punish my life for tainting of my love.
> (5.1.130–34)

Note that, like many male friends, including Valentine in *Two Gentlemen of Verona*, Cesario places his friendship above any "wife." The extravagance of Cesario's love simultaneously recalls the great sacrifices in idealized friendships and offers her the chance to speak of her heterosexual passion. The former is just as important as the latter, especially at this moment when both coincide and promise the total emotional and physical alliance that Montaigne suggests that women and men cannot achieve. Orsino's response when

Olivia reveals her marriage to "Cesario" recalls the prose narratives of true friendship as well. He renounces his claim to Olivia and leaves her to his friend, albeit with the warning that Cesario's lack of constancy has destroyed his amity with Orsino as effectively as Sebastian's apparent betrayal undoes his friendship with Antonio.

The appearance of Sebastian at this moment provokes Orsino's amazement but revives audience awareness that the twins represent an unusual mutual identity of male and female. Implicated in amity with one of these two persons, Antonio responds, "How have you made division of yourself? / An apple cleft in two is not more twin / Than these two creatures" (1.5.215–17). As Cesario and Sebastian embark on their lengthy litany of mutual identification, the twinning on stage raises the possibilities of likeness and reveals the advantages of difference. Cesario/Viola's refusal to embrace without her "woman's weeds" sustains her male identity and her status as a twin; thus Cesario continues to participate in both amity and heterosexual love.

This conflation continues as Orsino reveals that Cesario's passionate approach to amity has apparently characterized their relationship in a sustained, unproblematic way: "Boy, thou hast said to me a thousand times / Thou never shouldst love woman like to me" (5.1.260–61). Cesario's (now Viola's) answer verifies her former claims:

> And all those sayings will I overswear;
> And all those swearings keep as true in soul
> As doth that orbèd continent the fire
> That severs day from night.
>
> (5.1.262–64)

Cesario reiterates the declarations that Orsino has accepted as the devotion of the "true" male friend but presents those "swearings" as a woman. Viola's oath never to "love woman like to [Orsino]" is a declaration of amity – the male friend's promise never to love a woman over his friend – that stands in for a vow of heterosexual love and fidelity – the wife's promise never to love any man before her husband. His/her sworn fidelity allies this figure to the youth of Sonnet 20, whose "eye is less false in rolling" (4) and whose love for women is an important threat throughout the sonnets. More important, Orsino himself maintains their amity by continuing to call her Cesario even though he has promised that Viola will become her "master's mistress" (5.1.314), a comment that draws together amity and homoeroticism in ways echoed in the sonnets.

Reading Cesario and Orsino's amity as the visible, convincing expression of their mutual love illuminates several features of Shakespeare's engagement with amity and heterosexual love in *Twelfth Night*. First, the likeness of the twins enables both Cesario's access to amity and Sebastian's and Antonio's reinforcement of that relationship. Second, while Cesario's amity apparently does not invoke the sexual danger that Lelia in the *Gl'Inganni* source tale anticipates about being summoned as her "master's" bedfellow (Bullough 1968, 304), Cesario's erotic yearning for Orsino does allow to "bodies, share of the alliance" which Montaigne imagines as the benefit of involving women in amity (2005, 147). Finally, Cesario's frustrations within amity underscore early modern assumptions about the inequality of men's and women's love which supposedly disqualify women from "loving-friendship" with male beloveds. Cesario's achievement of open passion and reciprocal devotion with Orsino argues that women "are as true of heart as" men (2.4.105), and that sexual passion can co-exist with amity.

The play's proposed union between Orsino and Cesario thus simultaneously desexualizes amity and presents sexual union as its ultimate realization. The strength and passion of their friendship break the impasse of Orsino's doubled commitments to his all-male household and his heterosexual union; their amity authorizes Orsino's "share in this most happy wreck" (5.1.259), that is, his marriage to Viola. On the verge of becoming the "master-mistress" of Orsino's passion, Cesario embodies and imaginatively resolves the problems posed in Sonnet 20 as well as the challenges to male friendship in Shakespeare's comedies. In *Twelfth Night*, the best male friend is a woman and the most desirable wife is the loving male friend.

Works cited

Bray, Alan. "Homosexuality and the Signs of Male Friendship in Elizabethan England." *History Workshop Journal* 29 (1990): 1–19.

Bullough, Geoffrey. *Narrative and Dramatic Sources of Shakespeare*. Vol. II: *The Comedies, 1597–1603*. London: Routledge and Kegan Paul, 1968.

Charles, Casey. "Gender Trouble in *Twelfth Night*." *Theatre Journal* 49 (1997): 121–41.

Elyot, Sir Thomas. *A Critical Edition of Sir Thomas Elyot's The Boke Named the Governour.* Ed. Donald W. Rude. New York: Garland Publishing, Inc., 1992.

Johnson, Nora M. "Ganymedes and Kings: Staging Male Homosexual Desire in *The Winter's Tale*." *Shakespeare Studies* 26 (1998): 187–217.

Maslen, R. W. "*Twelfth Night*, Gender and Comedy." In *Early English Drama*. Ed. Garrett A. Sullivan, Jr. et al. New York: Oxford University Press, 2006.

McLuskie, Kathleen. "The Act, the Role, and the Actor: Boy Actresses on the Elizabethan Stage." *New Theatre Quarterly* 3 (1987): 120–30.

Montaigne, Michel de. *On Friendship*. New York: Penguin, 2005.

Osborne, Laurie E. *The Trick of Singularity: Twelfth Night and the Performance Editions*. Iowa City: University of Iowa Press, 1996.

——. "Cutting up Characters in Trevor Nunn's *Twelfth Night*." In *Spectacular Shakespeare: Critical Theory and Popular Cinema*. Ed. Courtney Lehmann and Lisa Starks. Cranbury, NJ: Associated University Presses, 2002: 89–109.

Patterson, Steve. "The Bankruptcy of Homoerotic Amity in Shakespeare's *The Merchant of Venice*." *Shakespeare Quarterly* 50 (Spring 1999): 9–32.

Pequigney, Joseph. "The Two Antonios and Same-Sex Love in *Twelfth Night* and *The Merchant of Venice*." *English Literary Renaissance* 22 (1992): 201–21.

Sargent, Ralph M. "Sir Thomas Elyot and the Integrity of *The Two Gentlemen of Verona*." *PMLA* 65 (1950): 1166–80.

Shannon, Laurie. "Nature's Bias: Renaissance Homonormativity and Elizabethan Comic Likeness." *Modern Philology* 98 (2000–2001): 183–210.

——. *Sovereign Amity: Figures of Friendship in Shakespearean Contexts*. Chicago: University of Chicago Press, 2002.

Thijssen, J. M. "Twins as Monsters: Albertus Magnus's Theory of the Generation of Twins and Its Philosophical Context." *Bulletin of the History of Medicine* 61 (1987): 237–46.

6 Masculine plots in *Twelfth Night*

Goran V. Stanivuković

Manhood . . . consisteth in measure and worthiness, in fearing to hazard without hope.

Robert Greene, *Gwydonius* (2001, 125)

In this epigraph from Greene's romance, masculinity is imagined as exhibiting balance and caution, and as something that can be controlled. In contrast, in *Twelfth Night*, a romance that shares a few details[1] with Greene's work, masculinity is the subject of melancholy, disguise, and comedy. Yet, since so much of the action in *Twelfth Night* depends upon discovering the meaning of masculinity, what is and is not a man, one could say that this play is one of the most masculinist of Shakespeare's romances. From Malvolio's early estimate of Cesario as "Not yet old enough for a man, nor young enough for a boy" (1.5.150–51) to Orsino's juxtaposition of gender, from Cesario to Viola, in the revelation scene at the end of the play – "Cesario, come – / For so you shall be while you are a man; / But when in other habits you are seen / Orsino's mistress" (5.1.375–78) – masculinity continues to puzzle, entertain, and dominate the stage. But since it is one of the characteristics of Shakespearean romance to twist and obscure the ways of understanding a normative discourse, masculinity in *Twelfth Night* is not represented as normative, in terms in which it was understood in the Renaissance, as heroic and reproductive. Rather, this version of normative masculinity is constantly challenged. Critics have written eloquently and persuasively about the instability of gender categories in this play, particularly with reference to how the anatomical gender was conceptualized in the Renaissance. Yet, the ways in which the plot of this romance imagines masculinity indicate more the influence of romance literature than the popular medical theories of gender. By 1602, when the first performance of *Twelfth Night* was recorded, the English print market had already been flooded with popular prose romances, whose narratives of chivalry and maturation pit the masculinity invested in courtship against a more archaic form of masculinity whose value is gained on the battlefield.[2] It is within the context of popular romances, especially their masculine-oriented narratives that I want to read the ways in which the plot of *Twelfth Night* imagines and challenges masculinity.

Writing about the proximity of cultural notions of masculinity and their imaginative representations in Shakespeare, Bruce R. Smith argues that "the relationship between dramatic fictions and social realities was, and is, a *reciprocal* matter: Shakespeare's plays represent masculine identity in ways that must have been recognizable from everyday life even as they set up models of action and eloquence that a man might want to imitate" (Smith 2000, 41; Smith's italics). But what if the fictionalized masculine agency in *Twelfth Night* is more closely modeled not on the everyday reality but on the humanist literature which narrates precisely the kind of plots and actions that resemble the plot and events in *Twelfth Night*? The humanist literature that I have in mind here is not the learned literature of Shakespeare's Italian sources, but widely circulating texts that belonged to what Simon Palfrey calls "an intertextual, cross-cultural, folk humanism" (1999, vii). Palfrey refers to the public plays in which the large and varied audiences would have been able to recognize echoes of the Bible or John Florio's dictionary. But I would add prose romances to that list of familiar texts, because they were a product of popular culture that was cheaply produced, widely circulated on the print market, and read by all classes.[3]

The story of a shipwrecked youth seeking service in a noble household in a small fictional country in the eastern Mediterranean, a story featuring a cross-gendered disguise and complications ensuing from it, is not just the story from Shakespeare's Italian and Latin sources, *Gl'Ingannati* (by the Accademia degli Intronati di Siena), Ariosto's *I Suppositi*, and Terence's *The Eunuch*, but also of prose romances, especially Emanuel Forde's *Parismus* (1598). I would argue, in fact, that in Forde's popular romance Shakespeare found the model for a plot centering on masculinity he was to write in *Twelfth Night*. Erotic risks, misunderstandings, misreadings, and accidents in representing masculinity in this play correspond to the ways in which masculinity is imagined in the plot of *Parismus*, a romance based on the motif of falling in love with a stranger, as is the case in *Twelfth Night*. Errors in understanding masculinity in *Twelfth Night* are instances of what Terence Cave, writing about the accidental nature of the plot in *Twelfth Night*, calls "the cognitive confusion on which the action of the play is based" (1990, 277). Looking at the plot of Shakespeare's romance in this way opens up a way to approach masculinity from the angle of textual transmissions, not anatomical discourses about gender.[4] My point, however, is not that Shakespeare merely imitates the discursive and textual strategies of plotting masculinity in prose romances, but that, in order to shape his own plot for the best theatrical entertainment, he re-imagines the masculine plots in prose fiction, turning masculinity from a celebrated category into the source of comedy. The ways in which plot becomes an index of various aspects of masculinity in *Twelfh*

Night remind us of the extent to which, in this comedy, plot and character are intricately connected. Indeed, as Alexander Leggatt says: "in *Twelfth Night* each set of characters has a plot to tend to, and is largely kept within the confines of that plot" (1974, 222). My earlier point about *Twelfth Night* as a masculinist play becomes even more apparent if we compare *Twelfth Night* to Forde's romance. Though addressed to and targeting both young men and women, prose romances, including *Parismus*, were primarily masculinist texts because of their insistence on the narrative of chivalric combat and praise of the violent masculinity of the knight.[5]

Despite the textual affinities between *Parismus* and *Twelfh Night*, scholars have only acknowledged Forde's work as a possible source for Shakespeare's play.[6] Thus, Stanley Wells and Roger Warren, recent editors of *Twelfth Night*, have observed that Forde furnished Shakespeare with "the names of his two heroines," the disguise, and "tenderness."[7] While it might be that Shakespeare got the names of the two heroines from Forde, however, neither heroine is structurally similar to its counterpart in Shakespeare, even though Violetta cross-dresses as a page. In fact, only Olivia appears both in Forde and Shakespeare; Viola's counterpart in Forde is Violetta. And Forde's Olivia is a queen, determined, as a Renaissance mother would be, to marry her daughter Laurana to Parismus, a young man of noble parentage. Violetta is a daughter of the merchant "Signior Andrugio, a Citizen" (Q4v). Although she possesses both the emotional resourcefulness and life energy of Viola, she is well grounded in her feminine sexuality, even when in disguise. Thus, while I acknowledge an apparent similarity between the two female characters in Forde and Shakespeare, I suggest that a further correspondence between these two texts is at the level of plot. This aspect of similarity, however, does not make Shakespeare an imitator of Forde, but a commentator on the kind of masculine plot Forde's romance promotes.

The love plot of *Parismus* is simpler than that of *Twelfth Night*, mostly because the complications of desire and sexuality, prominent in Shakespeare, are not central to Forde. Instead, in line with the romance strategy, Forde focuses on the heroic virtue and prowess of the eponymous hero. In addition, Parismus is in love with Laurana, who does not cross-dress, while his friend Pollipus woos Violetta, without taking any notice of the fact that she is cross-dressed as a page. But her disguise is not the source of confusions, as Viola/Cesario's is. This is a curious moment in *Parismus*, in which cross-dressing does not incur erotic anxiety; in fact, it is not even observed. Thus, while the status of *Parismus* as a *source* for *Twelfth Night* is only apparent, its importance as a *textual resource* that informs the plot of *Twelfth Night* is assured both by the shared tradition of romance, to which Shakespeare's and Forde's texts belong, and because of the structural and rhetorical similarities of their plots. My starting point, then, is that in *Twelfth Night*, Shakespeare comments on the romantic plot of *Parismus* in ways that re-write the representation of masculinity in that romance.

Janet Adelman has recently challenged, on the grounds of partial historical accuracy, the Galenic one-sex model based on the male gender as a norm, frequently invoked by critics to illuminate the flexibility of gender categories in *Twelfth Night*. Post-structuralist, especially new historicist, scholarship on gender has also come under criticism from another direction, one that replaces the materialist for rhetorical reading of the body in *Twelfth Night*. Thus, in a compelling essay about the body in *Twelfth Night*, Lorna Hutson questions the new historicist arguments about the Galenic one-sex model as a context for interpreting gendered identities, desire, and sexuality in this play. She argues that this model of reading obscures the important fact that "such traditional conceptions of sexual honor, credit, and wealth" were being "rapidly transformed by the technology of persuasion," or credit, represented in Shakespeare's plays (1996, 146). Because of this shift, Hutson's argument continues, the issue in plays such as *Twelfth Night* is not so much the emergence of identity and fantasies about the anatomical body, but "men's discursive ability to improvise social credit, and credibility" (147). Hutson demonstrates that Shakespeare imagines the body through the rhetorical strategies of credibility, as they are presented in the Italian humanist plays (Shakespeare's sources) about the confusing identities and separated twins (151). Thus, in her discussion of humanist arguments about the disguised body in *Twelfth Night*, Hutson shifts the argument of the play from the gendered-specific desire to the rhetorical strategy of proving credibility in order for a young man to gain access to a noble household and to marriage opportunities.

While offering an alternative approach to our reading of the disguise in *Twelfth Night*, however, Hutson leaves out of her discussion prose romances and the influence of their exemplary narratives on the shaping of the masculinity plot in this play. Although it is undeniable that the Italian sources Hutson analyzes enabled the representation of the body in *Twelfth Night*, popular romances produced around the same time as Shakespeare's romance were thematically, structurally, and ideologically closer to dramatic romances than humanist texts that targeted a limited, courtly, and learned culture. The influence of romances, then, complements the humanist sources of *Twelfth Night*. As Helen Cooper cautions, "the grounding of Renaissance literature in the great classical authors (in particular Ovid and Virgil), or in contemporary European works (Ariosto, or the Italian *novelle* that were endlessly pillaged for the plot of plays), are misleading: not because they are wrong, but because they are not enough. Alongside those works, which were accessible only to the intellectual elite unless or until they were printed in English translations, was a mass of stories available to everyone who could read English or hear it read to them"; for self-conscious writers of the Renaissance, Cooper continues, such stories "were a way of thinking, not just about spinning new plots" (2004, 7). Reading masculinity in *Twelfth Night* as a commentary on its display in *Parismus* means not just approaching the idea of Shakespeare's sources in a new way but also expanding the meaning of

Shakespeare's plot by suggesting that it registers, through Forde, the cultural shift from chivalric to romantic masculinity that occurred in the sixteenth and seventeenth centuries.[8] Thus, masculinity in *Twelfth Night* is shaped in proximity to chivalric masculine representations in the prose romance. Approaching *Twelfth Night* in this way means reading it more as a popular play that might have appealed to a popular audience of the middling sort, concerned with upward social mobility, similar to those of romance heroes and heroines.

In his Dedication to Sir Robert Ratcliffe, Earl of Sussex, Forde describes the gist of his fiction as "Honours Triumphe," whose purpose is to present "the viewe of those admired gifts of true Nobilitie, that abundantly adorne" his dedicatee's "Vertuous inclination" (A3r). Forde announces his work as a fiction ("a Fancie") that promotes honorable actions and offers it not just as an endorsement of aristocratic virtue but also as a model of such virtue to be followed by his readers. There is difference between, on the one hand, the honorable and virtuous values of the Knight, Forde's dedicatee, and, on the other, Sir Toby, "the knight's in admirable fooling" (2.3.75), and Sir Andrew, who professes he is a "true knight" (2.3.51), though out of tune and with "[a] contagious breath" (2.3.52), as he is quickly reminded by Sir Toby. Sir Toby and Sir Andrew, as I will show, represent a travesty of chivalry, but Forde's dedicatee is supposed to separate honorable acts from acts of militant violence in his treatment of the narrative as an example of virtuous conduct.

Since in *Twelfth Night* masculinity is mostly a subject of conversation and less of action, it is worth remembering Cesar Barber's comment that "It is amazing how little happens in *Twelfth Night*, how much of the time people are merely talking, especially in the first half, before the farcical complications are sprung" (1963, 242). Yet, in those instances when masculinity is shown in action, it appears to comment on Forde's romance, reminding us how representations in this play depend more on rhetoric than action. To be a knight, a heroic man, in *Twelfth Night* is often the reverse of what a man is in Forde's romance, where the eponymous hero, Parismus, confirms his valor, prowess, and honor in chivalric encounters with other knights, outlaws, and pirates. But while it is not the act itself but the value conveyed by it that romances insist on, in *Twelfth Night* it is both the structure and the value of (pseudo)chivalric encounters that give meaning to its masculine plot. What is honor and what the meaning of manhood is in *Twelfth Night* becomes a subject of conversation and dialogue as well as action. Both Forde's and Shakespeare's romance, therefore, shape the meaning about masculinity through the plots of their texts. As Barber reminds us, in Shakespeare's romance "[i]t is not the credibility of the event that is decisive, but what can be expressed throughout it" (1963, 241). In *Parismus* and *Twelfth Night* masculinity is displayed in chivalric actions and in the travesty of those actions respectively. This suggests two competing ways in which prose romances and drama commented on the shift from heroic to romantic masculinity. Humorous heroic masculinity suited better the entertainment quality of dramatic romances, while the nostalgic re-imagining of chivalry was better adapted to the printed book and reading whose purpose was both instruction and entertainment.

In chapter XIV in *Parismus*, in an episode equivalent in structure but opposite in its expressive meaning to a corresponding one in *Twelfth Night*, in which Sir Andrew Aguecheek and Viola/Cesario enter into a duel, Parismus fights the chief outlaw, Zoylus:

> At last *Parismus* beeing inraged at the valour of his enemie, and knowing it was now [O2r] no time of dalliance, because he sawe the outlawe beginne to faint, assayled the valiant *Zoylus* so fiercely that he could scarcely withstande his furie, and soone had dyed by the unconquered arme of *Parismus*, but that the Outlaw had receyved such a wound by the hand of *Ramon*, that he fel downe dead under his horse, which somewhat refreshed *Zoylus*, for that *Ramon* taking the aduauntage, also assailed *Parismus*, which draue him to his uttermost shifts. At last he espied a peece of armour broke from *Ramons* arme, in which place hee gaue him such a wounde, that hee let his horse raynes fall, and his steede being at libertie beganne to wonder disorderly about the lists, *Zoylus* in the meane time, beeing well refreshed with the ayde of *Ramon*, strooke such a forcible blowe at *Parismus*, that it pearced his armour on his left arme, and lighted so full on his Thigh, that hee was greeuouslie wounded, which blow, turned *Parismus* sences into that extreame furie, that with all his force, striking with both his hands at *Zoylas*, he smote him on the head with such furie, that he fell downe from his horse: at which blow all the fielde showted, and *Parismus* sworde burst.
>
> (O2v)

While this narrative invokes both the heroic and horrific aspects of a knightly combat,[9] it assures Parismus's victory and promotes the values – honor, valor, and prowess – he embodies throughout the romance. This episode's structural counterpart in *Twelfth Night*, however, turns what starts off as a chivalric clash into a parody of chivalry and heroic masculinity. In scenes involving multiple duelists, we witness a duel between Viola/Cesario (and Sebastian in 4.1) and Sir Andrew, and Antonio and Sir Toby. Fabian imagines Sir Andrew as "the knight . . . incensed against you [Viola/Cesario] even to a mortal arbitrement" (3.4.251–52), promoting his champion further as "the most skilful, bloody, and fatal opposite that you could possibly have found in part of Illyria" (3.4.257–59). Sir Toby, too, praises Sir Andrew as "quick, skilful, and deadly" (3.4.217–18) and hails him as a knight, "dubbed with unhatched rapier and on carpet consideration, but he is a devil in private brawl" (3.4.227–29). Yet the duel proves the opposite, since Sebastian defeats him very quickly: "there's for thee [Sir Andrew], and there, and there" (4.1.25). In the manner of Zoylus, whose attack on Parismus's comrade in arms turns "Parismus['] sences into that extreame furie" (O2r), so Fabian announces Sir Andrew's violent fury to Viola as "the knight . . . incensed against you even to a mortal arbitrement" (3.4.251). In a similar vein, Sir Toby presents Viola/ Cesario as a deadly knight to Sir Andrew:

> he's a very devil, I have not seen such a virago. I had a pass with him, rapier, scabbard, and all, and he gives me the stuck-in with such a mortal motion that it is inevitable; and on the answer, he pays you as surely as your feet hits the ground they step on.
>
> (3.4.264–68)

This mighty aspect of Viola/Cesario is enough for Sir Andrew to reject the fight – "Pox on't, I'll not meddle with him" (3.4.270) – demonstrating the absence of honorable prowess and heroic virility, even though after a subsequent duel he ends up with the wounded head, which is the sort of wound often reserved for the opponent in romances, as the above example from *Parismus* illustrates. While the account of Parismus's clash with Zoylus and Ramon echoes with the rhetoric of fury, the clamor of clashing arms, and the groans of wounded men, the language of the duel in *Twelfth Night* characterizes a comic reversal of the militant eloquence from Forde, where the death metaphor is used to invoke humor ("at this moment [Sir Andrew] is so implacable that satisfaction can be none by pangs of death and sepulcher. 'Hob nob' is his word, give't or take't," says Sir Toby [3.4.229–31]). At this point, *Twelfth Night* comments on the kind of a chivalric clash – of one knight instigating a battle with another – that *Parismus* promotes, in Viola's remark on the cause of the duel with Sir Andrew she is about to face: "I have heard of some kind of men that put quarrels purposely on others, to taste their valour. Belike this is a man of that quirk" (3.4.234–36). Sir Toby's denial of this statement ("Sir, no" [3.4.237]), however, suggests that a different kind of duel is about to take place. As a cultural practice exemplifying and proving virility, the duel has already started to be regarded as a crude behavior and rude fashion in a culture of civil courtesy and polite manners. If, in *Parismus*, the knightly clash promotes heroic valor, in *Twelfth Night* it legitimizes the resistance to chivalric violence and promotes masculinity tamed by passions, not spurred by its militancy. Characters playing chivalric knights in this comedy, then, appear to be an "aesthetic anachronism" (Smith 2000, 45), insofar as they imitate a heroic stance that has gone out fashion. Shakespeare's farcical knights are humorous because they attempt to emulate the masculinity of violence that can no longer be accommodated by the period in which masculinity and honor are categories of the social rank, not militant display. It comes as no surprise, then, that when Sir Toby urges Viola to "forswear to wear iron about" herself (3.4.243), she reacts with surprise: "This is as uncivil as strange" (3.4.244). And masculine violence is something to which Olivia, too, disapproves, referring to the duel as "uncivil and unjust" (4.1.51). These responses, which capture female shock at masculine violence, are tempered, though only just, by the clash between Orsino and Antonio in 5.1. When faced with Antonio, Orsino, the lover, can easily resort to the symbolism of war and the language of ire when he confronts Antonio: "That face of his I do remember well, / Yet when I saw it last it was besmeared / As black as Vulcan in the smoke of war" (5.1.45–47). However, Antonio, the "salt-water thief" (5.1.63), as Orsino has just called him, offers not a combat of words in return, but, justifying his presence in Illyria, reveals to the audience the full account of his story of Sebastian: he and the youth lived together for three months. Here is Antonio: "Today, my lord, and for three months before, / No int'rim, not a minute's vacancy, / Both day and night did we keep company" (5.1.89–91). Their cohabitation "day and night" within the private space for homosocial intimacy represents part of the masculine queer plot in *Twelfth Night*. Antonio's reference to his living with Sebastian draws attention to the intimate nature of that cohabitation precisely because it is the account of an action that has not been shown in the play.

Scene 4 of act 3 is a memorable comic scene in *Twelfth Night* mostly because of Sir Andrew's buffoonery that accompanies his pseudo-heroic posture and Sir Toby's inadequacy as a soldier-knight. Yet, there is something more to this scene. What *Twelfth Night* takes from *Parismus* is the exemplifying force of a chivalric combat as disruptive of civility, as a need to tame "upper-class violence" (Peltonen 2003, 67). But *Twelfth Night* emphasizes the inappropriateness of militant masculine violence by showing low-class men fight as if they were knights. It is partially through this violation of decorum (not just the clumsiness of the combatants), then, that heroic masculinity is also mocked in this play. To be a man in *Twelfth Night* means not to fight, not even to fight well, but to be made aware of how out of place chivalric posturing is in the world of romantic wooing. The chivalric masculinity of *Parismus* and its comic reversal in *Twelfth Night* capture, in differing ways, the spirit of times that considered the masculine violence of chivalry an ideal of the past. Forde's narrative represents nostalgia for the world of chivalry that was still part of the historical memory of his times. In turning the chivalric mode to comedy Shakespeare, however, reminds us of the other side of the reception of chivalry in the sixteenth and seventeenth centuries oriented towards civic humanist virtues: disapproval of the late medieval culture of chivalric violence.[10] Samuel Daniel captures well that shift from the heroic English past to its emasculated present, when he describes the late sixteenth century as the time "not of virility as the former [of the Plantagenets], but more subtle" (A3r). It is his time's subtlety, its softened virility emerging with the decline of the knight that Shakespeare sees just as the perfect material for comedy. In the scene that I have just discussed, Shakespeare criticizes chivalric violence and mocks civic masculinity parading as chivalric.

Even the setting for the duel determines the status of masculinity in romances. While the combat in *Parismus* takes place in an open outside world, a type of location that Cooper identifies as the "masculine space" (2004, 53), the pseudo-chivalric encounter in *Twelfth Night* occurs in the orchard within the merry and idle, feminine world of Olivia's household. The emasculated knight involved in the "triumph" of this un-chivalric clash turns into the caricature of chivalric masculinity, without being aware of it. Here is Sir Toby on the subject:

> Go, Sir Andrew. Scout me for him at the corner of the orchard like a bum-baily. So soon as ever thou seest him, draw, and as thou draw'st, swear horrible, for it comes to pass oft that a terrible oath, with a swaggering accent sharply twanged off, gives manhood more approbation than ever proof itself would have earned him.
>
> (3.4.170–75)

It is the swagger and swearing, not valor and honor, that define masculinity at this point. These acts are a burlesque of heroic masculinity and the play could be said to lament the loss of heroic comportment in a world in which romantic masculinity has replaced the chivalric masculine ideal of militant valor.

The locus of much current criticism on the meaning of gender and erotic desire in *Twelfth Night* has been Viola's cross-dressing. While the motif is not uncommon in romantic comedies, including Shakespeare's Italian sources and Terence's *The Eunuch*, structurally Viola's disguise as the page Cesario resembles Violetta's disguise in the page Adonius in *Parismus*. A curious difference between the effect of disguise in Forde and Shakespeare shows that while in *Twelfth Night* it is cross-dressing itself that raises suspicion about the anatomical gender underneath the clothes (witness Orsino's early enthusiasm about the "[d]ear lad" with whom "all is semblative a woman's part" [1.4.30–34]), in *Parismus* the narrative does not question the biological gender, but wrongly gendered eloquence: a boy is not supposed to speak wisely, as a man would. Shortly before this scene, which reveals that Violetta is a woman in man's disguise, Pollipus listens to "her" long account of Parismus's heroic actions and his love for Laurana. After Violetta/Adonius finishes speaking, Pollipus is confused about the page's sophisticated use of the "conceits" and wondered "to see such wisedome in a Boy: but by reason that shee was taken to bee no other than a Boy, hee entred into no deeper consideration of her actions" (Dd3r). It appears that the gendering of the boy by using "shee" and "her" indicates the uncertainty about gender. It is more apparent, in fact, that Pollipus is less confused by the effeminacy of the boy (which is not surprising given the history of gendering the boy figure in literature as master-mistress-like) than by the fact that the boy speaks as a wise man.[11] Masculine disguise in *Parismus* is a narrative device by which pleasure is deferred until the end. But if the narrative does not question the gender, only the stage of maturity, it is because disguise, like rhetoric, is here employed to take control of a woman's body, which is a narrative strategy that befits a masculinist narrative of the formation of patriarchy.[12] The larger context of the scene explains Pollipus's surprise. Namely, the content of Violetta–Adonius's story is the separation of Parismus from Laurana and the pain the separated lovers experience as they quest for each other. That story contrasts the present moment when two separated lovers, Pollipus and Violetta, are actually finding each other, without knowing it yet. The story of a missing friend's beloved is thus juxtaposed with the scene of lovers getting together, and the rhetoric about the suffering because of the separation is replaced by an actual union. Thus, the story of the amorous constancy of Parismus and Laurana also provides a model for the union of Pollipus and Violetta, about to occur while Violetta is still in the page's disguise. It is another instance of re-imagining masculinity in the romance, neither through masculine apparel,[13] nor through chivalric acts, but through the character's ability to speak persuasively in romantic situations.

In *Parismus* disguise is a transparent stratagem that does not self-consciously play with the gendered body behind male clothes, a strategy that *Twelfth Night* comments on. In chapter XVII, when Parismus dons palmer's disguise, he makes it known to Violetta only; similarly, Parismus is the only character aware of Violetta's disguise into the young page Adonius. Yet, when in the last chapter, Violetta/Adonius spends a night of amorous play with Pollipus and is in the morning discovered in bed with him by Parismus, the disguise does not become a source of same-sex titillation. Although surprised by the recognition of Adonius's real gender, Pollipus says in a matter-of-fact way:

> I know not what to coniecture, nor how to behaue my selfe, nor whether I should call you *Adonius*, or *Violetta*, considering how unlikely it is she should be so kind to me, and how certaine I am that *Adonius* hath done me manifolde pleasures. Then sweate *Violetta* (if you are shee) resolue mee of this my doubt, being thereby driue[*n*] to that hopefull despaire, that I know not whether my fortune bee better or worse then it was.
>
> (F4r)[14]

To this Violetta, "thinking a little back" (F4r), replies: "Pardone mee deere *Pollipus*, for I am your unworthie friend *Violetta* that haue in this disguise, made trial of my fortune [*and*] your friendship" (F4r). The scene resembles the recognition moment at the end of *Twelfth Night*, when Viola's disguise is revealed but Orsino does not seem to be confused by the error of gender, confirmed in his lines to Viola: "since you called me master for so long, / Here is my hand, you shall from this time be / Your master's mistress" (5.1.315–17). Apart from the structural similarities between these two scenes, they are also closely related by the absence of anxiety over sexual confusion. In

Parismus, this absence is further emphasized by the fact that a long narrative block that precedes the recognition scene involves a detailed account of soft pornography describing the night Violetta–Adonius spends in bed with Pollipus. So, at the end of both *Parismus* and *Twelfth Night* cross-dressing does not either compromise masculinity or incur anxiety over the object of erotic desire. Clearly, in *Parismus*, the status and stability of masculinity are not dependent upon either clothing or disguise. In that, this romance resists the kind of warning against the danger of the excess of apparel on masculinity, expressed in a homily by the Bishop of Salisbury, which warns that "many men are become so effeminate, that they care not what they spend in disguising themselves" (quoted in Smith 2001, 242). Even though the homily implies that appropriating new fashions, not cross-dressing, is either a foreign habit or transgresses one's social rank, the intent is to draw attention to the deception and danger to masculinity weakened by (hence metaphorically disguised in) luxurious clothing.

Parismus's melancholy has its counterpart in Orsino, also a lover who quests for his desired object from the opening to the closing scene. But Shakespeare increases the dramatic meaning of Orsino's love for Olivia by complicating Orsino's desire with the introduction of Viola cross-dressed as Cesario. Forde specifies the locus of sorrow in Parismus: the loss of Laurana to the Tartarian pirates in a tempest. After a tempest separated Laurana from Parismus, together with Pollipus and Violetta–Adonius, he is washed ashore on the "Desolate Iland" (S1r) and starts blaming "the compasse of [his] reason" (S1v) that failed him in salvaging Laurana. Yet, while Parismus curses the sea as an enemy that separated him from his beloved and shipwrecked the rest of their crew on a desert island, Pollipus pleads "patience" and "most prudentlie gouerned himselfe" (S1r), suggesting that only further travel, not lament, can lead to "the happie chaunce [that] we can once finde out . . . that is become of Laurana." In the meantime, he urges, "let us endure the searche for her diligently, for I vowe, that if shee be any where to be founde, I will never desist trauaile" (S2r). The effect of this speech so "reuiued *Parismus*, that hee althogether abandoned that effeminate kinde of griefe and lamentation" (S2v). The narrative of *Parismus*, thus, contrasts the effeminizing "inward sorrow" (S2v) that emasculates heroic men to the virile and prudent masculine resoluteness that proposes pragmatic action in the episodes of a heroic display of power. This contrast indicates what constitutes masculine agency and prowess, capturing the sense that "Masculinity . . . is knowable only in terms of the things it is not," of which Bruce R. Smith identifies, in the early modern period, four: "women, foreigners, persons of lower social rank, and sodomites" (Smith 2000, 104). Yet, one could say that all four categories are present in *Twelfth Night*, if we consider the Antonio–Sebastian relationship as potentially sodomitical.[15]

What characterizes masculinity in the shipwreck episode is the constancy and determination with which Pollipus treats his friend's mission, when melancholy overtakes him. In contrast, Feste criticizes Orsino's "changeability and inconstancy" (Shakespeare 1995, 138):

> Now the melancholy god protect thee, and the tailor make thy doublet of changeable taffeta, for thy mind is a very opal. I would have men of such constancy put to sea, that their business might be everything, and their intent everywhere, for that's it that always makes a good voyage of nothing.
>
> (2.4.72–76)

In fact, throughout *Twelfth Night*, Orsino's masculinity is determined more by his relationships with Cesario as an object of his desire and his pose of a melancholy lover than by his actions. In fact, his melancholy displaces him from the world of action into the sphere of emasculating contemplation, as he confirms to Cesario:

> For boy, however we do praise ourselves,
> Our fancies are more giddy and uniform,
> More longing, wavering, sooner lost and worn,
> Than women's are.
>
> (2.4.31–34)

If, in *Twelfth Night*, to be a man is not to be a woman, the kind of man closest to a woman is the man in love. And just as Pollipus is willing to endure any labor on his way to help his friend find his abducted beloved, Laurana ("I will neuer desist trauails until I can come to heare some happie tidings of her abode" [S2r–v]), so is Antonio willing to encounter danger if it brings him closer to Sebastian, as he says to him: "I do adore thee so / That danger shall seem sport, and I will go" (2.1.42–43). There is something of a heroic stance characteristic of the lover-knight from prose romances that characterizes Antonio's and Pollipus's roles. It is determination that gives both Antonio's and Pollipus's masculinity heroic qualities that distinguish them from the two lovers, Orsino and Parismus (in the scene in which he is overtaken by love) rendered passive (by love), inward-looking, and lacking in energy and resoluteness. *Twelfth Night* rejects the stereotype of noble humanist masculinity as an ideal and even attractive object of love, which is clear in an exchange between Viola and Olivia, in a scene in which Viola promotes her master Orsino to Olivia:

> *Olivia.* How does he love me?
> *Viola.* With adorations, fertile tears,
> *Olivia.* With groans that thunder love, with sighs of fire.
> Your lord does know my mind, I cannot love him.
> I suppose him virtuous, know him noble,

Of great estate, of fresh and stainless youth,
In voices well divulged, free, learn'd, and valiant,
And in dimension and the shape of nature
A gracious person; but yet I cannot love him.
(1.5.246–50)

Olivia's catalogue of Orsino's superlative qualities invokes not just an ideal Renaissance nobleman but also, by implication, an eligible marriage opportunity to any Renaissance woman looking to be married. Yet, although the dramatic situation dictates that Orsino be rejected – so that the titillating emotional thrill of the actions and verbal exchanges between Viola and Olivia can continue – Olivia's remarkable praise of him only enhances the sense of cultural loss for not accepting that masculine ideal. But in doing so, Olivia's rejection also resists both the cultural stereotype of an ideal aristocratic male – which suits a play that undermines other cultural stereotypes, such as sexuality, gender, class, honor, and entitlement – and privileges the uncertainty of the ambiguous masculinity of a low-status page. But there may be more to Olivia's rejection of Orsino. What makes Viola a more attractive object of amorous exchanges is, among other attributes, "actions" (1.5.282), as Olivia says of Viola's acts and behavior. Viola's resoluteness and perseverance, like Pollipus's and Antonio's determination, are presented as attractive qualities that give Viola vital energy. It is that energy that Orsino interprets as desire in Viola's attraction to him in their initial meetings. And it is that verve and amorous energy that make Viola an attractive character in the audience's eyes. As models of an active agency upon which the development of the plot depends, Pollipus and Antonio are privileged over the languishing passivity of the lover defined by the lack of action. Similarly, it is at the point at which Parismus's heart is tormented (S2r) by his thoughts of the abducted Laurana that Pollipus acts and moves the plot forward. Despite the fact that masculinity is a subject of conversation in *Twelfth Night*, it is Cesario's performed masculinity that in fact moves the plot forward, just as it is Parismus's and Pollipus's determination to be united with their beloveds that moves the plot of *Parismus* towards the romance's desired end: marriage and the restoration of order.

What we, then, witness in *Parismus* and *Twelfth Night* are two different, if at times overlapping, approaches to masculinity in a genre that is ultimately concerned with marriage, reproduction, and the establishment of household. While Forde's narrative insists on the heroic status of men until the end, masculinity in *Twelfth Night* is reassessed in actions that compromise and test the limits of masculine definitions. Shakespeare's play appeared at the time when romantic masculinity invested in courtship and household management took over as a representational (and cultural) model from the heroic masculinity of the earlier heroic times. But the late sixteenth- and seventeenth-century nostalgia for chivalry that prevails in both dramatic and prose romances of the period survives in *Twelfth Night* in such a way that the play opposes heroic masculinity by parodying it, and promotes and mocks forms of romantic masculinity in a variety of plot situations, such as courtship, seduction, marriage, or queer bonding. This variation in the representation of masculinity is the reason that *Twelfth Night*, despite its focus on the cross-dressed body and its sexual signification, is in fact more interested in social status than sex, because the culture has started to define masculinity more according to parentage and social rank and less according to heroic achievements. Those characters who have socially risen by their actions rather than birth – Maria, Sebastian, and Viola – indicate the play's interest in promoting individual agency over gender. In juxtaposing the scenes of effeminate romantic masculinity of Orsino with the parodic heroic masculinity of Sir Toby and Sir Andrew, *Twelfth Night* sets up competing interpretations of events that reimagine the shift from heroic to romantic masculinity. And while *Twelfth Night* makes Orsino's romantic masculinity the subject of comedy, it does not subject to either criticism or mockery Antonio's melancholy homoerotic masculinity. By leaving Antonio (somewhat awkwardly) without a mate at the end of the play, the play makes his separateness a reminder that not all forms of masculinity belong to the expected cultural categories that fit the conventional ending of romance bustling with matrimonial ceremonies and happiness.

Notes

1. There are also similarities between *Twelfth Night* and Robert Greene's romance *Gwydonius* which have not yet been assessed. For example, the male character in the subplot of Greene's romance, Orlanio, reacts to Gwydonius, a shipwrecked youth seeking service in his household, just as Orsino does when Cesario appears at his door requesting service. Here is Greene: "Orlanio, hearing this dutiful discourse of Gwydonius, marking his manners, and musing at this modesty, noting both his excellent courtesy and exquisite beauty, was so inflamed with friendly affection towards this youth that not only he accepted of his service but also preferred him as a companion to his son Thersandro, promising that since he had left his country and parents for this cause, he would so countervail his dutiful desert with favor and friendship as he should never have cause to accuse him of ingratitude" (2001, 97). While the reference to Orlanio's son is a departure into a more clearly normative household from Orsino's melancholy and solitary dukedom, the impulse to respond to a shipwrecked youth with such inflamed and affectionate enthusiasm resembles the affective basis of the corresponding dramatic situation in *Twelfth Night*. The setting and geography of *Twelfth Night* was also influenced by Barnabe Riche's fiction *Brusanus* (1592) and Thomas Goodwin's translation from Latin of William Caxton's romance *Blanchardine* (1595).
2. While Elizabeth Foyster, in *Manhood in Early Modern England*, offers an account of the socio-historical changes that masculinity underwent in the sixteenth and seventeenth centuries, Lorna Hutson documents this shift as reflected in imaginative literature of that period, in her book *The Usurer's Daughter*.

3. For romance reading classes, see Newcomb (2002).
4. Stephen Greenblatt's essay "Fiction and Friction"; Thomas Laquer's influential book, *Making Sex*; and Catherine Belsey's essay "Disrupting Sexual Difference: Meaning and Gender in the Comedies" have been hugely influential of this line of criticism.
5. Romances came out of the crusades, nostalgia for the world of Christian chivalry, overseas exchanges and contacts between (Western and Eastern) men, and anti-Turkish sentiments. The East, as Constance Relihan (1997) has argued, is excised from *Twelfth Night*, though it resonates in the background of Illyria as a Venetian colony in the eastern Adriatic.
6. See, for example, Stanley Wells and Roger Warren's edition of *Twelfth Night* in the new Oxford Shakespeare series of individual plays (Shakespeare 1995, 13). Throughout this essay, I quote *Twelfth Night* from this edition.
7. Wells and Warren provide a brief account of the shared motifs between Forde's romance and Shakespeare's play (1995, 18–19).
8. Since "Apolonius and Silla" as a source for *Twelfth Night* has been the subject of a numerous studies, as documented in two bibliographies of criticism on early modern prose fiction prepared by James L. Harner, I will leave it out from my discussion.
9. Writing about the decline and transformation of the chivalric culture from medieval to Tudor times, Arthur B. Ferguson posits, in the chapter "Chivalry and the Education of the Citizen" of his 1960 book, that the sixteenth-century citizen would look back to the culture of militant chivalry of the medieval period both with nostalgia for a heroic past and horror of the violence that culture entailed (182–221).
10. Arthur B. Ferguson (1960 and 1965) writes persuasively about the perception of late medieval chivalry in the humanist sixteenth century.
11. Stephen Orgel makes a distinction between the cultural gendering of boys, women, and men (1996a, 68–73).
12. Patricia Parker (1987) explores the link between the rhetoric of economics and the control of a woman's body in *Cymbeline* and in the "lexicon of merchandizing" (130) in *Twelfth Night*.
13. Orgel (1996b) discusses the relationship between emasculation and effeminacy, and male clothing in the visual culture's representations of masculinity.
14. The pagination in the last chapter is erroneously set as the signature F.
15. This relationship has been read as homoerotic and potentially sodomitical by Joseph Pequigney (1985, 22–23), Paul Hammond (2002, 97–100), Mario DiGangi (1997, 38–42), and Jonathan Goldberg (1992, 108, 142).

Works cited

Adelman, Janet. "Making Defect Perfection: Shakespeare and the One-Sex Model." In *Enacting Gender on the English Renaissance Stage*. Ed. Viviana Comensoli and Anne Russell. Urbana and Chicago: University of Illinois Press, 1999: 23–52.

Barber, C. L. "Testing Courtesy and Humanity in *Twelfth Night*." In *Shakespeare's Festive Comedies*. Cleveland and New York: Meridian Books, 1963: 240–61.

Belsey, Catherine. "Disrupting Sexual Difference: Meaning and Gender in the Comedies." In *Alternative Shakespeares*. Ed. John Drakakis. London and New York: Methuen, 1985: 166–90.

Cave, Terence. *Recognitions: A Study in Poetics*. Oxford: Clarendon, 1990.

Caxton, William. *The moste pleasaunt historye of Blanchardine, sonne to the King of Friz, & the faire lady Eglantine Queene of Tormaday*. Trans. Thomas P. Goodwin. London: William Blackewall, 1595.

Cooper, Helen. *The English Romance in Time: Transforming Motifs from Geoffrey of Monmouth to the Death of Shakespeare*. Oxford: Oxford University Press, 2004.

Daniel, Samuel. *The First Part of the Histories of England*. London: Nicholas Okes, 1612.

DiGangi, Mario. *The Homoerotics of Early Modern Drama*. Cambridge: Cambridge University Press, 1997.

Ferguson, Arthur B. "Chivalry and the Commonwealth." In *The Indian Summer of English Chivalry: Studies in the Decline and Transformation of Chivalric Idealism*. Durham, NC: Duke University Press, 1960: 105–41.

——. *The Articulate Citizen and the English Renaissance*. Durham, NC: Duke University Press, 1965.

Forde, Emanuel. *The First Part of Parismus the Renowmed Prince of Bohemia*. London: Thomas Creede, 1598.

Foyster, Elizabeth A. *Manhood in Early Modern England: Honour, Sex and Marriage*. London and New York: Longman, 1999.

Goldberg, Jonathan. *Sodometries: Renaissance Texts, Modern Sexualities*. Stanford, CA: Stanford University Press, 1992.

Greenblatt, Stephen. "Fiction and Friction." In *Shakespearean Negotiations: The Circulation of Social Energy in Renaissance England*. Oxford: Clarendon Press, 1990: 66–93.

Greene, Robert. *Gwydonius, or The Card of Fancy*. Ed. Carmine G. Di Biase. Ottawa: Dovehouse Editions, 2001.

Hammond, Paul. *Figuring Sex between Men from Shakespeare to Rochester*. Oxford: Clarendon Press, 2002.

Harner, James L. *English Renaissance Prose Fiction, 1500–1660: An Annotated Bibliography of Criticism*, 2nd edn. Boston: G. K. Hall, 1978.

——. *English Renaissance Prose Fiction, 1500–1660: An Annotated Bibliography of Criticism (1984–1990)*. New York: G. K. Hall, 1992.

Hutson, Lorna. "On Not Being Deceived: Rhetoric and the Body in *Twelfth Night*." *Texas Studies in Literature and Language* 38 (1996): 141–74.

——. *The Usurer's Daughter: Male Friendship and Fictions of Women in Sixteenth-Century England*. London and New York: Routledge, 1994.

Laqueur, Thomas. *Making Sex: Body and Gender from the Greeks to Freud*. Cambridge, MA, and London: Harvard University Press, 1992.

Leggatt, Alexander. *Shakespeare's Comedy of Love*. London and New York: Methuen, 1974.

Newcomb, Lori Humphrey. *Reading Popular Romances in Early Modern England*. New York: Columbia University Press, 2002.

Orgel, Stephen. "Call Me Ganymede." In *Impersonations: The Performance of Gender in Shakespeare's England*. Cambridge: Cambridge University Press, 1996a: 53–82.

——. "Masculine Apparel." In *Impersonations: The Performance of Gender in Shakespeare's England*. Cambridge: Cambridge University Press, 1996b: 83–105.

Palfrey, Simon. *Late Shakespeare: A New World of Words*. Oxford: Clarendon Press, 1999.

Parker, Patricia. "Rhetorics of Property: Exploration, Inventory, Blazon." In *Literary Fat Ladies: Rhetoric, Gender, Property*. London: Methuen, 1987: 126–54.

Peltonen, Markku. *The Duel in Early Modern England: Civility, Politeness and Honour*. Cambridge: Cambridge University Press, 2003.

Pequigney, Joseph. *Such is My Love: A Study of Shakespeare's Sonnets*. Chicago and London: University of Chicago Press, 1985.

Relihan, Constance C. "Erasing the East from *Twelfth Night*." In *Race, Ethnicity, and Power in the Renaissance*. Ed. Joyce Green MacDonald. Madison, NJ: Fairleigh Dickinson University Press, 1997: 80–94.

Riche, Barnabe. "Apolonius and Silla." In *His Farewell to Military Profession*. Ed. Donald Beecher. Ottawa and Binghampton, NY: Dovehouse Editions and Medieval and Renaissance Texts and Studies, 1992: 180–201.

Shakespeare, William. *Twelfth Night*. Ed. Roger Warren and Stanley Wells. Oxford: Oxford University Press, 1995.

Smith, Bruce R. *Shakespeare and Masculinity*. Oxford: Oxford University Press, 2000.

——, ed. *Twelfth Night*. Boston and New York: Bedford/St. Martins, 2001.

7 Post-communist nights

Shakespeare, essential masculinity, and Western citizenship

Marcela Kostihová

Since the Velvet Revolution of 1989, Shakespeare's *Twelfth Night* has become one of the popular staples in Czech theatres, offering Czech audiences a variety of productions in venues ranging from student stages to outdoor festivals to the National Theatre. Among the multiple contemporary foci generated by recent Czech interpretations of the play, masculinity stands out as perhaps the most complex and yet unexamined site of convergence between the Renaissance text and the current socio-political context. In my analysis, I am interested in post-communist Czech interpretations of the discourse of masculinity this play emphasizes in the keen competition between various masculine models for prominence and partnership. I foreground the practices of staging Antonio and Sebastian, two characters who simultaneously exhibit the most traditional masculine traits and affection for each other, presenting contemporary directors with the challenge of representing a complex and socially acceptable Renaissance bond to a subtly and subversively homophobic audience likely to read the characters' desires, if their speech is unedited, as evidence of emasculating homosexuality.

Considering Shakespeare's global function as a powerful cultural icon and a nation-building tool, an analysis of traditionally controversial masculinities in recent Czech Shakespeare productions reveals political struggles attendant on the process of redefinition of post-communist Czech nationhood and of the identity of the individual. In the anxiety produced by the unraveling of an already unstable system wherein communist ideology competed with a resistant undercurrent of ambiguously defined Czechness that hailed from Czech historic roots and traditions, Shakespeare has served as a welcome repository of universal truisms about human nature that could be used to negotiate instability and confusion. My analysis of Shakespearean masculinity presented in two recent Czech productions, Enikő Ezsenyi's *Twelfth Night* in the National Theatre (2001) and Viktor Polesný's *Twelfth Night* at the 2005 Summer Shakespeare Festival, exemplifies not only general understanding of masculinity in Shakespeare, but also the complex process of unstable redefinition of post-communist Western identity. Ultimately, I suggest that Czech Shakespeare productions reveal a great anxiety about the potential of widening the definition of masculinity to include alternative identities or behaviors. Despite the extensive West-initiated changes to the legal system accompanied by suitable public discourse, these *Twelfth Night* productions betray a deep ambivalence about accepting homosexuality as one of the natural variants of human behavior and identity.

When it comes to gender roles in general and masculinity in particular, the decade following the Velvet Revolution teemed simultaneously with multilayered change energized by the promise of a "free future" and, inevitably, with much tension, anxiety, and confusion. The culture on the whole seems to have gleefully rejected the communist-imposed requirements of gender equality on all levels of social existence, looking to replace them with more acceptable, arguably "Western" notions of gender and sexuality. Such notions would keep with the two-fold desire to "return" into the fold of (Western) European countries and also a return to essential Czech nationhood, overshadowed by four decades of Soviet ideological presence. The renegotiations have been unavoidably complicated by the lack of clear perception of what such nationhood might entail. They have uncovered, instead, the complex cultural constructions of national identities dependent on dominant perceptions of the national historical continuum, dominant ideologies of individual and collective identity, and political affiliations to other national entities. Overall, post-communist perceptions of gender, in stark contrast to the theoretical communist gender equality, seemed to prefer a more essential view of the sexes that often reminds Western researchers of traditional patriarchal values.

The redefinition of post-communist Czech citizenship – and masculinity at its center – straddles an ideological conflict of differing perceptions of the West. One is upheld as essential "Westernness" that can serve as a future cultural model, the other perceived as the existing cultural and political models of the established "Western" nations, perhaps originally rooted in the essential Westernness but ultimately corrupted by the process of cultural and political developments. While the Czech Republic had intensively lobbied for admittance to the Western European Union, it has simultaneously sought to establish individual, well-delineated national identity that can be seen as separate (and preferably superior to) existing cultural models. Much popular cultural smugness has rested on resisting the rhetoric of "political correctness" of the established West, attended by multiculturalism, feminism, and other forms of widening perceptions of national belonging and agency. Such resistance to hybridity is not unusual in countries recovering from longstanding state, cultural, political, and ideological domination by (an)other national entity, as Edward Said points out in the introduction to *Culture and Imperialism*. In arguing that nation and culture become, in such tense historical moments, often as enmeshed as to seem indistinguishable, (re)building a nation on paths that are to "return" it to its "culture and tradition," Said argues that "these 'returns' accompany rigorous codes of intellectual and moral behavior that are opposed to the permissiveness associated with such relatively liberal philosophies as multiculturalism and hybridity" (1994, xiii).

The desired "return to tradition," paradoxically hailed by many as a "return to Europe," is fueled by a complex, non-homogeneous set of conflicting ideologies, perceptions, and material experiences. For instance, whereas post-1989 government attempted to institute a number of gender-specific codes and laws that would "enable" women to withdraw from the work force into the domestic sphere (a strategy that was meant as a convenient gendered solution to rising unemployment), the simultaneous cuts in state funding for social services, housing construction, as well as inadequate wages, made it impossible for most women to become fully-fledged homemakers, even if they wished such self-transformation. Moreover, though resistant to an expectation of a prescribed communist gender role, women have grown up to expect a society that assumes their material equality: equal access to all strata of education, equal access to social and economic resources, equal pay for equal work, as well as state subsidized health-care and day-care. Instead of withdrawing from public life into traditionally acceptable domestic roles, many women have become viable, widely successful, and threatening competitors for men in the workforce. As elsewhere in the developed world, the average age of marriage has steadily increased from early to late 20s, while the birthrate has steadily fallen. A noticeable proportion of young Czechs has opted out of family formation altogether.

These trends have resulted in an increasingly recognized and documented, widespread existential frustration in the male population, confused by the gradual loss of their inherent position in the culture and frustrated by the marred expectation of a more prosperous future. The onset of capitalism, for the overwhelming majority of men, has resulted in heightened work expectations and a lower standard of living. This "male identity crisis," as political scientist Jacqui True maps out, "is a product of widespread masculine anomie, reflected in the rising male suicide and mortality rates, alcohol abuse, and unemployment and crime rates across the region" since "men have experienced greater stress and difficulty in adjusting to the new economic system than women" (2003, 71). While Czech men do not suffer as much as men in other countries of the post-communist block (such as Russia or Hungary), the crisis of masculinity is palpable, resulting, for instance, as I have argued elsewhere, in rising rates of domestic abuse (Kostihová 2005).

Moreover, in an analysis of post-socialist gender formations in East and East-Central Europe, Susan Gal and Gail Kligman traced the dependence of transitional definitions of nationhood and citizenship on culturally sanctioned perceptions of sexuality which are intimately interlinked with state reproductive policies:

> "citizens" are in many cases implicitly recognized as deserving of that title, and of the set of attendant "rights" by their display of particular

> forms of state-sanctioned, legally acceptable, usually reproductive sexuality. And conversely, the reproduction of citizens is seen as beneficial, judicious, necessary for the future, while the reproduction of those not recognized as such – for instance, immigrants or stigmatized minorities – is seen, for that very reason, as dangerous, out of control, and polluting.
> (Gal and Kligman 2000, 23)

In other words, the process of drawing ideological boundaries around a fledgling nation struggling with the aftermath of Soviet occupation draws on common perceptions of belonging and exclusion. Such perceptions, in turn, depend on unhindered continuation of its constituents through proliferation of its citizenry. Non-reproducing homosexuals, for instance, can be charged with withdrawing their reproductive support for the nation, while homosexuals with a desire to reproduce within the legal framework of the post-communist state threaten the newly redefined social policies on proper (essentially and traditionally conceived) heterosexual reproduction. Not surprisingly, in many Eastern European states, negotiations about citizenship inevitably resulted, as Gal and Kligman attest, in government promises "to uphold the unchanging forces of natural gender order" (2000, 29).

When it comes to understanding male identity and men's relationships with each other, the Czech population in the midst of this identity crisis is reluctant to accept homosexuality as one of the normal variants of human behavior. On the one hand, the culture has largely condoned the communist taboo of the issue; on the other, it has felt the pressure of the West, represented by the European Union, to grant all Czech citizens, including homosexuals, equal human rights. On February 2, 1994, the European Parliament advised its member states to alter their legislations to include homosexual partnership as a protected category and voted by a close majority for same-sex adoption. Though not an explicit requirement for admission to the EU, such "advice," together with similar guidelines about racism and sexism, clearly registered with the society and resulted in rapid, if mostly surface, changes in Czech legislation. During the years immediately following the EU recommendation, there were three attempts to legalize registered partnerships: 1995, 1998, and 1999. Each time, the legislation failed by a narrow margin of two or three votes. A workplace anti-discrimination law was not passed till January 1, 2001. As of December 16, 2005, the Czech Senate – under the pressure of the European Union to which the Czech Republic now belongs – initiated a draft of a law that would provide limited benefits to same-sex couples.

Yet, popular resistance to what is perceived as normalizing the abnormal weakens reluctantly if at all. The anxiety about homosexuality is intimately embedded in the masculinity and "good" citizenship crisis that seems to undermine traditional masculine identities in favor of disorderly gender relations that threaten to create a disorderly society. In addition to men who have forsaken their rightful dominant positions within nuclear heterosexual families and given too much of their power to women, these anxieties target men who have chosen to withdraw from nuclear families altogether and formed alternative, exclusively male communities and partnerships. Far from being concerned solely with the unorthodox gender roles homosexual men are perceived to create (consider, for instance, the myth of the softened, feminized, passive partner paired exclusively with a more masculine "top"), these anxieties uncover a deeper-seated concern with the future of a society no longer exclusively organized in neatly defined heterosexual families and, most importantly, a concern with flawed citizenship at odds with traditional forms of understanding core Western values.

Culturally, the Czech "return to Europe" has resulted in a wealth of creative expression, in which Shakespeare plays an indispensable part. In the social arena of Czech art, one of the prime sites of "culture," the dilemma of representing homosexuality uncovers a deep rift between what is perceived to be True, or "high" art, reportedly representative of humanity itself, and popular "low" art, supposedly bringing the sensation-hungry audiences snippets of latest Western fashions. The steady progression toward legalization of domestic partnership may suggest an increasing tolerance for homosexuality in the Czech culture, indeed reflected in more frequent representations of homosexuality in popular art. For instance, a theatre well known for performing popular American musicals recently produced two pieces with explicit homoerotic and homosexual themes, Jerry Herman and Harvey Fierstein's *Bird Cage* (1998), and Henry Mancini and Blake Edwards's *Victor-Victoria* (2002). Excitingly scandalous for the general Czech audiences, these productions sold enough tickets to sustain the theatre for several seasons. Yet, as much as the audiences flock to see the latest Czech remake of famous Broadway musicals-cum-Hollywood blockbusters, they are deeply ambivalent about sanctifying representations of homosexuality in productions of Shakespeare, the transcendentally universal repository of core models for humanity. For instance, a 2001 rendition of the *Sonnets*, historically the first not to muddle pronouns so that the poems would seem to express heterosexual love, was greeted by a stubborn refusal by theatre critics to review the performance and a rapid decline in audience attendance.[1] Because this performance was artistically sound and its script adhered closely to the pronoun-accurate new translation of Shakespeare's *Sonnets* by a celebrated scholar Martin Hilský, both reviewers and audience recognized that a silent boycott was the only effective response that would preserve the status quo. This suggests that the population at large, as represented by varied theatrical audiences, would prefer to understand homosexuality as a temporary, Western, fleeting "politically-correct" trend that must not threaten the deep-seated understanding of Czech national identity.

Recent performances of *Twelfth Night* are neither as scandalously spectacular as Czech versions of US musicals nor as unambiguously challenging as the 2001 production of the *Sonnets*. As such, they exemplify recent concerns with new definitions of citizenship reflected by a Shakespearean lens. The two recent productions I discuss – Enikő Ezsenyi's *Twelfth Night* in the National Theatre (2001) and Viktor Polesný's *Twelfth Night* at the 2005 Summer Shakespeare Festival – exemplify this conflict and, further, reflect an intriguing divide along the parameters of genre and venue in their representations of masculinity and – in particular – the relationship between Antonio and Sebastian.[2] Prominent, reputable, and well-attended theatres, I found, though eager to present a "contemporary" Shakespeare to affirm that they continue to move "with the times," seem to shy away from exploring the intensity of the characters' emotional commitment to each other, downplaying their interactions and editing their lines. Small theatres, perhaps eager to draw audiences with new material, seem far more likely to take risks in presenting unorthodox readings of Shakespeare's plays, but even there much care is taken that such productions relegate non-traditional masculinities into the realm of the exotic, fantastic, and even ridiculous.

The text of *Twelfth Night* lends itself particularly well to the explorations of various forms of masculinity. Its multiple, sometimes overwhelming references to and examination of manhood suggest that the worth of individual male characters – and their suitability for successful coupling – rests on the kind of masculinity they inhabit. Orsino, though seemingly the most eligible of all bachelors – as Olivia admits herself (1.5.227–31) – is too dangerously close to the stereotype of the soft, effeminate aristocratic courtier, far more invested in a courtly embodiment of the suffering lover than his professed beloved. Sir Toby's lack of resources coupled with his love for drink nearly disqualifies him from the eligible pool. Wealthy Sir Andrew Aguecheek is weighed down by slow wits. Malvolio is hindered by his servant status and undue ambition. Finally, Cesario suffers from his professed eunuch identity. All of the characters fail in the ultimate test of masculinity in their shortcomings as *soldiers*. Their swordsmanship – the ultimate marker of the degree of the phallus they possess – is less than admirable and results in public shaming of various degrees.

The two bachelors who do satisfy – at least initially – Renaissance requirements of eligibility and manhood are Antonio and Sebastian, both of whom do not hesitate to protect their selves, honors, and each other by valiant sword-wielding. These two characters also like each other to a degree that reminds us of a relationship between lovers. In particular, Antonio asserts that for the past three months "no interim, not a minute's vacancy, / Both day and night did we keep company" (5.1.83–85). Deeming himself bewitched (5.1.64), Antonio does not hesitate to risk his life following Sebastian to Orsino's hostile territory, since Sebastian's absence would "murther" him (2.1.35). As he sums it up, he gave Sebastian his "love, without retention or restraint, all his in dedication" (5.1.69–70). Sebastian corroborates this account, proclaiming that, even in his supposed post-nuptial bliss, any time apart from Antonio "rack[s] and torture[s]" him (5.1.203).

Significantly, Antonio's exclamations of love parallel Cesario's, as s/he marches to seemingly certain death at Orsino's hand (5.1.115). Similarly careless of preserving his/her life, Cesario proclaims that he "most . . . willingly . . . a thousand deaths would die" for him whom he loves "More than I love these eyes, more than my life, / More by all mores than e'er I shall love wife" (5.1.122–26). Aptly, this speech, etched into Orsino's memory, ultimately brings Cesario the husband s/he desires once s/he sheds gender ambiguity and turns woman again (252–53). Unlike Viola, Antonio fails to earn a husband by his proclamations of love for Sebastian, though he perhaps retains the position of Sebastian's bosom friend. After all, the ending of the play does not provide a clear delineation of any of the characters' emotional trajectories, and Antonio's textual silence could equally signal either his dismissal from the play (a common interpretation in current productions) or his complacent figuration as Sebastian's primary male companion in no competition with Sebastian's marital duties to Olivia.

The potential for longevity of Antonio and Sebastian's relationship past the closing of the play is further strengthened by Renaissance discourse of friendship and masculinity, wherein same-sex affection between two "bosom" friends, often expressed in language that we may consider erotic, functioned as a pinnacle model of true loyalty. In a world of innate inequalities, where all are bound to frameworks of vertical service, a voluntary, mutual – and sometimes sexual – relationship between men of similar social standing marks one of the few venues for a genuine connection. Contrary to twentieth-century terminology, the label "effeminate," in the Renaissance, applied to a man who spent – or desired to spend – a disproportionate amount of time away from the masculine pursuits of arms and exercise in the company of women (like *Twelfth Night*'s Orsino). In contrast, a man who spends his time in male company has an opportunity to grow to true masculinity and arms. As Stephen Orgel pointed out in *Impersonations*, Antonio is one of the exemplary "real" men in the Shakespearean canon, a position buttressed by his complete independence from women (1996, 81). Sebastian's continued allegiance to this "fighter/pirate – and lover of boys" may balance Sebastian's initial subservience to Olivia's wishes and ensure the preservation and further development of his masculinity.

Examining Renaissance popular knowledge of these characters, Cynthia Lewis has argued in *Particular Saints* that Renaissance audiences most likely greeted Shakespeare's Antonio and Sebastian with comfortable recognition of a stereotypical pair, who functioned as a model of steadfast friendship. Drawing on medieval and Renaissance hagiography of St. Anthony and St. Sebastian, both of whom eventually became patron saints of a complex network of hospitals caring for those suffering from painful incurable diseases ranging from St. Anthony's fire to syphilis, Lewis argues that

> By the late sixteenth century, the names Antonio and Sebastian alone must have provided a literary-theatrical shorthand to an audience that,

> upon hearing them, would recall a host of possibilities for and expectations of these characters. Most significantly, the audience would have instinctively associated Antonios with extravagant love and with the difficulty of expressing such love as human beings in the human sphere, which is bound by constraints.
>
> (Lewis 1997, 15–16)

In other words, a theatrical pairing of Antonio and Sebastian would have immediately signaled to the audience an imminent representation of characters who struggle to express their literally transcendental love for each other within acceptable earthly boundaries, limited both by human nature (bodies) and nurture (acceptable cultural norms).

Modern directors of *Twelfth Night* productions face a paradoxical dilemma of interpreting the play in a context in which perceptions of masculinity, individuality, and sexuality have changed so profoundly that a one-to-one correspondence with the Renaissance meaning of Shakespeare's text is no longer possible. Because of the current political climate wherein both masculinity and homosexuality are contentious at best, any interpretation of Antonio and Sebastian's relationship in a contemporary production is political. Individual performances thus reflect an uneasy intersection of a director's reading of the text and willingness to challenge the text's history on the stage and in literary criticism, as well as the unsheddable baggage of Shakespeare's author function as the genius of "all time." While no interpretation can approximate the complex Renaissance understanding of masculinity in *Twelfth Night*, these performances speak volumes about current tensions between traditional and redefined views on what makes or breaks a "true" man. Further, in the Czech Republic, the questions attendant on new definitions of masculinity make visible the minute details of the process of constructing a new "Western" identity, an identity (perhaps wishfully) taken for granted in most of the "developed" world.

Enikő Ezsenyi's production at Stavovské Divadlo, one of the stages of the Czech National Theatre, though in many ways presenting an alternative view of the play, let the homoerotic themes present in the text lie by the wayside. Contemporary in setting, which happens to be a run-down wintery country farm, this version comes across as a spectacle of stunning stage design and costumes. It underscores the themes of wealth, leisure, and relaxation and, most notably, sex. Almost every instance of Shakespeare's sexual innuendo seems to have been not only duly noted, but also transformed into a corresponding (mostly non-verbal) stage action. Figure 7.1, for instance, captures the production's unambiguous take on the nature of Sebastian and Olivia's connection. Catching them, literally, in the passionate act, Ezsenyi's *Twelfth Night* removes any doubt about the sincerity of Sebastian's sexual ardor for Olivia. The only sexual innuendos that are conveniently omitted are those suggested between the potential same-sex couples, Olivia and Cesario and

Figure 7.1 Olivia and Sebastian, *Twelfth Night*, director: Enikő Ezsenyi, 2002. Courtesy of Hana Smejkalová, photographer.

Antonio and Sebastian. Again, elaborate non-verbal action guides the audience in viewing the possible same-sex connection as volatile and violent (see Figure 7.2, overleaf).

In this setting, Antonio appears more interesting as a wealthy, hypermasculine but ultimately socially deviant, gun-toting blade-swinging drug lord than an object of or subject to affection regarding Sebastian who, in turn, is freed from the emotional complexity of multiple commitments. Antonio functions as a mere detached spectator to Sebastian's commitment to Olivia who subsequently blends into the celebratory wedding fray of act 5. The relationship between Antonio and Sebastian does not serve any particular purpose in the

Figure 7.2 Antonio and Cesario, *Twelfth Night*, director: Enikő Ezsenyi, 2002. Courtesy of Hana Smejkalová, photographer.

play beyond moving the plot forward, thus effectively erasing homosexuality as a positive variant of normal male identity, behavior, and sexuality.

The context of Ezsenyi's *Twelfth Night* makes this erasure profoundly political. Though this production seems carelessly frivolous, and has been dubbed repeatedly as such by disenchanted reviewers,[3] it cannot help taking a political stance by its mere presence at the National Theatre, where the play has a significant stage history. Shakespeare's *Twelfth Night* prematurely closed a season on August 31, 1944, the night before the Fascist regime shut down Czech theatres to repress subversive nationalistic expression. This closing performance is still remembered as profoundly tearful and emotional (Přibyl 2001b, 80–81), anchoring the endangered Czech nation to the higher transcendental values of Shakespeare's text. Once the war ended in May 1945, *Twelfth Night* rapidly returned to the stage on June 20, 1945, barely a month after Soviet tanks rolled into Prague.

In the communist years, the play served further subversive political purposes, centering around Malvolio's supposedly detestable surrender to institutional and political powers (Přibyl 2001b, 84). This view of Malvolio quickly lost its salience in the post-communist era, as the old political framework for understanding the play crumbled together with the old political regime, and the society entered the general confusion of the 1990s. Ezsenyi's production marked the first *Twelfth Night* at the National Theatre in 36 years and the first since the fall of communism. The stakes of a politically charged tradition of interpretation are inevitably high, and the director encountered the challenge of creating a "post-political" version of this well-loved play in a supposedly free democratic culture which professes no need for politics in art.

The confused and piecemeal enactment of the play, we could argue, ultimately does succeed in portraying the absolute fragmentation of post-communist Czech culture. The production seems unsettlingly disjointed, wherein none of the characters are developed into coherent theatrical – not to mention psychological – wholes, and Ezsenyi's *Twelfth Night* becomes a series of loosely organized, independent shots, crafted to amaze by their theatricality, slap-stick acrobatics, and unconventional exposure of body parts. In this context, Sebastian's simplified model of masculinity, that denies his character emotional complexity, indicates only one of the shortcuts the production makes in trying to grapple with the instability of the Czech post-communist culture. The presence of such a fractured production of Shakespeare, a repository of the essence of universal human nature, in the Czech National Theatre, a space traditionally reserved for artistic explorations and validations of the Czech national spirit, implies the current lack of coherence of the essence of Czech nationhood in general and its building blocks – individual identities – in particular. Fittingly, Ezsenyi's *Twelfth Night* was one of the last productions staged before a drastic change in National Theatre leadership in 2004.

In contrast to the highly structured and institutionalized space of the National Theatre, the Summer Shakespeare Festival is a relaxed affair. Staged annually since the mid-1990s in a Renaissance courtyard of a palace in the Prague Castle complex, the plays are billed as high profile "summer entertainment" during the regular theatre "off season," wherein audiences can relax watching high art performed by some of the most celebrated stars of the Czech theatre that they otherwise may glimpse on the film screen. Viktor Polesný's *Twelfth Night* followed suit in 2005 with a cast of high-profile actors

Figure 7.3 Antonio and Sebastian, *Twelfth Night*, director: Viktor Polesný, 2005. Courtesy of Agentura Schok.

and an interpretation of the play that most reviewers found "entertaining." Compared to Ezsenyi's version, Polesný's production focused on coherent plot development and distinctive presentation of consistent individual characters, including those usually considered minor.

For instance, the summer *Twelfth Night* uniquely foregrounds the serious implications of Sir Andrew Aguecheek's courtship of Olivia and highlights his devoted attention to Sir Toby. This ineffective adoration combined with the realization of Olivia's utter indifference to both his suit and his mere existence results in a portrayal of explicit – and laughable – masculine failure, further underscored by frequent comparisons with the ambiguously gendered Cesario. These comparisons then seamlessly crystallize in Cesario's and Aguecheek's staged sword fight in act 3, which makes visible the implicit competition for the embodiment of manhood, one ultimately rooted in the question of the size of the fighters' swords. The two who wield swords effectively and resolutely appear in this performance as a loyal pair (see Figure 7.3). Antonio leads as an older, experienced, wise, and weather-worn seaman, fully aware of the implications of his actions – wielding all of Shakespeare's original lines, traditionally cut in most performances – in proposing to wager his life for Sebastian's proximity. Sebastian's erratic behavior seems rooted in grief for his supposedly drowned sister as well as confusion about the intensity of his connection to Antonio. His positive reaction to Olivia's insistent wooing is reminiscent of a child ushered into a candy store rather than a self-propelled quest for a partner.

In short, unlike other performances of *Twelfth Night*, Polesný's version invites the audience to contemplate the possibility of a complexity of masculinities that stretch beyond the twentieth-century equation of masculinity and exclusive heterosexuality. Antonio and Sebastian, after all, are simultaneously the most masculine and accomplished of the *Twelfth Night* roster and explicitly affectionate toward each other.

In addition to not shying away from a potentially confusing portrayal of Antonio and Sebastian, this production prods further into the assumed centrality of masculinity to human existence. At the close of the play, twentieth-century performances of *Twelfth Night* traditionally make Olivia gleefully accept Sebastian as a rightful substitute – and decided masculine improvement – for the reluctant Cesario. This happy resolution of the dilemma of a woman being in love with a cross-dressed woman is also traditionally accompanied by non-verbal evidence of Olivia's embarrassment at her attachment to Cesario, now unveiled as a "maid." In Polesný's production, Olivia's affection remains with Cesario whom she had passionately kissed earlier in the play, marking one of the first female same-sex kisses in Czech Shakespeare (Figure 7.4), and she shows considerable distress having realized that she has married her beloved's substitute. In that sense, this production radically departs from the tradition of *Twelfth Night* interpretation as well as traditional understanding of gender identity and masculinity. After all, it is

Figure 7.4 Cesario and Olivia, *Twelfth Night*, director: Viktor Polesný, 2005. Courtesy of Ivo Mičkal, photographer.

clear that, in this version, the most eligible bachelorette is not sure that she indeed "needs a man" in her life and is more than ambivalent about the fact that she has been positively tricked into attaching herself to a virtual stranger.[4]

As much as the production breaks out of the mold of asserting traditional models of masculinity as the exclusive template of "normal" male behavior, it simultaneously carefully contextualizes the stage action in frameworks that detract from the urgency of the production's cultural implications. The minimalist outdoor stage (Figure 7.5), used as a backdrop to the entire play, continuously superimposes an aura of the "unusual" and frivolous. Constantly moved and manipulated (the seams of the backdrop reveal where the two smaller wings swing forward), the set of the play further evokes an atmosphere of playfulness and eroticism, presenting the action as delicate yet provocative sexual stimulation, rather than serious discourse.

The sense of erotic playfulness and general entertainment is echoed by the reviewers. Despite the director's and dramaturge's repeated public claims (in varied interviews) that their *Twelfth Night* is a "romantic comedy about love with a bitter melancholic undercurrent and problematic happy end" (rh 2005, 11), as if by mutual consent, none of the performance reviews comment on any of the sexual relationships that nudge the status quo. The reviews generally connect the subtitle, "what you will," with the various forms of love

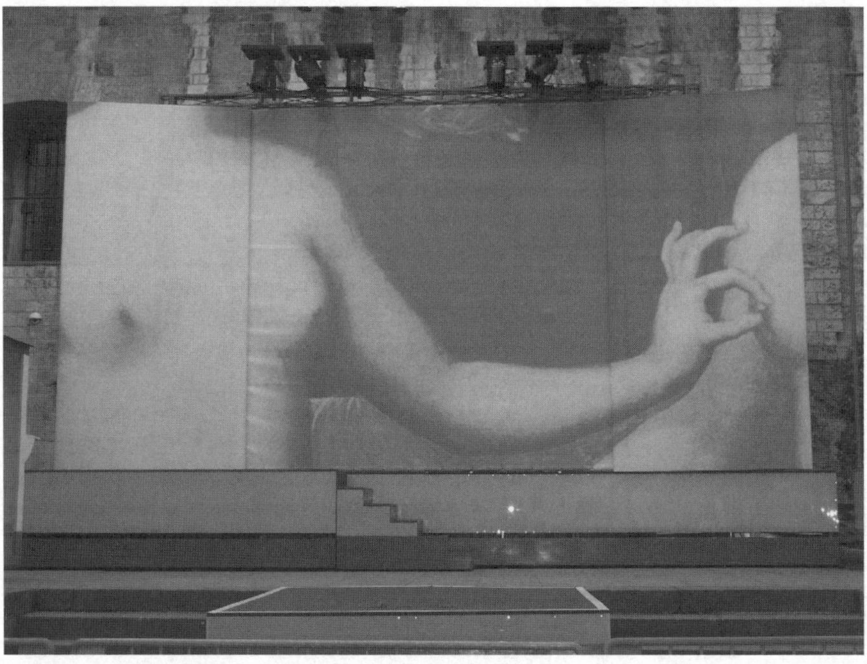

Figure 7.5 Backdrop for Polesný's *Twelfth Night,* stage designer: Petr Matásek. Photographed by author with permission of Agentura Schok.

presented in the play. Some, like Saša Hrbotický's review, exemplary of this approach, even capitalize on the argument of the heterogeneity of erotic expression in this play, stating that the entire play is built on "narratives of various forms of love, ranging from self-deification to selfless self-sacrifice, and, as is typical for the author [Shakespeare], this is enriched by multilayered interpretive possibilities" (2005, 7). Nevertheless, the variety of "love," as described by the reviewers, amounts to the fairly homogeneous complicated and largely unsuccessful heterosexual courtships, led by the connection of Viola to Orsino and the unhappy attraction of Olivia to Cesario. While varied interpretations of the unsuccessful courtship of Olivia by Sir Andrew and Malvolio seem integral to most of the reviews, few mention Sebastian as a happy substitute for Cesario and *none* admits Antonio's existence.

Instead of reading the main characters' ambivalent relationship to their eventual marriage partners as a venue of problematizing the play's generally accepted happy heterosexual resolution, acknowledging the "problematic happy-end" foregrounded by the production's director and dramaturge, reviewers who comment on the production's ending invariably express disappointment with what they perceive as shortcomings in direction or even individual acting skills. Simona Polcarová, for instance, comments on the lack of space that Orsino's character negotiates in this particular production that results in the disappearance of his "confused emotions toward the disguised Viola" which in turn causes the unfortunate result that "the two couples of lovers at the end . . . therefore have the unexpected effect of a fist in the eye" (2005, 15). Similarly, Josef Mlejnek is critical of Viola's diminished attraction to Orsino, which seems lost in light of her "confusion over Olivia's infatuation" as well as of Orsino's seeming lack of interest in Viola at the end, whom he accepts as a suitable face-saving substitute (2005, 3–4). Overall, the reviewers, either unaware of the production's alternative interpretive possibilities or unwilling to disturb the otherwise pleasantly coherent summer entertainment, underscore the view that Polesny's *Twelfth Night* is "a light comedy without an original interpretation, which does not seek to challenge the specific [Summer Shakespeare Festival] audience" (jš 2005, 1).

The response of the reviewers attests not only to the production's tentative presentation of unorthodox behaviors in Shakespeare, but also to the reviewer's own function within a cultural context in which alternative masculinity – positively presented in Shakespeare – is hardly thinkable. Turning a blind eye to the potentially disturbing elements of the production, the reviews turn to issues traditionally brought up in *Twelfth Night* productions, bolstered by the worn-out claim to the "endless multiplicity of interpretive possibilities" ascribed to Shakespeare's genius. In this specific context, I would like to propose, it is this claim to multiplicity in Shakespeare's Greatness that paradoxically intervenes in the interpretive process in significant ways and reduces the number of "viable" readings to those that are acceptable in a given cultural context. The mere weight of Shakespeare's reputation, the sheer volume of Shakespearean scholarship and stage history, most of which aims to distill the essence of human nature Shakespeare's work presumably encompasses, fuel readings of Shakespeare's texts that are profoundly political in sanctifying – or seeking to unsettle – a dominant status quo.

When we examine *Twelfth Night* performances and focus on the various renditions of masculinity they offer, it becomes clear that Shakespeare – despite the text of the play – is handled in ways that, at best, reflect larger confusions about masculinity in the post-communist Czech culture and represent this confusion as profoundly detrimental to the future developments of the country. At worst, these productions reinforce the traditional status quo presented as a template for a viable future of the Czech society. In their ambivalent stance toward homosexuality, the productions signal that the Czech culture in general, however willing to tolerate homosexuality either in the abstract or in the exaggerated representation that is to entertain, seems committed to marginalizing both representations of homosexual desire and homosexuality itself. Willing to extend homosexuals the rights necessary to pass under the watchful eye of the European Union and appease its pressure for legislation of equal human rights, the culture has been so far unable to allow the issue into its field of vision as an everyday reality. In this context, the unwillingness to accept positive representations of homosexuality in Shakespeare plays speaks to both the centrality of Shakespeare to an understanding of Czech national identity, and the unacceptability of homosexuality as a viable form of masculinity.

Notes

1. In interviews, the director, Tomáš Pavlík, and two principal actors, František Kreuzmann and Rostislav Tvrdík, revealed that initially performances sold out, in accordance with the tradition of Czech *Sonnet* stagings. The audiences disappeared once the erotic "bent" of the performance became known. Despite repeated invitations of reviewers, no reviews were published.
2. Between 2000 and 2005, four different theatres staged *Twelfth Night* in Prague alone; in addition to the two I discuss in this essay, *Twelfth Night* was performed at theatres ABC (1999) and Pidivadlo (2002). Since Czech theatres generally function on the repertory model, most of these performances ran for several consecutive seasons and, therefore, at one time or another, competed for the audience's attention. The two I chose for analysis in this limited space were particularly telling for their explicit implications in the nation-building process (Ezsenyi's *Twelfth Night* at the National Theatre) and wide popularity (Polesný's Festival *Twelfth Night*). In terms of exploring masculinity, I found these two performances to be representative of the four versions collectively.
3. A respected Shakespearean, Milan Lukeš, faults the performance for "gags" and attempts to make Shakespeare accessible to the populace which "go so far as to overtake an identifiable contemporaneity by some futuristic vision that is an especially uncomfortable manifestation of outward modernization" (2002, 55). Theatre critics who produce weekly ratings of current performances in *Divadelní*

Noviny awarded Ezsenyi's *Twelfth Night* 2.55 stars out of 5, on a scale where 3 equals "worth seeing" and 2 "at one's own peril" ("Kritický žebříček"2001, 3). Vladimír Mikulka renamed the play "Twelfth Night, or whatever we thought of" (2001, 5), pointing out the jumbled nature of the production, while, in another review, he laments the audience's eagerness to return to see the performance, particularly its explicit sexual content (2002, 25–38, particularly 34).

4. As in most androcentric societies, homosexuality in the Czech Republic is discussed primarily in regards to male–male relationships. This does not indicate that lesbian relationships are explicitly more tolerated or respected; largely, they seem invisible. When made visible (and political), such as in Polesný's *Twelfth Night*, they are simultaneously "sexy" and threatening of masculinity.

Works cited

Gal, Susan and Gail Kligman. *The Politics of Gender after Socialism.* Princeton, NJ: Princeton University Press, 2000.

Kostihová, Marcela. "Katherina 'Humanized': Abusing the 'Shrew' on Prague Stages." In *World-wide Shakespeares: Local Appropriations in Film and Performance.* Ed. Sonia Massai. New York and London: Routledge, 2005: 72–79.

Lewis, Cynthia: *Particular Saints: Shakespeare's Four Antonios, Their Contexts, and Their Plays.* Newark: Delaware University Press, 1997.

Orgel, Stephen. *Impersonations: The Performance of Gender in Shakespeare's England.* Cambridge: Cambridge University Press, 1996.

Přibyl, Daniel. "Anglická inscenační tradice." In *William Shakespeare: Večer tříkrálový aneb cokoli chcete.* Prague: Národní divadlo, 2001a: 56–65.

——. "Večer tříkrálový v Národním divadle." In *William Shakespeare: Večer tříkrálový aneb cokoli chcete.* Prague: Národní divadlo, 2001b: 67–86.

Said, Edward. *Culture and Imperialism.* New York: Vintage Books, 1994.

Shakespeare, William. *Twelfth Night: Texts and Contexts.* Ed. Bruce R. Smith. Boston and New York: Bedford/St. Martin's, 2001.

True, Jacqui. *Gender, Globalization, and Postsocialism: The Czech Republic after Communism.* New York: Columbia University Press, 2003.

Reviews

Hrbotický, Saša. "Večer Tříkrálový humor ani tempo nepostrádá." *Hospodářské Noviny* (July 25, 2005): 7.

jš. "Shakespeare nepřeje dovoleným." *Nedělní Svět* 11: 27 (July 3, 2005): 1.

"Kritický žebříček." *Divadelní Noviny* 18 (May 25, 2001): 3.

Lukeš, Milan. "Shakespeare současný a současnější." *SAD* 1 (2002): 46–61.

Mikulka, Vladimír. "Aneb cokoliv nás napadlo." *Divadelní Noviny* 17 (2001): 5.

——. "Lidem se to líbí – a hotovínko." *Kritická příloha k Revolver Revue* 22 (2002): 25–38.

Mlejnek, Josef. "Přízemnost versus láska ve Večeru Tříkrálovém." *Mladá Fronta Dnes* (June 27, 2005): 3–4.

Paterová, Jana. "Večer plný omylů a lásky: Letní shakespearovské slavnosti 2005 zahájily komedií Večer tříkrálový." *Lidové Noviny* (June 27, 2005).
Polcarová, Simona. "Polesný vsadil na legraci." *Rovnost* (July 26, 2005): 15.
rh. "Shakespearovské slavnosti už zkouší Večer Tříkrálový." *Právo* (April 21, 2005): 11.
"Viktor Polesný: Režírovat Shakespeara je velké dobrodružství." *Time In* 3: 7 (June 30, 2005): 78–80.

Interviews

Kreuzmann, František. *The Sonnets*. Montmartre. June 3, 2002.
Pavlík, Tomáš. Director: *The Sonnets*. Montmartre. June 3, July 12, 2002.
Polesný, Viktor. Director: *Twelfth Night*. Letní Shakespearovske Slavnosti. June 2005.
Tvrdík, Rostislav. *The Sonnets*. Montmartre. June 3, 2002.

Performances (listing by directors)

Dubský, Robert. Henry Mancini and Blake Edwards: *Viktor-Viktorie (Victor-Victoria)*. Hudební Divadlo Karlín, June 15, 2002.
Ezseny, Enikő. William Shakespeare: *Večer Tříkrálový* (*Twelfth Night*). Stavovské Divadlo. June 24, 2002.
Hlaučo, Miroslav. William Shakespeare: *Večer Tříkrálový* (*Twelfth Night*). Pidivadlo (VOŠ Herecká). May 28, June 18, 2002.
Pavlík, Tomáš. William Shakespeare: *Sonety (The Sonnets)*. Divadlo Montmartre (Divadlo ve Městě). June 9, 2002.
Polesný, Viktor. *Večer Tříkrálový* (*Twelfth Night*). Letní Shakespearovske Slavnosti (Summer Shakespeare Festival). June–August 2005.
Schejbal, Milan. *Večer Tříkrálový* (*Twelfth Night*). Divadlo ABC. 1999–2006.

8 Beyond the "lyric" in Illyricum

Some early modern backgrounds to *Twelfth Night*

Elizabeth Pentland

Critics of *Twelfth Night* have long treated Shakespeare's setting for the play, Illyria, as an exotic and unfamiliar locale associated with literary romance, lyricism, and illusion. Leah Marcus remarks in *Puzzling Shakespeare* that "Illyria was scarcely familiar territory, more significant, perhaps, for its evocation of like-sounding exotica – Elysium, delirium – than for concrete geopolitical associations" (1988, 161). Kenneth Muir has similarly suggested that Illyria was a "conveniently obscure location" and Geoffrey Bullough refers to it as "that little-known coast" (quoted in Stanivuković 2004, 404). While most current editions of the play point out that Illyria "could be found on a map" in Shakespeare's time (Smith 2001, 10), or that the name "could still be used to refer to part of the Adriatic coast – roughly Dalmatia – at the time under the dominion of the Venetian republic" (Elam 2008, 71), most tend to agree with Keir Elam's assessment that there are "few traces in the comedy of this heritage" (Elam 2008, 71). The result has been a critical tradition that treats Illyria as a place that, in many respects, "resembles nothing more than Shakespeare's England" (Elam 2008, 75), or that is "also very much a country of the mind, or a nowhere place, whose name simultaneously suggests and combines the words illusion and lyrics, both very present in the comedy" (Laroque 2005, 211; cf. Warren and Wells 1994, 9). While all of these critics point to important elements of the play's language, setting, and performance, including the musical or sonorous qualities of the name itself – Bruce R. Smith goes so far as to suggest that "in a theater without illusionistic scenery, Illyria is more a soundscape than a landscape" (2001, 10) – this continuing emphasis on Illyria as a "mythical" place (Elam 1996, 31) has tended to divert our attention away from what Shakespeare's earliest audiences would have known about the real history and geography of the region. Shakespeare's choice to move the action of *Twelfth Night* from Constantinople or Ancona,[1] where his sources were set, to the coast of Illyria (frequently glossed as "Sclavonia" by early modern writers) was not motivated by a desire for mystery or obscurity, but for reasons that had everything to do with the region's concrete historical and geopolitical associations.

Figure 8.1 "Pannoniae, et Illyrici Veteris Tabula," map from *Parergon*, in Abraham Ortelius's *Theatrum Orbis Terrarum*, Antwerp, 1595 (by permission of The Huntington Library, San Marino, California)

Scholars have only recently begun to reconsider the significance of Elizabethan cultural knowledge about Illyria and the Adriatic for plays like *Twelfth Night* and *The Comedy of Errors*. Some critics have dismissed this kind of archival work as a waste of time, citing what Manfred Pfister has called a "law of diminishing returns" (Laroque 2005, 212), but recent work by Sara Hanna and Goran V. Stanivuković suggests that there is, in fact, still much to be learned about these regions, and about the geographic sensibilities of Shakespeare and his contemporaries. Their research suggests not only the wealth of the early modern archive on Illyria but also the double nature of Illyria for the English imagination, as a locus of classical antiquity on the one hand (see Figure 8.1), and as a "modern" Adriatic region (see Figure 8.2), on the other, that English and European travelers passed through on their way eastward or southward to other destinations. Hanna's 2002 study focuses primarily on ideas about Illyria that emerge from the works of classical history and geography that were translated into English during the sixteenth century – Pliny, Pomponius Mela, Dionysius Periegetes, Solinus, Herodotus, Thucydides, Appian of Alexandria, and others. Stanivuković, on the other hand, looks at the question of Illyria's reputation in England through the lens

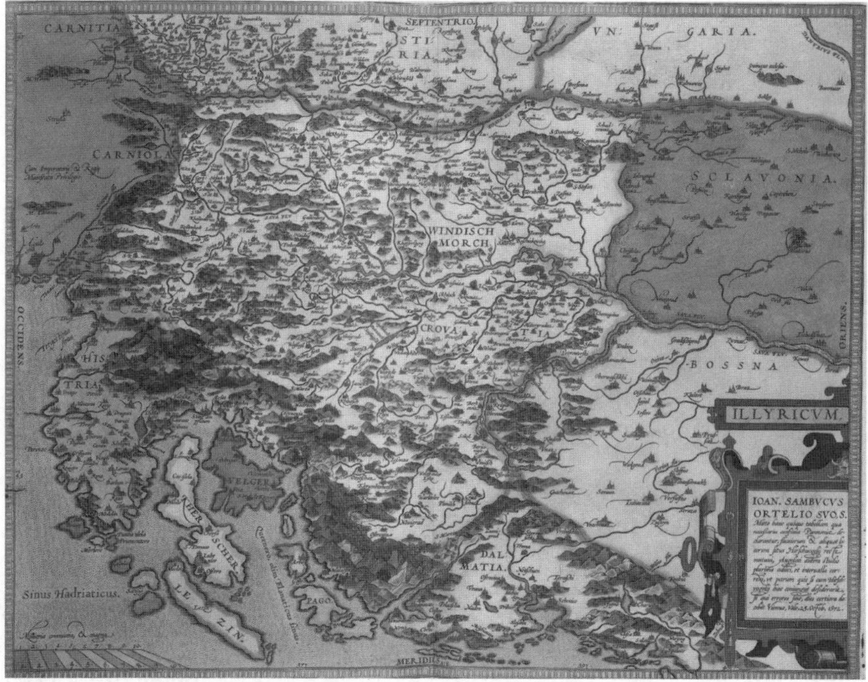

Figure 8.2 "Illyricum," map from Abraham Ortelius's *Theatrum Orbis Terrarum*, Antwerp, 1595: following 92 (by permission of The Huntington Library, San Marino, California).

of early modern travel narratives and geographical compendia, asking what the English had to say about this distant and apparently exotic land and how much contact Londoners might have had with "Illyrians" or Illyrian subject matter around the time that *Twelfth Night* was being written and performed.[2]

Both critics, for different reasons, come to similar conclusions: that there was less information circulating about Illyria in early modern England than there was about "any other part of the Mediterranean including north Africa" (Stanivuković 2004, 401), and that the small amount of information available in fact offered "very little insight" (Hanna 2002, 21) into the history or culture of Greek Illyria, Roman Illyricum, or early modern Sclavonia. As Stanivuković observes of travelers' accounts like Nicolas Nicolay's *Navigations, Peregrinations and Voyages, Made into Turkie*, or those published in Richard Hakluyt's *Principal Navigations*, "it seems that the narrators merely glanced at the region" (2004, 401) – perhaps because Illyria or the eastern Adriatic was, as Bruce R. Smith puts it, "no one's intended destination" (2001, 115). Never, in itself, "a final destination of western travelers; it was a coastline one sailed along" (Stanivuković 2004, 401). However, while it does seem that Shakespeare's contemporaries knew less about Illyria than about, say, Venice or Constantinople, we would be wrong to assume that it was as "obscure" or "mysterious" a setting to them as it has been for modern readers or audiences of *Twelfth Night*.

As several critics have pointed out, the Illyrian coast was considered dangerous for travelers – and this may explain why "knowledge of the eastern Adriatic was always partial, based more on imagination than on experience" (Stanivuković 2004, 401). From the time of the Greek geographer Strabo, it had been known for its sudden storms and treacherous shoals, and the thousands of islands that lined the coast had long been associated with piracy. Cosmographers and travelers observed that certain places along the coast, like the Gulf of Quernero, were famous for shipwreck (Thevet 1575, 779).[3] In the early seventeenth century, Shakespeare's contemporary William Lithgow described how his ship had been surprised by a "deadly storme" as it sailed along the Adriatic coast near Ragusa:

> when wee entred in the Gulf of *Cataro*, we fetched vppe the sight of the Ile *Melida*, called of old *Melignа*: Before wee could attayne vnto the Hauen, wherein our purpose was to stay all night, wee were assayled on a sodayne with a deadly storme: In so much, that euerie swallowing waue threatened our death, and bred in our breasts, an intermingled sorrow of feare and hope.
>
> (Lithgow 1614, D3r)

In the early modern period, moreover, the presence of the Turk[4] and the continuing wars among the Venetians, the Ottomans, and the Habsburgs may have added to the perception that – with the exception of Ragusa (modern-day Dubrovnik), the principal city on the Illyrian coast and the source of the name of the pirate Ragozine in *Measure for Measure* (Clubb 1989, 12) – Illyria was not a place to linger.

The limited information provided about Illyria (and Ragusa) in travelers' accounts and geographical compendia was usually derived from a fairly predictable set of sources, and this too has led to the perception that relatively little was known about the region. The knowledge that was disseminated through these works, however, had become so commonplace by the late sixteenth century that references to Illyria,[5] or Sclavonia, and its history could be found in some surprising places: in addition to a great number of classical works that circulated in early modern England, from Caesar's *Gallic Wars* and Ovid's *Metamorphoses* to late Roman histories like that of Procopius, we find works like Donne's *Satyre II* (in a possible allusion to Ovid or Juvenal) referring to the harsh sound of "scolding" Sclavonians (1633, 331),[6] or the second part of Marlowe's *Tamburlaine the Great* mentioning both the Sclavonians (among the forces of the Hungarian king, Sigismond) and the Illyrians (among the peoples "revolted" to the Anatolian king, Orcanes) in its opening scene (F3v–F4r).[7] The fourth volume of Belleforest's *Histoires*

Tragiques that contains the story of *Vne Fille Romaine Se Vestant en Page* ("A Roman Girl who Dressed as a Page"), which Shakespeare probably consulted for *Twelfth Night*, also includes the tale of *Theodore Zizime Ragousien* (set, as the title might suggest, in Ragusa); Reginald Scot's *Discoverie of Witchcraft* contains a marginal gloss (derived from Pliny) on the bewitching eyes of the ancient Illyrians (485);[8] and tracts defending or celebrating the "regiment of women" – including John Leslie's *Defence of the Honour of the Right Highe, Mightye and Noble Princesse Marie Quene of Scotlande*, John Bridges's *Defence of the Gouernment Established in the Church of Englande* and, much later, Heywood's *Gynaikeion* – allude to a famous Illyrian queen, Teuta (or Teuca), whose defiance of the Romans was recorded in the histories of Polybius, Livy, and Florus.

Shakespeare's references to Illyria outside of *Twelfth Night* are relatively few, but they reflect an awareness of the region's ancient reputation for trade and piracy. Most editors of the play, as a result, make some mention of "the traditionally warlike character of the Illyrians and especially to their notoriety for piracy" (Elam 2008, 71), noting Suffolk's reference in *2 Henry VI* to "Bargulus the strong Illyrian pirate" (4.1.106–8).[9] Interestingly, Shakespeare's reference to Bargulus, which is typically traced to a passage in Cicero's *De Officiis*, probably post-dates *Twelfth Night*, since the lines read differently in the earliest editions of the play. Both the first and second quartos of *2 Henry 6* refer not to Bargulus but to "mighty *Abradas*, / The great *Macedonian* Pyrate" (Shakespeare 1600, F2v), a phrase likely taken from Robert Greene's *Penelope's Web* ("*Abradas* the great *Macedonian* Pirat thought euery one had a letter of mart that bare sayles in [the] Ocean," [1587, E3v]).[10] Sometime after 1600, Shakespeare changed the name and literary genealogy of his pirate, but he chose nevertheless to preserve the reference to a long history of commerce and piracy on the Adriatic. Similarly, the allusion in *Measure for Measure* to "Ragozine, a most notorious pirate" (4.3.71) suggests that the playwright was well aware of the dangers of the Illyrian coast and the nation's ages-old reputation for thieving or pillaging at sea ["escumer la mer"] (Belleforest 1575, 1829).

As for Bargulus (or Bardylis), there is more to the story than Cicero's famous reference to him as "Bargulus, Illyricus latro" might suggest. Accusations of piracy, whether in the classical world or the early modern one, often expressed complex personal or national antagonisms and, in this respect, Roman attitudes toward Illyria were no exception. Edward Sugden notes that Bardylis "was first a collier, then a pirate, and finally King of Illyria. He was defeated and killed by Philip of Macedon, the father of Alexander" (1925, 263). The source for Sugden's biographical note is not offered, but references to Bardylis survive in classical works like the massive *Library of History* of Diodorus Siculus, which remains, to this day, an indispensable source for accounts of Philip of Macedon's early career and his wars with the Illyrians.

In *Twelfth Night*, Shakespeare gives us Antonio, whom Orsino calls a "Notable pirate" and "salt water thief" (5.1.69). We learn in the play's third act that Antonio cannot walk the streets of Illyria "without danger" (3.3.25), having done some notable "service" in "a sea-fight 'gainst the Count his galleys" (3.3.26–27). The "service" of which he speaks could be construed as naval service for a rival city, or as piracy; either way, it has clearly involved the capture and looting of Illyrian ships. As Antonio observes:

> It might have since been answer'd in repaying
> What we took from them, which for traffic's sake
> Most of our city did. Only myself stood out,
> For which if I be lapsed in this place
> I shall pay dear.
>
> (3.3.33–37)

We learn more about Antonio's activities in act 5, when Orsino's officer identifies him as "that Antonio / That took the *Phoenix* and her fraught from Candy" (or Crete), and "he that did the *Tiger* board / When your young nephew Titus lost his leg" (5.1.60–64). The names Antonio and Titus lend an antique or Roman quality to these reports of sea-fights in Aegean, Ionian, or Adriatic waters, recalling not only the ancient piracy mentioned by geographers like Strabo and Ptolemy, but more specifically the Illyrian campaigns against neighboring kingdoms in Greece, and their notorious attacks on Roman ships during the third century BC.[11] The name "Titus" may be linked to the story of the Illyrian queen Teuta, who beheaded a Roman Ambassador by that name. "Antonio," on the other hand, calls to mind Marcus Antonius – frequently characterized by Cicero as a "latro" (thief or brigand) in the *Philippics* – and his infamous retreat from the Battle of Actium, which took place off the Illyrian coast in 31 BC.[12] Although Antonio tries to "shake off these names" (5.1.73), and denies he ever "was thief or pirate" (5.1.74), Shakespeare effectively turns the tables, here, on centuries of Roman propaganda.

Of course Shakespeare, having read his Hakluyt, would have known that not everyone who sailed the Adriatic was a pirate or bore a "letter of mart." In the sixteenth and seventeenth centuries, English and European pilgrims on their way to Jerusalem also sailed from Venice, frequently stopping over at Ragusa or harboring along the coast during inclement weather. As early as 1511, the *Pylgrymage of Sir Richarde Guylforde* described for English readers the commonwealth of Ragusa, with its "su[m]ptuous buyldynge" and "grete Relyques" (Anon. 1511, B1r–v; Torbarina 1964, 35; Stanivuković 2004, 404).[13] Later pilgrims, like the Englishman John Locke, who sailed past Ragusa on his way to Jerusalem in 1553 (Hakluyt 1599, I3v) or the Frenchman de Vergoncey, whose *Pelerin Veritable* recounts a similar voyage along the Adriatic coast in the early seventeenth century, also made a point of describing the city and its environs. Diplomats and adventurers – some of them better known for their activities in the New World – also passed through the region on their way to Constantinople and the Levant: a French traveler named Jacques Gassot published an account of his voyage from Venice to Constantinople in 1547, noting that he sailed along the "Golfe de Trieste ancienement appellé Illyricus sinus" on his way (1550, B1v);[14] English ambassador Henry Austell spent three days in Ragusa en route to the court of Amurath III in 1586 (Hakluyt 1599, R2r); Sir Anthony Shirley and Captain John Smith each spent time in Ragusa in 1601 (Kostić 1975, 595); George Sandys passed through in 1610, and, as we have seen, William Lithgow survived a "deadly storme" in the Gulf of Cataro shortly thereafter. English commercial activity in Ragusa began to grow after 1600, and in 1603, according to historian Veselin Kostić, "the first agent of the Levant Company," a man named Ralph Ingilson, "applied to the Ragusan government for permission to trade in their town" (1975, 593).

Ragusa was known across Europe as a city of considerable wealth and culture during the sixteenth century. Its monuments and antiquities, mentioned by English writers as early as 1511, were documented in some detail by well-known French travelers, translators, and cosmographers including Nicolas Nicolay, André Thevet, and François Belleforest. Drawing on the work of Nicolay and perhaps also on Marin Barleti's *Historie of George Castriot, Surnamed Scanderbeg*, Ortelius described Ragusa as a city "famous for the Mart" (1606, 92) . Similarly, George Sandys observed that Ragusa, "heretofore *Epidaurus*," was "a commonwealth of it selfe, famous for merchandize and plentie of shipping" (1615, 3). And in a passage that suggests the importance of the city as a cultural crossroads, François Belleforest observed in his 1571 tale of *Theodore Zizime* that Ragusa was more prosperous than ever, living under its own laws and attracting merchants "from all nations":

> although the city has always been greatly renowned, and abundant both in people and in wealth, it has never triumphed more than it does at present, enjoying its laws and its privileges, governed by its magistrates, flourishing in policy like Venice, its Senate and its Empire neither subject nor answerable to any prince. It is certainly true that for the maintaining of traffic and peace, and for the free access to the sea as far as the Levant, where they have most of their trade, they are tributaries of the Great Turk, just as the Venetians pay tribute and homage for their islands, though they pretend otherwise. For the continuous commerce that takes place in Ragusa, therefore, one sees merchants there from all nations, and above all Greeks, who feel safer there than they do among the thieving Janissaries of Constantinople.[15]
>
> (Belleforest 1571, 467–68)

Figure 8.3 "Merchant of Raguse" from Nicolas Nicolay's *Navigations, Peregrinations and Voyages*, London, 1585: 137 (by permission of The Huntington Library, San Marino, California).

As some critics have remarked, *Twelfth Night*'s Illyria "relentlessly excludes the figure of the merchant" (see Figure 8.3) (Malcolmson; quoted in Elam 1996, 31). It also seems somewhat "removed from the mercantile society of the city-states" (also 31) associated with its Italian analogues.[16] The play is nevertheless replete with allusions to shipping, piracy, and trade, from the famous "Mistress Mary Accost" scene that features language of "boarding" and "assailing" to another early wooing scene, in which Olivia "proceeds (ironically) to divide her body according to a commercial schedule" (Sawday 1995, 202). In fact, the "marriage" of wooing and commercial themes in the play suggests an underlying awareness of Illyria's importance not only as a mercantile center but as a cultural crossroads where merchants and travelers of "all nations" mingled, and religions, social practices, and gender paradigms not only coexisted but could be subjected to the scrutiny of historians, travelers, moralists, and playwrights. As Bruce R. Smith observes in his recent edition of the play,

> In Sandys's own day, the region stood just at the contested border between Christendom and Islam, between Austria and the Ottoman empire. As such it occupied liminal space between "us" and "them" that can also be apprehended in Shakespeare's play with respect to sexual mores if not religion. Sandys is careful to note that the Christian inhabitants of the region were able to secure their peace only by paying tribute to the Turks.
>
> (Smith 2001, 126)

Shakespeare's contemporaries were well aware of Illyria's situation at the crossroads of several competing political and mercantile empires. It was, in fact, Ragusa's reputation for cultural mixing that drew Belleforest's attention as he reflected upon the differences between French customs in love and those of the Italians and the Turks.

It is difficult to imagine Shakespeare working closely with source texts in as many as three volumes of Belleforest's *Histoires Tragiques* and not so much as glancing at some of the other stories in the collection.[17] The tragic story of *Theodore Zizime Ragousien*, which appears in the same volume as the acknowledged source for Riche's *Apolonius and Silla*, tells how Theodore, a Greek merchant living in Ragusa, falls "desperately" in love with his best friend's wife and, being spurned by her, stabs himself to death. *Theodore Zizime* is framed by Belleforest as a story about the miseries of extreme passion or disorderly love ["Amour desreiglé"]; in his preface, the Frenchman claims that he went all the way to Sclavonia to find this tale so his readers would see "how far this natural folly has spread its Empire" ["combien loing ceste folie naturelle estend son Empire"] (Belleforest 1571, 466). The multicultural setting of the story, which in fact comes from Bandello, provides Belleforest with an occasion to reflect on the relative merits of Italian and

Turkish custom, as against the "too courteous" manners ["les façons de faire trop courtoises"] of his French compatriots. The Turks and the Italians, he tells his readers, "let none but themselves look upon their wives." ["ne laissent voir leur femmes qu'à leurs yeux mesmes"] It is not "jealousy that moves them to do this, and keep this sex closely confined," the author explains, "but rather it is compassion, for that they have hearts so susceptible to new Impressions that when they see some rare beauty set before their eyes they become enslaved to it." ["ne pense point que ce soit ialousie qui les esmeut à ce faire, & tenir si precieusement ce sexe clos en sa chambre, ains plustost la compassion qu'ils ont des coeurs si aisez à receuoir nouuelles Impressions, afin que s'ils voyoient quelque rare beauté leur estre representee à l'oeil de la veuë ils n'en deuinssent les esclaues"] (Belleforest 1571, 470). Should the object of their affection prove unattainable, however, "they risk falling into some great madness and utterly forgetting themselves" ["n'en pouuant iouyr fassent en danger de tomber en quelque singuliere folie & oubly de soymesme"] (Belleforest 1571, 470). Interestingly, none of these comments about the customs of Sclavonia are to be found in Bandello's version of the tale; they, along with the description of Ragusa that I quoted above, were added at the time of translation by Belleforest.

As among the Turks and Italians, Belleforest tells his readers, the custom in Sclavonia is to keep women covered and confined. Nicolas Nicolay, who may have provided Belleforest with certain details of Ragusan life, had reported just a few years earlier that the women of the city "doe goe very seldome abrode out of their houses, but do loue to be looking out at the windowes to beholde the goers by. As for their daughters are kept so close shut in, as they are not to be seen by no manner of wise" (1585, S4r). Importantly, though, the Greek merchants living in Ragusa are free to follow their own custom. Belleforest suggests that if Demetrius had kept his wife in her room "according to the custom of that country" ["suyuant la coustume du païs,"], his friend Theodore would not have become so hopelessly enslaved to Cassandra's beauty and good graces (Belleforest 1571, 470–71). As Belleforest presents it, Sclavonia (or Illyria) is a place where men are more susceptible to beauty, less able to withstand their passions, and, once in love, more likely to forget themselves or commit some great folly (470) – just as Malvolio does in *Twelfth Night* with his yellow stockings, cross-gartering, and speeches on "greatness" in 3.4, which seem like "very midsummer madness" to the bewildered Olivia. Orsino, similarly, having fallen in love with Olivia at first sight and been hounded by his passions ever since (1.1.18–22), displays all the susceptibility to "new Impressions" and "rare beauty" that Belleforest attributes to the Sclavonians.

If, as Belleforest suggests, with their Turkish and Italianate practices, the modern Slavonians seemed effeminate or especially prone to amorous folly, their ancient Illyrian counterparts had been ranked among the best warriors in the world – as famous for their military prowess, according to

Trogus Pompeius, as the Carthaginians, the Romans, and the Sicilians (Justinus 1578, 125). According to Ortelius, classical authorities concurred on this point:

> *Appian* nameth the people *Incolas bellicosissimus*, a most warlike and couragious people. *Liuy* saith that they are a very hardy nation both by sea and land: *Florus* and *Strabo* maketh them cruell and bloudy men, and much giuen to robbe and steale. *Iulian* the Emperor in his discourse *de Caesaribus*, testifieth plainly that they are one of the stoutest and valiantest nations of all *Europe*.
>
> (Ortelius 1606, xvii verso)

Another authority, Herodian, observed that the Illyrians were "of great and tall bodies prompte and redy to warre and murder," but also "are they of dul and grosse capacitie: where by they do not easelye perceyue what a man craftelye speketh or worketh" (1556, H2v; cf. Ortelius 1606, xvii). The aspiring emperor Septimius Severus, we are told, won the support of the Illyrian army in the final years of the second century by contrasting their reputation for "valiaute prowesse," "talnes of person, warlycke exercises, [and] fyghting hande to hande" with the cultural decadence of the Syrians, who, he claimed, were "chiefly addictede vnto iestes and playes" (Herodian 1556, H3v). Some of Shakespeare's contemporaries held similar opinions about the Slavonians: William Lithgow observed, in the early seventeenth century, that these men "are of a robust nature, martiall, and valiant fellowes, and a great help to maintain the right and liberty of the Venetian state" (1614, D4r).

The "riotous" Illyrians of *Twelfth Night* are decidedly more interested in singing, dancing, and late-night revelry than they are in martial pursuits, however – a state of affairs that mirrors not only the perceptions of Barnabe Riche (who complained about the decline of military discipline and the rise of effeminate French and Venetian fashions in Elizabethan England) but also those of François Belleforest, who comments, as we have seen, on the effects of Turkish and Italianate cultural influence in Ragusa. Certainly when Sir Toby boasts (ironically) that his friend Sir Andrew Aguecheek is "as tall a man as any's in Illyria" (1.3.20), he appears to refer to the kinds of stereotypes recorded by Ortelius. But while his penchant for late-night drinking with Sir Toby may be consistent with the Illyrian reputation for being "great wine bibbers" and "much giuen to drunkennesse" (Ortelius 1606, xvii verso), Sir Andrew's professed delight in "masques and revels" (1.3.113–14) and his boast that he has "the back-trick simply as strong as any man in Illyria" (1.3.123–24) turn nearly all the stereotypes about the warlike Illyrians on their heads. Indeed, the decline of martial discipline in Shakespeare's Illyria supplies much of the play's comedy, as when Fabian warns Cesario (who, although his name recalls a Roman famed for making "the fierce nation of the *Illyrians* . . . tame,"[18] confesses he is "no fighter") that Sir Andrew is "the most skillful, bloody, and fatal opposite that you could possibly have found in any part of Illyria" (3.4.266–69).

Ancient Illyria was further associated in early modern English writing with independent women and female rule. The story of the Illyrian Queen Teuta's resistance to Rome, though it is never mentioned by critics or editors of *Twelfth Night*, turns out to have been especially interesting to Elizabethan readers and writers. Known principally through the works of Polybius, Pliny, Livy, Florus, and Appian of Alexandria, the example of Teuta (who reigned for three years following the death of her husband in 231 BC) often figured prominently in sixteenth-century writings on the "regiment of women." Thomas Lanquet's *Epitome of Chronicles* published in 1549, is among the earliest English printed works to mention Teuta, noting that she "slue the Romayn ambassadors" and that she "flourished" in 229 BC before the Roman "consules toke many citees and subdued both the roialme and the quene" the following year in the "warres of Illyria" (68v). Almost 80 years later, Gabriel Richardson summarized the early history of Illyria in his compendious *Of the State of Europe*, arguing that:

> The *Romanes* were the first knowne forrainers, who invaded, and subdued this country. In the yeare of Rome 524 hapned their first warre with Queene *Teuta*, occasioned through her pride, and cruelty, killing one of their Embassadours, sent vnto her, and a pretence of the pyracies of the nation, and of their iniuries done vnto the neighbouring *Grecians*, managed by the Consuls Cn: *Fulvius Flaccus Centimalus*, and *A. Postumius*;[19] the successe whereof was the ouerthrow, & subjection of the Queene, (amercyed with a yearely tribute, and the losse of the greatest part of her kingdome) and the setting vp of *Demetrius Pharius*, their confederate in the warre.
>
> (Richardson 1627, X4r)

Richardson, like every other writer of the period, draws heavily on the works of Appian, Florus, and Polybius for this account.

Despite the harsh criticisms leveled at Teuta by these Roman writers,[20] the ancient queen's example proved useful to sixteenth-century defenders of women's right to rule. In 1569, for example, John Leslie cited Teuta's reign (among others) in the third book of his *Defence of the Honour of the Right Highe, Mightye and Noble Princesse Marie Quene of Scotlande* in order to argue that "the regimente of whomen ys conformable to the lawe of God and nature":

> As for Europe, as yt ys better knowen to vs, so therein haue we with all greater store of examples of this kinde of gouernemente. In Epire, yt appearethe by Olympias dawghter to Pyrrhus: In Macedonia where a woman called also Olympias succeded after the deathe of Alexander

> the greate: Yea and in the greate and famouse empire of Constantinople, where Irene, Theodora, Zoë an other Theodora, and Eudocia were the cheyf and highe magistrates . . . More ouer yt appeareth that the Illyrians and Slauons were ruled by Quene Teuca . . .
>
> (Leslie 1569, 131v)

A few years later, in his *Pilgrimage of Princes*, Lodowick Lloyd praised Teuta's reign in terms designed to suggest parallels with England's own Virgin Queen. Blithely ignoring the imputations of willfulness or tyranny in accounts by Polybius and others, Lloyd found much to praise in the Illyrian queen and her resistance to Roman infringements on her sovereignty:

> famous *Teuca* Queene of the *Illiryans*, gouerned hir subiectes after the death of hir husbande king *Argon*, which being warred on diuers times by the Romanes, infringed theyr force, broke theyr bonds, discomfited their armies to hir perpetuall fame & commendacion: shee gouerned the people of *Illeria*, no lesse wisely, then she defended the puissaunt force of the Romanes stoutly, shee liued (as histories report) as soberly and chastly without the company of man, as shee gouerned hir countrie wisly and stoutelye without the councell of man.
>
> (Lloyd 1573, 13r)

Similarly, John Bridges, arguing in 1587 that "the gouernment of women is not a thing vnaccustomed, euen to the most valiant nations," noted that "the Romane hystorie dooth celebrate Theuta, which gouerned the Liburnians, as her that durst make worke for their Citie" (Aaa2v). On the other hand, Sir Walter Ralegh, closely following Polybius, observed in his *History of the World* that "*Teuta* gaue her people free libertie, to rob all Nations at Sea, making no difference betweene friend and foe; as if shee had beene sole Mistresse of the salt Waters" (1617, 412). And Thomas Heywood's *Gynaikeion* mentioned the queen no fewer than five times, telling how "*Teuca* the wife of *Argon* tooke vpon her the soueraigntie, shee was queene of the Illyrians, a warlike nation, whome she wisely gouerned, by whose valour and fortitude she not only opposed the violence of the Romans, but obtained from them many noble victories" (1624, X1v). Heywood also noted (without disapproving) an incident that must have recalled, with some irony, Elizabeth's own rebuke of the Polish ambassador in 1597: according to Livy and Florus, Teuta had violated the laws of nations by putting to death the Roman ambassador Tytus (or Titus) Corrancanus "because hee spake to her freelie and boldlie" (V1r).

Although Teuta is never mentioned by name in the play, *Twelfth Night*, already replete with the language of commerce, shipping and piracy, foregrounds its own concern with the "regiment of women" through the figure of the Illyrian heiress Olivia, who remains "sole Mistresse" of her household after the deaths of her father and brother. The character of Olivia is of course largely modeled upon a similar character in Shakespeare's source stories, Riche's *Apolonius and Silla* and Belleforest's tale of the *Fille Romaine Se Vestant en Page* (based, in turn, on a novella by Bandello), but it is only in the Illyrian setting chosen by Shakespeare that her self-imposed chastity and imperiousness can effectively recall both an ancient queen and an early modern one. Just as Teuta was famed for living "soberly and chastly without the company of men" after the death of her husband, and for governing her country "wisly and stoutelye without the councell of man," Olivia, we learn, "hath abjur'd the [company] / And [sight] of men" (1.2.40–41) after her brother's death, veiling herself like a "cloistress" and vowing to refuse even the most eligible of suitors for seven years. As Sir Toby remarks early in the play, "She'll none o' th' Count. She'll not match above her degree, neither in estate, years, nor wit; I have heard her swear't" (1.3.109–11). Indeed, recalling the spirit of Elizabeth I's own negotiations with the duke of Anjou in the late 1570s, Olivia offers to marry Sebastian only on the condition that he submit to her rule: "come, I prithee, would thou'dst be ruled by me" (4.1.64).[21]

The historical association of ancient Illyria with a "chaste" queen whose pirates and policies were a thorn in Rome's side certainly complements a critical tradition that has often viewed Shakespeare's Illyria as an exotic stand-in for London's Whitehall (Hotson 1986), "a fairyland with back-streets" (Warren and Wells 1994, 9; quoting reviewer Hugh Leonard), or a locale that "resembles the rural England of landed gentry and country mansions far more than it does any Mediterranean court society" (Elam 1996, 31). Indeed, scholars have often glanced at Elizabeth I in discussing Olivia's household or the gender dynamics of the play more generally. While, as Viola herself notes, Shakespeare's Illyria is not quite the "Elizium" of Spenserian mythography, the play does find a neat opportunity – in relocating the action from Rome, Ancona, or Constantinople to the coast of Illyria – to comment upon a parallel history of female rule in a "barbarous" sea-faring nation that had long been famed for its resistance to Roman imperialism.

Shakespeare and his contemporaries thus knew far more about Illyria (or Sclavonia) than most readers and playgoers do today. Nearly all of the works I have surveyed here on the subject were available in some form to English readers before the first recorded performance of *Twelfth Night* in 1602; only a few would have required access to foreign books or a working knowledge of French, Italian, or Latin. While other Mediterranean regions were certainly more familiar to Shakespeare's audiences, Illyria was not as "conveniently obscure" as critics like Muir have suggested. On the contrary, information on Illyria was to be found across an impressive range of published works and genres in late Elizabethan England, from histories, travel narratives, and cosmographies to political tracts, verse satires, romances, novellas, and, of course, stageplays. Shakespeare's Illyria has become, for modern critics and directors of *Twelfth Night*, a place of lyricism, illusion, and exotic fantasy;

but even as we extoll the "lyric" in "Illyricum," we should not forget that Illyria was also famous to Elizabethans as a commercial and cultural crossroads where Italian, Turkish, and Greek practices mingled with local custom, and as an ancient kingdom with a long and fascinating history of piracy, resistance to Rome, and female rule.

Notes

1. Constantinople is the setting for Barnabe Riche's *Apolonius and Silla*, an established source for *Twelfth Night*. Riche's source, François Belleforest, sets his version of the story (a translation of Bandello's novella *Nicuola innamorata di Lattanzio*), in Rome and Ancona, Italy.
2. See also an earlier version (Stanivuković 2002) published in *Shakespeare's Illyrias: Heterotopias, Identities, (Counter)Histories*, a special volume of *Litteraria Pragensia* edited by Martin Prochazka.
3. Thevet even suggested that it was called Il Carnaro "because of the great carnage wrought by shipwrecks in this gulf." [à cause du grand carnage qui s'y fait par les naufrages contraints qui aduiennent dans ce goulfe"]. All translations from Thevet and Belleforest in this essay are my own.
4. For more on Illyria's association with the Turk, see Patricia Parker (2008).
5. There were, in fact, no fewer than 17 variant spellings of "Illyria" or "Illyricum" in English usage during the sixteenth century, many of them found in translated works like those mentioned here.
6. See Ovid's *De Tristibus*, Book 2, Elegy 1: "Sometimes Germania doth rebel, sometimes *Illerians* raile, / *Rhetia* and the *Thracian* land, with ciuill warres assaile" (1572, 13v). Juvenal also alludes to a "loud *Liburnian*" in his fourth Satire; Dryden's gloss observes that "Some say that the People of this Country, which is part of *Illyricum*, the *Romans* made their Cryers, because of ther lowd Voyces" (Dryden 1693, 62, 69 n. 13).
7. The ancient Illyrians had a reputation for political inconstancy and rebellion. Trogus Pompeius was of the opinion that "the *Illirians, Thracians, Dardanians*, & other Barbarous nations were of minde unconstant, and of promise unfaithfull" (Justinus 1578, H2r–v); Appian describes how "*Caesar Augustus* . . . had made the fierce nation of the *Illyrians*, so oft rebelling, tame" (1578, 289); and Ralegh mentions that the Illyrian queen Teuta put down a rebellion early in her reign (1617, 413). Mercator drew on this tradition when he referred to the Illyrians as "unconstant, envious, seditious" (quoted in Hadfield 2005, 10).
8. Ortelius observes that "*Isogonus* in *Pliny* writeth that there be a kinde of men amongst these which doe bewitch with their eies, and doe kill such as they doe beholde and looke vpon any long while together" (1606, xvii verso).
9. Unless otherwise indicated, all citations from Shakespeare in this essay refer to the Riverside edition.
10. Greene used the phrase again two years later in his *Menaphon* (1589, sig. E3v). The name Abradas has not been traced, and is thought to be Greene's invention.
11. See especially Appian, Florus, and Polybius on Illyrian piracy under Queen Teuta; Belleforest's *Cosmographie Universelle* offers an early modern commentary on this historical material and Ralegh's *History of the World* includes several chapters on the Illyrian wars based on Polybius.
12. Cicero uses the word "latro" no fewer than 33 times in the *Philippics* in connection with Antonius and his activities; in the thirteenth *Philippic*, moreover, he

refers to Antonius as an "arch-pirate" ("archipirata"). The Battle of Actium was described in Lucan's *Pharsalia*, an epic account of the Roman civil wars, and in Plutarch's *Life of Marcus Antonius*, which was Shakespeare's principal source for *Antony and Cleopatra*.

13. Several critics have suggested that Sebastian is alluding to the antiquities of Ragusa when he urges Antonio to "go see the relics of this town" (3.3.19) so that they may "satisfy" their "eyes / With the memorials and the things of fame / That do renown this city" (3.3.22–24; see Stanivuković 2004, 404, Torbarina 1964, 35).
14. Gassot was terrified by the winds along the treacherous Gulf of Quernero; his ship escaped this peril only to be pursued by pirates until it reached the coastal city of Iara (Zadar) (1550, B2r).
15. Or "quoy que ceste cité eust tousiours esté fort renommee, & abondante & en peuple & en richesses, si ne fust elle iamais plus triomphante qu'elle est à present, iouïssant de ses loix & priuileges, gouuernee de ses magistrats, florissante en police tout ainsi que Venise ayant son Senat, & Empire non sujet & iusticiable à aucun prince. Bien est vray que pour le maintenement du trafic & auoir paix, & libre accez sur mer iusques en leuant ou ils font le plus de leur trafique, ils sont tributaires au grand seigneur de Turquie, comme aussi les Venitiens ne sont sans luy faire & tribut & hommage de leurs isles quelque contenance de grandeur qu'ils facent. Pour la frequente marchandise donc qui se fait à Ragouse on y voit des marchans de toutes nations, & sur tout des Grecs, comme se voyans plus asseurez là, que parmy les voleurs Ianissaires du prince de Constantinople."
16. See Keir Elam and Louise Clubb on the play's Italian analogues. Clubb points out that "the coastal city of Ragusa, the Dalmatian Venice, . . . was the setting of some commedie" (1989, 12).
17. Stories from the third, fourth, and fifth volumes have been named as principal or possible sources for *Much Ado About Nothing*, *Twelfth Night*, and *Hamlet*, respectively.
18. The quote is from Appian. See note 7, above.
19. Spelled "Posthumus" in Ralegh's *History of the World.*
20. Florus, for example, complained that the "dishonour" to Rome was the greater because these events had taken place "in a womans reigne" (1619, 134–35).
21. Susan Doran argues that Elizabeth reopened the marriage negotiations with Anjou in 1578 "to entice him away from military adventures" in Flanders, probably hoping "that the negotiations themselves would be sufficient to make Anjou do her bidding" (1996, 147); she later suggests that Elizabeth thought "the only possibility for controlling him personally was by accepting his hand in marriage" (191).

Works cited

Anon. *This Is the Begynnynge and Continuaunce of the Pylgrymage of Sir Richarde Guylforde Knyght*. London, 1511.

Appian. *An Auncient Historie and Exquisite Chronicle of the Romanes Warres, both Ciuile and Foren*. London, 1578.

Belleforest, François. *Le Qvatriesme Tome des Histoires Tragiques.* Turin, 1571.

——. *La cosmographie vniverselle de tovt le monde*. Paris, 1575.

Bridges, John. *A Defence of the Government Established in the Church of Englande for Ecclesiasticall Matters*. London, 1587.

Clubb, Louise George. *Italian Drama in Shakespeare's Time*. New Haven, CT: Yale University Press, 1989.

Donne, John. *Poems, by J. D. with Elegies on the Authors Death*. London, 1633.

Doran, Susan. *Monarchy and Matrimony: The Courtships of Elizabeth I*. London: Routledge, 1996.

Elam, Keir. "The Fertile Eunuch: *Twelfth Night*, Early Modern Intercourse, and the Fruits of Castration." *Shakespeare Quarterly* 47 (1996): 1–36.

——, ed. "Introduction." *Twelfth Night, or What You Will*. The Arden Shakespeare, series 3. London: Cengage Learning, 2008.

Florus, Lucius Annaeus. *The Roman Histories*. London, 1619.

Gassot, Jacques. *Le Discours du Voyage de Venise à Constantinople*. Paris, 1550.

Greene, Robert. *Penelopes Web*. London, 1587.

——. *Menaphon*. London, 1589.

Hadfield, Andrew. "Introduction: Shakespeare and Renaissance Europe." In *Shakespeare and Renaissance Europe*. Ed. Andrew Hadfield and Paul Hammond. London: Thomson Learning, 2005.

Hakluyt, Richard. *Principal Nauigations, Voyages, Traffiques and Discoueries of the English Nation*. London, 1599.

Hanna, Sara. "From Illyria to Elysium: Geographical Fantasy in *Twelfth Night*." *Litteraria Pragensia* 12 (2002): 21–45.

Herodian. *The History of Herodian*. Trans. Nicholas Smyth. [London], 1556.

Heywood, Thomas. *Gynaikeion: or, Nine Bookes of Various History Concerninge Women*. London, 1624.

Hotson, Leslie. "Illyria for Whitehall." In *Twelfth Night: Critical Essays*. Ed. Stanley Wells. New York: Garland Publishing, 1986: 89–105.

Justinus. *The Abridgement of the Historyes of Trogus Pompeius*. Trans. Arthur Golding. London, 1578.

Juvenal. *The Satires of Decimus Junius Juvenalis. Translated into English Verse by Mr. Dryden, and Several Other Eminent Hands*. London, 1693.

Kostić, Veselin. *Ragusa and England, 1300–1650*. Belgrade: Serbian Academy of Sciences and Arts, 1975.

Lanquet, Thomas, Thomas Cooper, and Robert Crowley. *An Epitome of Chronicles*. London, 1549.

Laroque, François. "Shakespeare's Imaginary Geography." In *Shakespeare and Renaissance Europe*. Ed. Andrew Hadfield and Paul Hammond. London: Thomson Learning, 2005.

Leslie, John. *A Defence of the Honour of the Right Highe, Mightye and Noble Princesse Marie Quene of Scotlande and Dowager of France*. [London], 1569.

Lithgow, William. *A Most Delectable and Trve Discourse, of an Admired and Painefull Peregrination from Scotland, to the Most Famous Kingdomes in Europe, Asia and Affricke*. London, 1614.

Lloyd, Lodowick. *The Pilgrimage of Princes, Penned Out of Sundry Greeke and Latine Aucthours*. London, 1573.

Marcus, Leah S. *Puzzling Shakespeare: Local Reading and Its Discontents*. Berkeley: University of California Press, 1988.

Marlowe, Christopher. *Tamburlaine the Great*. [London], 1590.

Nicolay, Nicholas. *The Navigations, Peregrinations and Voyages, Made into Turkie*. Trans. T. Washington. London, 1585.

Ortelius, Abraham. *Theatrum Orbis Terrarum*. Antwerp, 1595.

——. *Theatrum Orbis Terrarum: The Theatre of the Whole World*. London, 1606.

Ovid. *The Thre First Bookes of Ouids De Tristibus*. Trans. Thomas Churchyard. London, 1572.

Parker, Patricia. "Was Illyria as Mysterious and Foreign As We Think?" In *The Mysterious and the Foreign in Early Modern England*. Ed. Helen Ostovich, Mary Silcox, and Graham Roebuck. Newark: University of Delaware Press, 2008: 209–33.

Ralegh, Sir Walter. *The History of the World*. London, 1617.

Richardson, Gabriel. *Of the State of Europe*. Oxford, 1627.

Sandys, George. *A Relation of a Journey Begun Anno Domini 1610*. London, 1615.

Sawday, Jonathan. *The Body Emblazoned: Dissection and the Human Body in Renaissance Culture*. London: Routledge, 1995.

Scot, Reginald. *The Discovery of Witchcraft*. London, 1584.

Shakespeare, William. *The Whole Contention Betweene the Two Famous Houses, Lancaster and Yorke*. London, 1600.

——. *The Riverside Shakespeare*. 2nd edn. Ed. G. Blakemore Evans et al. Boston: Houghton Mifflin Company, 1997.

Smith, Bruce R., ed. *Twelfth Night: Texts and Contexts*. Boston: Bedford/St. Martin's, 2001.

Stanivuković, Goran V. "'What Country, Friends, Is This?': The Geographies of Illyria in Early Modern England." *Litteraria Pragensia* 12 (2002): 5–20.

——. "Illyria Revisited: Shakespeare and the Eastern Adriatic." In *Shakespeare and the Mediterranean*. Ed. Tom Clayton, Susan Brock, and Vicente Forés. Newark: University of Delaware Press, 2004: 400–415.

Sugden, Edward H. *A Topographical Dictionary to the Works of Shakespeare and His Fellow Dramatists*. Manchester: Manchester University Press, 1925.

Thevet, André. *La Cosmographie Vniverselle*. Paris, 1575.

Torbarina, Josip. "The Setting of Shakespeare's Plays (with Special Reference to Illyria in *Twelfth Night*)." *Studia Romanica et Anglica Zagrabiensia* 17–18 (1964): 21–59.

Warren, Roger, and Stanley Wells, eds. "Introduction." *Twelfth Night, or What You Will*. The Oxford Shakespeare. Oxford: Oxford University Press, 1994.

9 Domesticating strangeness in *Twelfth Night*

Catherine Lisak

We commonly perceive the "stranger" as someone from elsewhere (*OED*, 1.a.) or as someone "else." The distinction arises from the domestic social structure wherein the stranger circulates. This act of identification combines the appropriation and segregation of otherness, the hosting and holding hostage of otherness. It implies the psychological process of a "disowning projection" (English and English 1958, 3), that is, a "projection onto the venerated or despised other of human possibilities not yet developed or rejected for the sake of something else by the defining group" (Fiedler 1973, 44). Strangeness thus understood broadly includes the "foreigner" whose status of alterity also depends upon the dichotomy of the insider/outsider. "Strangeness" and "foreignness" may be interchangeably used when denoting a person who originates from (or owes allegiance to) a country that is not his country of residence. However, it is interesting to note that "the word *foreigners* is not at all common in the sixteenth century; *strangers* is the normal expression. Indeed the first three examples of the former word in *OED* (that is, up to 1637) are all qualified by the latter word, as if to provide a clue to the meaning" (Hunter 1964, 412 n.). Adding to this linguistic footnote, Hoenselaars contends that "in *The Three Lords and Three Ladies of London* [Robert] Wilson is the first author before 1637 to use the concept of 'foreigner' ('Foriners,' line 54) without simultaneously qualifying the term by referring to strangeness" (1992, 253–54 n.). This piece of evidence, dating back to the 1580s, shows how the word "foreigner" seems ready to branch off from the umbrella term "stranger," perhaps because both words are considered to be synonymous and of equal strength; perhaps because their recognized difference in meaning signals an increasingly vexed conflation. A case in point is *Sir Thomas More* (1592–93), where we are made aware of the original etymologically grounded meanings of "stranger," "foreign," and "alien." Indeed, "the terms 'stranger' or 'aliens' denoted those from overseas, whereas 'foreigners' meant those who were not free of the City; the latter were not permitted to trade within the City boundaries although they did so extensively in suburbs like Southwark" (Hill 2005, 12–13). At the very least, these linguistic distinctions adumbrate the complex relationships that the notions of foreignness and strangeness entertain with the English domestic landscape.

Such waxing distinctions do not impair the plastic boundaries of strangeness; quite the contrary. The domestic scene that lets in the stranger may stretch the size of a nation or contract the size of a household – in which case the stranger, as one who is not in the place where his home is, may represent a visitor "staying for a time," in contradistinction to the members of the household (*OED*, 3.a.), or an alienated friend who has been away for a long time. Estrangement from the host community implies a degree of familiarity either lost or yet to be won. Often, the strange or estranged acquaintance is far-traveled (having wandered beyond the domestic periphery and rubbed shoulders with the unknown) and so will have proved as much a stranger amongst "them" as he or she has become a stranger to "us." Consequently, being a stranger can simply constitute an "occurrent" phenomenon – an incidental state dependent upon circumstances or some chance encounter – or it can be dispositional, as when the stranger is a stranger in blood, that is, not a "relation." Defining strangeness and the different phenomena it captures becomes a matter of perspective, as the meaning relies on who the defining group is.

In this essay, I investigate how *Twelfth Night* puts the stranger's case to its audiences through rotating platforms that enable playgoers to change places and identify (alternatively or simultaneously) with one strange party and/or the next. Generally, I argue that however much *Twelfth Night* staged "the encounter of the Illyrians with strangers and foreigners" (Stanivuković 2004, 409), it would have been hard for Shakespeare's playgoers to sort out who the stranger actually was. After all, the audience is faced with native Illyrians, like Orsino and Olivia, who resemble "neighboring Elizabethan aristocrats" (Warren and Wells 1994, 9) on the basis of their lifestyle, while others, like Sir Toby Belch or Sir Andrew Aguecheek, have "thoroughly English names" (Smith 2001, 116). Then there are such newcomers as Viola, to whom the audience is drawn closer than to any other character in the play. The fact that this character never really comes across as a stranger, to the playgoers at least, makes her representative of the equivocal nature of the stranger. She may begin her career in Illyria as an outsider and an intruder, but Viola swiftly shifts the spotlight of strangeness onto Illyria, in such a way that her "foreignness" ultimately acts as a dramatic ploy, requiring that "the question of identity [be] put not *to* the foreigner but *by* the foreigner" (Wilson 2005, 8). The captain, in turn, is only a stranger of a sort, as we learn he is shipwrecked close to home, having been "bred and born / Not three hours' travel from this very place" (1.2.22–23).[1] Such an ambivalent posture not only becomes the captain's role, which consists in introducing both Viola and the playgoers to a foreign land without alienating either from their sense of self or place in the world; it also typifies the intrinsically contradictory nature of strangeness in *Twelfth Night*.

The encounter of strangeness and domesticity is a stock situation in many comedies throughout the sixteenth century. Concerning *Twelfth Night*, it has been argued that, like *The Comedy of Errors*, *Love's Labour's Lost*, and *Much Ado About Nothing*, the play abides by an "alternate pattern." Rather than depart from court to wander into a strange green world, the characters keep to their domestic bounds where they are visited by strangers and find themselves tackling the outsider (or stranger) from within (Hawkins 1967, 67–68). It has also been shown that the play revolves around the admittance of a stranger within two aristocratic households: Orsino's palace and Olivia's stately home (Smith 2001, 116). The burden of this essay is that *Twelfth Night* portrays strangers in a remarkably original light, by conjuring dramatic stereotypes while blurring national distinctions. I begin by examining Illyria's multiple codes involved in domesticating strangeness (its rules, customs, prejudices, or hostilities). These are deployed and put to the test as Viola and Sebastian reach a foreign land and cross the threshold, first as unwelcome outsiders, then as guests (*OED*, "guest," informs us that its Old Teutonic derivatives *gasti*-z and WAryan *ghosti*-s are from the same root as the Latin *hostis*, which originally signified the "stranger" as well as the "potential enemy") while the hosts (*hospes*) extend their courtesy to these "visiting" strangers. I continue by analyzing the ideological drift between foreignness and strangeness and the way early modern drama repatriates strangeness and cancels the reductive characterizations based on the native–foreigner dichotomy. In a third section, I seek to investigate the meanings ascribed to strangeness in a play where foreignness is let off the hook (despite its action being set on the continent) and where the initial friction between the newcomers and the strange natives they discover is contained or "domesticated." My final section aims to show the feasibility of multiple perspectives and projections, by arguing that Illyria might be interpreted as an outlandish representation of Renaissance "core middle England" (or central London) that offers scenarios of the foreigner's reception and integration; or that, conversely, the twins' fortunes and misfortunes might be interpreted as portrayals of the Englishman abroad (as a tourist, settler or conqueror). In this final part, I argue that the play establishes a virtually symbiotic relationship between the domestic audience and the dramatic stranger. Throughout, I address characterization and the construction of identity, especially the way both Viola and Sebastian invite us to review the meaning of strangeness and weigh the definition and generic role of the "stranger" in early seventeenth-century drama.

* * *

The stranger who travels to foreign lands heads towards some appointed place, often another's homeland, with the aim of discovery, trade and commerce, or as a refugee of war. Strangers of this sort are imbued with a sense of direction and purpose. In *Twelfth Night*, however, the shipwrecked twins have neither. They seem to be going nowhere (there is no mention of any initial destination or design) and where they come from is something of a conundrum, as Feste unwittingly suggests in a dismissive remark: "who you are and what you would are out of my welkin" (3.1.58–59). In fact, the twins' geographical indeterminacy is not depicted as a source of anxiety either for them or the audience. Neither Viola nor Sebastian seeks a route back home. Nor do they treat Illyria as a port of call or behave as passers-by. Rather, they maneuver their way into the host community and become "settlers" a century before the word came to mean what it does today, carving their destinies out of the accidental: Viola as a servant and messenger, Sebastian as a protégé and perambulator, and both, ultimately, as aristocratic spouses home and dry and here to stay.

Their being set off-course remains downplayed to the point of irrelevance, perhaps because the shipwreck itself is "such a transparent plot device that an audience immediately forgets it" (Duncan-Jones 2001, 154). The novelty of a situation that has Viola and Sebastian follow in the footsteps of the Ovidian chief literary models, Cadmus and Harmonia, or meet with the same initial fate as Shakespeare's double set of twins, Antipholus and Dromio, in *The Comedy of Errors* (1594), had long since worn off for seventeenth-century characters and playgoers alike. While it is right to emphasize the convenient, codified nature of the shipwreck – its technical use being "to get the characters into place" (Auden 2000, 153) "and to provide Viola with a reason, albeit a flimsy one, for her disguise as 'an eunuch'" (Duncan-Jones 2001, 154) – it seems important not to discount the mythical motif and ritual dimension that subsume this dramatic convention. By pairing Illyria and Elysium, Viola draws the audience's attention to the landscape of liminality to which the shipwreck has introduced the characters. This plot device lays the groundwork for structures of transition that run through the play: transitions from life to death and from childhood into adulthood. It serves as a rite of passage, the first of many to inform poetic allusions and ritualize dramatic action in three phases – "separation, transition, and incorporation" (Liebler 1995, 117–18) – all of which are standard in romantic comedy and anthropological patterns. Thus the shipwreck separates Viola from Sebastian – an initial phase in which Viola's sense of loss shifts towards a sense of wonder as she inquires about her new circumstances and surroundings. "What country, friends, is this?" (1.2.1); "And what should I do in Illyria?" (1.2.3): contained in these questions are feelings of strangeness and estrangement that convert into a readiness to seek definition and self-determination. They prefigure a phase of transition crystallized in the disguised protagonist, Viola/Cesario, that "poor monster" (2.2.33) whose strangeness serves "the form of [her] intent" for the time of a play. Intimating the third phase of incorporation or domestication is the stranger's decision to take part in the life of the new-found community by stating: "I'll serve this duke" (1.2.55).

Viola enters the service of the noble duke by an act of *comitatus*. Orsino's domestication of the stranger to whom he offers shelter and employment does not represent "an optional manifestation of polite behavior," but "an absolute requirement of aristocracy" (Liebler 1995, 206). In contrast, the way Viola crosses Olivia's threshold emulates the traditional end-of-year mumming game. She stands "fortified against any denial" (1.5.146–47), putting to the test her host, who must face up to "the imperative of kindness to strangers by enacting the right of even the uninvited to cross the threshold of the house" (Wilson 2005, 13). Mummery involves "maskers who engineer encounters with the unmasked in the form of house-visits." By appearing in disguise, Viola clearly plays the game, since what the mummer should be at that point "is 'not himself'" (Twycross and Carpenter 2002, 82). On the other hand, Olivia's hiding behind a mask (or veil) to receive her visitor seems to flout the social skills required of a hostess. Hence Viola's insistence that Olivia abide by the custom: "Good madam, let me see your face" (1.5.233). *Twelfth Night* makes it the stranger's prerogative to expose strangeness within the host community by showing that misrule resides not outside the gates but within the home: "The rudeness that hath appeared in me have I learned from my entertainment" (1.5.217–18). When incivility culminates in a potential duel, Viola takes stock of the domestic situation, which she styles "as uncivil as strange" (3.4.257). Olivia and Orsino, each in turn, are made to face their own domestic strangeness, as their friendly intruders induce them to let down barriers, open their gates, unveil their faces – "we will draw the curtain" (1.5.236) – and unclasp "the book even of their secret soul" (1.4.13–14), until they uncover (and discover) their own estrangement to themselves.

It might fall to strangers to expose the uncouthness of their hosts, though by "strangers" we cannot simply understand the newcomers or unfamiliar faces. There are those autochthones that inveigh against another's obstinate incivility throughout, especially in matters of love. When Duke Orsino and Lady Olivia finally stand face to face, they pull no punches. Olivia, who finds no virtue in Orsino's show of outlandish obstinacy, responds to his provocation – "Still so cruel?" (5.1.109) – by deriding his constancy in unrequited love: "Still so constant, lord" (5.1.109). In an inability to domesticate either Olivia's heart or his own, Orsino rails against what he perceives to be her "ingrate" non-compliance with his game of love. His lover's complaint is to no avail while her scorn strikes a bitter chord: "What, to perverseness? You uncivil lady" (5.1.109–11). The frenzy of exalted strangeness that unfolds takes the estranged nobility away from their long-drawn-out emotional deadlock, which has proved damaging to civility generally. There may be "something decidedly improper about the perverse erotic excitement . . . and something irreducibly strange about the marriages . . . The strangeness of the bond between virtual strangers is matched by the strangeness of Orsino's instantaneous decision to marry Cesario – as soon as 'he' can become Viola by changing into women's clothes" (Greenblatt 1997, 1765). Despite this comedy of vertigo, the play precipitates both lady and lord into the arms of a set of look-alike strangers with remarkable and natural ease – "But nature to her bias drew in that" (5.1.258) – while comfortably, and comfortingly, ensuring that the twins remain on a social par with their hosts: "Be not amaz'd, right noble is his blood" (5.1.262).

Not all strangers fit into the Illyrian social framework so neatly. The play shows little mercy for Antonio, the marginal character who frets for the peregrine Sebastian and for "what might befall your travel, / Being skilless in these parts: which to a stranger, / Unguided and unfriended, often prove / Rough and unhospitable" (3.3.8–11). Antonio's show of hospitality (as one who has no shelter to offer other than his guardianship and friendship) is epitomized by his gentlemanly apology – "Pardon me, sir, your bad entertainment" – a courtesy Sebastian duly returns: "O good Antonio, forgive me your trouble" (2.1.32–33). Yet when Cesario (Viola), whom he takes to be Sebastian, lets him down, Antonio equally suffers the ultimate indignation of unrequited love and a shattering sense of betrayal. To top it all, Cesario puts his "strange speech" down to "distraction" (5.1.64–66). This subplot reveals to what extent the play opposes different degrees of strangeness by playing strangers against strangers in spite of themselves.

Twelfth Night deploys a double framework that swiftly absorbs a newcomer's strangeness while enabling the natives' idiosyncratic eccentricities to break through. The foreigner's striking ability to become integrated within the community is counterbalanced by the stark, undomesticated antics of some of the Illyrian residents. There is Olivia's uncle (and guest), who refuses to comply with household *boundaries*, a point hammered home by each word in Maria's injunction: "You must confine yourself within the modest limits of order" (1.3.8–9). And while Sir Toby is out of bounds, Sir Andrew is out of order in wanting to win Lady Olivia's affections. Sir Toby has persuaded his friend to settle in Olivia's household for a month – Sir Andrew would rather have tiptoed respectfully away early next morning. Sir Andrew complies, but ultimately, he is not spared Sir Toby's verbal flagellation and humiliation in front of Olivia. In fact, *Twelfth Night* turns uncouthness into a staple feature of Illyrian domestic policy, represented by Sir Toby and Co., especially when it comes to keeping each other's strangeness in check. Thus, while rallying the hired fool for his protracted absence without leave and his estrangement from the household, Maria, Olivia's maid, brandishes the threat of rough justice: "my lady will hang thee for thy absence" (1.5.3–4). We also witness Olivia's resident guests and servants team up to condemn her steward to solitary confinement and utter humiliation, to punish him for presuming to win Olivia's heart and climb the social ladder.

Left to their own devices, all characters, each in his and her own way, take it upon themselves to tame or hold at bay the strangeness in others while readily cultivating their own. Malvolio would have Toby "amend" his "drunkenness" (2.5.73) in order to remedy his extravagance and disorderly behavior yet claims to be eager to capitalize on his own "trick of singularity" (2.5.151). His ambition ultimately goes to his head and turns into a swaggering intoxication of the will: "I will be proud . . . I will baffle Sir Toby, I will wash off gross acquaintance" (2.5.161–63); "I will be strange" (2.5.171); "I will smile; I will do everything that thou wilt have me" (2.5.178–79). Sir Andrew Aguecheek's *modus operandi* is of a similar order. He would unhesitatingly "beat" Malvolio "like a dog" (2.3.141) if he believed him to be a Puritan, yet preposterously advertises his own marginality: "I am a fellow o'th' strangest mind i'th'world" (1.3.110–11), unwittingly confessing that: "Methinks sometimes I have no more wit than a Christian or an ordinary man has" (1.3.82–83). There is also Feste, who grows impatient as he mistakenly believes that Viola/Cesario (in actual fact Sebastian) is putting on an act: "I prithee now, ungird thy strangeness" (4.1.15–16). Yet he, too, pretends to be someone else when he appears dressed as a visiting curate come to castigate Malvolio. The desire to strip others of certain attributes (a veil, the bottle, pen and ink) incites the Illyrians to indulge in self-conscious, exuberant misrepresentations of the self, and the general manufacture of another identity, through apparel (concealment, disguise or cross-dressing), designation or appellation – "Thou shalt present me as an eunuch to him" (1.2.56).

* * *

Viola's introduction to Illyria appeals to our childlike sense of wonder. Memories may have needed prodding on Candlemas (February 2) 1602, but there were undoubtedly those amongst the Middle Temple students attending the performance in the Great Hall who would have responded to Viola's question, "Know'st thou this country?" (1.2.21), with as much assurance as the Captain – "Ay, madam, well," perhaps recalling some classroom lesson, like Cicero's reference to "Bargulus Illyrius latro" (*De Officiis*, 2.11.40) or Ovid's mythical account of the parents' plight to recover their child lost at sea (*Metamorphoses*, Book 4). Viola's other frame of reference is more informal, and more homely – information acquired by parental word of mouth. Her inquiry about the run of the country: "Who governs here?" (1.2.24) results in a familiar name that she had already come across in her past family conversations – "Orsino! I have heard my father name him" (1.2.28).

The Middle Temple audience would have relished the thought that *Twelfth Night* had been produced "under the auspices of the Middle Temple Treasurer whose nephew, Sir Robert Shirley, was 'the fencer to the Sophy' (3.4.248) saluted in the text" (Wilson 2005, 18). They would have applauded Fabian's comment as he watched Malvolio fall straight into Maria's epistolary trap: "I will not give my part of this sport for a pension of thousands to be paid from the Sophy" (2.5.180–81). But despite regaling the privileged students with fantasies of wealth brought back home, *Twelfth Night* indulges only up to a point in the armchair traveler's call of faraway lands. It has been suggested that underpinning Feste's disguise as "Sir Topas the curate" is an old-hat literary allusion to Chaucer the poet, who in "ironic self-presentation . . . makes a joke of his own unimpressive role as 'Chaucer the pilgrim'" (hear *peregrinus*, foreign, or strange). In *The Tale of Sir Topas*, the poet "makes himself the teller of a story so old-fashioned and tedious that the other pilgrims don't want to hear it out" (Duncan-Jones 2001, 156). If we read act 3 scene 4 with this interpretation in mind, we find that the cameo role of the passing traveler goes to the fictional storyteller of old rather than to the real life explorers and commanders of recent times. Chaucer's tales may no longer have been a match for the narratives of the Anthony Shirleys of this world, but in Shakespeare's play, Chaucer's traditional storytelling wanderer (Sir Topas) is granted the privilege of making an appearance as a character in his own right, possibly as a synecdoche for Chaucer himself, whereas William Barentz's stage presence, for instance, boils down to the allusive and metonymic "Dutchman's beard."[2]

The play taps into the "new map," delivering the discoveries it recorded of the East Indies and of Novaya Zemlya by the Dutch (Gillies 1994, 50), in a casual and allusive fashion, through metaphors and metonymies – a rhumb line, the outlines of a drawing, or an "icicle" for the Arctic. The wonders of this new geographical knowledge are summoned to illustrate the uncomfortable moods that prevail between characters. This is how Fabian intimates Olivia's increasingly cold indifference when he rebukes Sir Andrew: "you are now sailed into the north of my lady's opinion, where you will hang like an icicle on a Dutchman's beard" (3.2.24–26); this is how, further on, Maria's map of Malvolio's face changes, not without sarcasm, a smile into a *risus sardonicus* – "he does smile his face into more lines than is in the new map with the augmentation of the Indies" (3.2.75–77), thus drawing the line between knowledge (the audience's) and extravagance (the characters'), between derision (Maria's) and delusion (Malvolio's). Shakespeare's handling of new world discoveries is double-edged because he exploits their wondrous effect on the crowd while toning down, through clownish smiles, their potential to interpellate existing assumptions. It could be said that Shakespeare negotiates the emotional impact of novelty onto established ways of thinking by turning the subliminal into instruments of caricature. Introducing strangeness into the home becomes a process both enchanting and unsettling. If a map is "symbolic of both structure and *communitas*," its lines also "inscribe fissures along which crisis occurs" – a crisis of identity, by which even the definition of the "human" is "destabilized" (Liebler 1995, 198). Mapping Malvolio's smile becomes, indeed, a way of portraying "that borderline figure who defines the limits of the human" (Fiedler 1973, 15).

It is easy to imagine the topic of the Indies or the Polar North spicing conversations in melting-pot Renaissance London, very much as it does the play's dialogue, with ironic semiotic motifs woven into the lines. *Twelfth Night* is replete with living language, vernacular, provincialisms, and fashionable phrases, as when it refers to school lessons: "and *diluculo surgere*, thou know'st" (2.3.2–3), to popular games like the "tray trip" (2.5.190), and to such oddities as the notorious "bed of Ware in England" (3.2.46). Anchoring the action in local common knowledge, the play acknowledges that, at the turn of the century, London was not only supplying a growing market for exotic travel books: it was also selling literature on regional curiosities and a body of domestic mythology, and sometimes feeding on the foreigner's vision of England to do so. Thus, Ludwig of Anhalt-Köthen, a German prince who had toured England in 1596, was the first to bring the eccentric bedstead to national (and international) notice (Furness 1964, 204), a detail even John Norden's own *Description of Hertfordshire* (1598) did not supply.[3] Another contemporary publication circulating at the time was Richard Lynche's translation of Giovanni Nanni's *Travels of Noah into Europe* (1601). The primitive ethnographic vision of the world also receives an ironic echo in *Twelfth Night*. Indeed, it falls to Sir Toby, a parochial character, to allude to Illyria's antediluvian past, Europe's shared ancestor and the world's universal progenitor: "And they have been grand-jurymen since before Noah was a sailor" (3.2.14–15). Such details make characters like Sir Toby sound comfortably familiar to an English audience while Shakespeare's Illyria shares attributes in common with the "very rude, / uncivile, obstinat, and barbarous" people (Nanni 1601, sig. Gr) that the traveling Samothes domesticated and civilized, importing even the language that Cadmus would later transport to Greece and to Ovid's Illyry. Viola's role might be compared to that of a mythical moderator in her relation to the domestic characters of the play. Her initial strangeness operates as a mediating factor between wilderness and wonder as she enters Olivia's household offering her peaceful intercession: "I bring no overture of war, no taxation of homage; I hold the olive in my hand: my words are as full of peace, as matter" (1.5.211–14). She too seems to "curbe or bridle their naturall fantasies and disordinat affections" and tame the uncivil in Illyria "by faire and gentle demeanures," inspiring marvel amongst the audience at "so straunge alterations" (Nanni 1601, sig. Gr) in a way that rehabilitates the notion of strangeness.

* * *

What makes a play seem strange or foreign to its audience? Hunter argues that Marlowe's *Massacre at Paris* (1593) and Chapman's political plays, many of which are set in France, are not "foreign" in that "they are self-consciously un-English": being set outside of England, they allow for "the pursuit of political and religious conflicts that could not be safely dealt with in an English setting," while remaining sufficiently realistic to "avoid the escapist emphasis of Ruritanian settings" (Hunter 1964, 45). This suggests that a play is received as "foreign" when it does not offer the audience an opportunity to peer into the theatre of contemporary domestic issues, because its locale is either too close for comfort or too far-fetched.

There is much in *Twelfth Night* that makes Illyria come across as a Ruritanian "imaginary kingdom of central Europe" (*OED*), at one remove from reality. Stanivuković explains how "despite its actual presence on the cultural map of Mediterranean Renaissance, the eastern coast of Adriatic remained, for the English, a land of mystery and imagination" (2004, 406). However, this element of escapism is counterbalanced by parochial national awareness and insular linguistic mannerisms with which a turn-of-the-century audience might easily have identified. Shakespeare's Illyria is not so much "self-consciously un-English" as self-consciously Illyrian. It is self-referential in its end of sentences: "as any man in Illyria" (1.3.20, 114, 121); "as any in Illyria" (1.5.26–27); "in any part of Illyria" (3.4.272); "if there be any law in Illyria" (4.1.34). Even Malvolio, desperate to be acknowledged for his sanity and to be welcomed back into society, asserts, "I tell thee I am as well in my wits as any man in Illyria" (4.2.110–11).

Other mannerisms in Shakespeare's Illyrian vernacular consist in fashionable appropriations of foreign phrases that enhance the speaker's sense of sense and draw our attention to the character's powerful stage presence, by changes in the rhythm and sound of speech. Sir Toby Belch particularly enjoys flaunting his wide-ranging knowledge of those fashionable foreign words that had made their way into the English language in some form or other: "Kikshawes," "galliard," "sink-a-pace," "cubiculo." Corruptions such as "Castiliano vulgo" (1.3.42) may remain utterly obscure, except to Sir Toby, but it is when his continental dialect is most appropriately used, as in, "*Pourquoi*, my dear knight?" (1.3.89), that Sir Andrew is left guessing the meaning of the simplest of words: "What is *pourquoi*? Do, or not do?" (1.3.90). Toby's Illyrianisms may be those of a braggart though, more to the point, they conjure up a picture of a well-traveled, quick-witted Englishman, who flaunts his knowledge the better to flout the ignorance of his close entourage.

Sir Toby's relation to foreignness has both retrospective and proleptic depth. Seen against the mirror of the past, Sir Toby Belch's drinking habits, his name even, recall such dramatic filiations as the foreign and bibulous Vandalle, a character from William Haughton's *Englishmen for My Money, or A Woman Will Have Her Will* (1598). Vandalle is, indeed, "an unmannered though rich rustic type with a tendency to belch in his beloved's ear, [who] like his compatriots in other plays . . . is no teetotaller" (Hoenselaars 1992, 55–56). From a contemporary angle, it would seem that history has bequeathed Sir Toby's florid use of foreign words to the illiterate, self-made entrepreneur, epitomized by the 1980s' British sitcom anti-hero, Derek Trotter and his multicultural cockney dialect in *Only Fools and Horses*. Though Del Boy's soppy French phrases and general linguistic inadequacies cut no ice with the traveled man, they pepper his language – as in "what we have here is a case of *je ne sais quoi, pourquoi*" – in a way that keeps his friends guessing, as Sir Toby does Sir Andrew, and gives him the upper hand over the cavemen down at The Nag's Head. Following the same rules of comedy as his ancient counterpart, the sitcom's wheeling-and-dealing rogue refuses to "confine," altogether evading income-tax and this "pina-colada lout" shares with Toby the propensity for alcoholic sprees. Both stock characters appear in a double act, Derek's brother, Rodney "the dipstick," standing as a modern version of Sir Andrew, with the added distinction that unlike Sir Andrew – "O, had I but followed the arts!" (1.3.92–93) – Rodney's the one "with the GCSEs in art" (Sullivan 2003).

Malvolio's characterization also draws deeply upon the ways certain characters in Tudor and Elizabethan drama were given license to explore foreignness. There is a vice character, in particular, in the Tudor *Enterlude of Welth and Helth* (1554–57), that might very well be perceived as Malvolio's old English namesake: Ill Will. It is not just the name that links the character to Malvolio. Ill Will (like other characters in the play) berates the intemperance of the parasitical and unlikable Fleming, Hance Berepot, as Malvolio does Sir Toby's Dutch courage. Moreover, just as the anonymous dramatist makes his character resort to disguise, Shakespeare dresses up Malvolio. Ill Will pretends to be "un spuanardo compoco parlauere" (sig. D3r) to avoid Good Remedy, who having already expelled Hance from the kingdom, seeks Ill Will to punish him for having wreaked havoc in the country. Malvolio dons cross-garters and yellow stockings, not to avoid attention, but on the contrary, to attract it, so as to be fast-tracked to Olivia's privileged life. Where the Tudor interlude was mildly attempting to pass off a native as a foreigner, for his own safety, *Twelfth Night* takes the comic device of the Englishman impersonating a foreigner and gives it a twist. The play dons its character full of ill will in a send-up of English attire, thus precipitating his marginalization and segregation from the household – he is literally shut up and held hostage by his entourage. In addition, his garments are both highly formal and somewhat old-fashioned; cross garters, especially, were worn by the Lord Chamberlain, patron of the Order of the Garter, as well as "old men, Puritans, pedants, footmen, and rustic bridegrooms" (Linthicum 1936, 264). He thus appears no better than the common "pedant that keeps a school i'th'church" (3.2.72–73). In fact, there is nothing foreign about Malvolio, either before or after his change of guise. However strange he may seem in appearance or behavior, he comes across, down to the wire, as an Englishman of a sort: the parody of a pedantic Puritan.

In both cases, the characters' endeavor to look or sound singularly different (strange or foreign) backfires. But as Hoenselaars explains, "to be taken for a Spaniard still involved certain privileges not to be expected by other foreigners like Hance Berepot. Considering the fact that Queen Mary's husband, Philip of Spain, resided in England when the play was performed at court during the winter of 1554/5 and that he most probably attended the performance, it is not unlikely that Ill Will's choice of disguise was meant to be interpreted as a shrewd attempt to capitalize on pro-Spanish sentiments prevailing in court circles" (Hoenselaars 1992, 41). There is nothing shrewd in Malvolio's spectacular outfit and behavior, which he wears on what he believes to be the epistolary demand of Olivia. To be branded as "a sort of

Puritan" and show willful divisiveness in a way that recalls Martin Marprelate's antics would not have gone down well in 1602. The religious controversy had after all started around the issue of dress, in 1566, before culminating in a war of tracts, during the Armada Autumn of 1588. But Malvolio is a character forgiven and pitied, who partakes just as much of the century's tradition of "English criticism – in prose, poetry, and drama – of the Englishman's fondness of new and foreign fashions" (Hoenselaars 1992, 164) than he does of the political and religious controversy. As a type character on the English stage, Malvolio's only excites ridicule because his fashion is neither new nor foreign, but old-fashioned and sectarian.

Following up on the comparison, it might be said that when Feste, disguised as a curate, denies Malvolio "some ink, paper, and light" (4.2.113–14), he re-enacts the punitive measures bishops (and editors) took against the Puritan movement. Similarly, Maria's letter functions like the tracts themselves, which had become "evidence . . . of how reality and distorted perceptions and projections of reality, fact and fiction, theatre and life, could interact" (Collinson 2002, 390). Fabian makes a similar comment, when observing the gulled Malvolio: "If this were played upon a stage now, I could condemn it as an improbable fiction" (3.4.128–29). Malvolio's exit line serves as a reminder that as we return to the final merriments of comedy, we should not forget the elephant in the room. His outburst resounds as a final portentous call-up cry, warning that every dog will have its day: "I'll be revenged on the whole pack of you" (5.1.377). And indeed, in 1602, "the idea . . . that [the Puritans] had lost the argument or had nothing more to say [was] mistaken . . . the accession of James I [would reactivate] hopes of reform and the redress of grievances" (Collinson 2002, 391).

Another Shakespearean character had similarly stormed out of *The Merry Wives of Windsor* (1597), a few years before, exclaiming "by gar, I'll raise all Windsor" (5.5.208). The French physician Doctor Caius had been repeatedly subjected "to the wiles and schemes of the English characters" in his pursuit of Anne Page (Hoenselaars 1992, 58) for being utterly foreign, just as Malvolio is victimized by his domestic entourage for being utterly aloof and estranging others. Yet what transpires in the comparison is a turn in the trend, for it is no longer a character's foreignness that leads to his being ill-treated in *Twelfth Night*, but his strangeness or "singularity" – a characteristic that will later cost Shakespeare's final tragic hero, Coriolanus, his consulship, his residence in Rome, his life in Corioles. In this romance, by contrast, characters are still relatively secure. Through placing the setting in a foreign country, *Twelfth Night* emancipates foreignness from strangeness. Foreignness no longer systematically carries with it the idea of strangeness, any more than strangeness systematically implies foreignness.

* * *

Twelfth Night does not truly display ethnocentricity. It refers to a familiar English world, even while evoking some other world – other, because from some other land or some other time. There are puns and riddles that betray a tension in its broadest sense, a tension which is sometimes resolved, and sometimes not, between the inlanders and the "strangers." In Toby's mouth, foreignness as a metaphor for suspicion and unreliability also turns native. "My lady's a Cataian" (2.3.76), it has been demonstrated, refers metonymically to home-bred "big-talking" travelers, like Humphrey Gilbert and Martin Frobisher, whose tales were not always reliable: "Cataian" has been identified as an over-determined signifier "for someone whose speech is not to be trusted (that is, who makes empty threats or vain promises)" (Billings 2003, 7). The statement, "Malvolio's nose is no whipstock, my lady has a white hand, and the Myrmidons are no bottle-ale houses" (2.3.27–29), offers contrastive combinations, in which the foreign-sounding name is juxtaposed with the familiar, domesticating handle of a whip and the artificiality of the legendary Myrmidons clashes with the downrightness of the customary bottle-ale houses.

The phrase "my lady has a white hand" (an appropriate characteristic for a woman) surrounds the aristocratic, landowning, isolated maid with a covetous and competitive male entourage. The effect is unsettling. The lady stands between the whip and the bottle, between the stick and the ale-house. It is no wonder that Olivia appears circumspect about whom she lets in. When asking, "What is he at the gate, cousin?" (1.5.117–18), Olivia leaves the unknown visitor waiting outside, as the questions move from Sir Toby to Malvolio: "what is he?" (1.5.128); "What kind o'man is he?" (1.5.152); "What manner of man?" (1.5.154); "Of what personage and years is he?" (1.5.157). Such questions may not concern strangeness per se, but they suggest that the degree to which a character is treated like a stranger depends on his rank and ways. Where Viola's questions in act 1 scene 2 express with acute open-mindedness her wish to understand the basic pattern of a group in a process of assimilation and social adjustment, Shakespeare's gated community betrays both nervousness in letting others in and apprehension about not being let in. In anticipation of another rebuff from Olivia, Duke Orsino enjoins Cesario not to take no for an answer (as Valentine did): "Be not denied access, stand at her doors, / And tell them, there thy fixed foot shall grow / Till thou have audience" (1.4.16–18); "Be clamorous, and leap all civil bounds" (1.4.21).

At another level, Valentine's lines reveal his own anxiety at witnessing with what ease Viola has secured a domestic stronghold: "If the Duke continue these favours towards you, Cesario, you are like to be much advanced: he hath known you but three days, and already you are no stranger" (1.4.1–4). Valentine betrays a possible loss of faith in his master's love as well as fear of the newcomer's potential ruthlessness: "You either fear for his humour, or my negligence, that you call in question the continuance of his love" (1.4.4–5). Viola's intention to play and sing (as Cesario) to the Duke makes her a professional rival to Valentine. Being admitted into Olivia's household, she becomes a contender for the hand of the aristocrat in the eyes of Sir Toby. Her role as a messenger is even received as a threat by Feste, who feels the need to reassert his generic role as a go-between, as he remarks: "I would play Lord Pandarus of Phrygia, sir, to bring a Cressida to this Troilus" (3.1.52–53). The stranger who integrates himself into the Illyrian community socially, through employment, provokes nervousness amongst those natives taken aback by the disturbing skill with which the stranger has turned domestic. When the same stranger enters that community intimately, through love and marriage, he is received as a menace by master and servant, by the social-climbers, the "love-brokers" (3.2.36), and the unrequited lovers.

Strangeness turns native, and is repatriated, in another way. There is a growing trend in comedies, after 1595, "to present the foreigner as a surprising mirror of English characters" (Hoenselaars 1992, 66), in ways that make inveterate foreign vices seem native. Flemish, Dutch or German dipsomania progressively becomes an English characteristic, especially when the Englishman travels abroad (except in *Hamlet*, where it is resolutely Danish). In *The Weakest Goeth to the Wall* (1600), Barnaby Bunch drinks the Fleming Jacob to bed, making his final exit to the pub, while in *Thomas Lord Cromwell* (1602), Hodge, who only goes to work once having taken his draught, enters Antwerp expressing a thirst for English beer. Within such a context, Sir Toby comes across as an Englishman abroad on regular drinking sprees, who will typically claim, "I'll drink to her as long as there is a passage in my throat, and drink in Illyria" (1.3.38–40). Madness also treads the stage as another form of strangeness that progressively evolves into a typical English trait. In 1601, Shakespeare's gravedigger in *Hamlet* alleges that all Englishmen are mad (5.1.149–50). Insanity may have become a characteristic of the common Englishman; yet such strangeness of the mind is rampant in Illyria. Interestingly, it is Sebastian, the stranger or traveler, who is shown fending off madness, that is, the feeling of strangeness brought about by the errors of the plot, at every encounter. He dismisses Feste – "I prithee vent thy folly somewhere else" (4.1.10) then beats back Sir Andrew, before exclaiming "Are all the people mad?" (4.1.25). The ultimate irony is that, as he progressively catches up with Viola, he feels that madness could well catch up with him. Immediately before agreeing to marry Olivia, he thus confesses, "that I am mad, / Or else the lady's mad" (4.3.15–16). The criterion for such "disorders" becomes so blurred that even Olivia will concede, "I am as mad as he / If sad and merry madness equal be" (3.4.15). The element of madness, which brings home to us the difficult questions of identity and recognition, definitely has its place in the comic pattern, as *The Comedy of Errors* had already revealed. In *Twelfth Night*, however, it also populates the foreign country of Illyria with characters so familiar as to sound and look more English than foreign. To this extent, it might be suggested that the play looks towards those plays of the seventeenth century like *The Pilgrim* (1621) by John Fletcher that "satirically portrayed English character types in a foreign setting" in "what became a tradition of English madmen peopling the continent of Europe in English drama" (Hoenselaars 1992, 166).

* * *

Domesticating strangeness means having to decide not only between "madness" and "wonder" (4.3.3 and 5), but also between the unworthy in mankind (ignorance) and the worthy – the humane. In *Sir Thomas More*, the eponymous protagonist invites in the first instance the rioters, and through them, the playgoers, to imagine themselves in exile: "Why, you must needs be strangers" received by a nation "of such barbarous temper" who breaks out "in hideous violence" and "spurns" aliens "like dogs." The conclusion is outfront, disturbing even: "What would you think / To be thus used? This is the stranger's case, / And this your mountainish inhumanity" (2.3.141–50). In *Twelfth Night*, Sir Toby's final encounter with Sebastian shows him ready to draw and break out in violence against the stranger. Olivia is made to realize that Sir Toby's lack of domesticity signals not only caterwauling but a fortress mentality, as she is given to witness in outrage his boorish reception of the stranger she loves. Not only is this a wake-up call for Olivia, but it also marks a stage in the play where "the degenerate Illyrian 'politician' is ripe for domestication" (Ungerer 1979, 94). She publicly castigates Sir Toby as an "ungracious wretch, / Fit for the mountains and barbarous caves, / Where manners ne'er were preach'd!" (4.1.47–48). The lesson from *Sir Thomas More* seems to echo in her lines. It really is not clear whether Olivia exclaims, "Out of my sight!" and "Rudesby, be gone!" (4.1.48, 50), in the heat of the moment, or whether she finally chooses to act upon her moral, noble (contrary to ignoble) standards, and to boot Sir Toby out altogether of her home in righteous indignation.

As this last of the romantic and festive comedies unfolds, its spectators are made to feel foreign, estranged, or strange, for the play continually challenges their sense of what it means to be human. *Twelfth Night* incites the audience to accompany the protagonists past their frontiers only to make them discover they are being led closer to home through a wide range of scenarios that all seem to ask how fares "the stranger that is within thy gates."[4] The answer, like audience perspective, seemingly varies with the ebb and flow of the castaways' lot, the midsummer madness of resident characters, and the cross-tide of subplots, though it unremittingly transpires that strangers "R" us. Swimming under the surface of *Twelfth Night* Illyria is a projection of England, "a romance land to which England displaces its own unruliness and vices . . . its own provincialism vis-à-vis the civilized Renaissance Europe" (Stanivuković 2004, 409). In fact, the play transports several stock national traits back to the continent, though not a familiar part of it, in a way that enables the playgoers to feel they are watching England through a looking glass, as its "nonsense" logic cancels the Anglo-foreign dichotomy. Old Tudor contests that opposed the foreigner's vice to the native's virtue, as in *Welth and Helth*, no longer prevail. If *Twelfth Night* is a comedy "whose humor targets both the English and the foreigners, both *us* and *them*" (Stanivuković 2004, 411), more often than not, *we* and *they* merge communally and morphologically into a complex state of being.

Notes

1. The edition I have used throughout this essay is the J. M. Lothian and T. W. Craik's 1975 edition.
2. "But where . . . is there any indication in the plays of Elizabeth's reign that the seamen's services achieved glorious recognition?" (Lindabury 1931, 161). "Though it was only a matter of time before the Elizabethan newly engaged abroad . . . would become integrated into the drama" (Hoenselaars 1992, 77).
3. The Bed of Ware received mention only in John Taylor's *The honorable, and memorable foundations, . . . of divers cities . . . of this kingdome, etc.*, London, 1636.
4. *Geneva Bible*, 1560, Deuteronomy 5: 14.

Works cited

Auden, W. H. *Lectures on Shakespeare.* Ed. Arthur Kirsch. Princeton, NJ: Princeton University Press, 2000.

Billings, Timothy. "Caterwauling Cataians: The Genealogy of a Gloss." *Shakespeare Quarterly* 54 (2003): 1–28.

Collinson, Patrick. "Literature and the Church." In *The Cambridge History of Early Modern English Literature*. Ed. David Loewenstein and Janel Mueller. Cambridge: Cambridge University Press, 2002: 374–98.

Craik, T. W., ed. *The Merry Wives of Windsor. The Oxford Shakespeare*. Oxford: Oxford University Press, 1990.

Duncan-Jones, Katherine. *Ungentle Shakespeare. Scenes from His Life.* London: Thompson Learning, 2001.

English, Horace Bidwell, and Ava Champney English. "Projection." In *A Comprehensive Dictionary of Psychological and Psychoanalytical Terms*. London: Longmans, Green & Co., 1958.

Fiedler, Leslie. *The Stranger in Shakespeare*. London: Croom Helm, 1973.

Furness, Horace Howard, ed. *Twelfth Night, or What You Will.* By William Shakespeare. A New Variorum Edition of Shakespeare. New York: Dover Publications, 1964.

Gillies, John. *Shakespeare and the Geography of Difference*. Cambridge: Cambridge University Press, 1994.

Greenblatt, Stephen, ed. *Twelfth Night. The Norton Shakespeare*. New York and London: Norton, 1997.

Hawkins, Shearman. "The Two Worlds of Shakespearean Comedy." *Shakespeare Studies* 3 (1967): 62–80.

Hill, Tracey. "'The Cittie is in an uproare': Staging London in the Booke of Sir Thomas More." *Early Modern Literary Studies* 11 (2005): 2.1–19.

Hoenselaars, A. J. *Images of Englishmen and Foreigners in the Drama of Shakespeare and His Contemporaries. A Study of Stage Characters and National Identity in English Renaissance Drama, 1558–1642*. London and Toronto: Associated University Presses, 1992.

Hunter, G. K. "Elizabethans and Foreigners." *Shakespeare Survey* 17 (1964): 37–52.

Liebler, Naomi. *Shakespeare's Festive Tragedy: The Ritual Foundations of Genre*. London and New York: Routledge, 1995.

Lindabury, R. V. *A Study of the Patriotism in the Elizabethan Drama*. Princeton, NJ: Princeton University Press, 1931.

Linthicum, M. Channing. *Costume in the Drama of Shakespeare and his Contemporaries.* Oxford: Oxford University Press, 1936.

Lothian, J. M., and T. W. Craik, eds. *Twelfth Night.* The Arden Shakespeare. London: Metheun, 1975.

Sir Thomas More: A Play by Anthony Munday and Others. Ed. Vittorio Gabrieli and Giorgio Melchiori. The Revels Plays. Manchester: Manchester University Press, 1990.

Nanni, Giovanni. *Travels of Noah into Europe*. London: 1601.

Smith, Bruce R., ed. *Twelfth Night, or What You Will: Texts and Contexts*. Boston and New York: Bedford/St. Martin's, 2001.

Stanivuković, Goran V. "Illyria Revisited: Shakespeare and the Eastern Adriatic." In *Shakespeare and the Mediterranean: The Selected Proceedings of the International Shakespeare Association World Congress, Valencia, 2001*. Ed. Tom Clayton, Susan Brock, and Vicente Forés. Newark: University of Delaware Press, 2004: 400–415.

Sullivan, John. *Only Fools and Horses*. The Complete Series 6. Directed by Tony Dow. Produced by Gareth Gwenlan. BBC Worldwide Ltd, 2003.

Twycross, Meg, and Susan Carpenter. *Masks and Masking in Medieval and Early Tudor England.* Aldershot: Ashgate, 2002.

Ungerer, Gustav. "'My Lady's a Catayan, We Are Politicians, Maluolios a Peg-A-Ramsie,' (*Twelfth Night*, II, iii, 77–78)." *Shakespeare Survey* 32 (1979): 85–104.

Warren, Roger, and Stanley Wells, eds. *Twelfth Night, or What You Will.* Oxford Classics. Oxford: Oxford University Press, 1994.

Wilson, Richard. "Making Men of Monsters: Shakespeare in the Company of Strangers." *Shakespeare* 1.1 (2005): 8–28.

10 Staging the exotic in *Twelfth Night*

Nathalie Rivère de Carles

In his appraisal of the relationship between the dramatic and the exotic A. P. Riemer states that "the distortions and the rearrangement of everyday life in most comedies represent artistic necessity – the discovery of an ideal landscape in which playfully ambivalent concerns find a proper and comfortable environment" (1980, 65). Illyria is an unclear destination hesitating between reality and fiction. One could argue that other Shakespearean comedies fictionalize their own geographical situation, but *Twelfth Night* seems to take the process a step further in featuring a mythical country which has disappeared in the turmoil of history. This is not Italy, Greece, Spain or Austria; this is Illyria, the land of the exotic. The creation of an ideal landscape which exists only in a mythological intertext or in other plays (*2 Henry VI*, 4.1.107) as a fictional counterpart to familiar spatial landmarks is essential to the dynamics of the performance because it provokes the audience's wonderment.

Murray Levith points out that although editors trace back the place name, Illyria, to Golding's translation of Ovid's *Metamorphoses* and locate it "in present-day Yugoslavia [. . .]; the feel and ambience of Orsino's dukedom is decidedly Italian" (1989, 11). Thus, the geographical indeterminacy of the play's setting is an essential feature of both the plot and the staging. Indeed, this spatial license enables Shakespeare to superimpose English and non-English influences within the action but also allows a complete scenographical flexibility. In his study of the directorial choices in recent performances of *Twelfth Night*, Michael Billington notes that

> Stage history suggests there is a constant debate about how the play should be staged. Does Illyria yield up its secrets to realism or to the imagination? Between the archeologically exact terraced gardens of Beerbohm Tree at one end of the scale and the neo-Elizabethan simplicity of William Poël at the other there seems to be an infinite number of options.
>
> (Billington 1990, ix–x)

Twelfth Night is paradoxically a very challenging play to stage, precisely because of the strangeness of its location. According to each period of history it will be performed in, productions will have to opt for a different dramaturgy of the exotic. However, the indeterminacy of Illyria and the ensuing scenographic flexibility of the play is one of the main reasons of its appeal to modern directors. The spatial and temporal license of *Twelfth Night* enables directors and actors to reach a wide audience. This intrinsic adaptability of the play is at the origin of this essay. *Twelfth Night* can be set in an incredibly varied amount of geographical contexts. Yet, as the play is originally located in an imaginary though very southern European environment, it seems interesting to observe how the play's spatial flexibility and exoticism could translate when directed and performed on the continent.

The concept of alienation is central to both plot and setting in *Twelfth Night*: the play is set in a foreign space; some of the characters themselves appear to be strangers in this space, and the playwright juxtaposes an English and a non-English onomastics, preventing a clear identification of the geographical context. Nevertheless, throughout the centuries, the play, originally destined to English audiences, widened its reach and started to focus increasingly on its initial plot: the landing of strangers on alien shores. The play about foreigners lost in a foreign land became a foreign play. Indeed, the inclusion of Shakespeare into the repertories of various continental companies changed the perspective on the exotic play. What was exotic for an English audience was not necessarily what would titillate continental spectators' curiosity.

The absorption of *Twelfth Night* in the continental repertoire questions the exoticism of the play. If Illyria is of a continental origin, the exotic has to find new means of expression than the southern European clichés. Continental directors often opt for minimalist décor to build up the indeterminacy of Illyria. The exoticism of the reverie thus created is reinforced by the confusion of the temporal landmarks and of the spectators' senses.

Such a play on dramaturgy raises the issue of the relationship between the exotic and theatricality. The search for innovative techniques to stage the exotic sometimes ends in a dialogue between the director and dramatic art. The issue is whether metatheatricality is an actual signifier of the exotic or its very limitation.

"A perspective that is and that is not" (5.1.109): *Twelfth Night* through the continental looking glass

Shakespeare's text remains inconclusive as far as the spatial context is concerned. To Viola's anxious question "What country, my friend, is this?" the Captain of their wrecked ship answers laconically, "This is Illyria, lady" (1.2.1–2). Neither the stage directions nor the cues help the audience to imagine Illyria. Shakespeare counted on the foreign onomastics to convey a sense of exoticism. However, the evolution of staging and the development of a directorial and spectatorial taste for imposing stage settings altered the initial dramaturgy of the exotic. If Shakespeare seemed to rely on words and maybe on costumes, later theatre companies opted for a more visually explicit exoticism. Hence, it is not surprising to witness major alterations of the Shakespearean script when adapted on the continent. After the example of William Davenant, who rewrote *Macbeth* in 1673 to fit the requirements of the Restoration theatres, continental poets adapted Shakespeare's text to their own *zeitgeist*. *Twelfth Night* entered the continental repertoire as a doubly exotic text: the plot was drawn from an English playwright and the original script had to be made more continental.

After the translation of the complete works of Shakespeare by Pierre Letourneur (1776–83), nineteenth-century France took a growing interest in the Bard's plays. Victor Hugo translated poetically all of Shakespeare's plays (1859–66) and contributed to the increasing appeal of the Elizabethan playwright. Nonetheless, this new appreciation of the Bard's drama implied some unfaithfulness to the original. Indeed, the spirit and the scenography of the English Renaissance were adapted to fit nineteenth-century French audiences' expectations.

Twelfth Night did not enter the French repertoire under its name but as *Le Conte d'Avril* (April's Tale). This 1885 play by Auguste Dorchain retained only the Orsino–Viola plot and dropped the vengeful intrigue against Malvolio. In short, Dorchain kept the openly exotic part of the play. Indeed, Shakespeare's comedy concentrated the familiar features of Englishness in this secondary plot, while the intrigue revolving around Orsino, Viola/Cesario and Olivia remained sufficiently indeterminate to be remodeled to continental taste.

Thus, Dorchain repossessed the play and gave it continental visual overtones. The opening stage direction set the scene in a professed "imaginary Illyria" with "sixteenth-century style setting and costume" [author's translation]. Yet, the décor implied by the plethoric stage directions was definitely continental:

> A square with some trees. – Downstage, on the right, an inn with a vine arbour under which are a table and chairs. – Upstage, a cabaret. – On the left, Olivia's pavilion and adjacent to it the outside wall of the duke's park. The door of the pavilion opens on a marble threshold with a double staircase.
>
> (Dorchain 1885, 1.1.0.1–4; author's translation)

The inn and the cabaret were straightforward continental elements, as well as the sense of an outdoor life conveyed by the furniture. Of course, for a French audience, this would not have looked remotely exotic. Strangeness had to find other means of expression and that is what Dorchain showed in his closely scenographed script.

His version of *Twelfth Night* aimed at being strictly followed by directors. The play was performed twice in the same theatre, in 1885–86 and in 1918–19 and seemed to respect Dorchain's indications in both cases. The 1885 edition shows the performance at the Théâtre de l'Odéon by Marc Porel (director) and M. Foucault (scenographer) was faithful to the script.

The threefold structure contained in the first stage direction of the play recalls the medieval stage organization when the performance area was divided in several scaffolds or mansions, enabling a continuous act thanks to a simultaneous staging. The protean nature of the Illyrian world is enhanced by this obvious fragmentation of the perspective. The spectator's gaze is constantly redirected to a different space attached to sometimes opposite characters. The semi-circular set plays with the depth of the proscenium stage and draws an implicit line between the plebeian world of the inn and the cabaret on the right, and the aristocratic houses of Olivia and Orsino on the left. Such a layout does not seem really surprising from a social point of view. The symbolic partition between the two worlds is really significant. Yet, the exoticism is brought up by the strange proximity between the noble house of the virtuous Olivia and the cabaret. Even Orsino's land is strangely close, thus turning Illyria into a compact although eclectic territory. The strange nature of Illyria is conveyed, first, by its versatility – the play is organized around five changes of perspective – and, second, by its pastoral influence. The initial global perspective on Illyria is swiftly replaced during act 2 by a more suitable décor for a bucolic love story,

> The Duke's park. Trees, statues and lilacs groves. At the centre of the stage, a bush and a marble bench.
>
> (Tableau 1.2.0.1–2; author's translation)

and its nocturnal version during act 4,

> The Duke's park. – Same perspective as in act II, but at night, under a moonlight.
>
> (4.0.1–2; author's translation)

Dorchain concentrates his plot on the noble characters and their love entanglements but he pays his tribute to Renaissance literature by replacing the exotic indeterminacy of Illyria by an Arcadian perspective. The pastoral theme, characteristic of Shakespeare's *As You Like It*, is chosen to replace *Twelfth Night*'s Mediterranean marvelous. While Shakespeare was relying on indeterminacy and foreign onomastics in order to create exoticism, Dorchain plays with a literary tradition. The introductory stage direction focused not only on the fictional aspect of space but also on the chronological gap between audience and characters. The spectators are given the impression that they are watching the stage version of a Renaissance pastoral, for the sixteenth-century-style costumes strengthen the poetic quotation. The exotic is here provided by the transfer of Illyria into an entirely fictional environment and above all into a different temporal stratum. The exotic shock is predicated on both the literary allusion and the travel in time.

"Is there no respect of place, persons, nor time in you" (2.2.79)

When Malvolio complains about Toby Belch's breach of the household etiquette, he is actually addressing the core issue of the play: the whirligig of the *Ego*, *Hic et Nunc*. Wonderment in the play is engendered by the turning upside down of both the identity of the characters and the spatiotemporal landmarks. In 1914, Jacques Copeau's production offered the audience the first non-traditional performance of the Shakespearean comedy. The stylized set was matched by anachronistic costumes. Viola's Renaissance-style white doublet with thin black stripes was counteracted by Louis Jouvet's Aguecheek and his sky-blue top hat and Feste's pink and blue garb and lobster claws-shaped red cap. The shock between the resolutely modern set (quoted in Billington 1990, xv), the phantasmagorical clothes and the remnants of the Renaissance explored the core of Shakespeare's deliberate confusion of time, space, and identity in *Twelfth Night*. In his article on the relationship between Shakespeare and European geography, François Laroque raises the question of the "geographic palimpsest." He argues that the Shakespearean imaginary geography is both "synonymous with escape, detour, or indirection for characters in quest of liberty or identity" and "indissociable from a topography of time" (2004, 151). The turmoil of the sense and the senses illustrated by Malvolio is the dramatic version of the questions raised by exoticism. The displacement of the action in foreign lands and indefinite time is the theatrical response to the characters' ontological wanderings. Hence, it seems necessary to have a closer look at the scenographic strategies used by contemporary continental directors to convey the comic disorder of space, time, and self.

Antonio Latella uses the same confusion of space and time as Copeau in his own 2004 adaptation of *Twelfth Night*, *La dodicesima notte, o quel che volete*. He reverses the Elizabethan tradition of an all-male cast by turning it into an all-female one and replacing the Shakespearean theatrical tradition with that of the *commedia dell'arte* (Figure 10.1). Feste is a female Harlequin, Olivia is Columbine and all the other characters are dressed as Italian Renaissance comedians. Latella switches from one Renaissance to another. Nevertheless, he is not aiming at an archeological performance or at an Italianized version of an English Renaissance play. He follows Shakespeare's own prescription: he shows no respect for time, place, or persons. He

Figure 10.1 *La dodicesima notte, o quel che volete*, director: Antonio Latella. Théâtre municipal, Avignon 2004. Photograph: Hervé Bellamy.

acknowledges the sixteenth-century origins of *Twelfth Night* but displaces its initial theatrical context by turning the play into one of the *commedia dell'arte* repertoire. This subtle temporal and spatial movement is the impulse to a more radical dramaturgy bringing the play into a visual and aural temporal continuum.

In his directorial notes, Latella defines his first contact with the Shakespearean comedy as a spatiotemporal riddle: "For the first time, I am faced with a comedy which is set in an instant, which is set neither in a specific place nor in a specific time" [author's translation]. Latella defines his staging of *Twelfth Night* as the "reflection of a dream" [author's translation]. He borrows the indeterminacy of the oneiric world as a modern echo of Shakespeare's own spatiotemporal ambiguity. The exoticism is once more conveyed in this performance by juxtaposed temporal strata. The twenty-first-century audience has to face its own theatrical memory and witness the revival of a tradition.

However, the awkward sense of an indeterminate space is the real source of the exotic. The familiarity of the spectators with the *commedia dell'arte* is altered by the choice of white aerial balloons attached to the reclining stage. The impression of evanescence due to the strong contrast between the white spheres and the dark background invites the spectators into a reverie. The space of the play is the world of dreams. This dramatization of imagination is strengthened by a horizontal stage tempted by verticality. The actors seem suspended in the air like dreamlike fairies or about to slide off the stage. The absence of firm spatial landmarks strengthens the impression that the story is set in an unfamiliar world. The oneirism implied by the mythical Illyria has found its dramatic expression. The play's exoticism lies in the dream-quality of the performance of a script detached from its time and space.

This indeterminacy is the contemporary answer to Shakespeare's own geographical vagueness in *Twelfth Night*. The point is to drag the audience into a purely illusory world where imagination is at work. In *A Midsummer Night's Dream*, Shakespeare unveils the challenging role of the artist when confronted with an imaginary unknown: "as imagination bodies forth / The forms of things unknown, the poet's pen / Turns them to shapes" (5.1.14–17). The exotic has to be given a dramatic shape whether it fits the evanescence and irrationality of fancies or it imposes an unusual frame onto the Shakespearean script. Latella chose an oneiric environment close to Peter Brook's suspended performance of the *Dream*, but Declan Donnellan and the Russian group of Cheek by Jowl chose another strategy. Donnellan's play on time is of a fairly different nature. He transfers Shakespeare's script into the world of another playwright, Anton Chekhov.

The play was first created in 2003 for the Chekhov International Theatre Festival and has been on a world tour since then. The scenographical choice of Nick Ormerod, designer of the Cheek by Jowl Company, is a transfer of the Illyrian plot into the setting of *The Cherry Orchard* (Figure 10.2). The set bears the Brechtian feature of simplicity. The stage is carefully delimited by geometrical lines on the floor, defining the inside and the outside of the Illyrian world. Within these lines will alternate Orsino's and Olivia's palaces and Antonio and Sebastian's wanderings. The space is neutral enough to enable a rapid change of action and the performance rhythm increases so dramatically that a scene is hardly finished before the following one starts. The superimposition of Shakespeare's sixteenth century and Chekhov's early twentieth century is not enough for Donnellan, and he deepens the temporal

Figure 10.2 From bottom, Dmitry Dyuzhev as Aguecheek, Sergey Mukhin as Sebastian, Alexander Feklistov as Sir Toby, Igor Yasuovich as Feste and in the background, Alexey Dadanov as Olivia, Cheek by Jowl, Barbican, London, 2006. The fight between Sebastian and Aguecheek, Act 5. Photograph: Keith Pattison. Copyright Cheek by Jowl.

tumult by imposing a frenetic pace to the performance. The exotic springs from this confrontation between the familiarity of twentieth-century chronological landmarks and the strangeness of a rapidly flowing performance. This rhythmic unsteadiness is reinforced by the linguistic shock caused by actors playing in Russian. The foreign musicality of the Russian language replaces the melody of the Elizabethan iambic pentameter. Yet, the use of the Russian language and of a Chekhovian characterization gives a different and typically Russian identity to the play, adding to the confusion of time and space. For instance, Sir Toby is given a thoroughly more excessive character. He becomes the stereotypical alcoholic who abuses physically the weaker ones, as in the scene where he beats up Maria before apologetically fondling her face and hiding in shame beneath a table. Donnellan and his actors are crossing a dramatic threshold and completely adapt the Shakespearean script to the target Russian dramatic context, its refinement and its violence. Belch's original verbal unkindness about Maria, "She's a beagle true bred, and one that adores me" (2.4.145), is now turned into sinister brutality. This *Twelfth Night* is decidedly that of a displaced Slavic geography. If Donnellan hybridizes his production by retaining the Renaissance all-male cast for the show and by allowing several incursions of an even closer modernity with a very 1970s Aguecheek into his *belle époque* frame, it is only to trap his audience into this Russian Illyria, this other world that mirrors the madness of our world.

To illustrate the confusion of time, space, and the self, Donnellan also adds an aural exoticism to the performance. Vladimir Pankov and Alexander Gusev's sound design mirrors the bewilderment of both characters and spectators. The music announces the action and sets the general mood of the performance, without replacing the action itself. The whole cast enters the stage at the beginning of the play to the sound of samba music played live by the actors as an invitation for the audience to enter the festive spirit of the play. For instance, soft bossa rhythms illustrate Orsino's love-talks, and Cesario starts dancing while playing an instrument. Yet, the boy's passionate routine is opposed to the serious devotion of Orsino's other attendants. The comic contrast instantly deflates the self-absorbed languidness of his new master.

The comic side of the play is also characterized by its own music. Feste is granted a few songs hesitating between cabaret music and tango. The latter style is the trademark of the cunning party formed by Sir Toby, Maria, Aguecheek, and Feste. The contrast is puzzling between the musical background and the spatiotemporal frame but once more contributes to the impression of oneirism. Donnellan offers the audience a dream version of *Twelfth Night*. As in a reverie, he is allowed to use all the ingredients he fancies regardless of chronology or realism.

Latella even goes further and opts for a clash of musical genres. While Donnellan's sound designers chose a coherent Latin atmosphere with South American rhythms, Latella aims at shocking his audience's ears. Beethoven's *Seventh Symphony* alternates with *Besame Mucho*; Bach gives way to *Che Gelida* and the soundtrack to *West Side Story*. *Twelfth Night* is now granted a global physical geography. The exoticism of the play was in the names, but for a Mediterranean audience, the exoticism is in the expansion of the Latin otherness and its confrontation with Northern European musical tradition.

This global view of exoticism can be puzzling for the audience if it is only superimposed on the performance. An alternative to this hyperbolic musical escapism could be the reintegration of the musical element in the text itself as prescribed by the Shakespearean script. *Twelfth Night* contains ten songs and the musical medium is definitely part of its aesthetic shape. In her 2004 adaptation of the play for Théâtre 13 in Paris, Anne Bourgeois developed this feature of Shakespeare's play and used music to convey the exotic. The composer Fred Pallem chose Eastern European folkloric music to create the melody of Illyria, and Bourgeois gave this melody a further role in the play. A dialogic song staging Malvolio's entrapment replaced act 2 scene 5. Thus, she tried to recapture the Renaissance use of musical accompaniments during plays. This technique of intertwining text and tunes is known as *parlando* and participates in the exotic shock of this palimpsest of aesthetic genres. Andrew Gurr exemplifies *parlando* by quoting from a performance of Beaumont's *Knight of the Burning Pestle* at the Blackfriars in 1607: "the hero's father, an anti-merchant figure called Merrythought, sings almost all his words to popular songs from ballads. He uses more than thirty different tunes, mostly fitting their opening lines into his replies in a kind of *parlando*" (1980, 83). When music enters dramaturgy, it can be either as a background or an incidental element or as a new mode of communication within the script. The danger occurs when music tries to explain the text and overwhelms the audience's senses. The technique of *parlando* prevents such a hyperbolic use of the aural environment because the music is not superimposed on the text but merged in the dialogue. This simultaneity provides at the same time wonderment and entertainment without burdening the performance.

Exoticism is born of the sense of originality caused by transversal dramaturgies. However, whether directors choose the English Renaissance as a mirror for the exotic or some other eclectic scenographical strategies to convey the strangeness at the core of *Twelfth Night*, they ask the same fundamental question: is the audience ready to enter the illusory world of drama? Given this constant necessity to renew the staging of the exotic, would it not be that the ultimate form of exoticism is metatheatricality?

"If this were played upon a stage now, I could condemn it as improbable fiction": the exoticism of metatheatricality

The confrontations of the multiple cultural references of the author, the director, the actors, and the spectators engender the exotic. Its emergence is a problematic one which obliges drama companies to ponder theatricality. In their introduction to *Twelfth Night*, Roger Warren and Stanley Wells focus on the protean nature of the play's setting:

> Each of these aspects of Illyria – the geographical or Mediterranean, the specifically English, the magical, and the sense of a country of the mind – can be illustrated by the prominence each has been given in notable stagings.
>
> (Shakespeare 1995, 9)

They also imply that all those aspects are raised separately or together by theatre productions and that the strangeness of Illyria is a dramaturgical issue. Thus, it seems that the question at the core of the staging of the exotic is that of the genre and the techniques of the theatre. Turning the argument on its head, some directors actually create exoticism by reminding the audience of where they are. The entrance into the exotic world of Illyria is achieved through various degrees of explicit references to theatricality. Some use the Bard and the theatre of his time as the form of the exotic content, while others use the theatre as the very embodiment of the exotic and scatter metatheatrical reminders throughout their productions. Both these scenographical strategies coalesce into a third one which consists in the confrontation of various theatrical influences. The aim of this more or less open metatheatricality is to build a stage image of the mythological reverie which constitutes Illyria. Exoticism is a dramatic signified, but the signifier, i.e. the performance, is also a form of exoticism *per se*.

Theatre plays on its familiar shape to seduce the audience and then offers a sometimes unfamiliar spectacle. Shakespeare's Illyria is a sort of *mise en abyme* of this paradox. It bears exotic features as well as streaks of London local color. The imaginary world is ridden with references to the concrete English Renaissance world such as the Elephant (an inn in Southwark), Mistress Mall's picture, the spinsters, and the knitters in the sun. From a continental point of view, this opens a new exotic perspective for directors and scenographers. *Twelfth Night* is also known for its displaced Englishness as well as its non-English exotic perspective, and its adaptation by continental theatre companies often retains the English side of the play. Shakespeare and his time become the exotic.

As for the director Anne Bourgeois, the aim of her 2004 production was clearly asserted in the program. The performance was to be "a festive celebration of the Shakespearean madness, in the tradition of Elizabethan drama with masques, songs and musicians on stage" [author's translation]. Bourgeois's concern was to retrieve the techniques and the energy of Elizabethan drama. The latter *is* the exotic; that's why she made a point in preserving the original dramatic form of the play.

Bourgeois relied on the stereotypical image of the Elizabethan sparsely furnished stage to create her own scenography: a backcloth, a long bench dividing the stage longitudinally, and a set of two ropes encircling the whole and delimiting a liminal zone between the Illyrian space and the audience (see photos of this production at http://www.lavirgule.com/documentation/

images-et-sons/saison-04-05-la-nuit-des-rois.htm). She borrowed the main features of English Renaissance theatres and transferred them onto the box stage of the Théâtre 13. The stage was reduced thanks to those ropes arranged in a semicircle. The stage size was as limited as that of an Elizabethan outdoor theatre and the actors had to fit their performance to this contrived space. Hence, the use of the backcloth as the possible extension of the stage and the material embodiment of the play's peripeteias became a necessity. That curtain recalled the hanging(s) hiding the central opening in the tiring-house wall. This secondary space stood for an alternative playing area and was often used as a way to fragment and complicate the action (see Hosley 1959, 35–46; Gurr 1980, 147, 149ff.). This fundamental element of Elizabethan dramaturgy illustrated the metamorphosis of the proscenium stage into an open stage.

Illyria is a "closed world" (Hawkins 1967, 63) symbolized by the ropes encircling the characters. Those ropes put the mythical space at a distance from the reality of the spectators. Nonetheless, the striking element in the representation of Illyria as a remote island was the central opening in the middle of the semicircle formed by the ropes. Symbolically, Bourgeois and her scenographers, Elise Roche and Philippe Mathieu, wanted to reintroduce the notion of an open stage allowing a more direct communication between the performers and the spectators. This continental Shakespearean Illyria is a "space that simultaneously joins and divides the stage and audience" (Styan 2000, 27). Hence, instead of a full enclosure of Illyria within the box-stage, this visual rupture of the frontier symbolically invited strangers in, whether they were the survivors of a shipwreck or the spectators themselves.

This reinterpretation of the Elizabethan theatrical features and tradition contributed in creating the general impression of an exotic setting for a strange account of love, humiliation, and comic revenge. The English Renaissance dramaturgy was chosen here to challenge the audience's imagination. Changing the theatrical codes with which the spectators are familiar is a form of exotic dramaturgy that some directors will push to its limits as we will see hereafter.

Whether the audience is attuned to the Elizabethan stage architecture and dramaturgy or not is not a central issue when a director chooses Shakespeare as the signifier of the exotic. The gap between the spectators' expectations and the actual performance suffices to create the distancing effect that enables the exotic to develop. This strategic choice is somehow prescribed by the play itself for it revolves around the confusion of the sense and the senses. Hence, for continental directors, the key to *Twelfth Night* exoticism is to be found in a puzzling dramaturgy upsetting the familiar aesthetic landmarks of the audience.

The experience of the theatre requires the same *modus essendi* as the exotic: the suspension of disbelief. This suspension allows the audience to enter the world of illusion as deliberately as they would a reverie. Theatre also requires the spectators to be conscious of the dramatic illusion. The paradox of this experience is that it requires proximity and distance, disbelief and a form of aesthetic consciousness – varying from one spectator to another and ranging from the simple awareness of being in a theatre to a deeper knowledge of the dramatic genre.

The opening act of Donnellan's Russian production plays on a clear metatheatrical mode so as to warn the audience that it is entering a physical as well as a fictional otherness. The empty white stage is suddenly invaded by the entire all-male cast to the sound of music. They scatter themselves orderly around the stage so they can face each part of the three-sided amphitheatre. Suddenly, the music stops and an actor is chosen and taken outside the geometrical lines on the floor representing Illyria. Other actors dress him up as a woman. Then, they renew the act with two other actors. Thus, Viola, Olivia, and Maria, who were only textual fantasies, are given a theatrical shape. They are fashioned in the margins of the stage. This deliberate directorial choice is a reminder for the audience of the Elizabethan theatrical tradition of an all-male cast and a reassertion of the illusory nature of drama. Donnellan and his actors signal the spectators they are entering an alien world where their rational and sensual landmarks will be challenged. At the end of this metatheatrical dumbshow, most of the cast disappear to re-enter the stage fully dressed in their respective costumes. This interlude is the threshold leading to the theatrical world. It marks for both the players and the spectators the entrance into the Illyrian exoticism.

This fusion of the exotic and the theatrical emerges again at the end of the play when the characters are faced with the reunited twins. The anxiety provoked by this most strange sight constitutes a theatrical climax. The twins embody the exotic within the exotic, and Illyria sees its own strangeness in this physical mirror. In awe, the Illyrians gather into a compact mass of bodies leaving the unnatural symmetry outside. The actors' bodies now stand for the exotic Illyria. They seem assembled in a human jigsaw puzzle, speaking and moving together. Their comic whereabouts enhance both theatricality and exoticism. The exaggeration in the actors' gestures and mimicry reminds the spectator of the artificiality of what they see. The distance thus created gives again the impression that Illyria is a mythical world where the laws of non-dramatic reality do not apply.

Nonetheless, the temptation of theatre as the exotic can lead to a radical formalism. The strategy of putting theatricality and metatheatricality at the core of the scenography of the Illyrian exoticism may shift the attention from the content of the play onto its form. Certain productions choose to use the performance of *Twelfth Night* as a means to convey new or renewed dramatic techniques to a varied audience. The exotic perspective becomes thoroughly different. The interest lies in the dramatic techniques rather than in the cooperation of the performance with a narrative. The indeterminacy of *Twelfth Night*'s environment opens a wide range of possibility as far as the scenography is concerned. As the exotic is the main characteristic of Illyria, continental directors can explore exotic techniques. Non-Western theatrical forms are the ultimate means to stage the exotic.

This is Ariane Mnouchkine's strategy in her 1982 adaptation of *Twelfth Night* for the Théâtre du Soleil at La Cartoucherie in Paris. She chose to value the performing techniques and a certain conception of theatre rather than the play itself. The exoticism inherent to the Shakespearean play became a pretext for conducting a radical research on theatrical forms. Mnouchkine's production was grounded on theatricality. The ultimate form of exoticism seemed to be the constant confrontation of the spectators with the dramatic illusion.

The organization of the theatrical space strengthened this strategy. La Cartoucherie was divided into three halls: the first one was the foyer while the two others gathered the stage space and the audience. From their seats, the spectators were faced with both the immense barren stage made of a striped straw carpet and sumptuous veils at the back and, on their right, the tiring-house framed by blue curtains where the actors could be seen dressing up for the play. Mnouchkine insisted on the stage space as a theatrical reminder.

Theatre was the Other *par excellence*. The exotic was not where you were supposed to find it, i.e. the performance of the plot, but in the theatrical forms used for the performance. Mnouchkine once declared that Shakespeare's era did not have strong theatrical forms (Williams 1999, 93) and that's why she had to resort to Asian theatre. Hence, she decided to dress her actors with culturally-composite costumes. They were a mix of Elizabethan doublets, medieval skirts, and cloaks suggesting kimonos. The make-up and the masques on the actors' faces belonged to the *commedia dell'arte* and to Japanese, Indian, and Balinese theatrical traditions. Those oriental theatrical forms were not only blended together in the costumes but also emerged as major influences on the movements of the actors and the use of props and music (Neuschäfer 2002, 145–50). Jean Alter describes these juxtapositions of theatrical forms as "a theatre-within-the-theatre strategy pushed to the extreme" (1988, 82). The exotic is now in the perception of the body, of the stage space, of the costumes rather than in the collaboration between the dramatic narrative and its scenography. This is the moment when *Twelfth Night* disappears behind the search for a universal form of theatre.

Mnouchkine used the same stage space and scenographical strategies for the three Shakespeare productions she directed between 1982 and 1984. The particularity of *Twelfth Night*'s exoticism was then completely annihilated because of the symmetrical scenographies used for the two historical plays, *Richard II* and *1 Henry IV*. The fact that *Twelfth Night* is set in a mythical space disappeared because of the repetitive scenography. If *Twelfth Night* had been the only production to require non-Western theatrical forms to create the exotic, the dramaturgy could have been considered as a stage realization of the fictional Illyrian world. Nonetheless, the point was not to convey the strangeness of the play's universe but that of the theatrical world.

Mnouchkine's *Twelfth Night* testified to no in-depth work on the narrative;

the emphasis was laid on the choreography, on the relationship between the actor and his/her body. Unlike Peter Brook who borrowed from the Oriental mythologies and philosophies and merged them into the Shakespearean script, Mnouchkine divided herself from the content, to retain only the technicalities of Oriental theatres (Neuschäfer and Serror 1984, 76). The hyperbolic theatricality modified considerably the understanding of *Twelfth Night*. Mnouchkine, who was working with her own translation of Shakespeare, seemed to have rewritten the script mainly to the benefit of an exploration of pure theatrical forms. Shakespeare's characterization was even altered to the point of destruction in order to promote theatre for the sake of theatre. George Bigot, who played Orsino, Richard in *Richard II*, and Prince Hal in *1 Henry IV*, developed a body language which fitted all three characters. The same technique was used by Odile Cointepas, who played Olivia, the Queen in *Richard II*, and Lady Kate in *1 Henry IV*. Such a choice resulted in creating one-dimensional characters and in denying the variations implied by the original scripts. The acting techniques replaced the text in performance. Theatricality overwhelmed the play itself and the story disappeared behind the invention and ideas of the acting company.

Josette Feral defines Mnouchkine's dramaturgy as the victory of theatricality: "Formal and perfectly stylized, [these artistic forms] put realism at a distance and promote an artificiality conferring a purely theatrical dimension on both the narrative and the characters" [author's translation] (1998, 225). Exoticism is not a scenographic strategy to question the self but the means to achieve a thorough understanding of the essence of theatre and theatricality. This is the limit of the dramaturgy of the exotic: when the exotic content of *Twelfth Night* is supplanted entirely by the exotic theatrical forms.

In *Every Man out of his Humor* (1599), Ben Jonson illustrates the proximity between the exotic and art: "magicke Witchcraft, or other such exoticke artes" (4.3.25). This essay focused only on the relationship of exoticism and the scenography of *Twelfth Night*, according to three main lines: the presence of the exotic in dramatic narratives, the strategies to bring the exotic out of the page onto the stage, and the directorial quest for an apt aesthetic embodiment of the exotic. Choosing the continental perspective since the first introductions of *Twelfth Night* into the European dramatic repertoire was a deliberate strategy to discuss fully the exoticism of this play and its limits. As the continent was used as the geographical locus of the exotic in Shakespeare's play, studying the continental productions of this play seems to help to encompass the perspectives on otherness in a more objective manner. It is now possible to avoid centering the debate on the Mediterranean and its imagery, but to focus on the dramatic potentialities of an exotic text. Stephen Greenblatt notes the historical "use of symbolic technology" (1991, 12) so as to represent otherness. Staging is an instance of this symbolic technology. When working in full collaboration with the text, dramaturgy helps the spectators questioning their own time, place, and identity.

Works cited

Alter, Jean. "Decoding Mnouchkine's Shakespeare (A Grammar of Stage Signs)." In *Performing Texts*. Ed. Michael Issacharoff and Robin F. Jones. Philadelphia: University of Pennsylvania Press, 1988: 75–85.

Billington, Michael. *Directors' Shakespeare: Approaches to Twelfth Night*. London: Nick Hern Books, 1990.

Bourgeois, Anne. *Les nouvelles du 13*, 6. Paris, February 2004.

Davenant, William. *Macbeth, A Tragedy: With all the Alterations, Amendments, Additions, And New Songs. As It Is Now Acted at the Dukes Theatre*. London: Clark, 1674. Wing S2930.

Dorchain, Auguste. *Conte d'Avril*. Paris: Alphonse Lemerre Editeur, 1885.

Feral, Josette. *Trajectoire du Soleil*. Paris: CNRS, 1998.

Greenblatt, Stephen. *Marvelous Possessions, The Wonder of the New World*. Oxford: Clarendon Press, 1991.

Gurr, Andrew. *The Shakespearean Stage 1574–1642*. Cambridge: Cambridge University Press, 1980.

Hawkins, Sherman H. "The Two Worlds of Shakespearean Comedy." *Shakespeare Studies* 3 (1967): 62–80.

Hosley, Richard. "The Discovery-Space in Shakespeare's Globe." *Shakespeare Survey* 12 (1959): 35–46.

Jonson, Ben. *Every Man out of His Humour*. London: Stansby, 1600. STC 14751.

Laroque, François. "Shakespeare et la géographie imaginaire de l'Europe." In *Proceedings of the Conference "Shakespeare et l'Europe."* Société Française Shakespeare, 2004. Ed. P. Kapitaniak. Paris: Atenor, 2004: 151–72.

Latella, Antonio. *Note di regia*. www.teatrostabile.umbria.it.

Levith, Murray J. *Shakespeare's Italian Settings and Plays*. New York: St. Martin's Press, 1989.

Neuschäfer, Anne. *De l'improvisation au rite: l'épopée de notre temps. Le Théâtre du Soleil au carrefour des genres*. Frankfurt: Peter Lang, 2002.

——, and Frédéric Serror. *Le Théâtre du Soleil, Shakespeare*. Cologne: Prometh Verlag, 1984.

Riemer, A. P. *Antic Fables. Patterns of Evasion in Shakespeare's Comedies*. Manchester: Manchester University Press, 1980.

Shakespeare, William. *Twelfth Night*. Ed. Roger Warren and Stanley Wells. World's Classics. Oxford: Oxford University Press, 1995.

——, *King Henry VI Part 2*. Ed. Ronald Knowles. The Arden Shakespeare. London and New York: Routledge, 1999.

——, *A Midsummer Night's Dream*. Ed. R. A. Foakes. Cambridge: Cambridge University Press, 2003.

——, *Twelfth Night*. Ed. Elizabeth Story Donno. Cambridge: Cambridge University Press, 2004.

Styan, J. L. "Stage Space and the Shakespeare Experience." In *Shakespeare in Performance*. Ed. Robert Shaughnessy. Basingstoke: Macmillan, 2000: 24–41.

Williams, David. *Collaborative Theatre: The Théâtre du Soleil Sourcebook*. London: Routledge, 1999.

Productions

Le Conte d'Avril. Marc Porel (director). Théâtre de l'Odéon. Paris, 1885–86.

La dodicesima notte, o quel che volete. Antonio Latella (director). Teatro Stabile dell'Umbria. Verona, 2004.

La Nuit des Rois. Jacques Copeau (director). Théâtre du Vieux-Colombier. Paris, 1914.

La Nuit des Rois. Ariane Mnouchkine (director). Le Théâtre du Soleil. La Cartoucherie. Paris, 1982. [First performed at La Cour du Palais des Papes. International Theatre Festival. Avignon, 1982.]

La Nuit des Rois. Anne Bourgeois (director). La Troupe du Phénix. Théâtre 13. Paris, 2004.

Twelfth Night. Declan Donnellan (director). Cheek by Jowl. Barbican Theatre. London, 2006. [First performance of this production given in May 2003 at the Pushkin Theatre in Moscow.]

11 "The text remains for another attempt"

Twelfth Night, or What You Will on the German stage

Christa Jansohn

Twelfth Night, or What You Will "is difficult to cast, difficult to direct, and especially difficult to design," observes Michael Pennington (2000, 18), and John Gielgud recalls in his memoirs that he has "seen so many bad productions and never a perfect one" (1979, 176). In 1836, the German Romantic poet and celebrated translator of Shakespeare, Ludwig Tieck, gave a detailed and convincing explanation for this in his novella *The Young Master Carpenter*:

> Every note is sounded in this unique work; farce and fun are not spurned, lowness itself is touched and hinted at, but just the same, the poetic, the desire, the notes of love, and with it so much poetic obstinacy, madness, wisdom, delicate jokes, and profound thoughts within the entertainment, so that the poem, like a large, multicolored butterfly, flutters through the pure blue skies, mirroring its golden gleam against the sun and the colorful flowers, and whoever wants to catch it to take a closer look, beware only of brushing off any of the delicate fragrance of the most tender pollen since even the smallest loss will suffice to spoil the beauty that seems like a breath into the air. This is . . . why so few people who otherwise believe that they understand the great poet or at least admire him know what to make of his comedies.
>
> (Tieck 1988, 389–90; unless otherwise indicated all translations are my own)

Tieck, Gielgud, and Pennington with their lifelong experience as translators, actors, and directors of Shakespeare's plays should certainly know. Not only does this most beloved comedy require a carefully balanced ensemble of a dozen actors of more or less equal power (Pennington 2000, 22), but it also requires the right balance of "the romance of the play with the cruelty of the jokes against Malvolio" (Gielgud 1979, 176), as well as a sophisticated interlocking of space, motion, and event, which means "that time perception is not only a function of direct textual references but the effect of bodies moving in space in certain ways . . . [o]r on occasion, of bodies not moving in space" (Smith 2005, 62).

In German productions of *Twelfth Night*, the multiple ways in which time is experienced depend to a considerable degree on the translation, which frequently requires more time than the estimate of 2.4 seconds per line of the original (Smith 2005, 59), but, more importantly, the instability of the text in a foreign language offers added possibilities for directorial experiments. This is also supported by the fact that most German versions of the play dispense with the main title and base their interpretation on *What You Will* (*Was Ihr Wollt*) as the most familiar German title, often disregarding the delicate equilibrium between the contrasting elements of the play and putting too much emphasis on "misrule" and "What You Will" in the sense of "make of it what you will but don't take it too seriously."

Twelfth Night was and is frequently performed on the German stage, not only during the nineteenth century but also throughout the twentieth and twenty-first centuries. Between 1911 and 1935 the German *Shakespeare Jahrbuch* listed 3914 performances (Stroedel 92). After the Nazis took over, an average of 12 productions per year were staged in Germany between 1933 and 1938, with a total of 135 productions for this entire period (Eicher 2000, 303); between 1947 and 1975 another 4423 performances of *Twelfth Night* made this comedy the most popular Shakespeare play in Germany; it was number six on the list of the most frequently performed plays, following Lessing's *Minna von Barnhelm* with 6058 performances, Goethe's *Faust I, II* with 5646, Kleist's *The Broken Jug* with 5552, Schiller's *Mary Stuart* with 4657 and his *Intrigue and Love* with 4469 performances (*Was spielten die Theater?* 1978, 32). Between 1975/6 and 1980/1 there were 849 *Twelfth Night* performances in West Germany; only in 1976/7 and 1979/80, however, was it the most popular Shakespearean play. At the turn of the twenty-first century – according to the statistics of all theatre productions in the German-speaking countries (including Austria and Switzerland) – *Twelfth Night* was still immensely popular but had been superseded mainly by *Hamlet*, *A Midsummer Night's Dream*, and *Romeo and Juliet.*

So far there is no book-length study of the German performance history of *Twelfth Night*. This essay therefore can only provide a brief and certainly not exhaustive survey of some German productions. It attempts to show how directorial choices have shaped the play in performance, by focusing in particular on the changing conceptions of the stage design, the age of the main characters, and the costuming. Certain developments and trends as well as the instability of the text in performance can be highlighted, but further and more detailed studies will be necessary to place these productions in their cultural and historical context without running the risk of stereotyping and/or simplifying the reception of *Twelfth Night* in the German theatre. The reader who is especially interested in the striking differences between the German and English productions is referred to the detailed accounts in the critical editions and studies of key productions by Paul Edmondson (2005, 30–66), John R. Ford (2006, 127–63), Michael Pennington (2000), Lois Potter (1985,

43–72), Stanley Wells (1976, 43–63), and the accounts of actors (Donald Sinden as Malvolio and Zoë Wanamaker as Viola) in *Players of Shakespeare* (vols. 1 and 2) as well as *Directors' Shakespeare: Approaches to Twelfth Night*, ed. Michael Billington (1990).

Twelfth Night in the nineteenth century

During the nineteenth century August Wilhelm Schlegel's elegant, imaginative, and at the same time wistful and melancholic rendering of *Twelfth Night* (*Der Heilige-Drey-Königs-Abend, oder Was ihr wollt*; Leipzig, 1797) stressed the charm, light comedy, and lyricism that supported an interpretation, often described as "romantic" though in fact "the style and tone of the finished result is in general harmony with the diction of 'classical' serious drama of the entire Goethe era" (Habicht 1993, 45–47). For Schlegel the Shakespearean drama was understood as organic poetry in which "each formal detail must be seen as being calculated to serve the total effect . . . Hence a faithful rendering of the original requires attention not only to semantic meaning, but also, and more importantly, to aesthetic form . . . The major part of Schlegel's formal attention appears to have been absorbed by matters of verse and rhyme, and also by Shakespeare's compact, bold and emphatic style," but tended to overlook many additional phenomena "such as quibbles, indecencies, metrical irregularities, etc." (Habicht 1993, 45–47 and Paulin 2003, 299–329). The result was a smoothing of the original, very often associated with and reduced to a harmonious "romantic" style.

That the approprate recitation of these "romantic" words should be the primary basis for any production of Shakespeare was particularly emphasized by Karl Leberecht Immermann's stage for *Twelfth Night* in 1840. He did without any elaborately realistic or would-be "historical" setting but provided a bare stage that allowed the audience to concentrate fully on the actors and their words. It offered "the most intimate proximity with the listeners," which altogether comprised not more than 200 people. The width of the fore-stage also gave the actors much more room than a narrower, deeper scenic stage which enabled them to make the complex relationships and the complexity of the action more apparent by obvious "clear, light groups" (Immermann quoted in Williams 1990, 182).

In *The Young Master Carpenter* Tieck describes an imaginary production whose main characteristics were again its purity and lack of definite locale in order to give the audience free access to Shakespeare's poetic words and his "imaginative world":

> The stage made a pleasant impression and visibly announced that it was created for a festive occasion. The upper balcony or gallery . . . supported by free-standing pillars, the ionic capitals of which were elegantly gilded.

> Below was the smaller, inner stage, hidden by curtains of red silk. The steps were also designed with colorful coverings, so that the stage could be itself, whatever one wanted.
>
> (Tieck 1988, 418; see also Asper 1974, 134–47 and Williams 1990, 179)

A very plain and simply designed *Twelfth Night* was also put on stage by the Meiningen Court Theatre in 1874, the most celebrated German theatre company of the last decades of the nineteenth century. Throughout the first half of the twentieth century this production served as a model with its rich inclusion of instrumental music and songs and its simple set:

> only twice was a shallow space inserted, once for a room in the duke's palace and once for a room in Olivia's house. On stage left stood Olivia's house; a flight of nine descending steps ending in a narrow veranda led into the garden in the back, set off from the street by a fence . . . The backdrop showed a garden landscape and a half-hidden building. In front of the house were a bench and garden properties. Doors and windows were practicable, the windows transparent to allow the candlelight inside to fall into the garden and mix with the moonlight . . . For the first time in Germany the actors of *Twelfth Night* wore Elizabethan dress.
>
> (Koller 1984, 154)

Twelfth Night in the Third Reich

In the Weimar period (1919–33) and later during the Third Reich (1933–45) this traditional "romantic" pattern did not undergo significant changes. Only a few directors attempted a more experimental approach, e.g. the Leipzig director, Detlef Sierck, who directed the play in Berlin at the Volksbühne in September 1934 with a new and much disputed translation by the playwright and dramaturge Hans Rothe (Anders 1935, 161–62). Rothe's intimate knowledge of the theatre made him take much greater and more daring liberties with the original than any other translator before him: "he did away with old-fashioned elisions and usual inversions, simplified the syntax and used a modern vocabulary" (Hortmann 1998, 88). Praised by the actors as eminently speakable, it was heavily criticized by scholars (in particular the German Shakespeare Society) and was finally banned from the stage by Joseph Goebbels in 1936, decreeing the Schlegel translation the only legitimate one.

Gustav Gründgens's production of 1936/7 was a much greater success than Sierck's version. His choice of Schlegel's translation was from the start a statement of his directorial intention and in close agreement with the visual design of his concept. He used *Der Heilige-Drey-Königs-Abend, oder Was ihr wollt*, modernizing, omitting, and rearranging only some few words and passages in order to bridge the gap between Shakespeare's language and the classical German taste and to highlight the poetic elegance and timeless wit of his production. He placed "the story in the ambience of Mediterranean country houses on the shores of a sunny Illyria, . . . with Orsino, profoundly in love with love; Olivia, wrapped in her *Weltschmerz* and black robe" inside, a brilliantly versatile performance by Marianne Hoppe as Viola and Malvolio, played by the already famous comedian and movie star, Theo Lingen – bursting with self-love and affectation. Gründgens's sparkling and inventive interpretation of the play was based on the subtle balance of form and style, charming perfection, stylistic artistry as well as deliberate artificiality without any topical or historical references (Hortmann 1998, 128–31; Kühlken 1972, 32–48). It was, in fact, his answer to the official program of "blood and soil" (Hortmann 1998, 131).

Twelfth Night in post-war Germany

After World War II *Twelfth Night* continued as one of the most popular of Shakespeare's plays in Germany, and, for a while, the majority of directors went on with a prevailing poetic and enchanting interpretation, mostly using Schlegel's translation. Only a few reviewers criticized this neo-romantic, often nostalgic approach. The social, political, and linguistic context had changed, and soon critics began to demand more up-to-date translations to achieve a more contemporary confrontation with the text (Günther 1963, 19–21, and "Umgang mit Shakespeare" 1963, 27–33); in consequence, new translations (by Richard Flatter, Hans Rothe, and Rudolf Schaller) were used, but there was still some reluctance about the unequivocal assertion of contemporary relevance. In 1949 the influential theatre critic Friedrich Luft insisted on a new approach to the comedies with a new translation (Luft 1962, 109). Six years later he doubted whether it was appropriate to perform *Twelfth Night* in the bleak post-war period at all:

> it seems to me that the age is not disposed to the numbingly sweet confusion of these creations of laughter and sighing as it was once upon a time. As if the serene adagio and scherzo did not sound as unashamedly delightful as it once did . . . Can it be that there is a shifting of values?
>
> (Luft, *Die Neue Zeitung* 17, 1954, quoted in Rice 1987, 92–93)

This "shifting of values" was certainly achieved by Fritz Kortner's version, first performed at the Kammerspiele in Munich in 1957 and, five years later, at Berlin's Schillertheater. Kortner heavily revised Schlegel's translation, cut the text, and used excessive theatrical methods. Maria's three-minute fully orchestrated aria of laughter after her triumph over Malvolio was only one notorious example of the visual and tonal surprises (Hortmann 1998, 212). In

1963 the performance was hailed by the newly founded theatre journal *Theater Heute* (1960) as the "production of the year" whose theatrical and unconventional qualities made it the "most inspiring and freshest" interpretation. It was praised for its loss of traditional elements and original interpretation ("Unsere Aufführung des Jahres" 1963, 35, with 46 photos from the Berlin performance and an interview with Kortner 36–48). It was, however, also criticized for the "precisely calculating intellect of the director" and as "overbred artistry" which did harm to the original (*Kölnische Rundschau*, October 12, 1962), and one reviewer even used the headline "Not by Shakespeare but a good Kortner" (*Kölner Stadt Anzeiger*, October 12, 1962). Others stressed the carefully thought-out conception, "full of imagination and loving attention to detail. But the comedy and the magic of his production would have unfolded themselves even more wonderfully within a set that was clear, stylistically consistent and more severe" (Rischbieter 1962, 19). Whether this was an implicit criticism of Kortner's decision to transfer Shakespeare's fantasy world to a specific location (Yugoslavia) or whether the reviewer thought that the theatricality of the performance did not need a specific reference to reality is difficult to say.

After this immensely successful production directors frequently attempted to find a compromise between fantasy and localizing actuality. They also tried to get away from the cabaret-like or even slapstick interpretations and preferred to focus rather on those elements previously by-passed in productions, such as the loneliness, disillusion, insecurity, and isolation of the characters as well as their untrustworthiness and even madness.

Illyria on the German stage in the later twentieth and the early twenty-first century

On the more recent German stage Illyria has certainly stimulated different illusions, if not disillusions. The stage for Shakespeare's comedy often has suggested anything but a sweet and colorful imaginary country. It was not *What You Will* that was the focal point, but rather "the director's will." Often the traditional translation by Schlegel was employed as play-text, radically modernized, or else more recent translations were used, the best known being those by Thomas Brasch, Erich Fried, Frank Günther, Reinhard Palm, Bernhard K. Tragelehn, and Michael Wachsmann.

In this new age of "director's theatre" – East and West – the required "updating" was achieved at the expense of the wistful illusion of Illyria. A convincingly melancholic atmosphere was evoked by productions in Weimar in 1995 and 2005 (German Nationaltheater). The first (1995, directed by Katja Paryla) was set on a ship (of fools), the second (2005, directed by Anna Sophie Mahler) in the foyer of a hotel, with red plush chairs and a hushed atmosphere (see Figure 11.1). The foyer and the ship were places of transit, of waiting, homelessness, and non-commitment. Everything in a hotel seemed stiff and anonymous; even the alcoholic Sir Toby appeared in a wheel-chair and the music also underscored the general note of tiredness, interrupted only by the musical versatility of the fool, who handled the piccolo trumpet, synthesizer, mouth organ, and concertina with equal virtuosity. The mood of weariness was also taken up in the programme notes by the dramaturge:

> Yes, we are tired; we have seen all that before, passed it many times, cracked every joke once too many, recited to ourselves each of these infinitely melancholy soliloquies, nobody listening, nobody paying attention . . . Well, so be it. But we do not want to die. This is why we play and joke. Those who despair have no other choice.
>
> (Winnacker 2005, 5)

At Ingolstadt in 2000, the play was also set in a hotel (Großes Haus, directed by Peter Rein). Only here the place seemed run down. The walls showed poisonous verdigris, the stairs plush-red, brothel-like, and, like other doors, leading nowhere. The air-conditioning fan had stopped working and

Figure 11.1 Olivia (Elke Wieditz) disputing with her negligent fool (Marco Morelli, *left*) with Malvolio (Burkard Wolf) discreetly in the background. *Was Ihr Wollt*, first night, June 11, 2005 at the Großes Haus, Weimar. Director Anna Sophie Mahler, set Gisela Goerttler, costumes Ursula Leuenberger, translation Thomas Brasch; duration 2½ hours. Photograph Wonge Bergmann.

the neon advertisement flashed in gaudy colors at uncoordinated intervals something like "Desire." Here, too, the hotel was a scene of alienation. Men and women were living next door to each other and still didn't know one another.

The ship of the 1995 production in Weimar also underlined the idea that none of the characters was able to get any firm hold on the ground. There was no land in sight, the ship had them all captured; it was a staged apocalyptic mood, while the lonely, intelligent fool played the ferryman and soft, sad, and melancholy saxophone-tunes set the rhythm of the production.

In another production, directed by Reinhardt Friese for the Landesbühne Wilhelmshaven (2006), all of the action was steeped in a permanent fog and the dominant color was black. There were long chromium poles from which, at a lofty height, historical costumes were hung and worn by the actors. Sir Toby entered as a pale skinhead, Sir Andrew as a comic Einstein in pyjamas with red balloons fixed to his belt, and Malvolio seemed a parody of the court official in the Disney classic *Cinderella* (see Figure 11.2).

The Münster production set the action in a bar (Städtische Bühnen, 2002, directed by Karin Neuhäuser). All the characters were stranded in a desolate dancing bar whose splendour had had its day, like the red velvet wall coverings suggesting nothing but hopelessness. The red bulbs flashing "Illyria" next to the unendingly long counter did not even manage all the letters of

Figure 11.2 Was Ihr Wollt, first night, January 7, 2006 at the Landesbühne, Wilhelmshaven. Director Reinhardt Friese, costumes and set Diana Pähler, translation Horst Laube; duration 3 hours. Photograph Volker Beinhorn.

the alphabet. In this bar, reminiscent of Edward Hopper, Olivia was dancing, with the urn in her arms, sailors were getting drunk, and sexual contacts were arranged over the telephones on the tables.

These productions lacked subtle nuance, but could still be provocative. In Peter Eschberg's 1987 production in Bonn, the lovers were locked into a strictly stylized inner room; in Heinz Kreidl's production at the Staatstheater in Darmstadt (1994), high walls shut off the empty space and light from the sidelines. It was only in the background that we could recognize the outline of the shore, a rainbow in the sky, and in front nothing but a desert of sand. In Jens Schmidl's Giessen production (2005), any suggestion of pomp was dispensed with and nothing but a deep and spacious stage was provided, consisting of a large curved floor and a trench with stairs near the front. A similar image of Illyria was presented in a production at Nordhausen (1994), directed by Monica Querndt. Here Illyria was a large dance-hall with six doors and wide windows. Whoever was stranded there just mixed with the rest. With a snap of his finger the fool began the play, and the characters dressed in fanciful costumes began to move like mechanical clockwork. They gave an impression of dressed-up puppets, and yet they could show their pain at this mechanical existence. The audience might also have been surprised when Maria swept up the "sea" of the preceding scene – a blue silk cloth – and threw it into a bucket (Bremen Shakespeare Company 1988); or when, at the end of the play, "a peacock-blue scarf, Orsino's meagre sign of ducal dignity, remained on stage all on its own" (*Frankfurter Allgemeine Zeitung*, February 28, 1974 on Alfred Kirchner's production in Stuttgart).

Twelfth Night had also provoked loud, at times garish displays of color symbolism. In his Nuremberg production (1975), Wolfram Mehring decided to use a stage area with dark and heavy silk bordered at the back by a black gallery of archways, only changed by lighting. At the center he put inviting and seductive yellow, red, and blue silk cushions from *Arabian Nights* – a mild, somnambular setting for a night-time fairytale.

Completely different bright colors could be seen in the performance of the Weimar National Theatre in 1986 which offered a most coherent and highly artificial image of Illyria, a kind of "wishful Utopia contrasted to the more inhibited and humdrum modes of everyday life" (Hamburger 1998, 410): "A stage horizon of sky and sea blue over an ochre-colored sloping surface, porcelain-colored camels and palm trees on the stage shining in violet shades" evoked "the image of a peculiar, unreal, rigid coastal landscape with a touch of Mediterranean exotic flair," in which during the letter scene finally the "dream ship [appears] on the azure horizon" (*Thüringer Tageblatt*, April 3, 1986). This was the only GDR production with a happy ending. It did "at least in part serve as a metaphor for overt, free relationships involving spiritual *and* physical interdependence" (Hamburger 1998, 410).

Shakespeare's vague definition of the setting was completely done away with in Johannes Schaaf's production at the Munich Residenztheater in 1970.

Here Illyria was an entirely artificial stage set with sparse props. It was limited by high, auburn, vertically curved pieces of scenery that reminded one of the sandstone pillars of a castle while the reflecting plastic material created a detachment from the realistic associations: "Three or four props had to carry the action. A heap of sand, for instance, served as a playground for the comic characters, as a salvaging beach for the shipwrecked, as a garden for the romantic couple. A pink plastic bath tub covered with a tiger's fur also proved usable in a similar way" (*Spandauer Volksblatt*, March 21, 1970).

Another stage set (Berlin Volksbühne, 1981) appeared especially surreal: the imaginative Hungarian director, István Iglódi, had "a mighty hill made of cushions put up on stage and a catwalk built through the auditorium . . . and from there hangs an enormous red cloth and a great number of suspended balls descend" (*Neue Zeit*, February 6, 1981). This set, which was underlined by rock music, drove the actors to a display of acrobatic performances on the mountain of cushions. In contrast, Wilfried Minks, in his Hamburg production (1974), created merriment with an undertone of sorrow. Here, *What You Will* virtually turned into a black comedy. The concept was simple and resolute:

> The place of performance is a cave of mourning lined in black. At the front there is a sitting area for Orsino, who not only keeps goldfish in a bowl but also domestics trembling with fear. At the back, we see part of a cemetery flanked by the stairwell of an apparently abandoned fashionable building site, also in mourning. In between there is nothing but a bashed concert grand piano which turns into the chief prop; as a toy for the melancholic tinkling of Olivia, as a private bar for the low-life scenes, drowning in habitual drunkenness, and, at the end, as a hiding-place for Malvolio, and a cage for the exorcistic nonsense.
>
> (*Frankfurter Allgemeine Zeitung*, October 8, 1974)

Where literature is the food of love, there is Illyria. This was made the motto of a production in Schauspielhannover in 2004 (directed by Sebastian Nübling), where the first scene was acted on a bare stage, and then a huge wall of packed bookshelves ascended from below and descended again at the end. According to the set designer, it extended to "10 metres in length, 5 metres in height and 1.5 metres in depth and contained more than 4500 books in German, collected by donations" (Gerstner 2004/5, 12) (see Figure 11.3). The inhabitants of Illyria lived among the bookshelves, climbing up and down them. Everything was created out of language and literature – even the theatre itself. Malvolio sat to the left, reading cheap love-stories under a standard lamp, steadily provided with fresh supplies by tequila-drinking Maria. It was out of Malvolio's dream and Maria's bottle that Illyria was generated. All of them were addicted to reading romances, though the Fool only read the happy endings of love-stories, and it became apparent in the course of the action that love itself was dependent on the continual

Figure 11.3 *Was Ihr Wollt*, first night, November 20, 2004 at the Schauspielhannover. Director Sebastian Nübling, costumes and set Muriel Gerstner, translation Thomas Brasch; duration 3 hours. Photograph Thomas Aurin.

nourishment from books: "We are creatures of language – it is not we who are masters of language – it is language that masters us. This is the experience of the heroes of Illyria" (Gerstner 2004/5, 13). At the end they all vanished again into the bookshelves, and these were sunk back below ground; only Maria's tequila bottle remained on the bare stage. It was a logical, consistent concept, with its own dynamism, true to the play's poetic character and not reliant on melancholy or farce and where the Fool was the only rational creature. This concept was also underlined by the translation of Thomas Brasch whose version did not daub over the original with arbitrary everyday jargon, but paid due reverence to Shakespeare's poetic form.

The eclecticism of the visual effects evoking a post-modern Illyria was especially pronounced in Niels Peter Rudolph's Bonn production (2002), where "the scenic design was lavish though furnished in a seemingly arbitrary mixture of styles: the high platform in the middle serving as Illyria's seashore and multi-purpose stage within the stage . . . a Corinthian column in one place, a life-sized white horse made of papier mâché, in another, in front of it a medieval suit of armour" (*General-Anzeiger*, September 16, 2002). These properties, seemingly arranged by accident rather than design did not stress the suggestion of theatre workshops so much as the unreal dream atmosphere of a country where nothing was what it seemed to be.

The same eclecticism could be observed in Andrea Breth's 1989 production in Bochum, in which the audience was confronted with a veritable deluge of visual allusions, from Renaissance paintings and modern art to twentieth-century films, from classical myth and Christian hagiography to the theatre of the absurd. This production elucidated in a particularly striking way the recent tendency of contemporary theatre to replace traditional character concepts by visual appeals or at least to modify them in such a way as to pick up directly the great mass of images which modern audiences are permanently exposed to in the world outside the theatre. The modern theatre has become a "theatre of images" (Hortmann 1993, 243) rather than anything else; it intends, by such new artistic methods, to make the audience experience the existential reality of the fictional characters and actions. Of course, this can easily be perceived as an arbitrary mixing of Shakespeare's and the director's visions, and often causes provocation and protest.

"Not yet old enough . . .": age in *Twelfth Night*

The unconventional visions of some directors also apply to the characters' ages, which in many cases seem to be clearly specific in Shakespeare's text. Feste seems to belong to an older generation, since Olivia's father has already enjoyed his presence (2.4.12). The twins, Viola and Sebastian, for instance, were 13 when their father died (5.1.242–43); Malvolio describes Cesario as "[n]ot yet old enough for a man, nor young enough for a boy" (1.5.150–51), and Orsino is called "of fresh and stainless youth" by Olivia (1.5.248). According to the duke, women should be younger than their men (2.4.28–29), which in turn indicates the youthful age of Viola and Olivia.

As an assertion of the director's (or the company's) independent vision, such detailed statements were deliberately ignored in many German productions. Thus we encountered Olivia as an ageing aristocratic grand dame, greedily and somewhat frivolously pursuing the young Viola. We also met an Orsino who, as a no longer really young "long-locked Dürer-youth in an armchair from the fifties . . . [dreamed] of the love for Olivia by means of a reverberating throat microphone" (Bochum in 1989; *Stuttgarter Zeitung*, March 13, 1989). These ageing Orsinos and Olivias seemed to have missed out on too much in life, and for such lovers a great "happy ending" could only turn into helplessness and sorrow as in Dieter Dorn's production in Munich (1980), where the beginning of their relationships meant the end of their adventures. In an interview Dorn stressed his decision to choose older actors for the part:

> I wanted it to deal with me and my generation . . . For all these people it is the last chance when love and a new life may be still possible, but they all are dreadfully tense, each one is only concerned with himself and, for fear of death, grabs out for any other person, naturally grabbing the

> wrong person – nearly all of them grab the wrong one, don't they? There is no really fulfilled love in this play.
>
> (Jauslin 1982, 31–32)

But even young actors and actresses did not necessarily represent freshness of youth, love-stricken behavior, or genuine rapture. Their actions might have been determined equally by a weariness of life, disillusion, and an agonizing sense of resignation. Peter Löscher's production in Frankfurt am Main (1977) tried to highlight that with particular emphasis: "Here, Orsino is no longer an infatuated adult, but a boy out of the rock milieu. He lecherously licks his reflection in a mirror, then whips his naked back with a leather belt" (*Frankfurter Rundschau*, March 8, 1977). He later boastfully showed the belt off, and Viola licked up his blood and at the same time fumbled with his flies. These performances in Bochum, Munich, and Frankfurt were particularly eloquent instances of the directorial choice by means of the characters' ages to suggest an awareness of certain changes in our society's conception of love: the unreal and far-off Illyria is set against a complex present-day world with its own clichés.

Costumes

Drawing attention to the set and the characters' ages is, of course, not the only means of indicating the direction of a production; in addition the costumes can also be an important factor in support of a particular message. They may define the historical period as well as the social status of people, for example when Malvolio appears as a "black, smooth Puritan," Aguecheek as a "greenish immature fop," and Sir Toby Belch as a "greying, coarse, heavy knight" (Magdeburg, 1981; *Volksstimme Magdeburg*, September 24, 1981).

Costumes, however, can also be entirely timeless, sometimes even styleless. For example, in Dieter Dorn's Munich production of 1980 the costume noblesse of the aristocratic characters was altogether dispensed with. Orsino and Malvolio wore leotards and bathing suits, Viola and Sebastian shabby carnival costumes; and only Olivia was resplendent in striking gowns and decorative lace blouses while the low comedy characters were put "in inside-out outer clothing as caricatures of their roles" (*Der Tagesspiegel*, February 3, 1980). In the Bonn production (1987), Olivia had escaped from the Spanish Rococo period, suggesting a definite historical period. The director, Peter Eschberg, however, was particularly concerned to lay stress on the timelessness of the themes by mixing the ages and the social status evident in the performance.

There have also been cases of acting *without* costumes, especially during the "liberation fever" of the 1970s. This is again a phenomenon that productions in both West and East Germany have in common (always a little later in the latter), and, as the program notes make clear, with almost exclusively female nudes. In a production in Wuppertal in 1975, however, a naked Orsino stepped into the bathtub and, when towelling himself afterwards, gave Viola an opportunity to show her feelings without words. That a woman, too, can take a man into her bed (here Olivia and Sebastian) was at the centre of the Frankfurt production in 1977 with Orsino as a perverse rock youth. This symbolic reference to the dawn of the emancipation movement does not, of course, really go with Olivia's behavior when, stark naked, after a night with Viola's twin brother, she rushes to a priest in order to make him receive Sebastian's vow of fidelity. Her conduct, "first the orgasm, then the organ," seems, at least from today's perspective, tense and antiquated (*Frankfurter Allgemeine Zeitung*, March 8, 1977).

That the pleasure many directors took in nudity on stage had not died out at the turn of the twenty-first century was demonstrated in a Munich production by Matthias Fontheim (1995) which was fiercely criticized:

> This is how the play at the Residenztheater starts: dressed with nothing but a ring on his finger, the young man presents himself to the audience in all his pallor. Nobody knows why. It does not tell us of his lovesickness at any rate. Even though he covers himself with blankets, dresses himself in silk and velvet, this Orsino remains colorless right to the end, as his naked body at the beginning.
>
> (*Münchner Merkur*, February 2, 1995)

What You Will, or That's All One

The variety of the décor and costumes, the choice of age, period, and design in German productions have demonstrated how much liberty Shakespeare's text allows the director and actor. It presents the theatre and the audience with a score that contains much more than a simple comedy of confusion. Rather, it is open to all sorts of variations: it offers the music for gags, grotesque courting, for deception and self-deception, for bursts of laughter and absurdities, for the presentation of the feminine in the masculine, the masculine in the feminine, for frivolous lecherousness, wild desire, ecstatic ardour, but also for grief, melancholy, and an agonizing thirst for life; and all this concerned with only *one* topic, that of being in love and of folly, love often being nothing more than another form of folly. "[I]t's all one" (1.5.123), as Sir Toby aptly remarks. This can, after all, be applied to the whole play, and the programmatic subtitle of the comedy has not unjustly achieved the status of the chief and (usually) only title in German versions of the play.

As we look back on the history of *Twelfth Night* in the German theatre, two things are immediately apparent. One is the change from purely romantic to more realistic and even uncomfortable interpretations which often transferred the setting to a dire disillusioned Arcadia and the conventional "Happy Ending" disturbingly called into question. The other is the fact that even the less successful productions hardly ever failed to provide entertainment for the audience. There have been countless different approaches to *Twelfth Night*, each production provoking its own questions and solutions or, as Zoë Wanamaker concluded in her stimulating account of playing Viola at the RSC in Stratford (1983) and at the Barbican the following year: "the text remains for another attempt. I shall always be wanting to try it again" (1988, 91).

Works cited

Anders, Erika. "Theaterschau: Shakespeare auf der deutschen Bühne 1933/34. Eine Übersicht im Auftrage von Dr. Ernst Leopold Stahl." *Shakespeare-Jahrbuch* 71 (1935): 148–201.

Asper, Helmuth G. "Ludwig Tieck inszeniert *Was Ihr wollt.* Beschreibung und Analyse einer Fiktion." *Shakespeare-Jahrbuch* 110 (1974): 134–47.

Billington, Michael, ed. *Directors' Shakespeare: Approaches to Twelfth Night.* London: Nick Hern Books, 1990.

Edmondson, Paul. *Twelfth Night: A Guide to the Text and Its Theatrical Background.* Basingstoke: Palgrave Macmillan, 2005.

Eicher, Thomas. "Shakespeare und die Elisabethaner." In "*Theater im Dritten Reich.*" *Theaterpolitik, Spielplanstruktur, NS-Diktatur*. Ed. Henning Rischbieter. Seelze-Velber: Kallmeyersche Verlagsbuchhandlung, 2000: 297–316.

Ford, John R. *Twelfth Night: A Guide to the Play*. Westport, CT: Greenwood Press, 2006.

Gerstner, Muriel. "Die Erben Babels." *Was Ihr Wollt*. Programme. Schauspielhaus-hannover: Spielzeit 2004/5: 12–14.

Gielgud, John. *An Actor in His Time*. London: Sidgwick & Jackson, 1979.

Günther, Alfred. "Wie übersetzt man Shakespeare? Zu den Übertragungen von Flatter, Rothe und Schaller." *Theater Heute* 2 (1963): 19–21.

Habicht, Werner. "The Romanticism of the Schlegel-Tieck Shakespeare and the History of Nineteenth-Century German Shakespeare Translation." In *European Shakespeares.* Ed. D. Delabastita and L. D'huelst. Amsterdam: John Benjamins Publishing Company, 1993: 45–54.

Hamburger, Maik. "Shakespeare on the Stages of the German Democratic Republic." In *Shakespeare on the German Stage: The Twentieth Century*. Ed. Wilhelm Hortmann. Cambridge: Cambridge University Press, 1998: 369–475.

Hortmann, Wilhelm. "Word into Image: Notes on the Scenography of Recent German Productions." In *Foreign Shakespeare: Contemporary Performance*. Ed. Dennis Kennedy. Cambridge: Cambridge University Press, 1993: 232–53.

——, ed. *Shakespeare on the German Stage: The Twentieth Century*. Cambridge: Cambridge University Press, 1998.

Jauslin, Christian. "Dieter Dorns Shakespeare-Inszenierungen: Gespräch mit dem Regisseur." *Deutsche Shakespeare-Gesellschaft West Jahrbuch* (1982): 27–35.

Koller, Ann Marie. *The Theater Duke. Georg II of Saxe-Meiningen and the German Stage*. Stanford, CA: Stanford University Press, 1984.

Kühlken, Edda. *Die Klassiker-Inszenierungen von Gustaf Gründgens*. Meisenheim am Glan: Anton Hain, 1972.

Luft, Friedrich. "Shakespeares *Was Ihr Wollt*: Schlosspark-Theater." In *Berliner Theater 1945–1961. Sechzehn kritische Jahre*. Friedrich Luft. Velber bei Hannover: Erhard Friedrich Verlag, 1962: 107–9.

Paulin, Roger. *The Critical Reception of Shakespeare in Germany 1682–1914: Native Literature and Foreign Genius*. Hildesheim: Georg Olms, 2003.

Pennington, Michael. *Twelfth Night: A User's Guide*. London: Nick Hern, 2000.

Potter, Lois. *Twelfth Night. Text and Performance*. Basingstoke: Macmillan, 1985.

Rice, Jane C. "The Discussion of Shakespeare in Germany." Dissertation, Stanford University. Stanford, CA, 1987.

Rischbieter, Henning. "Kortner's Beispiel: *Was Ihr Wollt* zum Abschluß der Festwochen." *Theater Heute* 11 (1962): 19–21.

Shakespeare, William. *Twelfth Night, or What You Will*. Ed. Roger Warren and Stanley Wells. The Oxford Shakespeare. Oxford: Clarendon Press, 1994.

Sinden, Donald. "Malvolio in *Twelfth Night*." In *Players of Shakespeare 1: Essays in Shakespearean Performance by Twelve Players with the Royal Shakespeare Company*. Ed. Philip Brockbank. Cambridge: Cambridge University Press, 1985: 41–66.

Smith, Bruce R. "Ragging *Twelfth Night*: 1602, 1996, 2002–3." In *A Companion to Shakespeare and Performance*. Ed. Barbara Hodgdon and W. B. Worthen. London: Blackwell Publishing, 2005: 57–78.

Stroedel, Wolfgang. *Shakespeare-Pflege auf der deutschen Bühne vom Ende des Weltkriegs bis zur Gegenwart*. Weimar: Böhlau, 1938.

Tieck, Ludwig. *Romane: Der Aufruhr in den Cevennen. Der junge Tischlermeister. Vittoria Accorombona*. Munich: Winkler Verlag, 1988: 205–538.

"Umgang mit Shakespeare: Vier Regisseure und ein Übersetzer berichten über ihre Erfahrungen mit Shakespeare-Übertragungen." *Theater Heute* 6 (1963): 27–33.

"Unsere Aufführung des Jahres: 'Was Ihr Wollt' in Berlin." *Theater Heute* 4 (1963): 35–48.

Wanamaker, Zoë. "Viola in *Twelfth Night*." In *Players of Shakespeare 2: Further Essays in Shakespearean Performance by Players of the Royal Shakespeare Company*. Ed. Russell Jackson and Robert Smallwood. Cambridge: Cambridge University Press, 1988: 81–91.

Was spielten die Theater? Bilanz der Spielpläne in der Bundesrepublik Deutschland 1947–1975. Ed. Deutscher Bühnenverein. Bundesverband deutscher Theater. Remagen-Rolandseck: Verlag Rommerskirchen, 1978.

Wells, Stanley. "Royal Shakespeare: Studies of Four Major Productions at the Royal Shakespeare Theatre, Stratford-upon-Avon." *Furman Studies* (June 1976): 1–63.

Wer spielte was? Werkstatistik des Deutschen Bühnenvereins. Bensheim: Mykenae Verlag Rossberg, 1981–.

Williams, Simon. *Shakespeare on the German Stage*. Volume I: *1586–1914*. Cambridge: Cambridge University Press, 1990.

Winnacker, Susanne. "Illyrien." *William Shakespeare: Was Ihr Wollt. Komödie in fünf Akten*. Programme. Weimar: Schauspiel-Großes Haus, 2005: 4–5.

12 "What he wills"

Early modern rings and vows in *Twelfth Night*

Alan W. Powers

Books on Shakespearean comedy – like those by Cesar Barber, Theodore Weiss, Ralph Berry, W. T. MacCary, G. Beiner, and Michael Mangan – routinely conclude with a chapter on *Twelfth Night*, as if in this play Shakespeare's comic writing somehow culminates.[1] Even Erich Segal, in his dour presage of the *Death of Comedy*, notes how Shakespeare surpasses Lyly and Plautus in what he calls transvestite comedy: "*Twelfth Night* is arguably Shakespeare's finest comedy, the culmination of his 'first comic phase'" (2000, 310). Whether it is his "finest comedy" in a "comic phase" (as if the author were a teen taken with blue hair), certainly it is a rich text in several senses, offering a cascade of jewels or tokens; if for Barber the play tests courtesy with liberty, it also anticipates *Timon* as rigor tests generosity. Titled for a festal date in the Renaissance calendar, the one associated with Christmas gift-giving in imitation of the Magi, *Twelfth Night* also embraces other Renaissance ceremonies from which only vestiges remain.

Begin with Olivia's mourning, an elaborate ceremony at the time, as it still is in many traditional societies. Then there is the duel, and the offstage secret marriage. In these cases, the play abridges all three ceremonies, two being religious, and thus forbidden on stage. Another instance of ceremony – specifically, social ceremony – is the unlikely heart of the play's agon: Malvolio the steward's social position and all the behavioral decorum it implies – especially regarding Sir Toby. Similarly, Sir Andrew's mastery of dance suggests one kind of participation in a ceremonial society. Certain early modern ceremonies, for instance religious ones, were forbidden to the stage, for example marriage oaths – always distorted or offstage in the canon. Modern filmmakers universally ignore this prohibition, so narrated offstage marriages, like Petruchio and Kate's, take center frame. As we look at the early modern age and stage, we witness the onstage overlapping of dramatic and social conventions. If *Twelfth Night* undercuts certain ceremonial conventions, that is what comedy does. But it also sustains, perhaps surprisingly, some Renaissance ceremonies that held special appeal for illiterate listeners in the audience (Wrightson 1982, Raffel 1996).

Take, for example, vows and their usual tokens, rings. In pre-literate cultures, rings often served the same function as words in respect to vows. One might use either (and often both) rings and words to memorialize a vow. If one could not write to remember the words, a ring token served to remind, like a string tied to a finger. For the purpose of our analysis, rings fall under the broader aegis of Shakespearean tokens – from Ophelia's "remembrances" to Troilus's gift sleeve and Cressida's glove (a common Elizabethan token), from Orlando's "napkin, / Dy'd in blood" to Othello's famous handkerchief "dy'd in mummy which the skillful / Conserv'd of maidens' hearts." These other tokens suggest the real place of tokens in an oral culture that validated magic and feared forbidden ceremonies. Rings, too, were part of that culture, although their vestigial use in our modern culture abrades their original significance.

Tokens often accompanied oral contracts or vows. Both oaths and tokens are like bets, structurally. When one swears by something, or offers a token in collateral, one is offering to forfeit what one offers or swears by (Mauss 1954). In Shakespeare, common forfeits or oaths include "by my hand," or "by my father's soul" (both *HV* 3.2.90ff.); Bassanio enacts this very exchange a vow implies, "I will be bound to pay it ten times o'er / On forfeit of my hands, my head, my heart" (*MV* 4.1.208). Thus, oaths "by God" are not to be bandied lightly, offering as they do to forfeit all; on stage, Shakespeare often prefers to syncretize with "by the gods," especially after the 1606 Jacobean injunction against stage swearing (Gazzard 2009). Juliet, aghast at the prospect of liability and loss through vows, counsels Romeo:

> Oh, swear not by the moon, th'inconstant moon
> That monthly changes in her circled orb,
> Lest that thy love prove likewise variable.
> (*RJ* 2.1.151–53)

When Romeo asks what token she would accept, "What shall I swear by," Juliet enjoins, "Do not swear at all . . ." She would accept no token, nothing less than "by thy gracious self," but then demurs even at that:

> I have no joy of this contract tonight.
> It is too rash, too unadvised, too sudden,
> Too like the lightning which doth cease to be
> Ere one can say it lightens.
> (2.1.159–62)

In *Merchant of Venice*, Gratiano and Nerissa quarrel over the ring she gave him at their parting; Gratiano like Romeo swears by the moon, oh changeable forfeit. Gratiano swears that he gave the ring "to the judge's clerk," of course Nerissa in disguise. Gratiano's excuse, in the days before legal secretaries, and before women's education in the Latin of the law, and before fashionable suspicions of bisexuality, would have served as a plausible alibi. However, it is not good enough for the legal eagle Portia, who overhears and demands, "A quarrel ho already! What's the matter?" (*MV* 5.1.146)

In one of those excursuses on criticism that populate the plays, Gratiano defends himself by turning critic, or "lewd interpreter." He diminishes the verse or proverb inscribed on the ring. Using his literate criteria, he dismisses the ring's monetary and literary value as well as its symbolism in oral culture, its meaning. Gratiano says they quarrel:

> About a hoop of gold, a paltry ring
> That she did give me, whose posy was
> For all the world like cutler's poetry
> Upon a knife, "Love me, and leave me not."
> (5.1.147–50)

His critique of a token on its literary merit enacts the conflict between oral culture and literate judgment. As literate critics, when we come to elements of oral culture in the plays, we are in precisely the same danger as Gratiano, liable to dismiss the folk inheritance. Our very literacy may hinder or excuse us from understanding oral elements in the text like vows and tokens, proverbs, rhymes and mnemonic structures, gestures and non-verbal ceremonies.

Gratiano turns to his language training in order to deliberately misinterpret. He must know that a ring's meaning is not limited to the letters inscribed on it. He must know, because everybody knows *that*. The meaning of a ring is such common knowledge that it has even survived the Renaissance. But Gratiano, confronted with a personal failing – and the appearance of a larger one – turns literary critic and mounts the soap-box of Renaissance masculine literary-rhetorical training. According to the criteria of the literate, largely male culture, the ring was sentimental, a Harlequin romance, a motto roughly equivalent to those decals on pine boards available in souvenir shops, like "Home Sweet Home." The writing on the ring was "like cutler's poetry / Upon a knife"; the ring makes bad reading. But Gratiano's interpretive feint rests upon criteria from literate culture that are inadequate to how a ring means. Its meaning depends upon a nexus of oral customs and associations.

As we turn back to *Twelfth Night*, though ring tokens are offered throughout the canon, in no other comedy is one character, Viola/Caesario offered so many gems – five, by my count, though Sebastian intercepts two of them. Moreover, because of their relation to vows and secret meanings, rings in *Twelfth Night* take on meaning far from costume and adornment, *pace* Kerrigan: "Jewels and precious stones are typical of its [adornment's] highly external relationship . . . [They do not] express the organic nature of the person adorned" (2001, 107). Rings in *Twelfth Night* do indeed express the meaning and intention of the giver, if not of the person adorned.

The exchange of rings as spousal gesture, or subarration, occurs on stage in *Two Gentlemen of Verona*, *The Merchant of Venice*, *Cymbeline*, and offstage in *Romeo and Juliet*, *All's Well That Ends Well*, and *Twelfth Night*. Sometimes the woman initiates the token exchanges, as does Julia early in *Two Gentlemen*. The gift of ring by messenger takes place in *The Comedy of Errors*, *Two Gentlemen*, *Romeo and Juliet*, *The Merchant of Venice*, *The Merry Wives of Windsor*, and *Twelfth Night*. Often such messenger tokens are associated with shame, as when the sworn brotherhood in *Love's Labour's Lost* break their vows by messenger, or when Portia disguised as a justice succeeds in worrying Bassanio out of the ring whose loss would "presage the ruin of your love" (*MV* 3.2.173). Bassanio sends it by messenger, lamely mitigating his breach of oral contract. Occasionally messenger tokens mask true passion that must be hidden, as when Juliet sends Romeo her ring after Tybalt's murder, or even in *Merry Wives*, when Fenton, unacceptable to the father, requests, "Give my sweet Nan this ring" (3.4.99).

While we pursue rings as signifiers in early modern culture, particularly at the intersection of literate and oral cultures, we need not forget many other resonances of both the word *ring* and the object or prop. Curiously, I have not found much punning on this word amongst its various meanings: for instance, as a verb and a sound, famously in *Othello*, but also in histories like *1 Henry 6* and *2 Henry 4*; or as a formation, either in battle or in the emperor's cortege in *Julius Caesar*: "Make a ring about the corpse of Caesar" (3.2.159); or as a proto-Freudian reference to female sexual anatomy, say in Gratiano's ring allusions. In this last usage, *ring* may be the female equivalent of *stand* as a male erectile reference in the first scenes of both *The Taming of the Shrew* and *Romeo and Juliet*, and *Two Gentlemen of Verona* (2.5.21). In line with Shakespeare's familiar chastening of his comic sources (from frank Italian tales of adultery), Shakespeare appears to joke more easily about male sexuality, since Sly, Sampson, and Lance all pun on this anatomical detail of male sexual function.

Turning back to the early modern ring exchange in one of the earliest plays, the changeable Proteus needs no coaxing to send the ring he received from Julia to his new flame Silvia in *Two Gentlemen*; however, he chooses the disguised Julia to be his token-messenger. A prototype of Viola, Julia dutifully delivers the token: "And now am I, unhappy messenger, / To plead for that which I would not obtain, / To carry that which I would have refused" (4.4.97–99). Such rings and tokens enjoyed a prominence in the popular culture of Tudor England unsupported by canon law; as the historian Ralph Houlbrooke observes:

> The importance of the ring (and other tokens, such as glove, coins, and kerchiefs . . .) seems to have been much greater in the eyes of the parties, and more particularly in the eyes of male suitors, than it was in the view of the law.
>
> (Houlbrooke 1961, 60–61)

It is clear that *Twelfth Night* appeals to members of popular culture such as those male suitors in the audience for whom all the gift rings add plot suspense. Moving from the quotidian to the stage, one wonders about the size and scale of rings as props.

The medieval religious, with their own sense of theatricality, found it necessary to use oversized rings that all could see, and that fit over the required ceremonial gloves of twelfth-century abbots and abbesses: "I grossi anelli dal diametro gigantesco a noi conservati dal Medioevo, erano dai vescovi portati sopra i guanti nelle funzioni sacre e tenuti fermi da un anellino" [The rings of giant diameter we have from the Middle Ages were worn by bishops over their gloves for sacred functions and held secure by a smaller ring] (*Enciclopedia Italiana*, 241). Even among the laity, modern ring conventions did not apply: one extant engagement ring from the fifteenth century bears, instead of a jewel – which came in three centuries later – a helmeted head in relief. This is illustration #11 from *Enciclopedia Italiana*: "anello di fidanzamento del sec. XV" [fifteenth-century engagement ring] (244). Sometime over the 400 years between *Twelfth Night* and ourselves, Renaissance canon distinctions between spousals *de futuro* (or engagement) and spousals *de praesenti* (or marriage) became the material fact of diamonds for the former, and for the latter, gold bands. One suspects it is a late nineteenth-century convention pushed by the merchant interests in the diamond mines (Kanfer 1993).

Writing around the same time as diamond mining began in earnest – the 1870s – the Italian literary folklorist Antonio De Gubernatis discusses "*il toccamano*," or handfasting, and the use of the engagement ring, or *anulus pronubus* in Latin (1878, 102). Surely this is clerical adaptation of Roman custom, where proposals of marriage went through fathers. There would be no need for a ring signifying such a promise when it was contracted in such a setting. But as young people came to arrange, even partly, their own spousals, rings may have come to represent – and even to displace? – dowry negotiations. Prior to De Beers, the ring signifying the promise of marriage, the spousal *de futuro*, may well have been an inexpensive one full of sentiment. De Gubernatis notes that "a Roma, al tempo di Plinio, era solamento di ferro" [at the time of Pliny, such a ring could only be iron] (103). And he quotes an Italian popular song that suggests such a ring allows a "trial period" for the contract, allowing it to be broken until the ring is gold:

> Se siete sposo ancor non lo so io;
> Ancora siete a tempo a dirgli addio.
> Quando si vederò l'anello in dito
> Allor ci piglierò pena e partito.
> Quando si vederò l'anello d'oro,
> Allor ci piglierò partito e duolo.
>
> (De Gubernatis 1878, 103)

This little ditty says, "I sure don't know if you're hitched yet / Still you've time to say goodbye; / So, they see a finger ring, you bet / Then it hurts to say goodbye; / When they see a ring of gold, / Then to part brings griefs untold." So nineteenth-century Italian popular song made this distinction in rings, where the engagement ring was less an investment, all around (Cunnington 1963, Edwards 1855). The relative worth or "weight" of the contract is equated to the worth or weight of the jewelry. And this song seems to conflate the ceremonial subarration with the gold ring itself.

Not just on stage, intermediaries or messengers were commonly used to deliver gifts and tokens, as well as to negotiate marriage (O'Hara 2000, 65). In *Twelfth Night* we enjoy the spectacle of two ring-bearing intermediaries, two unlikely cupids or pandaruses, the spoilsport Malvolio and Viola/Cesario. Cesario, reluctant to win Olivia for Orsino whom she secretly loves, becomes just as reluctant to displace Orsino in Olivia's affections. Several of the Tudor marriage court cases in O'Hara suggest social analogs for elements in Shakespeare's plot. O'Hara's chapter on "The Language of Tokens" includes negotiating intermediaries, "forced" gift tokens, and the rejection of a token (a "neckercher") by casting it on the ground:

> the neckercher he thrust into her pockett which she took out and cast to him agen on the ground at Hithe [Hythe] fayer . . .
>
> (O'Hara 2000, 66)

In *Twelfth Night*, Malvolio serves as ring-bearer messenger to another messenger, Cesario, who does not accept the offer. Malvolio casts the ring onto the ground, perhaps in dramatic imitation of how he imagines it thrust upon his mistress Olivia.

> Come, sir, you peevishly threw it to her, and her will is it should be so returned. [*He throws down the ring.*] If it be worth stooping for, there it lies, in your eye; if not, be it his that finds it.
>
> (2.2.13–14)

Olivia has cast Malvolio in his familiar role as nay-sayer (or dramatically, as agelast): he believes he is returning, rejecting the gift. He plays this role with relish, but Viola/Cesario detects his true role as messenger-pandar. Picking up the ring once she is alone, Viola notes: "I left no ring with her. What means this lady? . . . None of my lord's ring? Why, he sent her none. / I am the man" (2.2.17, 24–25).

Olivia's use of the unwitting Malvolio here as nay-sayer anticipates his role throughout the play as "a kind of Puritan" or, what is the same, "a Brownist," one of the sect that would become the Congregationalists, and as such founded Massachusetts Bay Colony in 1630 while their London brethren shut down the theatres in 1642. It is in this light that Malvolio's harsh treatment becomes intelligible, quite beyond his role as blocking figure in comedy. To any American inheritor of Brownist Protestant culture, Malvolio is recognizably one of very few upward-mobile "Americans" in Shakespeare. (Valentine in *Two Gentlemen of Verona* might be another, courting the Duke of Milan's daughter Silvia – and possibly a third, Othello? The list probably extends to various carriers, attendants, and folks like Caliban – though he is arguably the heir of a large land-holder.) Malvolio plans to marry the boss's daughter, or in fact, in a very twenty-first century turn, the boss herself. And for this, he is treated, on the Jacobean stage, as a madman.

Incidentally, the Renaissance treatment of insanity shares two methods used in modern mental wards: first, like Malvolio, depressive patients today may also be treated chronobiologically, but instead of with darkness, with more daylight. Secondly, Malvolio, like the protagonist in Kesey's *One Flew Over the Cuckoo's Nest*, is quizzed. In the modern novel (and in medical school training at the time), proverbs are used as a touchstone to determine mental state; Malvolio has to answer the more taxing Renaissance interrogation about metempsychosis. Feste, disguising his voice as a curate, probes, "What is the opinion of Pythagoras concerning waterfowl?" (4.2.50). Malvolio gives the good Christian reponse, "I think nobly of the soul, and no way approve his opinion" (4.2.55). Though Malvolio appears to breeze through his oral exam on Pythagoras, Feste/Sir Thopas flunks him as a matter of zany theological – and ornithological – correctness; before Sir Thopas will discharge him, he must convert to Pythagoreanism: "Thou shalt hold th' opinion of Pythagoras ere I will allow of thy wits, and fear to kill a woodcock lest thou dispossess the soul of thy grandam."

For our analysis, Malvolio's own love exchange is missing an appropriate token. True, he receives an epistle, and written tokens are included in O'Hara's 403 gifts and tokens exchanged from 1542 to 1600 in Kent parishes. They amount to only 13 (about equal to gifts of "animals and foodstuffs"), mostly mentioned in depositions between 1580 and 1600. The giving of rings tops the popular gifts and tokens at 61 out of 403; gloves appear in 37 depositions. About one-fifth of the gifts and tokens in O'Hara's data fall under "metal and trinkets," rings accounting for most, but another 23 as well. Perhaps Valentine's advice to the aging suitor, the Duke of Milan (the prospective victim of his elopement plan), was common knowledge: "Win her with gifts if she respect not words. / Dumb jewels often in their silent kind / More than quick words do move a woman's mind" (3.1.89). Milan would not be pleased to hear this from his prospective son-in-law. But elsewhere, Shakespeare's use of tokens is, like some of his language, raised from common usage; no character in the canon receives a goat or a stoat, though Launce offers his flatulent dog in place of Proteus's lap-dog stolen in the marketplace (4.4.60).

So often in his plots Shakespeare doubles his source, for instance, two sets of twins instead of *Menaechmi*'s one. Here in *Twelfth Night*, messenger is added to messenger, and both are also, at points in the play, themselves lovers. Additionally, the supposed rejected token doubles as really a forced gift. O'Hara's collection of court cases features one that encapsulates the plot element of Olivia's desiring Cesario to return, though in Tudor actuality the message was delivered to a messenger: "She insisted that if Thomas Lambard would come to her again he would be even more welcome than before" (O'Hara 2000, 65).

When Viola does come again to Olivia, she has another jewel, the one given her by Orsino: "To her in haste; give her this jewel. Say / My love can give no place, bide no denay" (2.4.123–24). She also must still have the ring Malvolio threw towards her. At this point, she might be played as a traveling pawn-shop, a gentrified version of Autolychus in *The Winter's Tale*. Even in *Twelfth Night* we can learn economics, the advantage of the middleman/woman. She does not return either token – probably a plot device to keep the rich ambiguity of the gift-tokens in suspension. Like *A Midsummer Night's Dream*, *Twelfth Night* suggests omnivorous desire, and the sheer generosity, the fecundity of gift tokens in the play, reinforces this broad theme. (Much recent work helps here, such as Bruce R. Smith's edition of the play emphasizing the contexts of "what you will.") After Orsino's, the next token Viola receives – again as Cesario, but now the second for Cesario proper – is a locket, a portrait "miniature" from Olivia: "Here, wear this jewel for me. 'Tis my picture. / Refuse it not. It hath no tongue to vex you" (3.4.203–4).

Viola in cross-gendered disguise becomes what W. C. Fields called the "hypotenuse" in a love triangle – or actually, two triangles. Orsino loves Olivia loves Cesario; and Olivia loves Cesario loves Orsino. Does that make it a love hexagon, pentagon, or rhombus? And what is the geometry of love once Malvolio intrudes, less cross-gendered than cross-gartered? Malvolio loves Olivia loves Cesario loves Orsino: a clear quadrilateral. But once Cesario splits, like meiosis, into Viola and Sebastian, it's a pentagon, with Malvolio left out. Shakespeare's usual doubling compounds the proverb into four's company, but five's a crowd. In *Twelfth Night*, the playwright seems to have doubled the ring exchanges as well.

The fourth token begins act 4 scene 3. Carrying a pearl, Sebastian enters in a daze, doubting if he dreams, "For though my soul disputes well with my sense, / That this may be some error," as do so many characters in the canon like Antipholus of Syracuse, given a golden chain in *Comedy of Errors*, "This fellow is distract, and so am I / And here we wander in illusions" (4.3.42–43). Like Antipholus, Sebastian stands amazed to be caught up in the web of jewels that we have been tracing: "This is the air, this is the glorious sun, / This pearl she gave me, I do feel't and see't; / And though 'tis wonder that enwraps me thus, / Yet 'tis not madness" (4.3.1–4). He appears to "protest too much" his sanity. For the audience, this is a great leap forward in the plot, the first token not given to Viola/Cesario – though of course, Sebastian is mistaken for his sister in disguise.

Of the myriad tokens exchanged throughout the canon, we find more written tokens, more love poems, in Shakespeare than in historical records of the period – only some 3 percent in O'Hara's summary of Kent. Besides earnest poet-lovers like Valentine and even the reluctant Benedick, whose verses are used as evidence against themselves, there are poets like Parolles, Phebe, Berowne, Dumain, Orlando, and Touchstone. Versifying is highly gendered, heavily male, because poetics was part of schoolboy Latin training. But Shakespeare's women are fierce critics of men and their verses. Katherine in *Love's Labour's Lost* laughs at Dumain's efforts: "Some thousand verses of a faithful lover/ . . . Vildly compiled, profound simplicity" (5.2.50, 52). Five lines later, the Princess summarizes women's "practical criticism" of tokens: "Dost thou not wish at heart / The [gold] chain were longer, and the letter short?" Perhaps an exception, Rosalind, though a good critic – equaled only by Touchstone in that play – proves susceptible to verse.

It is not surprising that the great poet and dramatist should endow his lovers with literacy and a literary bent, one sometimes employed by the less literary, be they women untrained in poetics or servants. Even the literate Silvia in *Two Gentlemen* employs Valentine to compose a verse letter – to himself, an interesting variant on messenger-tokens like Viola's. In *Twelfth Night* the messenger is disguised, while in *Two Gentlemen*, the object of affection, the addressee, is hidden. *Twelfth Night* has the fewest male lover-poets of any comedy, but it does boast a competent female poet. Maria disguises the object of affection as did Silvia; she sends her deceptive letter and does include a tetrameter quatrain bearing the popular culture form, the riddle: "I may command where I adore; / But silence, like a Lucrece knife, / With bloodless stroke my heart doth gore / M.O.A.I doth sway my life" (2.5.87–90).

Malvolio partakes of the Renaissance love of such anagrammatic puzzles, such a word game, while this period's passion for those games may stem from the emergence of literate culture. Surely, Feste is a literate fool, as Mullini emphasizes in her book on the growth of Shakespearean fools as "corrupters of words": "C'è da notare che il *fool* sa leggere: questa caratteristica, che non appartiene invece al *clown* rustico e illetterato" (1990, 55) [One notes that the *fool* knows how to read; this quality does not belong to the rustic and illiterate *clown*]. Clowns need not read; using Mullini's distinction, we might call Juliet's Nurse the most complex clown figure in the canon.

The fifth, and final, jewel token exchange in *Twelfth Night* takes place offstage. The Priest attests in act 5: "A contract of eternal bond of love, / Confirmed by mutual joinder of your hands, / Attested by the holy close of lips, / Strengthened by interchangement of your rings . . ." (5.1.154–57). Olivia assumes she has married Viola/Cesario, who denies it, though she has received – and not returned – at least three tokens from Olivia. The marriage ring would be the fourth. In summary, the multiple and ambiguous gifting of tokens, largely from Olivia, but also from Orsino, raises the tone of *Twelfth Night* from everyday gifts such as those bought at fairs, or "fayrings." These tokens contribute to the overall poetic tone of the play, while grounding it securely in the popular culture of the day. To be fair, while the sheer fecundity of gifting here may raise the tone, Shakespeare carefully and metadramatically lowers the quasi-religious tone of his title when the only title reference becomes Sir Toby's drunken rendition of "O the twelfth day of December" (2.3.81). That same oral popular culture Shakespeare has used from his early comedies like *Two Gentlemen of Verona*, riddled as it is with oaths and breaches of oaths, tokens and gifts, the oral proclamation of "vanishment" (as Launce mispeaks it), the spoken word as bond (2.7.75), and the effort to compose written tokens, especially verse.[2]

Twelfth Night seems to leave behind the hyper-poeticality, the meta-criticality of plays like *Love's Labour's Lost* and *As You Like It*, both filled with written – indeed, verse – tokens. What if Malvolio had composed a foolish poem rather than a silly wardrobe? What if he had offered a ring to Olivia? One senses this would have been a very different play. For Olivia to reject Malvolio's ring would have breached the etiquette of the popular culture that, I argue, this play embraces. For Olivia to criticize Malvolio's poem instead of his dress would have placed us back in the world of *As You Like It* and *Love's Labour's Lost*. For Malvolio to have been considered mad for either his gift jewel or his poetry would antagonize the sacred givens of Elizabethan popular culture; whereas, for wanting to marry the boss's daughter – of course that was a crazed idea that would require centuries and voyages and New World colonies and a revolution to validate as social behavior.

In tying this play to the popular culture of early modern England, I have offered my partial answer to Barbara Everett's profound question about all, and especially the earlier, of Shakespeare's comedies, "Why do we take them seriously?" She observes that "at their best they achieve a lightness as far as possible from triviality" (Everett 1985, 294). My title puns on Shakespeare's subtitle by relating the festive gift rings in this comedy to the rings with which this essay, and Shakespeare's life, end. Rings have a resonance throughout the law court records, a resonance taken more seriously by the common and illiterate people than, indeed, by the courts themselves – who yet gave them almost the prominence of a spousal handshake (Powers 1996).

In the oral culture of Shakespeare's day, tokens memorialized and certified, just as legal words and documents did for the literate (Goody 1968; Wrightson 1982).[3] For instance, in *The Winter's Tale* Antiochus's death is attested not only by the shepherd's son's word, but by "a handkerchief and rings of his that Paulina knows" (5.2.66). The memorializing function of the token was used by Shakespeare himself when, in that written document that is his will (or, what *he* wills), he left money to his Stratford neighbors William Reynolds, Anthony Nash, Hamnet Sadler, and to his London colleagues Richard Burbage, John Heminges, and Henry Condell to buy memorial rings (Schoenbaum 1970, 45). Certainly the last three were literate, especially the two who oversaw publication of the First Folio. But even if all seven of his memorial ring-bearers were literate, Shakespeare chose to sign his passing with a ring, the appropriate gesture in the oral culture of Stratford in the early modern period.

Notes

1. Recently critics have added chapters on the Romances or Problem Plays, so that some conclude with *MFM* or *The Tempest.* C. Barber, T. MacCary, and R. Berry (who adds the romance *The Winter's Tale*) exemplify the former, K. Muir's *Shakespeare's Comic Sequence* the latter.
2. Harold Jenkins observes, "The most important source for *TN* . . . is *TGV*" (1965, 74).
3. Wrightson (1982). In East Anglian depositions from 1580–1700, gentlemen were 2 percent illiterate, merchants and shopkeepers 6–12 percent, poor artisans 88 percent, husbandmen 79 percent, laborers and servants 85 percent, and women 89 percent. See also Schofield (1968) and Cressy (1977).

Works cited

Barber, C. L. *Shakespeare's Festive Comedy: A Study in Dramatic Form and its Relation to Social Custom.* Princeton, NJ: Princeton University Press, 1968.

Beiner, G. *Shakespeare's Agonistic Comedy.* Cranbury, NJ: Associated University Presses, 1993.

Berry, Ralph. *Shakespearean Comedies: Explorations in Form.* Princeton, NJ: Princeton University Press, 1972.

Cressy, David. "Literacy in Seventeenth-Century England." *Journal of Interdisciplinary History* 8 (1977): 150.

Cunnington, C. Willet, and Phillis Cunnington. *Handbook of English Costume in the Seventeenth Century.* London: Faber and Faber, 1963.

Dasent, J. R., et al. *Acts of the Privy Council of England (1542–1625).* 21 vols. London: HM Stationery Office, 1890–1934.

De Gubernatis, A. *Storia comparata degli usi nuziali in Italia e presso gli altri popoli indoeuropei.* Milan: Fratelli Treves, 1878.

Edwards, Charles. *The History and Poetry of Finger-Rings.* New York: Redfield, 1855.

Enciclopedia Italiana. Vol. III. Istituto G. Treccani. Milan: Rizzoli, 1929–37.

Everett, Barbara. "Or What You Will." *Essays in Criticism* 35 (4) (October 1985): 294–314.

Gazzard, Hugh. "The Act to Restrain Abuses of Players." *Review of English Studies,* 2009. http://res.oxfordjournals.org/cgi/content/full/hgp066.

Goody, J., ed. *Literacy in Traditional Societies.* Cambridge: Cambridge University Press, 1968.

Houlbrooke, Ralph. *Church Courts and the People During the English Reformation.* Oxford: Oxford University Press, 1961.

Jenkins, Harold. "Shakespeare's *Twelfth Night.*" In *Shakespeare, the Comedies: A Collection of Critical Essays.* Ed. Kenneth Muir. Englewood Cliffs, NJ: Prentice-Hall, 1965: 72–87.

Journals of the House of Commons, Vol. 1, *From November the 8th 1547, in the First Year of the Reign of King Edward the Sixth, to March the 2nd 1628 in the Fourth Year of the Reign of King Charles the First*. Printed by Order of the House of Commons, 1800.

Kanfer, Stefan. *The Last Empire: South Africa, Diamonds, and De Beers from Cecil Rhodes to the Oppenheimers*. New York: Farrar, Straus and Giroux, 1993.

Kerrigan, John. "Secrecy and Gossip in *Twelfth Night*." In *On Shakespeare and Early Modern Literature.* Oxford: Oxford University Press, 2001: 89–112.

Kesey, Ken. *One Flew over the Cuckoo's Nest*. New York: Signet, 1963.

MacCary, W. Thomas. *Friends and Lovers: The Phenomenology of Desire in Shakespearean Comedy*. New York: Columbia University Press, 1985.

Mangan, Michael. *A Preface to Shakespeare's Comedies 1594–1603*. London and New York: Longman, 1996.

Mauss, Marcel. *The Gift: Forms and Functions of Exchange in Archaic Societies.* Trans. I. Cunnison. Glencoe, IL: Free Press, 1954.

Muir, Kenneth, ed. *Shakespeare: The Comedies*. Englewood Cliffs, NJ: Prentice Hall, 1965.

Mullini, Roberta. *Corrutore di parole: il fool nel teatro di Shakespeare*. Bologna: Cooperativa Libreria Universitaria Editrice Bologna, 1990.

O'Hara, Diana. *Courtship and Constraint: Rethinking the Making of Marriage in Tudor England.* Manchester and New York: Manchester University Press, 2000.

Powers, Alan W. "Meaner Parties: Spousal Conventions and Oral Culture in MFM and AWEW." *The Upstart Crow* 15 (1996): 35–47.

Raffel, Burton. "Who Heard the Rhymes, and How? Shakespeare's Dramaturgical Signals." *Oral Tradition* 11 (2) (1996): 190–221.

Schoenbaum, Samuel. *Shakespeare's Lives.* New York: Oxford University Press, 1970.

Schofield, R. S. "The Measurement of Literacy in Pre-Industrial England." In *Literacy in Traditional Societies*. Ed. J. Goody. Cambridge: Cambridge University Press, 1968: 311–25.

Shakespeare, William. *The Complete Works*. Ed. S. Wells and G. Taylor. Compact edn. New York: Oxford University Press, 1992.

Segal, Erich. *The Death of Comedy*. Cambridge, MA: Harvard University Press, 2001.

Smith, Bruce R., ed. *Twelfth Night or What You Will: Texts and Contexts*. Boston: Bedford/St. Martin's, 2001.

Wrightson, Keith. *English Society 1580–1680*. New Brunswick, NJ: Rutgers University Press, 1982.

13 Madness and social mobility in *Twelfth Night*

Ivo Kamps

In his *Optick Glasse of Humours* (1607), Thomas Walkington recounts the story of a "humorous melancholick scholar" who was afraid to come in the company of others because he believed "his nose was bigger then his whole bodie, and that the weight of it weighed down his head" (137). The title of Walkington's text and his diagnosis of the scholar as "humorous melancholick" draw the man's case into the humoral discourse that largely governed early modern thought about various types of mental illness. This medical discourse, which early modern physicians had inherited from ancient writers such as Galen and Aristotle, viewed madness in the context of what we would today call a "disease model," in which mental aberrations are understood in terms of a physical pathology (Ingleby 1982, 125–27). Specifically, early moderns believed that mental conditions resulted from a surplus or deficiency, or excessive digestion of one or more of the four humors that make up the human body. A melancholy or depressed individual, for instance, was thought to suffer from an excess of black, or of overly "concocted" or digested bile and possibly a deficiency of blood. Humor theory was not adverse to a consideration of other causes of mental illness, such as diet, behavior, witchcraft, demonic possession, fierce passions, and spiritual bewilderment, but a physiological condition was almost always viewed as central to the case.[1] Proposed cures for mental conditions therefore routinely sought to affect a physical change in the patient, a physical change that would bring about a proper balance between the humors and return the patient to mental health. One would therefore expect the melancholy scholar of Walkington's *Optick Glasse of Humours* to be treated for his delusions about the size of his nose with herbs, medicines, spiritual guidance, behavior regiments, or a dietary change. But nothing of the sort occurs in the continuation of the account, for Walkington submits that patients like this scholar are not only "out of temper for their organs of body, but their minds also are so out of frame and distract, that they are in bondage to many ridiculous passions" (134). To cure the man in question of his conceit,

> The Phisitions . . . invented this means, they tooke a great quantity of flesh, having the proportion of a nose, which they cunningly join'd to his face, whiles hee was a sleepe, then being waken they rased his skinne with a rasour till the bloud thrilled downe, and whiles hee cried out vehemently for the paine, the Physition with a jirke twitcht it from his face, and threw it away.
>
> (Walkington 1603, 137)

The intervention apparently succeeded and the scholar was cured. So instead of a "conventional" treatment addressing the physical pathology supposedly underlying the patient's "passions" and "conceit," we get a theatrical performance, a carefully planned act of deceit – a parlor trick, if you will. Walkington offers this case as one of the many "pleasant examples" contained in the records of the ancients, but what does the nature of the cure tell us about the Renaissance physician's conception of mental illness?

It appears that in order to restore the scholar to mental health the doctor temporarily accepts the "reality" of his patient's gargantuan nose. From within that reality, he then takes the logical step of cutting the nose down to proper size. Note that he shows the scholar an actual piece of flesh, not an imaginary portion of the scholar's imaginary nose, even though the pretense of cutting the imaginary flesh should be theoretically sufficient because the scholar clearly has the capacity to imagine a large physical object where there is none. The chunk of flesh serves to forge a link between the scholar's private, delusional reality and the reality of the physician (and rest of the community) in which a nose is no larger than it actually is. The deception is designed to bring about a gestalt shift in the scholar so that he will accept the community's sense of reality instead of his own.

Several other cases cited by Walkington reveal similar theatrical trickery. A different man "perswaded himselfe that he had no head" (135). In this instance the physician fastened a heavy steel cap to the man's skull, who soon "cried amaine his head ak't." The doctor triumphantly observed that for one's head to hurt, "thou hast a head belike." This, too, apparently led to a cure. Another patient who believed he was God was cured as follows. He was "pend vp on an iron grate, and had no meate giuen him at all, onely they adored him and offered to his deity the fumes of frankinsense, and odours of delicate dishes" (138). After a while, the man grew so hungry "that hee was faine to confesse his humanity, vnlesse he meant to haue beene starued." But "the most famous of all conceited fools," and "worthy to be canoniz'd" is a man who would rather die "then let his vrine goe" (139). This man believed that "with once making water he should drowne all the houses and men in the towne" (139–40). To make the man "vent his bladder," the physicians set "an old ruinous house" on fire, and told him that unless he put out the blaze the entire town would be in grave danger. "The man sente forth an abundant stream of urine, and so was recovered of his malady" (140).[2]

What these cases have in common is that there is little apparent interest in the underlying physical causes for their condition. The patients are diagnosed as suffering from a "conceit," or delusion, which may well stem from a humoral imbalance, but one that apparently does not require treatment of the body or the removal of root causes. To return the patient to mental health, the physician conjures up a little stage play that substitutes an alternate reality for the patient's,[3] and when the patient accepts this new reality (one man's urine cannot flood the world; my nose is now normal size; I must have a head because it hurts; and I must not be a god because I experience hunger), he appears restored to mental health. Or, to put it differently, the cure is achieved when the patient starts to perform an identity that conforms to the community's expectations. One may be tempted to say that these patients were cured because their delusions were displaced by a newfound grasp on reality – of things as they really are – but it may not be that simple. We must remember that the nose of the scholar does not actually change in proportion. All that really changes is his perception of his nose. The chunk of meat that was "removed" was never part of his nose. If anything, his new reality is based on the illusory removal of his illusory nose. Likewise, the man who is afraid to urinate must have done so countless times or he would have died long ago, and the man who believes he is god must have eaten many meals, giving him ample prior evidence that he is not divine. What has brought about their cure is a change in the manner in which they perceive themselves (based on a belief in a deception), and the manner in which that perception allows them to perform repetitively an identity acceptable to the community. The community understands men who eat, who urinate, and who have heads.

It is my contention that Shakespeare playfully explores the dynamics of madness, diagnosis, and cure, in the Toby, Maria, Malvolio plot of *Twelfth Night*. Like Walkington, Shakespeare posits a direct link between the performance of identity and madness. But whereas Walkington's physicians create theatrical illusions to return patients to sanity, Maria and Toby use analogous techniques to create the impression that Malvolio has gone utterly mad. If the patients in Walkington's text are tricked into abandoning their performances of madness, Malvolio is hoodwinked into performing lunacy.

Implicit in my argument so far has been a concept of human identity as a repetitive performance, borrowed from the work of Judith Butler, and before I continue my narrative I would like to make my terms more explicit. Drawing on the work of Michel Foucault, Butler claims that gender identity is not essential or biological but performative. Taking issue with the commonplace that gender is an interior condition that forms identity, she argues that "the inner truth of gender is a fabrication," "a fantasy inscribed on the surface of bodies" by various social discourses that produce only the truth effect of a "stable identity" (1999, 174). The key to maintaining the *truth effect* of a gender identity is the repetitive performance of specific "acts, gestures, [and] enactments" aside from which gender identity has no ontological status (173). Gender identity, therefore, has a reality only insofar as it bears the "corporeal signs and other discursive means" sanctioned by a particular society's dominant ideological mode(s).

If we accept Butler's formulation vis-à-vis *gender* identity, we may, without further argument, extend this formulation to identity *in general*.[4] We must also grant that even though identity is performed by a particular individual, there is every reason to believe that such a performance, while unique (in the sense that all individuals are different), does not solely originate within that individual. As Louis Althusser famously argued, all humans are interpellated as subjects by ideological structures that are beyond their control and are often even invisible to them (1971, 170–77). In other words, the performance of identity may be unique in ways that allow us to distinguish one subject from another and to recognize them as individuals, but it is socially homogeneous in the sense that it enacts upon individuals a society's ideological structures and dispensations.

The connection between the performance of one's *social* (or ideological) identity and ascriptions of madness is readily apparent when we consider the so-called "intelligibility" criterion discussed by psychiatrist David Ingleby. The bedrock principle of the intelligibility model is that people are judged mentally ill or deviant when "their conduct simply does not 'make sense'" (1982, 128). This is a deceptively plain assertion. Does not "make sense" to whom, and what is the precise meaning of "sense"? To explain the concept of "sense," Ingleby borrows Wittgenstein's concept of the "language-game," and argues that a community's members are connected, as would be the players in any game, by a set of public rules that its members know, even though they may not always be able to articulate them (129). When a player does not play by the rules of the game because he is ignorant of them, his behavior becomes unintelligible; or, by extension, if a member of a community fails to grasp and perform the basic rules of that community he or she may be judged abnormal by the other members. "Sense," or the absence of it, is inherently a "social construction" (129). Michael MacDonald, a historian of madness in the early modern period, underscores this very point when he observes that the *initial* diagnosis of madness was rarely made by physicians or psychiatrists but by "laymen" such as family members or neighbors, often on the basis of "popular beliefs" about the nature of mental illness (1981, 113, 114). We can be fairly certain that Walkington's scholar was first diagnosed by family or neighbors and not by a physician.

But we can refine the concept of intelligibility further. Ingleby's formulation applies primarily to a community's ability to judge any of its members mentally deviant, even if the member is personally unknown to those who pass judgment. We need not know anything personal, for instance, about the scholar with the enormous nose to know that he suffers from some type of mental disorder. But what about the person who is well known to his family and neighbors? When is he judged mad? The answer is not that this occurs when the person merely violates or ignores the rules of the community (which can often be explained away as harmless eccentric behavior) but when the person stops performing his or her identity as the community has come to expect of him or her over time. Shakespeare demonstrates this meaning of intelligibility in *Hamlet*, when Claudius says of Ophelia that she has been "divided from herself and her fair judgment" (4.5.86). What he means is that Ophelia no longer has access to the identity by which *they* knew her. She now speaks with the words of others (see Neely 1991, 323–26), and does not respond to the members of her community in the way she used to. Her words still have the power to move those who hear them, but "her speech is nothing," and meaning can only be derived when auditors "botch the words up fit to their own thoughts" (4.5.7, 10). *They* have to construct an identity and intentionality for her. She still physically resembles the daughter of Polonius, but she no longer acts or talks like "herself" because she is divided from that self.

That Shakespeare acutely grasped the role of intelligibility in diagnoses of madness in particular individuals who fail to perform their *known* identity is evident in one of his earliest plays, *The Comedy of Errors* (1589–93). Shakespeare's use of two sets of identical twins yields numerous moments of misrecognition between characters, leading to many diagnoses of madness, but it is important to recognize that Adriana is already deeply confused by her husband's unhusband-like behavior and has difficulty recognizing him *as* her husband before the twin brother appears. Luciana, Adriana's sister, seeks to comfort her by suggesting that "a man is master of his liberty" (2.1.7), and should not be expected to be home for dinner on time. Luciana argues that the social definition of "husband" is expansive enough to accommodate Antipholus of Ephesus's behavior. Adriana, however, is not concerned with a broad definition of the term "husband"; she laments *her* husband's unpredictable behavior and sees it as a sign of a fundamental rift in their marriage. "How comes it," she asks,

> That thou art thus estranged from thyself?
> Thyself I call it, being strange to me,
> That, undividable, incorporate,
> Am better than thy dear self's better part.
> Ah, do not tear away thyself from me!
> For know, my love, as easy mayst thou fall
> A drop of water in the breaking gulf
> And take unmingled thence that drop again,
> Without addition or diminishing,
> As take from me thyself and not me too.
> (2.2.118–28)

The image of marriage she posits is one of a union of inseparable souls, and by estranging himself from himself, Antipholus of Ephesus is not only estranging himself from her but her from herself. Their identities are linked and mutually dependent on each other and must be performed repetitively for their stability to continue. But it is the *in*stability of identity, of course, that intensifies as the play dramatizes various encounters between Adriana and her brother-in-law, Antipholus of Syracuse, whose very existence is unknown to her. Adriana invites her "husband" in for dinner and offers to "shrive [him] of a thousand idle pranks" (2.2.207), ostensibly to bring him back to his proper, socially recognizable role as *her* husband. But her efforts to transform her "husband" back into who he should be inevitably only bewilder Antipholus of Syracuse. "Am I in earth, in heaven, or in hell?" he wonders. "Sleeping or waking, mad or well-advis'd? / Known unto these, and to myself disguis'd?" (2.2.211–13). What Shakespeare is drawing on here is the social nature of human identity. Being known to others in a way that does not conform to one's own sense of identity (a sense that is itself rooted in the social context of his life in Syracuse) makes him unknown to himself – and to Adriana.

Adriana ultimately solicits the services of a charlatan exorcist, Dr. Pinch, to cast out the demons that have driven her husband mad. Pinch diagnoses that "the fiend is strong *within* him" (4.4.107; emphasis added), but the audience of course knows that there is nothing "within" Antipholus of Ephesus and that the claim of possession is spurious and a fraud (Greenblatt 1988, 114–15). As Stephen Greenblatt puts it, "Exorcism is the straw people clutch when the *world* seems to have gone mad" (115; emphasis added). Thus Shakespeare directs his audience to recognize that (at least in this instance) madness is not an internal, psychological, or humoral condition but an external social condition that is (mis)diagnosed by members of a community when someone's performance of self fails to meet that community's expectations of who that someone "is."

When Shakespeare writes *Twelfth Night* about a decade after *The Comedy of Errors*, he uses the figure of Malvolio to explore again how a community diagnoses madness when a person fails to perform his *known* identity, but he expands the concept of intelligibility to include Malvolio's failure to perform his *social* identity as a member of a certain class as well. What is more, in *Twelfth Night*, Shakespeare reverses the dynamic of attribution of madness that we saw in *The Comedy of Errors*. If *The Comedy of Errors* replicates the diagnosis of madness of those who fail to perform their identity in a way that makes them recognizable to other members of the community, *Twelfth Night* goads Malvolio into performing an identity that *makes* him unrecognizable to members of Olivia's household, resulting in a diagnosis of madness followed by his incarceration, and a mock exorcism intended to cast out the demons that supposedly possess him.

The basis for the confrontation between Malvolio and Sir Toby and Maria

can be found in Malvolio's problematic position as steward in
hold. The central issue for Toby is one of class. As a knight and
Countess Olivia, Toby outranks the commoner Malvolio in s
But within Olivia's household Malvolio the steward acts with
authority and is thus in a position to issue orders to Toby. Tha
on his mistress's behalf is clear when he seeks to put an end
gathering by Toby, Andrew, Maria, and Feste who, despite the household being in an official state of mourning, are engaged in a riotous drinking bout:

> Sir Toby, I must be round with you. My lady bade me tell you, that, though she harbors you as her kinsman, she's nothing allied to your disorders. If you can separate yourself from your misdemeanors, you are welcome to the house; if not, an it would please you to take leave of her, she is very willing to bid you farewell.
>
> (2.3.95–101)

But Malvolio does not merely attempt to exercise authority over his social betters; he is also the one who, ironically, introduces the issue of class into the confrontation. He accuses the raucous revelers of gabbling "like tinkers" and turning an aristocratic manor into "an alehouse" (2.3.87–89). The irony is double-edged because while it is true that Malvolio owes his position of authority precisely to his willingness to enforce the "respect of place, persons . . . [and] time" (2.3.91) that structure the world of Illyria and Olivia's household, it is these same structures that constitute the absolute limits of his own upward social mobility and that define him as a subordinate in rank to Sir Toby, Sir Andrew, and the gentlewoman Maria. Performing his identity as steward thus causes Malvolio both to exercise his proper role and to transgress it. Toby gets right to the heart of the matter when he mockingly interpellates the officious Malvolio by asking him, "Art any more than a steward?" (2.3.113–14). And within the hierarchical social structure of Illyria, Malvolio is indeed nothing more than a steward: a commoner and Toby's subordinate.

In order to put Malvolio back in his proper (social) place and remind him of his proper (social) identity, Maria devises a plan that will bring into the open Malvolio's transgressive desire for upward social mobility. Knowing of Malvolio's secret aspiration to marry Olivia and become "count Malvolio" (2.5.34), Maria forges a letter in Olivia's hand that implies that the countess is in love with Malvolio. The letter encourages him to pursue Olivia and display through various outward signs his love for her. Malvolio is to dress in yellow stockings, go cross-gartered, smile incessantly (something which he never does), discourse on matters of politics, act aloof, and speak condescendingly to other members of the household (2.5). The point of the scheme is to have Malvolio act so *out* of character that he will be declared mad and punished accordingly. There is an ironic appropriateness to the plan because, to Toby nd Maria, Malvolio's social ambition is a form of insanity, and what could be more fitting than to have him act out his desire and to be declared insane for it? It is one thing for Malvolio to harbor a secret desire for Olivia, but to act on his desire and to make it public is so ludicrously inappropriate that only a madman would do it (or so Maria and Toby believe). What is more, encouraging Malvolio to transgress the limits of place and propriety that have allowed him to rise to the position of steward will show him dismantling the very social hierarchy on which he has come to depend and which he has defended so vigorously in Olivia's name *and* his own interest.

That said, Malvolio seems perfectly capable of *performing* his desired social identity of a count. Before finding Maria's letter and following the incriminating recommendations in it, Malvolio paints a dignified if somewhat pompous picture of himself as count. He would "have the humor of the state," he says, and would tell Toby and the others that "I know my place as I would they should know theirs" (2.5.51–53). He tells us that he knows how to dress, how "to frown the while" at his inferiors, how to wind his watch for dramatic effect, and how to use his "prerogative of speech" to admonish Toby for his indecorous behavior (2.5.58–59, 69). There does not seem to be anything wrong with Malvolio's performance; it is just that it is the wrong performance for Malvolio as far as Toby and Maria are concerned.

Malvolio subsequently finds Maria's letter and tortures its words until he is convinced that Olivia loves him romantically. He assumes the identity of a courtly lover and embarks on a bizarre courtship of the countess. He flouts the principles of respect of place, persons, and time that have hitherto defined his subject position, identity, and the limits of his ascendancy in the household. He now acts as if "greatness" has been "thrust upon him" by circumstances (3.4.46–47). And yet, his erratic actions – his rudeness to household servants, his outlandish fashion sense, his bold and amorous talk to Olivia – could be explained as the harmless eccentricities of an aristocrat in love. Compared to Orsino's obsessive, self-indulgent love for Olivia, Malvolio's amorous overtures do not seem quite so outrageous. The main difference between them is one of class. Orsino is the aristocrat whose melancholy love makes him appear fashionable, sensitive, and profound, whereas Malvolio is a commoner who must be out of his mind to court someone above his station. Orsino conforms to a well-known literary type appropriate to his social rank, but Malvolio is "beside himself," an "overweening rogue" (2.5.29), so blown with imagination (2.5.41–42) that he has taken leave of his senses. But whether we laugh at Malvolio or believe that he is quite capable of acting the count, there is no denying that at Maria and Toby's instigation, Malvolio has assumed "corporeal signs and other discursive means" that have produced or interpellated him in a new way.

Very few of us will find Malvolio an especially sympathetic character, though Olivia makes it clear she values her steward greatly and asks heaven to "restore" him to sanity (3.4.48). Shakespeare also does not give us many reasons to disagree with Olivia's assessment that Malvolio is "sick of se love" (1.5.87), or with Maria's that he is nothing "but a time pleaser; an affection'd ass, that cons state without book and utters it by great swarths" (2.3.147–48). His loose association with the Puritan sect (2.3.139), known for its strictness and anti-theatricalism, is unlikely to signal the playwright's approval of the steward or to win him favor with Elizabethan audiences. But when Maria brands Malvolio as "a kind of puritan," she is not suggesting that he is a religious zealot intent on reforming the hierarchy of the Church of England; instead she "identifies the Puritan in Malvolio as a matter of social ambition and exaggerated self-worth" (Smith 2001, 320). As unattractive as Malvolio's ambition and self-love may seem, there is a possibility that Shakespeare shared Malvolio's desire for upward social mobility, leading Greenblatt to suggest that the steward may be "the shadow side of Shakespeare's own fascination with achieving the status of a gentleman" (2004, 82). Sometime after 1568, the year of his election as bailiff of Stratford, Shakespeare's father John sought the appellation of "gentleman" when he applied for a coat of arms, a distinction that he could lay claim to by virtue of his various offices in Stratford's civil administration.[5] William, as a common player, had no immediate right to this distinction, and when, in 1596, the application was finally granted, he could only put on the title as his father's son. That William valued his newly acquired status is undeniable because "he would sign his last will and testament 'William Shakespeare, of Stratford upon Avon in the country of Warwick, gentleman'" (Greenblatt 2004, 79).

That Shakespeare may have been ambivalent about his inherited rank emerges from the family motto that accompanied the newly acquired family crest and which he most likely wrote: *Non sanz droict*, which translates as "not without right." Greenblatt correctly senses a "touch of defensiveness" (2004, 79) in this formulation, which is perhaps not entirely secure in its assertion of preferment. Does the restraint of motto circumscribe both Shakespeare's own ambition and those of Malvolio, who is too much in love with his own aspirations?

Malvolio refuses to take part in the play's comedic resolution. This may validate Toby and Maria's rebuffing of the steward's upward social mobility. But when Malvolio vows to be revenged on the whole pack of them, Shakespeare insinuates that the ending of his play may not be the end of the story. The precise form of the aspiring steward's revenge is, of course, unknown, but that growing numbers of ambitious and adventurous commoners were making inroads into England's aristocratic ranks in Shakespeare's time is well known (see Stone 1967, 287–89; Elliott 1981). When Malvolio dreams of marrying Olivia, he cites the "lady of the Strachy [who] married the yeoman of the wardrobe" as his precedent (2.5.38–39). The lady of the Strachy has never been successfully linked to a historical person, but it is clear that in the context of the play she is supposed to be a real person, suggesting that Malvolio's mad desire is already historical reality. The battle to preserve an

nce between commoner and aristocrat may therefore already

elings of anger and the desire for revenge that Malvolio nal scene are vitally important, and they may signal Shake- t the genre of romantic or festive comedy can no longer credible *and* serve the social status quo. Ever since the publication of C. L. Barber's landmark study *Shakespeare's Festive Comedy* (1959), a number of critics have understood the many manifestations of social and gender reversals in *Twelfth Night* in the context of saturnalian holiday festivals. Barber argued that Shakespeare's festive plays explored the "social form of Elizabethan holidays," and that the basic "saturnalian pattern appears in many variations, all of which involve inversion, statement and counter-statement, and a basic movement which can be summarized in the formula, through release to clarification" (1959, 4). Barber's theory is perhaps best understood as a safety-value theory, which accounts for the way Elizabethan society allowed popular feelings of resentment, frustration, and anxiety to be expressed irreverently on specific days of the year, so that they would not lead to widespread disobedience or rebellion. The "release" of popular frustration on Halloween, Midsummer Eve, and the last day of the Christmas season, Twelfth Night, may be taken to "absurd extremes" (5), as the common people are encouraged to indulge their senses, to ridicule authority, and to flout everyday conventions, but the "clarification" to which this release ultimately leads is, according to Barber, a renewed understanding of everything and everyone's proper place in the rigidly hierarchical social order. In discussions of *Twelfth Night*, the spirit of holiday and reversal is generally associated with Sir Toby, Maria, Feste, the cross-dressing Viola, and the countess Olivia herself, once she unexpectedly falls head over heels in love with a woman dressed as a man. Malvolio is generally cast by these critics as the representative of order and propriety, as the killjoy who does not understand that there is a place for pleasure and "cakes and ale" in human society. He is the man who, if left in charge, would ban all holidays and thereby remove the Elizabethan safety valve and perhaps endanger the very stability of society itself.

But, more importantly, Maria's prank reverses the roles of the key players in this binary social drama. When Malvolio, encouraged by Maria's letter, pursues his ambition and woos Olivia wearing yellow stocking on his legs and a ridiculous smile on his face, he becomes a figure of misrule and courtly lover, while Toby becomes the voice of the establishment that says his niece "will not match above [or below] her degree" (1.3.107–8). And while Orsino, Viola, Olivia, Toby, and Maria are all disciplined into the societal norm when they enter into class and gender appropriate marriages and thus serve, uphold, and reproduce the social status quo, it is Malvolio's drive for upward social mobility that endeavors to make misrule *permanent* in the shape of an interclass marriage.[6] Identity may, as Butler suggested, be a "fabrication," "a fantasy inscribed on the surface of bodies," but that fabrication has clearly taken hold of Malvolio. When his hopes are dashed, he refuses to be brought back into the social dispensation that he has spent his professional life defending. He turns away from his career and the way in which that career has created and defined him. He refuses to perform the identity prescribed for him by society, and, in Althusserian terms, he refuses to be hailed by those who have authority over him; he escapes this particular moment of interpellation. And one wonders if his refusal is at all intelligible to the other members of Illyrian society, raising the possibility that in their eyes Malvolio may now seem *truly* mad.

Finally, let me put forward that Malvolio's hunger for social advancement may be less mad and threatening to Illyrian social stability than is the behavior of most other figures in the play. Carol Thomas Neely goes so far as to suggest that "Malvolio is punished for flaws others share" (2004, 152). Maria and Toby's charade, she submits, "draw[s] both laughter and condemnation onto Malvolio, and away from the erotic unruliness, gender fluidity, and willful marriages" of other characters in *Twelfth Night* (151). I am not sure that Malvolio and Orsino, Viola, Olivia, Toby, and Maria share the *same* flaw (for except for Malvolio none of them seeks an upwardly mobile marriage), nor do I think that their irresponsible behavior is entirely and successfully displaced onto Malvolio in the final act, but there is little doubt their behavior is potentially harmful to the stability and proper reproduction of Illyrian social formations.

When the play opens, Duke Orsino is engaged in an unproductive obsession with the Countess Olivia, who has emphatically rejected his romantic advances. The countess has in fact taken herself off Illyria's marriage market for a period of no less than seven years because she mourns the recent deaths of her father and brother. From the perspective of romantic comedy and orderly social reproduction, a match between duke and countess is highly desirable because it would ensure the production of an heir able to govern Illyria after Orsino's death. What is more, this should be precisely the time for Olivia to accept a mate as she, following the deaths of her father and brother, is left without a male authority figure in her life. Viola, distraught over the presumed death of her twin brother Sebastian, decides to seek employment with the duke as a eunuch singer. Disguising herself as male also removes her from the marriage market, and although she quickly falls in love with the duke, she takes no steps to recover her former gender identity and make herself available for marriage to the duke. Sir Andrew Aguecheek is engaged in a doomed attempt to win Olivia. Andrew is foolishly paying Sir Toby's massive bar tab in the hope that Toby's influence with his niece will further his courtship of her, but we realize instantly that Andrew does not stand a chance. Olivia herself suddenly falls in love with Cesario, not knowing that Cesario is really Viola disguised as a man. Her love may be genuine, but the sameness of their gender prevents them from fitting into the normative coupling required by romantic comedy. Finally, Captain Antonio's adoration of Sebastian is

ected in this context because it too cannot lead to marriage and ıction. When Olivia witnesses Malvolio's "mad" courtship of a direct parallel between their conditions: "I am as mad as he," ad and merry madness equal be" (3.4.14–15). And Sebastian, ıe complex web of misrecognition and misdirected desire, aptly asks, "Are all the people mad?" (4.1.26).

What rescues these characters from madness (in the eyes of society) is their ultimate willingness to forego their primary desire and to perform class-appropriate heterosexual unions, even if those unions appear haphazard and ill-prepared to us. Viola may still be sporting male attire when Orsino proposes to her, causing the gender ambiguity to linger, but the duke does reveal that "right noble is [Sebastian's] blood" (5.1.261). One may wonder how Orsino knows Sebastian's ancestry, but this information apparently needs to be made public before Viola can make him a suitable wife. Likewise, the sudden union between Sir Toby and Maria is sometimes viewed as a "cross-class marriage" (Neely 2004, 152), but Maria's status as Olivia's "gentlewoman" makes her more or less the social equal of the knight.[7] Andrew, a mere knight who hopes to marry above his station, Antonio the captain and commoner who adores the socially superior Sebastian, and Feste the clown (who may harbor a secret desire for the gentlewoman Maria), are all left out of the play's festive resolution. They appear to go away quietly. But not Malvolio. He self-righteously refuses to see it all as one big harmless prank, and he refuses to resume performing his former identity as steward.

The patients described in Walkington's treatise may have been tricked by a theatrical deception to assume identities approved of by the community, but Maria's script appears to have the opposite effect on Malvolio. Maria and Toby intended to "cure" (and punish) Malvolio by having him act out his socio-economic desires to the point of madness, but instead of shrinking back into his former self, Malvolio vows revenge on those who viewed his ambitions as madness. The physicians in Walkington's treatise con their patients into accepting an alternate reality that should result in a repetitive performance of a "sane" identity. Whether the patients are in fact cured or sane is not really established by the accounts. But that they come to accept the "truth effect" generated by the deception as their new identity is. Malvolio, on the other hand, may *never* have acted out his secret ambitions had he not been prompted by Maria and Toby. The repressed Malvolio was perfectly sane by Illyrian standards, and he might have continued to repeat his performance of the sour, repressed steward until the end of his days. But, like the physicians in Walkington's text, Maria and Toby have (albeit unwittingly) brought about a gestalt shift in Malvolio, by giving him a script by which to fashion himself anew, and produced the "truth effect" of a mobile identity. Is the old madness about to become the new sanity? Is this the vengeance of an emerging middle class? Should we look as far ahead as the Puritan Revolution? At the very least, there certainly appears to be a correlation between

Malvolio's transformation and the latent danger in conduct manuals such as Castiglione's *Book of the Courtier*, which, when obtained by the baser sort, could give almost anyone the manners, bearing, outward dignity, and "truth *effect*" of an aristocrat or gentleman. Walkington wrote that the cases he describes are of patients who are mad because "they are in bondage to many ridiculous passions" (1607, 134), but the madness inflicted on Malvolio appears precisely to have set free his passionate ambitions.

Malvolio displays his "truth effect" in part in the scene in which Feste, disguised as Sir Topas the curate, pretends to exorcize the demons that have driven Malvolio mad. If Malvolio looked utterly ridiculous as Olivia's courtly suitor earlier in the play, he is perfectly rational in the exorcism scene. It is Feste who speaks "bibble babble," not Malvolio (4.2.97). Malvolio's responses to Feste's questions are perfectly intelligible to everyone, *not just to those in on the joke*. Confined to a dark cell, Malvolio is told that his room is illuminated by light pouring in through bay windows, but he steadfastly insists that he is in the dark. When asked to explain Pythagoras's theory of the transmigration of the soul, he does so correctly, and properly denounces such beliefs as dishonorable to the human soul (4.350–56) (see Draper 2000, 188–89). When told he is mad, he steadfastly espouses his sanity. What is more, he refuses to falsify his answers in order to get out of prison. He asks Sir Topas to seek out Olivia and ask her for help, but Feste deliberate misunderstands the request and proceeds with the mock exorcism: "Out, hyperbolical fiend! How vexest thou this man! Talkest thou of nothing but ladies?" (4.2.26–27). What is the point of this? If Malvolio is convinced of his own sanity, and if the audience knows he is not mad, then why perform an exorcism? As Greenblatt has argued, exorcism had already become a ritual emptied out of metaphysical meaning, and had come to be regarded as outright fraud and "theatre" in Shakespeare's day (1988, 94–114). So what is purportedly being "exorcized" here? The logic of the Toby–Maria plot suggests an answer: social ambition is the demon inside Malvolio. But if Feste is not a real exorcist and if exorcism is a theatrical fraud, then Shakespeare may be telling us that the rise of commoners like Malvolio cannot be stemmed with empty, ineffective, passé ideas and rituals. How would the audience receive Malvolio's thirst for upward mobility? Does the fact that Malvolio appears lucid and rational to the audience in the exorcism scene mean that they are invited to give serious thought to a similar gestalt shift? Are they being asked to see the old madness as the new sanity? Maybe.

As he does so often, Shakespeare declines to provide us with an unambiguous answer to a vital question suggested by the main action of the play. Malvolio appears wisely to have abandoned his quest for marriage with Olivia in the drama's closing moments, so upward mobility in any immediate sense may have been taken off the table, but his letter to the countess (read aloud by Fabian) is surprisingly bold and continues to harp on the issue of class:

> "By the Lord, madam, you wrong me, and the world shall know it. Though you have put me into darkness and given your drunken cousin rule over me, yet have I the benefit of my senses as well as your ladyship. I have your own letter that induced me to the semblance I put on, with the which I doubt not but to do myself much right or you much shame. Think of me as you please. I leave my duty a little unthought of, and speak out of injury. The madly used Malvolio."
>
> (5.1.283–90)

These are hardly the words of a repentant man aware that he has grossly overstepped the boundaries of propriety. *You* have wronged *me*, he charges, and you should never have allowed Toby to exercise authority over me; my perception of the world is as sound as yours. The final sentence may hint at a touch of humility, but it also prominently asserts Malvolio's right to speak out as a wronged human being not bound by the strictures of class. Orsino, the voice of highest authority in the play, appears won over by Malvolio's words, and asserts, "This savours not much of distraction" (5.1.293). Orsino may not know the entire Malvolio story, and he is a most unlikely advocate for an aspirant middle class, but are his words not a tacit validation of the Malvolio project? One thing is certain: Malvolio does not take any of it back upon learning that Olivia was not directly involved; he will be avenged on *all* of them. And does Feste's melancholy song that closes the play – an odd conclusion to a festive comedy – not describe life as a journey of vanity, meaningless boasting, troubled marriages, drunkenness, and daily rain that all humans endure alike, regardless of class? Who, in such a world, is to deny Malvolio the right to fashion his own dream? The old aristocratic world may be fading, but Malvolio, and men like him, are here to stay.

Notes

1. See MacDonald (1981, 7). For an overview of humor theory, see Babb (1951, 5–20).
2. André du Laurens reports the same case in *A Discourse of the Preservation of Sight* (1599). See also Salkeld (1994, 8).
3. Robert Burton sanctions the use of "fair and foul means [and] witty devices" as established medical practice (2001, 109; see 109–15).
4. See Casey (1997) for an application of Butler's theory with the emphasis on gender and *Twelfth Night*.
5. See Sir John Ferne's *The Blazon of Gentry* (1586), quoted in Schoenbaum (1977, 38).
6. John Webster's Duchess of Malfi seems to make this very point when she marries her steward Antonio and calls him "a lord of mis-rule" (3.2.8).
7. Even if, as some have argued, Maria is of lower rank than Toby, it would seem that the knight's vulgar behavior would not place him far above Maria in the audience's eyes.

Works cited

Althusser, Louis. *Lenin and Philosophy*. New York: Monthly Review Press, 1971.

Babb, Lawrence. *The Elizabethan Malady: A Study of Melancholia in English Literature from 1580 to 1642*. East Lansing: Michigan State College Press, 1951.

Barber, C. L. *Shakespeare's Festive Comedy: A Study of Dramatic Form and Its Relation to Social Custom*. New York: Meridian Books, 1959.

Burton, Robert. *The Anatomy of Melancholy*. 1621. Ed. Holbrook Jackson. New York: New York Review Books, 2001.

Butler, Judith. *Gender Trouble: Feminism and the Subversion of Identity*. New York: Routledge, 1999.

Casey, Charles. "Gender Trouble in *Twelfth Night*." *Theatre Journal* 49 (2) (1997): 121–41.

Draper, R. P. *Shakespeare: The Comedies*. New York: St. Martin's Press, 2000.

Elliott, Vivien Brodsky. "Single Women in the London Marriage Market: Age, Status and Mobility, 1598–1619." In *Marriage and Society: Studies in the Social History of Marriage*. Ed. R. B. Outhwaite. New York: St. Martin's Press, 1981: 81–100.

Greenblatt, Stephen. *Shakespearean Negotiations: The Circulation of Social Energy in Renaissance England*. Berkeley: University of California Press, 1988.

——. *Will in the World: How Shakespeare Became Shakespeare*. New York: Norton, 2004.

Ingleby, David. "The Social Construction of Mental Illness." In *The Problem of Medical Knowledge: Examining the Social Construction of Medicine*. Ed. Peter Wright and Andrew Treacher. Edinburgh: Edinburgh University Press, 1982: 123–43.

MacDonald, Michael. *Mystical Bedlam: Madness, Anxiety, and Healing in Seventeenth-Century England*. New York: Cambridge University Press, 1981.

Neely, Carol Thomas. "'Documents in Madness': Reading Madness and Gender in Shakespeare's Tragedies and Early Modern Culture." *Shakespeare Quarterly* 42 (3) (1991): 315–38.

——. *Distracted Subjects: Madness and Gender in Shakespeare and Early Modern Culture*. Ithaca, NY: Cornell University Press, 2004.

Salkeld, Duncan. *Madness and Drama in the Age of Shakespeare*. New York: Manchester University Press, 1994.

Schoenbaum, Samuel. *William Shakespeare: A Compact Documentary Life*. New York: Oxford University Press, 1977.

Shakespeare, William. *The Complete Works of Shakespeare*. Ed. David Bevington. Glenview, IL: Forman, 1980.

Smith, Bruce R., ed. *Twelfth Night, or What You Will: Texts and Contexts.* Boston: Bedford, 2001.

Stone, Lawrence. *The Crisis of the Aristocracy, 1558–1641*. New York: Oxford University Press, 1967.

Walkington, Thomas. *Optick Glasse of Humours*. London: Martin Clerke, 1607.

14 *Twelfth Night* and the New Orleans Twelfth Night Revelers

Jennifer C. Vaught

The interlacing of Shakespeare's *Twelfth Night* and early modern festival customs remains striking to audiences and critics throughout North America and Europe.[1] Surprisingly few critics have discussed Shakespeare's great festive comedy in relation to the Louisiana traditions of Twelfth Night and Mardi Gras, one of the only regions in America that continues to cultivate these Carnival practices today.[2] The Anglo-Americans who immigrated to New Orleans and the surrounding areas were among those who perpetuated these religious (or sacrilegious) festivities that were celebrated for centuries in medieval and Renaissance England and Europe. The Crescent City contains numerous immigrants not only from France, Spain, Ireland, Catholic Germany, and Italy but also from the Middle Atlantic states. These American immigrants brought with them a distinctly English heritage. As Reid Mitchell argues, "New Orleans Mardi Gras is so often traced to its French or African-Caribbean origins that it is sometimes forgotten that Anglo-Americans lived in Louisiana with festive traditions of their own" (1995, 26). Both Shakespeare's *Twelfth Night* and Feast of the Epiphany celebrations by the Twelfth Night Revelers, the second oldest Mardi Gras krewe in New Orleans formally organized in 1870, include holiday practices of consuming cakes and ale and appointing a Lord of Misrule.[3]

Carnival festivities centered on feasting, drinking, and ritual inversions of rank often allow for the temporary release but ultimate containment of political tension within the existing social hierarchy or can spark popular rebellions leading to more permanent social reforms.[4] Those representative of the aristocracy in Shakespeare's *Twelfth Night* and the merchant class in the New Orleans Twelfth Night Revelers appropriate these festival practices originating among the folk in order to maintain their elite position above those they perceive as social inferiors.[5] The social mobility of those beneath them threatens their superior position within the existing status quo. Sir Toby Belch, who acts as Lord of Misrule at his niece Olivia's aristocratic house, resists the rise of a new breed of men defined by income rather than inherited rank. He refers to Malvolio as a "rogue" and wishes for a "stone-bow to hit him in the eye!" for his attempt to marry above his station (2.5.29, 46).[6] The Twelfth

Night Revelers revived the English and European figure of the Lord of Misrule as leader of their parades in an effort to return in a nostalgic fashion to the hierarchical medieval and Renaissance eras when social status was frequently determined by inherited rank, wealth, and property, including slaves. Although the Lord of Misrule was often played by a servant, the custom of appointing one served as a reminder of holiday festivities in royal palaces and aristocratic houses and thus provided the Revelers with a means of promoting themselves as members of an elite group (Mitchell 1995, 74 and Gill 1997, 88). Shakespeare's *Twelfth Night*, a play about aristocratic reactions to the rising middle ranks, and the Twelfth Night Revelers thereby expose the potentially conservative and violent underbelly of literary and cultural celebrations of the Feast of the Epiphany.

Shakespeare in *Twelfth Night* and the Twelfth Night Revelers appropriate and adapt similar folk, carnivalesque traditions surrounding the festival of Twelfth Night. Intertextual connections abound between this literary text and its larger cultural context, extending from medieval England and Europe to the post-Civil War Southern region in America. Although it is unclear whether or not the Twelfth Night Revelers selected their title with the intention of alluding to Shakespeare's *Twelfth Night*, we know that the names of both this early modern play and the New Orleans krewe refer to the Feast of the Epiphany celebrated on January 6. This date, which marks the end of the Christmas season, denotes the beginning of the Carnival period that culminates with Mardi Gras in France and Shrove Tuesday in England immediately before Lent. Thomas Dekker's *The Shoemakers' Holiday* (1599), the title of which denotes the October 25 Feast of St. Crispin, the patron saint of shoemakers, also refers to a "Pancake bell" marking the celebration of "Shrove Tuesday" with pancakes, beer, and wine (5.2.205). Juliet Dusinberre argues that the Clown Touchstone's mentioning of "pancakes" adds to her hypothesis that *As You Like It* was performed during Shrovetide at Richmond Palace on February 20, 1599 (1.2.62–63). She bases her convincing hypothesis on an extensive web of significant associations linking the play to this cultural event (2003, 371–405). In *All's Well That Ends Well* (1602–6) the Clown similarly alludes to this widely-celebrated English holiday known to modern American audiences as Mardi Gras when he states, "As a pancake for Shrove Tuesday, a morris for May-day" (2.2.23–24). In nineteenth-century New Orleans, Twelfth Night festivities were as elaborate as Mardi Gras celebrations there today and parallel early modern festive practices relevant to Shakespeare's play in a number of ways.

The King Cake tradition still practiced during Twelfth Night and Mardi Gras celebrations in contemporary Louisiana was well understood by Elizabethan and Jacobean audiences and customary during their festival of Twelfth Night. In fact, the name and concept of a "King Cake," which refers to a braided sweet bread with a hole in the middle, was widely recognized throughout medieval and Renaissance England and Europe. In *The Medieval*

Stage E. K. Chambers notes that the English Lord of Misrule, known as the Epiphany King in France, was crowned and referred to as a "Twelfth Night King" during the Feast of the Epiphany (1925, 407). In contemporary Louisiana the term "King Cake" originates from the traditional custom of electing a mock or temporary king or queen to lead the Twelfth Night or Mardi Gras festivities according to who finds the hidden bean (now a plastic baby representative of fertility) in his or her portion of cake. In medieval and early modern England the popular holiday figure of the King of the Bean was associated with the festive, communal practice of consuming a "Twelfth night cake" and the "wassail-bowl" (Chambers 1925, 260). John Aubrey, an English antiquary and writer of miscellaneous stories and folklore most widely known for his fieldwork linking Stonehenge to the Druids, reports in 1686–87 that "at Twelfth-tyde at night they use in the countrey to wassaile their Oxen and to have wasaile-Cakes made" (1881, 9). The Twelfth Night cake to which Aubrey refers was customarily baked with a hole in the middle so that it could be placed as a crown on the horn of the biggest and strongest ox (Henisch 1984, 17). Contemporary folklorist A. R. Wright further remarks on popular English Twelfth Night customs reminiscent of those practiced in nineteenth-century Louisiana: "During the twelve days ending on Epiphany, revels were held, and one of the most popular and jovial of these was the revel of Twelfth Night; the Twelfth Cake was cut, this being the preliminary step to the election of a King, a Queen, and other officers of the ceremonies" (1968, 51). Similarly, the New Orleans Twelfth Night Revelers choose their queen and maids-in-waiting at a ball by having them discover gold and silver beans in their portions of King Cake (Reinecke 1965, 47). The Lord of Misrule leading their parades during the Feast of the Epiphany is reminiscent of the aristocratic figure of Sir Toby Belch and his "cakes and ale" and serves as a direct link between these English and American festival practices (2.3.115).

Renaissance England holiday celebrations of Twelfth Night at court and within aristocratic households frequently included the folk motif of the King of the Bean. Although the traditional figure of the "king of the bean" is most widely known in medieval France, Chambers states that "payments to the 'King of Bene' . . . were made by James IV of Scotland between 1490 and 1503" as well (1925, 261). Mary Tudor, who reigned from 1553 to 1558, observed the "bean feast" that still exists in Louisiana in terms of the hiding of a bean or plastic baby in the King Cake (Reinecke 1965, 49). Bridget Ann Henisch remarks in her discussion of Twelfth Night festivities in England that one of the earliest literary uses of the bean and cake motif was "the shepherds' play devised in Queen Elizabeth's honour at Sudeley in 1592." She continues that in Ben Jonson's *Christmas His Masque* (1616) – an elaborate court entertainment – the "last and youngest in the line comes Babie Cake, followed by his Usher 'bearing a great Cake with a Beane, and a Pease'" (Henisch 1984, 45). Similarly, in the poem *Twelfth Night or King and Queene* from the *Hesperides* (1648), Robert Herrick exclaims, "Now, now the mirth comes / With the cake full of plums, / Where Beane's the *King* of the sport here" (1–3). Throughout the *Hesperides* Herrick refers to country and court festive practices that were associated with lower as well as upper classes but that were increasingly appropriated and controlled by the government and other conservative forces in seventeenth-century England (Marcus 1986, 8 and 19; Laroque 1991, 9).

Lords of Misrule, who reigned from November 1 (All Soul's Day) through Shrove Tuesday, similarly appeared not only in country folk festivals but also in courtly settings and the houses of gentlemen in early modern England (Phythian-Adams 1972, 67–69). Customarily, a servant acted as master of the household during the topsy-turvy holiday season and received a crown as well as the authority to give toasts and lead the drinking (Henische 1984, 18). This role, which could be appropriated for conservative and radical agendas, was frequently but not always played by those with relatively little political or domestic power (Stallybrass and White 1986, 14). English folk customs were often indistinguishable from those practiced at court and among the wealthy more generally. Chambers notes, for instance, that "nobles and even private gentlemen would set up a Lord of Misrule in their homes" in sixteenth-century England (1925, 404 and 418–19). C. L. Barber concurs that this holiday figure was commonly appointed in "noblemen's houses, and among great housekeepers" (1963, 25). Those at the "universities and the Inns of Court" also appointed Lords of Misrule (Chambers 1925, 407). The status of the Lord of Misrule most likely varied with the status of the master or mistress of the household. In John Webster's *The Duchess of Malfi* (1613) the Duchess refers playfully to her steward-turned-husband Antonio as "Lord of Misrule" (3.2.7). An estate steward such as Webster's Antonio or Shakespeare's Malvolio was usually a member of the lower gentry (Cahill 1996, 64 and Hainsworth 1992, 7). A Lord of Misrule was not necessarily a lowly-ranking servant but could be an aristocrat or gentleman depending on the social status of the ruler or householder. Sir George Ferrers, one of the authors of *Mirror for Magistrates*, served as Lord of Misrule at the royal palace under Edward VI for two Christmas seasons from 1551 to 1553 (Chambers 1925, 405).

A debauched aristocrat, Sir Toby Belch acts as Lord of Misrule in Olivia's house in *Twelfth Night*.[7] It is not unreasonable for him to assume this role because his social status is beneath that of his niece, a countess. Yet his rank differs dramatically from that of servants who frequently performed this festive role in Renaissance England. Typical of such a holiday figure, Sir Toby mocks figures of authority – though he is one himself by birth – and is the leader of bacchanalian revels at night (Billington 1991, 35 and 47). He exposes the cowardice of knights at court (3.4.237–38); pokes fun at a pseudo-scholar who takes pride in his ability to speak "three or four languages" (1.3.26); and refers to "politicians" in a derogatory sense (2.3.76). During his drunken revelry with Sir Andrew Aguecheek and Feste after midnight, Sir

Toby leads the singing of the Christmas ballad, "*O' the twelfth day of December–*," an appropriate lyric for a Lord of Misrule appointed during this winter holiday (2.3.85).[8] Shortly after singing a line from this and other popular ballads, Sir Toby exclaims to Malvolio, "Dost thou think because thou art virtuous, there shall be no more cakes and ale?" (2.3.114–15). His late night revelry with Sir Andrew and Feste culminates with Maria's devising the letter scheme intended to punish the killjoy, Malvolio. He inspires Sir Toby's wrath in part because of his intolerant objections to the festive practice of consuming "cakes and ale" during the holiday season. Puritans similarly attempted to suppress holiday customs with pagan or Catholic origins such as the revelry of the Lords of Misrule (Carnegie 2001, 410–11; Malcolmson 1996, 179). Malvolio tries unsuccessfully to suppress Sir Toby's bacchanalian singing of ballads with his cronies in this aristocratic setting that the steward accuses them of transforming into an "ale-house" (2.3.90).

Fundamental to the dispute between Sir Toby Belch and Malvolio is a conflict between ranks characteristic of Twelfth Night and Shrove Tuesday festivities among the populace in fifteenth- and sixteenth-century England. During the late medieval and early modern periods, Christmas and Shrovetide parades were potentially violent, riotous, and rebellious and exposed existing social tensions. As Antony Gash states in connection to his discussion of the unruliness of popular Shrovetide customs in fifteenth-century Norwich, "the King and Queen of Yule, riding at the start of the Christmas season, drew riot crowds with their bawdy and social satire" (1986, 86). During these Christmas-time parades that took place on January 6, it was customary for the Lord of Misrule to "cast gold and silver abroad" while riding on horseback, a ritual similar to the continuing practice of kings and queens casting beads to the crowds from Mardi Gras floats in New Orleans (Chambers 1925, 407). Yet early modern Twelfth Night and Shrove Tuesday parades were not necessarily inclusive or harmonious. Gash adds that in fifteenth-century Norwich "effigies of Lent could provide targets for festive missiles on Shrove Tuesday." In Norwich in 1443 the figure of the King of Christmas led a revolt of citizens against an Abbot responsible for closing two of the city's mills. This revolt stemmed from a larger conflict between wealthy merchants and discontented artisans, some of whom were the driving force behind the Christmas parades, over who would control the city's government and jurisdictional boundaries of buildings like the mills (Gash 1986, 85–86). The parade featuring the King of Christmas, a role played by one of the artisans defending his livelihood at the mills, metamorphosed into an organized rebellion against this particular abbot and the Church more generally.

Unlike this unruly artisan leading the Norwich revolt dressed as the King of Christmas, Sir Toby Belch is not acting on the collective interests of popular folk culture in his role as Lord of Misrule. He deliberately appropriates this role for politically conservative purposes during his "brawl" with Malvolio. As Countess Olivia's uncle he is of a higher social rank than Malvolio and objects vociferously to the latter's desire to marry his niece (4.2.85). Sir Toby reminds Malvolio of his "lowly" rank by exclaiming, "Art any more than a steward?" (2.3.113–14). Sir Toby's invocation of their difference in rank is suggestive of his anxieties about diminishing demarcations between aristocrats like himself and socially-mobile citizens like Malvolio. During the letter scheme in the garden where Olivia's steward is "caught" like a trout by "tickling," Sir Toby explodes rhetorically with "Bolts and shackles!" when Malvolio refers to him without his title of "Sir" – a further sign of his sensitivity to perceived threats to his social status (2.5.22, 56).

Although Sir Toby performs the role of Lord of Misrule for the communal Feast of the Epiphany, his political agenda of objecting to Malvolio's ambition for social mobility is not only conservative but also elitist and regressive. As Ivo Kamps argues in his essay in this volume, Sir Toby "becomes the voice of the establishment" by resisting the upstart's desire to move above his station within the existing social hierarchy. Sir Toby responds violently to the steward's ambitions to marry his way into the aristocracy by threatening to hit him in the eye with a "stone-bow," a catapult used for shooting stones (2.5.46). Throughout the play he refers to his social rank derisively by labeling him a "coistrel" (1.3.40), denoting a "base fellow" or "groom," and a "foul collier" (3.4.118), meaning a "dirty coalman" (Shakespeare 1985, 13 and 99). Immediately prior to the letter trick, they both refer to Malvolio as a "rogue," which was a term of abuse commonly applied to servants and a cultural trope for social mobility (*OED* 2.b. and Dionne and Mentz 2004, 1). Sir Toby exclaims, "Here's an overweening rogue!" and Sir Andrew concurs, "'Slight, I could so beat the rogue!" (2.5.29, 33). They adamantly but rightly classify his social status as lower than theirs.

The difference in rank between Sir Toby, Sir Andrew, and Malvolio contributes to the fiery conflicts between them. The steward insults Sir Toby and Sir Andrew by accusing them of acting like "tinkers" and "coziers" (2.3.89–91), despite their aristocratic titles (Shakespeare 1985, 49). Similarly, Olivia calls Sir Toby a "rudesby" and "ruffian"after he accepts Sebastian's challenge to a duel as revenge for beating Sir Andrew (4.1.50, 55). Sir Toby's threat to "throw" Sebastian's "dagger over the house" and his order that he "put up [his] iron" when Viola's brother attacks his friend indicate that Sebastian uses his dagger, a common method of chastising one's inferior, for pummeling Sir Andrew (4.1.27–28, 38; Northrop 1995, 192). Cumulatively, these insults and duels point to the blurring of the relative social status of Sir Toby, Sir Andrew, Sebastian, and Malvolio.[9] Despite Sir Toby's attempt to defend Sir Andrew from Sebastian, he describes him as an "ass-head," a "coxcomb," and a "gull" by the end of the play (5.1.204–5). Sir Andrew's gullibility and lack of wit, not his ownership of land and income of "three thousand ducats a year," ultimately determine his status in Illyria (1.3.22). Like the festive custom of "cakes and ale" under siege by the Puritans, the English system of determining social status by birth or rank rather than merit

rdy (Halpern 1991, 245). In America over 150 years later, the Twelfth Night Revelers appropriated the figure of the Lord of eader of their Feast of the Epiphany parades as a result of their r a rigidly hierarchical culture that they perceived as reminiscent and early modern Britain. Yet the very hierarchy they associated with ie times and longed for after the Civil War was itself beginning to crumble in Renaissance England.

Malvolio's ambitions to marry Olivia are not unprecedented in the realm of fiction. Fantasizing about his match with his lady Olivia, he muses, "There is example for 't: the Lady of the Strachy married the yeoman of the wardrobe" (2.5.39–40; Arlidge 2000, 17–19). Though Maria lacks an aristocratic title, Sir Toby admires her wit because of her letter scheme that humiliates Malvolio and exclaims, "I could marry this wench for this device" (2.5.182). Her witty "jest" functions as her "dowry" (2.5.184–85). Intelligence, not aristocratic birth or rank, makes her attractive to Sir Toby. He objects to the social aspirations of Malvolio because the steward would acquire the title of "Count Malvolio" and Olivia's estate through marriage and would possess considerable authority and wealth as a result (2.5.35). Unlike Maria, Viola, and Sebastian, all of whom marry somewhat above their stations, Malvolio is objectionable to Sir Toby because he would use his position as count to disrupt the festive traditions of "cakes and ale" and to impose his "ill will," the linguistic root of his name, on a community where he knows his place as his inferiors "should [. . .] theirs" (2.5.54; Malcolmson 1996, 171, 178). Malvolio's political vision that seemingly favors the underdog is ultimately as rigid and conservative as Sir Toby's. Ironically, he, too, harps on the importance of preserving distinctions between ranks. The steward is dissatisfied with his own place in the social hierarchy rather than the exploitative system itself. His desire for social mobility does not lead him to object in an egalitarian fashion to the hierarchical structure that oppresses others.

Both Shakespeare's *Twelfth Night* and the Twelfth Night Revelers, a krewe known for its spectacular street theatre, illustrate how popular festive customs such as "cakes and ale" and the revelry of a Lord of Misrule can be appropriated for conservative, elitist, and repressive purposes. *Twelfth Night* was well-known in nineteenth-century New Orleans where approximately 25 Shakespeare plays were performed a season until the end of the Civil War in 1865 (Roppolo 1983, 119). *Twelfth Night* was first performed in New Orleans on April 11, 1830 and subsequently on March 18, 1844; on March 26, 1861; during "the last week of February" in 1879; in 1892 and no doubt on other dates as well (Kendall 1952, 55, 164, 233, 390, 401). Interestingly, on January 7, 1870 in *The Daily Picayune* an advertisement for performances of Shakespeare's *Twelfth Night* at the Varieties Theatre in New Orleans and an elaborate description of the first procession of the Twelfth Night Revelers appeared on the first page of this newspaper. Readers of it were so familiar with the plot of this festive comedy that this particular reviewer refers to

Viola and her escapades rather than to the play title itself. Later in 1898 the Mistick Krewe of Comus, the first Mardi Gras krewe in New Orleans, centered its parade on "Scenes from Shakespeare" and included among the 20 floats one devoted to *Twelfth Night*. Although we do not know if the Twelfth Night Revelers were alluding to Shakespeare's play in particular, we do know that its members frequently made allusions to famous canonical texts. In 1872 their parade on "English Humor" featured scenes and characters from works by Chaucer, Shakespeare, Jonson, and Swift among others. For this particular parade their float on "Shakespeare, 1500 to 1600" included the comical figures of Dogberry in *Much Ado About Nothing*, the clown Touchstone in *As You Like It*, and Falstaff. Interestingly, one of the captions for their Tableau Ball entitled "The Apotheosis of Humor" was "the mob of gentlemen who wrote with ease" (Young 1931, 229). This elaborate parade and ball depicting numerous English writers of humor as "gentlemen" enabled the Revelers to promote themselves – however falsely – as members of the privileged aristocracy.

Together, Shakespeare's *Twelfth Night* and the New Orleans Twelfth Night Revelers, both of which feature Lords of Misrule and "cakes and ale," provide literary and cultural commentary on class conflicts that surface in terms of battles and duels.[10] As Sir Toby exclaims to Sir Andrew prior to the gulling of Malvolio, "we will fool him black and blue" (2.5.9–10). The advent of the Twelfth Night Revelers during Reconstruction exposed race as well as class conflicts in the Deep South immediately after the Civil War. As socially mobile members of the middle and upper-middle class, they attempted to promote themselves as the new aristocracy through elaborate expenditures at parades and balls.[11] They and other New Orleans krewes such as the Mistick Krewe of Comus paraded their desire for elite status by appropriating early modern festive practices from England and Europe and various aspects of canonical texts like Spenser's *Faerie Queene* and Milton's *Comus* and *Paradise Lost* (Rambuss 2000, 67). Mourning and melancholy provide another point of connection between the Twelfth Night Revelers and Shakespeare's play. During Reconstruction, members of Carnival and Mardi Gras krewes sought release from mourning their defeat during the Civil War through the "tonic" of holiday revelry, parades, and balls (Mitchell 1995, 57).[12] In *Twelfth Night* a number of figures mourn their loss of loved ones or respond to the end of the Christmas season with melancholy. Feste's melancholic songs about "What's to come is still unsure" and "Youth's a stuff will not endure" are cases in point. Many of Shakespeare's upper-ranking revelers in this festive comedy are drowning in their own tears or drink (1.5.137).

The Twelfth Night Revelers attempted to return to an imaginary age of chivalry and hierarchical order that would favor the elite white establishment in post-war Louisiana.[13] They emerged at a moment in American history when the middle and upper classes were experiencing acute economic and political threats from racially diverse lower classes. In 1868 the federal government called a Louisiana constitutional convention that produced a bill of rights granting African Americans the right to vote, desegregating the schools, and prohibiting discrimination in public transportation and accommodations. Members of the Crescent City Democratic Club, a white supremacist organization similar to the Ku Klux Klan and the Knights of the White Camellia, formed the Twelfth Night Revelers in 1870 immediately after the desegregation of public schools and other upheavals to the racially repressive Old South during Reconstruction (Gill 1997, 86, 88). The middle and upper classes in Louisiana were no longer masters over slaves and had temporarily lost the legal authority to disenfranchise people of color. With the end of Reconstruction and the withdrawal of Federal troops from Louisiana in 1877, however, all those perceived as black lost the right to vote and segregation returned to schools, entertainment venues, and forms of public transportation and accommodation. Mardi Gras krewes in New Orleans continued to exclude non-whites from membership and participation in their organizations until forced to do so over 100 years later by a city ordinance that in effect desegregated Carnival in 1992.

Although the medieval and Renaissance Lord of Misrule often inverted the existing class hierarchy of master over servant during the holiday season in a liberating fashion, the Twelfth Night Revelers led by a Lord of Misrule reinforced rather than diminished nineteenth-century class, gender, and racial inequalities. In 1873 their parade, "The World of Audubon," featured a float entitled "The Crows in Council" that viciously mocked African Americans serving on the Republican state legislature in Louisiana shortly after the Civil War (Young 1931, 109–10). According to the New Orleans *Bulletin* in 1876, their "The March of the Ages" parade featured a tableau entitled the "Present" with a "herculean Negro" facing the wrong way and another of the "Future" with Minerva dominating the Amazons, sarcastic allusions to developing civil liberties for African Americans and women. The *Bulletin* commented on the Lord of Misrule distributing programs to the crowd that explained the parade: "The general public generally speaking is not up to the classics, and when these pageants are understood they are more appreciated" (Mitchell 1995, 70 and 74). This reporter and presumably members of the Twelfth Night Revelers equated Greek and Roman mythological figures of Hercules, Minerva, and the Amazons with the "classics," the knowledge of which they believed differentiated the upper and lower classes. For the Twelfth Night Revelers and other Anglo-American, New Orleans Mardi Gras krewes, the printed word, cultural literacy in general, and familiarity with canonical texts became the means for enforcing rather than diminishing class distinctions. Shakespeare among other "classic" writers served as their ammunition for combating the aftermath of the Civil War and Reconstruction that they felt disenfranchised them. They viewed these canonical texts, many of which were written for diverse audiences, as the exclusive property of the elite. The Twelfth Night Revelers appropriated festival rituals as well as canonical texts in order to oppress rather than liberate those beneath them. Likewise, Sir Toby Belch as Lord of Misrule reinforces rather than inverts the existing social hierarchy by persecuting Malvolio for attempting to marry above his station.

In New Orleans the bayonets surrounding the Lord of Misrule on the invitations to the Twelfth Night Revelers Ball in 1875 conveyed the explosive political tensions between their merchant-class white members and those whom they feared were threatening their racially exclusive way of life (Gill 1997, 121). These invitations alluded to the Battle of Liberty Place on September 14, 1874 when 5,000 members of the Crescent City White League confronted 3,500 men, most of them African American, and more than 500 Metropolitan police in an attempt to unseat William Pitt Kellogg as Governor of Louisiana. The battle resulted in 100 men wounded and 25 men killed. Kellogg, who was known as a "Carpetbagger," was appointed Governor in 1873 by the federal government in place of the elected Confederate Lieutenant Colonel John McEnery. Perceived as an "outsider," Kellogg was also unpopular for appointing a number of African Americans during his administration. The White League rebels, whose former demand for Kellogg's resignation was denied, attempted to overthrow the existing government through physical force during the Battle of Liberty Place. By the end of the day on September 15, the White Leaguers "had occupied all the city's police stations and state arsenals, confiscating 1,600 rifles, 46,000 rounds of ammunition, and four cannon." They also replaced Kellogg with Confederate Colonel David B. Penn as Governor. The Confederate forces, however, surrendered on September 17 after receiving word that the massive federal reinforcements that President Grant had requested to restore the legitimate government were on their way to Louisiana (Dawson 1982, 170–74). After General Philip Sheridan, another federal appointee who assumed control of the Department of the Gulf on January 4, 1875, had declared the White Leaguers "banditti" on January 5 for their revolt, the Twelfth Night Revelers announced the cancellation of their Ball of 1875 by issuing these militaristic invitations (Gill 1997, 120–21).

Examining Shakespeare's *Twelfth Night* in tandem with the cultural phenomenon of the New Orleans Twelfth Night Revelers ultimately reveals the extent to which popular, festival customs can be appropriated by elite groups for conservative, repressive, and violent purposes. The aristocratic figure of Sir Toby and merchant-class members of this New Orleans krewe make use of carnivalesque elements often linked with folk, "grass-root" rituals to guard against their fears and anxieties of socially mobile individuals gaining those rights and privileges they view as exclusively theirs. "Cakes and ale" and Lords of Misrule are central to the literal and figurative wars they wage in an attempt to restore their "romantic" vision of a rigidly hierarchical world favoring them. A number of white supremacists who were members of the Twelfth Night Revelers were former masters of slaves before the Civil War.

After the "Lost Cause," they were deprived of mastery permanently, not only for the duration of the festive time of Carnival and Mardi Gras. Although folk celebrations of Twelfth Night, Shrove Tuesday, and Mardi Gras featured servants ruling masters temporarily, the Twelfth Night Revelers attempted to reinvert carnivalesque inversions of the status quo by reestablishing the social hierarchy of master over servant – a politically regressive rather than progressive move. Like the White Leaguers, who were armed with bayonets and cannons during the Battle of Liberty Place, merchant-class members of the Twelfth Night Revelers equipped themselves with satirical parades, exclusive balls, and canonical texts in order to attack those who largely succeeded in toppling their hierarchical pyramid in post-war Louisiana.

Notes

1. See Barber (1963, 3–15, 24–30, and 240–61); Bristol (1985, 140–41 and 202–4); Laroque (1991, 227–28 and 255–56); Gash (1995); and Cale-Feldman (1998, 215–28).
2. To the best of my knowledge only Reinecke discusses the parallel between Shakespeare's *Twelfth Night* and Louisiana holiday traditions (1965, 49). I am grateful to folklorist Marcia Gaudet, Dr. Doris Meriweather/Board of Regents Endowed Professor of English at the University of Louisiana at Lafayette, for referring me to this key source and a number of others for this project.
3. The term "krewe" refers to a group of individuals that organizes parades and balls during the Carnival season in New Orleans. Such krewes tend to feature large entourages of royalty during their parades.
4. See Zemon Davis (1975, 97–123); Le Roy Ladurie (1979, 229–63); and Underdown (1985, 44–72, esp. 47–48), for examples of riotous and rebellious carnivalesque celebrations. Burke cites a 1444 text written by French clerics who compared the usefulness of carnivalesque practices such as the Feast of Fools to providing an air-hole for a barrel to prevent it from bursting (1978, 201–2). See Kamps's discussion of Barber's safety-valve theory of "saturnalian holiday festivals" as providing a "release" of popular discontent but ultimately a "clarification" of "everyone's proper place" within the existing social hierarchy (Kamps, this volume, and Barber 1963, 4).
5. Interestingly, Hotson refers to those audience members who were watching Shakespeare's *Twelfth Night* during the Christmas holidays in 1600–1601 as "Twelfth Night revellers" (1954, 109). In the play itself Sir Andrew exclaims, "I delight in masques and revels sometimes together" (1.3.111–12). In addition, the Master of the Revels during the English Renaissance supervised and financed court entertainments and later became the censor of public plays.
6. All citations of *Twelfth Night* refer to the text edited by J. M. Lothian and T. M. Craik (Methuen, 1985).
7. Shakespeare scholars generally concur that Sir Toby Belch plays the part of the Lord of Misrule. See Bristol (1985, 202); Astington (1993, 126); and Gash (1995, 12). Spens (1916) is one of the first to note that the "resemblance of Sir Toby Belch to the titular Lord of Misrule is glaring" (41–42).
8. The twelfth day of December refers to the advent of Christmas and is perhaps a misquotation and comic error for the popular seventeenth-century ballad "The Twelve Days of Christmas": (Shakespeare 1985, 48–49).

9. As Kamps states, the "battle to preserve an absolute difference between commoner and aristocrat may therefore already be lost" in *Twelfth Night*.
10. In nineteenth-century New Orleans aggression during Mardi Gras celebrations sometimes took the form of duels: Mitchell (1995, 41).
11. Rambuss states that members of the secret society of Comus were "professionals and merchants" and largely "middle-class" (2000, 47 and 54).
12. Gill notes that a national economic depression deepened the woes of Confederates whose wealth and resources were already diminished by the war (1997, 105).
13. See Kinser (1990, 101) and Rambuss (2000, 61). According to Mitchell, "Carnival allowed white supremacists both to mock their enemies and to create a fantasy world in which they were absolute" (1995, 80).

Works cited

Arlidge, Anthony. *Shakespeare and the Prince of Love: The Feast of Misrule in the Middle Temple*. London: Giles de la Mare, 2000.

Astington, John. "Malvolio and the Eunuchs: Texts and Revels in *Twelfth Night*." *Shakespeare Survey* 46 (1993): 23–34.

Aubrey, John. *Remains of Gentilisme and Judaisme (1686–7)*. Ed. James Britten. London, 1881.

Bakhtin, Mikhail. *Rabelais and His World*. Trans. Hélène Iswolsky. Cambridge, MA: MIT Press, 1965.

Barber, C. L. *Shakespeare's Festive Comedy: A Study of Dramatic Form and Its Relation to Social Custom*. Princeton, NJ: Princeton University Press; New York: Meridian, 1963.

Billington, Sandra. *Mock Kings in Medieval Society and Renaissance Drama*. Oxford: Clarendon Press, 1991.

Bristol, Michael D. *Carnival and Theater: Plebian Culture and the Structure of Authority in Renaissance England*. New York: Methuen, 1985.

Burke, Peter. *Popular Culture in Early Modern Europe*. New York: New York University Press, 1978.

Cahill, Edward. "The Problem of Malvolio." *College Literature* 23 (1996): 62–82.

Cale-Feldman, Lada. "Engendered Heritage: Shakespeare's Illyria Travested." *Journal of Ethnology and Folklore Research* 35 (1998): 215–31.

Carnegie, David. "'Maluolio within': Performance Perspectives on the Dark House." *Shakespeare Quarterly* 52 (2001): 393–414.

Chambers, E. K. *The Medieval Stage*. Vol. 1. Oxford: Oxford University Press, 1925.

The Daily Picayune, January 7, 1870.

Davis, Natalie Zemon. "The Reasons of Misrule." In *Society and Culture in Early Modern France*. Stanford, CA: Stanford University Press, 1975: 97–123.

Dawson, Joseph G., III. *Army Generals and Reconstruction: Louisiana, 1862–1877*. Baton Rouge: Louisiana State University Press, 1982.

Dekker, Thomas. *The Dramatic Works of Thomas Dekker*. Vol. 1. Ed. Fredson Bowers. Cambridge: Cambridge University Press, 1953.

Dionne, Craig, and Steve Mentz, eds. "Introduction: Rogues and Early Modern English Culture." In *Rogues and Early Modern English Culture*. Ann Arbor: University of Michigan Press, 2004: 1–29.

Dusinberre, Juliet. "Pancakes and a Date for *As You Like It*." *Shakespeare Quarterly* 54 (2003): 371–405.

Gash, Anthony. "Carnival against Lent: The Ambivalence of Medieval Drama." In *Medieval Literature: Criticism, Ideology, and History*. Ed. David Aers. New York: St. Martin's Press, 1986: 74–98.

——. "Bidding Farewell to Carnival: The Politics of *Twelfth Night*." *Q/W/E/R/T/Y* 5 (1995): 11–19.

Gill, James. *Lords of Misrule: Mardi Gras and the Politics of Race in New Orleans*. Jackson: University of Mississippi Press, 1997.

Hainsworth, D. R. *Stewards, Lords, and People: The Estate Steward and His World in Later Stuart England*. Cambridge: Cambridge University Press, 1992.

Halpern, Richard. *The Poetics of Primitive Accumulation: English Renaissance Culture and the Genealogy of Capital*. Ithaca, NY: Cornell University Press, 1991.

Henisch, Bridget Ann. *Cakes and Characters: An English Christmas Tradition*. London: Prospect Books, 1984.

Herrick, Robert. *The Poetical Works of Robert Herrick*. Ed. L. C. Martin. Oxford: Clarendon Press, 1956.

Hotson, Leslie. *The First Night of Twelfth Night*. New York: Macmillan, 1954.

Kendall, John S. *The Golden Age of the New Orleans Theater*. Baton Rouge: Louisiana State University Press, 1952.

Kinser, Samuel. *Carnival, American Style: Mardi Gras at New Orleans and Mobile*. Chicago: University of Chicago Press, 1990.

Laroque, François. *Shakespeare's Festive World: Elizabethan Seasonal Entertainment and the Professional Stage*. Trans. Janet Lloyd. Cambridge: Cambridge University Press, 1991.

Le Roy Ladurie, Emmanuel. *Carnival in Romans*. Trans. Mary Feeney. New York: George Braziller, 1979.

Malcolmson, Christina. "'What You Will': Social Mobility and Gender in *Twelfth Night*." In *New Casebooks: Twelfth Night*. Ed. R. S. White. New York: St. Martin's Press, 1996: 160–93.

Marcus, Leah. *The Politics of Mirth: Jonson, Herrick, Milton, Marvell, and the Defense of Old Holiday Pastimes*. Chicago: University of Chicago Press, 1986.

Mitchell, Reid. *All on a Mardi Gras Day: Episodes in the History of New Orleans Carnival*. Cambridge, MA: Harvard University Press, 1995.

Northrop, Douglas A. "Shakespeare's *Twelfth Night*," *Explicator* 53 (1995): 191–92.

Oxford English Dictionary.

Phythian-Adams, Charles. "Ceremony and the Citizen: The Communal Year at Coventry, 1450–1500." In *Crisis and Order in English Towns, 1500–1700*. Ed. Peter Clark and Paul Slack. London: Routledge and Kegan Paul, 1972: 57–85.

Rambuss, Richard, "Spenser and Milton at Mardi Gras: English Literature, American Cultural Capital, and the Reformation of New Orleans Carnival." *Boundary* 2.27 (2000): 45–72.

Reinecke, George F. "The New Orleans Twelfth Night Cake," *Louisiana Folklore Miscellany* 2 (1965): 45–54.

Roppolo, Joseph Patrick. "Shakespeare in New Orleans, 1817–1865." In *Shakespeare in the South: Essays on Performance*. Ed. Philip C. Kolin. Jackson: University Press of Mississippi, 1983: 112–27.

Shakespeare, William. *The Riverside Shakespeare*. Ed. G. Blakemore Evans. Boston: Houghton Mifflin, 1974.

——. *Twelfth Night*. Ed. J. M. Lothian and T. M. Craik. The Arden Shakespeare. London: Methuen, 1985.

Spens, Janet. *An Essay on Shakespeare's Relation to Tradition*. Oxford: Blackwell, 1916.

Stallybrass, Peter, and Allon White. *The Politics and Poetics of Transgression*. Ithaca: Cornell University Press, 1986.

Underdown, David. *Revel, Riot, and Rebellion: Popular Politics and Culture in England, 1603–1660*. Oxford: Oxford University Press, 1985.

Webster, John. *The Duchess of Malfi*. Ed. Brian Gibbons. New York: Norton, 2001.

Wright, A. R. *British Calendar Customs*. Vol. 2: *Fixed Festivals: January–May, Inclusive*. Nendelm: Kraus, 1968.

Young, Perry. *Mistick Krewe: Chronicles of Comus and His Kin*. New Orleans: Carnivell Press, 1931.

15 Whodunit?

Plot, plotting, and detection in *Twelfth Night*

Cynthia Lewis

> it is clear that life is always in some way too fast for us, that it is a spectacle we can't interpret or a dumbshow difficult to word. The detective novel allows us to catch up a little by involving us in the interpretation of a mystery that seems at first to have no direct bearing on our life. We soon realize, of course, that 'mystery' means that something is happening too fast to be spotted. We are made to experience a consciousness . . . always behind and running; vulnerable therefore, perhaps imposed on.
>
> Geoffrey Hartman (1975, 215)

Twelfth Night, of course, is no detective novel. But, as a narrative, it exploits elements of detective fiction – a form little dreamt of in the early seventeenth century – for purposes both like and unlike those of the later genre. The play contains no corpse – the *sine qua non* of the detective story. Nor does it include what S. S. Van Dine, creator of detective Philo Vance, describes as a single, clear "culprit" (1947, 191). Its fabulous plotting, however – one of its most salient and famed features – resonates with detective fiction and is based largely on the characters' plotting in an effort to deceive one another. Such self-conscious internal plotting not only calls attention to the outer play's construction as artifice; it continually places the characters in a position to detect – to perceive past the obvious and put together clues so as to divine the truth.[1] Viola's soliloquy in 2.2 is a prime example. While the fatuous Malvolio cannot conceive that Olivia has been dishonest about where the ring came from, Viola quickly senses, upon having the ring thrust her way, that she has "charm'd" Olivia (2.2.18). Later, the revelers count on Malvolio's acknowledged "self-love" to prevent him from riddling past M.O.A.I. to understand that he is not beloved, but ridiculed (1.5.90, 2.5).

Many of Shakespeare's plot elaborations in other plays also stem from characters' internal plotting for the purpose of deceiving others, as in *A Midsummer Night's Dream*, *Much Ado About Nothing*, and *As You Like It*, to name a few. Almost as often, at least one instance of the characters' plotting becomes the hinge between a lighter and a darker tone – for example,

Oberon's manipulation of Titania, Don John's duping of Claudio and Don Pedro, and *Twelfth Night*'s prison scene (4.2). At the same time, these plays owe a great deal of their humor to the dramatic irony arising from innocuous or playful instances of misleading a character – the duping scenes of Benedick and Beatrice (2.3, 3.1), the lovers' mix-up in *Dream*, and the letter scene in *Twelfth Night* (2.5), as well as Viola's disguise. Many of these comedies end without the characters' ever becoming aware of the plots against them – for example, Helena, Demetrius, Beatrice, and Benedick. The pleasure that audience members take in these cases, whether outright laughter or smug satisfaction, derives largely from their privileged position: the audience knows more than the characters who have been fooled, even as the play closes. In an instance like Titania's, an audience might well react with discomfort or distaste toward Oberon's violative, covert means of getting his way.

At the conclusion of *Twelfth Night*, however, the characters' confusions, which the audience has known about up until the dénouement, are laid bare within the scope of the play, whether Olivia's and Orsino's mistaken perceptions, brought about by Viola's disguise; the true author of the letter dropped in Malvolio's path; or the identity of Sir Topas: "I was one, sir, in this enterlude – one Sir Topas, sir, but that's all one" (5.1.372–73). So much for the audience's superior stance.

By the time of Feste's closing song, in fact, dozens of revelations have occurred to the characters while nearly as many have been withheld from the audience. Some, like the fates of Malvolio and Antonio, are both obvious and crucial unknowns. Malvolio's reasons for imprisoning the sea captain in possession of Viola's clothes and the exact location of those clothes also escape explanation, and, although the characters seem certain that Viola will retrieve her outward female identity, the audience may be left wondering. Similarly, Orsino's command to "[p]ursue" Malvolio "and entreat him to a peace" implies more confidence in the prospect of the characters' easy reconciliation with Malvolio than the audience may share (5.1.380). Other, smaller questions that have emerged throughout the play are never answered – for example, why Viola first embraces the notion of disguising herself as a eunuch (1.2), then later appears as a boy page (1.4), and why Sebastian adopts a false name – Roderigo – that he exposes to Antonio in their first scene together, 2.1.[2] Shakespeare's vulnerability to forgetting details like Viola's initial choice of a eunuch's identity aside, the play would seem to include too many examples of unresolved plot elements to be construed as accidental.

Some critics have attempted to minimize or contextualize these loose ends, either asserting the play's final closure or justifying its lack of closure in artistic terms. The most vocal of these critics, Ejner J. Jensen seeks to demonstrate that some of the elements at the end deemed most problematic, like Orsino's easy acceptance of Viola/Cesario as his bride, are prepared for earlier in the play, as when Orsino and Viola "pre-enact a closeness" in 2.4 "that is promised but deferred in the actual closure of the play" (1991, 110). Jensen concludes that "closure in *Twelfth Night*, far from . . . being problematic, is a dramatically skillful realization of connections prepared for and pre-enacted in the play's earlier events" (117). Jensen, however, does not deal with all of the strands that remain unresolved in act 5 – for example, the matter of Antonio's fate – and perhaps oversimplifies others – for instance, by denying that Malvolio deserves much sympathy from the audience during and following 4.2 (114–15). Even more sanguine about the play's coherence, Trevor Nunn, who directed the movie version in 1996, has deemed *Twelfth Night* a "perfect," "complete" work of art, a judgment now canonized in the *Norton Anthology of English Literature*.[3] Anne Barton, who does not attribute quite such perfection to the play, nevertheless discusses its ending as an extension of Shakespeare's art. Comparing and contrasting *As You Like It* and *Twelfth Night* in terms of their balance between romance and realism – or between comic resolution and its qualifications – Barton finds less poise in the later play: "In *Twelfth Night*, . . . the fragmentation only hinted at in the last scene of *As You Like It* became actual, as Shakespeare began to unbuild his own comic form at its point of greatest vulnerability: the ending" (1994, 104).

Whether what Shakespeare is up to is "unbuilding" his own comic form is another matter, and one that I shall return to below, but the view implied by Barton that Shakespeare had somehow become weary of or unconvinced by the conventional comic resolution is common among audiences who find the play's ending jarring, amiss, or incomplete. I am arguing, though, that inconsistencies and mysteries of plot pervade not just the ending, but the entire play. Some audience members will simply be more sensitive than others to these elements, and, while many of the elements may be less obvious in the theatre, where the play glides by, than to a reader (and, by the same token, more obvious to a re-reader), I would argue that, whether consciously or subliminally, most audiences will pick up on at least some of them. Taken together, they constitute a critical mass. Why do they proliferate, what is their nature, and what is their purpose?

Most obviously, the unsolved mysteries of *Twelfth Night*'s plot cast audience members in a role much like the one in which the characters often find themselves – a kind of detective role. In most cases of characters (rather than the audience) being deceived, the question is one of identity – literally, who is who and who did what. Who gave whom the ring that Malvolio throws to Viola/Cesario in 2.2? Who wrote the letter in 2.5? To whom did Antonio give his purse in 3.3 and from whom does he attempt to reclaim it in 3.4? Who speaks to Malvolio in 4.2? Whom does Olivia marry? Who is who in 5.1? Yet the same audience members who may gloat, along with the revelers, over Malvolio's being tricked by the letter may eventually find themselves baffled, as Malvolio eventually becomes, by what they do not understand about the larger play or know about its outcome.

Pondering the plot's loose ends reveals that those matters, too, involve mainly identity and agency. So, for example, while the question of Sebastian's identity may be resolved in relation to the characters' experience within the play, why he ever needed to adopt the pseudonym "Roderigo" is an issue left dangling. Did he do so in order to protect Antonio from getting further enmeshed in his bad luck? How changing his name would protect Antonio, rather than himself, is not immediately evident. This apparently dead-end detail suggests another narrative – a sub-narrative – knowledge of which is shared between its participants, Sebastian and Antonio, but is unavailable to the audience. The sub-narrative involving the unnamed sea captain and Malvolio appears of the same ilk. Has Malvolio incarcerated Viola's confederate out of his general ill will, or did the captain, belying the "fair behaviour" that Viola once chose to believe in, deserve Malvolio's punishment (1.2.47)? Only Malvolio and the sea captain would know for sure.

* * *

The notion that these questions force is that *Twelfth Night* is more of a slice of life than is your average, everyday fairy tale or romantic comedy. Or, for that matter, detective story. As narrative theorist Peter J. Rabinowitz observes, detective fiction appeals to an audience through rewarding a reader's attempted detection with closure: "[Classical detective fictions] traditionally end with explicit solutions for those readers who have not been able to fill in the gaps on their own. In fact, the pleasure of the text in detective stories resides primarily in the reader's *inability* to figure out what has happened until told" (1987, 150). As Rabinowitz explains, the reader's expectations of coherence may be temporarily frustrated, but never truly in doubt (149–50); that a rational structure and explanation will ultimately prevail is one of the givens of detective fiction. The reader's intelligence, as Geoffrey Hartman asserts, may not compare to that of the "hero-detective," but a reader's ability to trust the higher intelligence of her "co-deductor" (to borrow Van Dine's word) and author is a chief source of pleasure (Hartman 1975, 219, Van Dine 1947, 190–91). In general, the plot of detective fiction provides the gratifying reassurance of knowing that, if life is crowded with too much information and too many options, the intimate intellectual contact between the individual audience and the author/detective will unveil a single, right "interpretation," a "thread of logic" (Hartman 1975, 207; Van Dine 1947, 190).[4]

Nearly all of this description applies to the conventions of romantic comedy, as well as detective fiction, and the profuse epiphanies at the end of a play whose very title alludes to Epiphany underscore the comic resolution of rampant confusion. The skill with which the playwright accomplishes the unraveling (a dénouement unmatched in spectacular complexity except by that in *Cymbeline* and possibly in *All's Well That Ends Well*) and the generosity of the romantic characters once their folly is exposed must help account for the assessment by some readers and theatre practitioners like Nunn that *Twelfth Night* is an artistic masterpiece. The satisfaction of watching how the playwright brings about the characters' discovery of truth is akin to discovering the truth itself, since the audience is still aligning itself as co-deductor with the author.

Conversely, the audience's understanding of many aspects of the play's plot is frustrated by a final proliferation of interpretation, creating an undertow to its artistic coherence. To use the terms of narratologist Emma Kafalenos, much information about the characters' plotting is "deferred" for them, while some knowledge of Shakespeare's plot is "suppressed" for the audience (1999, 35). The "narrative gaps" in the characters' understanding, in other words, are mostly "temporary"; many of those in the audience's are "permanent" (48). Kafalenos argues that permanent gaps can lend narrative "much of the open-ended play of signification characteristic of life," which itself "offers endless versions of fabulas that serve as configurations in relation to which we interpret, reinterpret, or . . . fail to reinterpret given events" (37, 59–60). Most basically, in the narrative pattern that she describes as lifelike, each new piece of information alters the audience's perception of what has come before, warranting a reinterpretation of previous assumptions. An audience member who embraces Marc Antony's funeral oration with the enthusiasm of a plebian only to recoil two scenes later when Antony, Octavius, and Lepidus mark various Romans for extinction exhibits what Kafalenos calls the "primacy effect" – that is, "our tendency to accept as valid the information we are initially given, even when that information is contradicted later in the same message" (57).

Elements of Antonio's backstory in *Twelfth Night* both illustrate this primacy effect and complicate it, since new information about the sea captain is often less clear-cut than my example of Marc Antony. Some new information about Antonio is itself muddled or contradictory, thus elaborating not only on character, as in Antony's case, but also doing so in ways that resist interpretation and enhance the audience's experience of Antonio's mysteriousness as lifelike.

In his first scene, Antonio is decidedly a lover, not a tyrant, offering himself as Sebastian's "servant" (2.1.35–36). At the scene's end, he attests only that he has "many enemies in Orsino's court," but does not say why (45). That explanation begins to surface in his next scene, 3.3, where he says that he was once engaged in a "sea-fight 'gainst the Count his galleys," but adds that his "service" in the fight actually involved no bloodshed, although it might have under other circumstances (26, 27, 30–32). But if the "quarrel" eschewed bloodshed, one might ask, what made it a fight (31)? Antonio intimates that, in an intense argument of principle with Orsino, he took property from the Count in order to register disagreement with him; when the others who also stole from Orsino restored his possessions in order to regain passage in waters governed by the Count, only Antonio "stood out" (33–37). Given what the audience knows at this point about Antonio's "sharp" "desire" to serve Sebastian and about his past entanglement with Orsino, Antonio might well appear a pacifist and conscientious objector to some unspecified injustice at the hands of a shady ruler (2.1.5, 4).

Orsino challenges that reading when he confronts Antonio in 5.1, but he does not exactly subvert it. He begins by giving Antonio credit for accomplishing as much as he did against his own "most noble . . . fleet" with only a "baubling vessel," even styling Antonio a hero (57, 54, 58–59). He goes on, however, to accuse Antonio of outright piracy, and his first officer, corroborating his commander's sense of injury, testifies that the fight at sea, contrary to Antonio's earlier narration, was indeed bloody, since "this is he that did the *Tiger* board, / When your young nephew Titus lost his leg" (69, 62–63). Now the battle appears to have been violent, though the officer does not confirm, but rather implies, that Antonio's action cost Titus his leg.[5] If Orsino's charges and his officer's innuendoes are true, Antonio's character is as blackened as his face "in the smoke of war" (5.1.53). But Antonio does not back down:

> Orsino, noble sir,
> Be pleas'd that I shake off these names you give me.
> Antonio never yet was thief or pirate,
> Though I confess, on base and ground enough,
> Orsino's enemy.
>
> (5.1.72–76)

The question "whodunit?" applies not only literally – as in who hurt Titus? – but also to the audience's impression of Antonio's character. Who *is* he?

Antonio's behavior toward Viola/Cesario amplifies the question. Believing that she is Sebastian, Antonio intercedes to rescue her in 3.4 with Christ-like language: "If this young gentleman / Have done offense, I take the fault on me" (312–13). His willingness to sacrifice himself for this youth recalls his extravagant generosity in giving Sebastian his entire purse, should he desire "some toy" (3.3.44). When Viola/Cesario refuses him the same purse in 3.4, offering him "half" her "coffer" instead, her reserve contrasts with Antonio's generosity even as that generosity eerily reverses itself (347). He harangues the boy for "deny[ing]" him at his time of need, implying that Sebastian owes him payment for rescuing him earlier at sea and for his "devotion" (347, 359–63). Antonio's unconditional love has overtones of account-keeping. In 5.1, when Antonio again mistakes Viola/Cesario for Sebastian, he again confuses the issue of his motive: "That most ingrateful boy there by your side / From the rude sea's enrag'd and foamy mouth / Did I redeem" (77–79). Despite many other suggestions that Antonio has freely restored Sebastian's life, without condition, Antonio here expects gratitude for his "dedication" to Sebastian (82).

Rabinowitz posits three ways that narrative coherence may be interrupted, the first two of which apply in Antonio's case:

> First, texts can be insufficient – that is, they can be apparently incoherent because of gaps in their fabric, holes that need to be filled in. Second, works can be overabundant – they can have a surplus of information that we need somehow to tame, including details that seem to contradict one another and that we need to reconcile.
>
> (Rabinowitz 1987, 148)

Paradoxically, the audience does not know enough to judge which of the several conflicting details and stories to believe about Antonio's actions and character. That Antonio's fate is the least resolved of any character at the play's end seems in keeping with the murkiness about him up to that point.[6] In contrast with Malvolio's sense of injury, which Orsino addresses (5.1.380), the chains that bind Antonio are not so much as mentioned. The first instance involves (indefinitely) deferred information; the second, suppressed information. Critics have discussed Antonio's imprisonment, which extends outside the narrative boundaries of the play, thematically, including the view that it sequesters his homoerotic feelings toward Sebastian to make room for the heterosexual unions requisite to romantic comedy.[7] But it also presents an obstacle to reading the play coherently, resisting the play's artificial unity.

* * *

The discrepancy between a formulaic, unified romantic comedy and a play that, like *Twelfth Night*, cracks a window on the disordered world just beyond its boundaries comes close, I think, to the difference between crime fiction and crime reporting. As someone who writes about actual crime, I am familiar with the frustration of not being able to discover whodunit.

Recently, I wrote about the best known unsolved homicide in the area where I live – Charlotte, North Carolina. The victim, a 32-year-old newly adoptive mother and NOW activist, was found by her husband in July of 1990, brutally slain in her dining room. To this day, a murder case can be made against each of two men: her husband and a handy-man who lived nearby and had done some work for her. My article, entitled "Either / Or," outlines the evidence against each man, as well as the intricate plot that ensued from the killing, including the arrest of the husband and the dismissal of the charges against him once the key piece of evidence was ruled inadmissible in court, and then the husband's suing the handy-man for wrongful death (and winning). As I state in the article, I wrote about the case in hopes that keeping it in the public eye might contribute to its being solved, and yet I leave my readers with only an open-ended story representing a far cry from *Law and Order*. Reviewing a few of the American TV crime shows that have recently clogged the air waves,

Nancy Franklin has written in *The New Yorker* that "by solving crimes that often seem mind-bogglingly mysterious or unsolvable," the programs "create the comforting illusion that competence – having the right tools for the job – will conquer all; they give us a handle on our chaotic, nonsensical world" (2003, 104). Real crime reveals that, although some criminals get caught, the course of justice never did run smooth and sometimes whodunit simply escapes human understanding.

Why would a playwright destabilize or threaten to dismantle this play's comic structure and coherence by introducing realistic threads of the plot that elude understanding? What might be the purpose of arousing an audience's frustration at not knowing or being able to find out? Exploring the riddles in *Twelfth Night*, in which the tug and pull in the play's narrative find reflection, helps to focus this question of artistic purposes. Richard Horwich asserts that riddles, as distinct from dilemmas, always have answers. According to Horwich, "riddles are seldom answered through the exercise of pure logic alone, and often require an imaginative leap or insight of some sort, but that is not to say that they do not primarily engage the intellect" (1977, 193). Described thus, resolving a riddle bears close resemblance to solving a crime. Indeed, like a detective story, a riddle engages one mind with another, the riddler initially wielding power over the solver, but the solution of the riddle resulting in the marriage of two minds. This use of temporary power to effect a balance of power between two people makes the riddle especially appropriate for a female character who is attempting to bring about a satisfactory marriage with a man who first needs a comeuppance.

Not surprisingly, then, riddles are often gendered female – when they are not assigned to clowns – as Horwich implies when he identifies Belmont with riddles (and Venice with dilemmas) (1977, 197). Horwich illustrates how Portia uses the wedding ring as a riddle both to exert control over Bassanio and to claim him, through a choice independent of her father's casket test, as a husband who is taught to be worthy of her (199). Similarly, Mariana and Helena (through Diana) both use riddles to confuse and then lay claim to Angelo and Bertram as their husbands (*Measure for Measure* 5.1.195–99, 203–4, *All's Well That Ends Well* 5.3.300–304). Rosalind, too, uses riddle-like catechisms both to instruct Orlando in the realities of marriage and to veil who she is, and she signals her unveiling in a similar mode, as when she says to Phebe, "I will marry you, if ever I marry woman, and I'll be married tomorrow" (5.2.113–14). More often than not, the solutions to these riddles reveal identity, whether who presided over the trial in Venice, who slept with whom, or who will marry whom.[8] Those solutions epitomize, and form part of, the narrative unity of romantic comedy.

Many riddles in *Twelfth Night* operate in much the same way. Viola's cryptic lines like "I am not that I play" and "I am not what I am" beg the very question of her true identity that Olivia bluntly asks in 1.5: "What are you? What would you?" (1.5.184, 3.1.141, 1.5.212–13). The control over Olivia that

Viola's language briefly allows her evanesces once her identity comes to light and she is claimed as an equal – a "sister" – by the woman she once deceived (5.1.326). Likewise, Feste's riddling catechism of Olivia in 1.5, by her own testimony, helps to "mend" her spirit even as it proves her a "fool" (1.5.71–74). The resolution of such riddles coincides with, even results in, the establishment of social harmony.

The glaring exception to the rule is the M.O.A.I. in Maria's forged letter. That it is a "fustian riddle" – where *fustian* is taken as "nonsensical" – does not stop Malvolio from forcing it to identify himself (2.5.108 and n. to l. 108).[9] That it is "fustian" in the sense of "bombastic" suggests why so many critical attempts at its solution have been launched. That these efforts, apparently aimed at outsmarting Malvolio by supplying the true solution to the riddle, ultimately conflict with one another as a group and fail individually to solve the riddle convincingly says much about how the lack of resolution, both to the riddle and in the plot, functions.

To read just some of the critics' proposed solutions to M.O.A.I. in succession is to be struck by how closely they resemble Malvolio's own overconfident and strained decoding. Lee Sheridan Cox at least humbly submits that his solution – "I am O (Olivia)" – may be the second answer of two to the riddle (the other being "Malvolio") (1962, 360). According to Cox, Malvolio's inserting himself in the letter where Olivia makes more sense may emphasize "the foolish self-importance of the steward" (360). Alistair Fowler holds that M.O.A.I. is an anagram for *omnia*, spelled variously as "oia," "oma," "oi", and, yes, sometimes "omia" (1992, 269). Fowler further reasons that *omnia* alone suggests the "religious commonplace" OMNIA VANITAS, or "all is vanity," which "Malvolio's vanity keeps him from recognizing" (270). In a 25-page article that sneers at all others' speculation while advancing his own, Peter J. Smith argues that M.O.A.I. very clearly alludes to John Harrington's *The Metamorphosis Of A Iax*, a title not only referring to what Shakespeare, the characters, and the audience thought about Malvolio, but also, Smith assures us, so well known at the time that no one would have missed the connection (1998, 1215–22). All of these submissions share the opinion that Malvolio deserves ridicule for failing to decode the riddle properly and an obliviousness to how closely anyone else who attempts to solve the same insoluble riddle resembles the steward. Only R. Chris Hassel notices that "The amusing point of the episode is that Malvolio is already so taken with his own attractiveness that he can convince himself Olivia loves him with neither wit nor humor enough to unravel the fustian" (1974, 356). Equally amusing are critical stabs at inferring meaning where none exists – none except irony toward the very practice of forcing sense from nonsense.[10]

* * *

If M.O.A.I. is a trap for desiring and even imposing erroneous meaning, it is also a miniature model of possible responses to the larger play's lack of complete resolution, as well as of Shakespeare's possible motives for skirting closure. Two interpretations of those motives strike me as compelling. The first possibility is that the playwright seeks to retain control over the audience, rather than surrender or share it at the play's end. The trick on Malvolio renders Maria such control over her nemesis while shielding her from detection, a mode that Feste continually exploits. While Feste's interaction with Olivia about her melancholy in 1.5 suggests genuine concern for her, most of his verbal play and trickery keeps him in command and "o' th' windy side of the law" (3.4.164). His wise foolery with Viola/Cesario in 3.1 exemplifies this pattern in that he walks a line between delighting and insulting her. In turning the wrong side of her sentences outward, he offends her more than once, first by wishing she would go away and then by ironically calling her "your wisdom" and almost losing her as an audience and benefactor: "Nay, and thou pass upon me, I'll no more with thee" (12–43). As Viola comments in her soliloquy after Feste's exit, he is a kind of "haggard"; he likes the upper hand (60–69).

He also makes every effort to protect himself. Like Maria, he remains absent during the letter scene, which could, at any moment, careen out of control and result in trouble for everyone present. When he finally joins the trickery in 4.2, he needlessly disguises himself, as Maria points out, as if taking every precaution possible to guard his identity (64–65).[11] His refusal at the opening of 5.1 to let Fabian look at the letter from Malvolio suggests the same desire to orchestrate events while remaining immune from censure; his reading of the letter in a voice of his choosing – as if Malvolio were literally mad – also exerts control over and skews the interpretation of events (1–7, 282–300). Feste delivers his final and passive aggressive "revenge" on Malvolio so as to maximize Malvolio's humiliation while minimizing his peril: his speech on the "whirligig of time" takes the other characters by such surprise that they hardly have a chance to address the public spectacle of Malvolio's folly in the moment (370–77). They simply watch in amazement as Malvolio stomps off stage, vowing his own revenge (378). Feste has pulled off a masterful reprisal, quite out of proportion to the injury he suffered from Malvolio's "bird-bolt" of an insult in 1.5, and he is never called to account for having "notoriously abus'd" Malvolio (1.5.83–89, 93; 5.1.379). The wonder is that his clean escape from responsibility is never cited as another disturbing loose end about the ending.

Other readers will perhaps see nothing objectionable about Feste's treatment of Malvolio, which the steward, granted, somewhat invites. Still others may not see Feste as the character in *Twelfth Night* most closely associated with the playwright. Many readings of the play, however, hinge on how Feste is understood – and with good reason.[12] His manipulations, including taunting the frantic Malvolio in a dark prison, raise questions of tone that radiate throughout the entire play. Whether menacing or innocuous, those manipulations amount to an artistry akin to Shakespeare's, and they imply that, where the whole play is concerned, we are mocked with art. Feste's example, that is, aligns the play with the dark prison and Malvolio with Shakespeare's audience, while Shakespeare withholds enlightenment from us much as Feste withholds light from Malvolio (4.2.104–17).

Perhaps a Shakespeare disillusioned by standard romantic comedy and, even more to the point, jaded by his uncritical audience's unceasing demands for ever more of the same would incline, as Anne Barton surmises, to "unbuild" his familiar comic endings and, in the process, tease and taunt his viewers. *Twelfth Night* may savor of Jonsonian dyspepsia – particularly the thinly veiled contempt for the audience – though it is encased in the conventional trappings of romance.[13] Like Feste's humor, which hits and hurts even while it evokes laughter, *Twelfth Night* virtually disguises its lack of narrative closure with extravagant claims to the coming of a harmonious "golden time," when all will be resolved through marriage and reconciliation with Malvolio (5.1.382). Even so, all that glisters is not gold, "for the rain, it raineth every day" (5.1.392).

That reference to "golden time," however, points to another reading of the fissured plot, in which the dark reading just explored lightens considerably. Put succinctly, it is the view that artifice is but a shadow of perfect knowledge of truth. To stop short of completing a work of art, to resist answering all questions and solving all riddles, could well bespeak humility, rather than either the urge to tease an audience through exercising power over its members or the presumption that everything can be known and resolved.[14] This stance would be especially appropriate for a play concerning Epiphany in its many forms, including the moment in which divine love is incarnated and thus made known to the world. In such a moment, all approximations to perfection fall aside in the face of the real thing, as in *The Winter's Tale*, where Hermione as statue gives way to the living Hermione (5.3.103). Art, in fact, becomes obsolete, unneeded, because a representation of truth like *Twelfth Night* no longer serves a purpose. In this reading of the play's relative incompleteness, as in the case of the unsolved murder I have tracked, the truth is out there, but unavailable here: it exists outside the scope of the plot; it escapes human apprehension. Antonio's fate, the mysteries of his past, and a myriad of similar dangling matters involving what's what and who's who continue to dangle. From this perspective, too, we are mocked with art – not as fools, but, rather, resembling the way that the Chorus speaks of the play *Henry V*: "Yet sit and see, / Minding true things by what their mock'ries be" (4.Chorus.52–53). Much as a play cannot fully embody human experience, so human experience can provide but a hazy reflection of what will come to light through the matrix of time, whether before or after this life.[15]

Frank Kermode has written that, in a postmodern culture, "we still feel a need, harder than ever to satisfy because of an accumulated scepticism, to experience that concordance of beginning, middle, and end which is the essence of our explanatory fictions" – fictions that "help us to make sense of our lives" (1967, 35–36, 3). The absence of such total concordance need not signify postmodern chaos, but may posit early modern faith in perfect revelation whose time has simply not yet arrived. When Orsino asks Viola/Cesario whether her fictional sister (a stand-in for her actual self) "died" of her unrequited "love," she responds with a riddle that not even she can fathom: "I am all the daughters of my father's house, / And all the brothers too: and yet I know not" (2.4.119, 120–21). Neither presuming to know nor doubting that she will, she simply concedes that the plot is partly out of her hands.

Notes

1. Susan Baker, who writes about the presence and effect of Shakespeare in modern detective fiction, states that the "classic detective story deals with problems of evidence, interpretation, and proof" (1995, 428).
2. Kristian Smidt speculates that at least some of these small incongruities result from Shakespeare having changed his mind about certain details during the writing process (1993, 66–67).
3. Nunn's exact words are, "I happen to think 'Twelfth Night' is a masterpiece, a perfect work of art. There are not many things you can say that about. 'The Marriage of Figaro,' I think Chekhov's 'Three Sisters' is that, Jane Austen's 'Emma,' Billy Wilder's 'Some Like It Hot.' For each of those, you say: 'That's it. It's complete'" (quoted in Marks 1996, 18). *The Norton Anthology of English Literature*'s introduction to *Twelfth Night* refers to it as "both the most nearly perfect and in some sense the last of the great festive comedies" (Greenblatt 2006, 1077).
4. Baker discusses how the detective (and, by extension, the reader) who can follow this logic becomes, in the scheme of detective fiction, morally superior to characters who cannot keep up with it (see, e.g., 1995, 442–45). Viola/Cesario makes a similar link among perceptiveness, intelligence, and integrity about Feste, who

   must observe their mood on whom he jests,
   The quality of persons, and the time;
   And like a haggard, check at every feather
   That comes before his eye. This is a practice
   As full of labor as a wise man's art;
   For folly that he wisely shows is fit,
   But wise men, folly-fall'n, quite taint their wit.
   (3.1.62–68)

5. As I have noted elsewhere, the very name Titus both confuses the morality and further fragments this narrative element by pointing in two directions: one toward the pagan avenger Titus Andronicus (and thus involving a slick self-reference on Shakespeare's part) and the other toward Titus, St. Paul's friend (Lewis 1997, 95).
6. In an entirely different context, Valerie Forman notices that "The story of [Antonio's] purse is also left unresolved" (2003, 123). Assuming that the purse "contain[s] what was stolen from Orsino" (120), she adds: "Unlike the handkerchief in *Othello*

or the chain in *Comedy of Errors* whose circulations are crucial to the plot, the purse in *Twelfth Night* has no causal relation to the events of the play. The purse occupies an unusual position in that it is simultaneously central to the plot complications – a sign of mistaken identities and of Antonio's identity or history – and yet irrelevant to the plot itself" (123). Her assumption exemplifies how the play invites audience members to fill in some of the narrative gaps that remain open to an audience's imaginative speculation.

7. See, e.g., Osborne (1994, 108–14) and Traub (1992, 130–44).
8. Horwich remarks about the riddles in *The Merchant of Venice* that they all "ask the central question of the play: who is Portia, and where is she to be found?" (1977, 199).
9. *Fustian* is glossed differently by various editors. *The Riverside Shakespeare* defines it as "worthless, nonsensical," the sense with which I am mainly working in my essay. The Arden (Lothian and Craik), Norton (Greenblatt), and Longman (Bevington) editions all favor the gloss of "bombastic."
10. Leah Scragg has also worked out a hidden meaning for the C, U, T, P in 2.5.87–91, explaining how the letters point to the truncated word "*cut-P – – – –*," or *cut-Purse* – a warning to original audience members to look about them (1991, 16).
11. Once assured that Malvolio cannot see him, however, Feste is emboldened to extend the ruse even after Sir Toby calls for an end to it for fear of getting caught (4.2.67–71).
12. One example of many would be Karin S. Coddon, who sees Feste as the key figure by which the play's ambiguous views of class are manifested (e.g., 1993, 317–18).
13. In a discussion of *Twelfth Night* and Jonson's *Every Man in His Humor*, which looks at similarities between Shakespeare's and Jonson's plot elements (more than at the issue of tone), Ruth Morse agrees with David Bevington that "Shakespeare did indeed 'seriously flirt with Jonsonian satire in *Twelfth Night* . . .'" (2004, 190).
14. In keeping with the play's open-endedness and noting that the recovery of Viola's "maiden weeds" depends upon Malvolio's being "entreat[ed] to a peace," John Kerrigan observes that, "Until the steward is reconciled, comedy will not be consummated. Just how he will be persuaded remains one of the secrets of the play" (2001, 111–12).
15. For a relevant discussion of the workings of Providence in the play, see Maurice Hunt (1993).

Works cited

Abrams, M. H., ed. *The Norton Anthology of English Literature.* 7th edn., 2 vols. Vol. 1. New York: Norton, 2000.

Baker, Susan. "Shakespearean Authority in the Classic Detective Story." *Shakespeare Quarterly* 46 (1995): 424–48.

Barton, Anne. "*As You Like It* and *Twelfth Night*: Shakespeare's Sense of an Ending." In *Essays, Mainly Shakespearean*. Cambridge: Cambridge University Press, 1994: 91–112.

Bevington, David, ed. *The Complete Works of William Shakespeare*. 4th edn. New York: Longman, 1997.

Coddon, Karin S. "'Slander in an Allow'd Fool: *Twelfth Night*'s Crisis of the Aristocracy." *SEL* 33 (1993): 309–25.

Cox, Lee Sheridan. "The Riddle in *Twelfth Night*." *Shakespeare Quarterly* 13 (1962): 360.

Forman, Valerie. "Material Dispossessions and Counterfeit Investments: The Economies of *Twelfth Night*." In *Money and the Age of Shakespeare*. Ed. Linda Woodbridge. New York: Palgrave Macmillan, 2003: 113–27.

Fowler, Alistair. "Maria's Riddle." *Connotations* 23 (1992): 269–70.

Franklin, Nancy. "Criminal Justice." *The New Yorker* 79.6 (March 31, 2003): 104–5.

Greenblatt, Stephen, gen. ed. *The Norton Anthology of English Literature*. 8th edn. Vol. 1. New York: Norton, 2006.

Hartman, Geoffrey. "Literature High and Low: The Case of the Mystery Story." In *The Fate of Reading and Other Essays*. Chicago: University of Chicago Press, 1975: 203–22.

Hassel, R. Chris. "The Riddle in *Twelfth Night* Simplified." *Shakespeare Quarterly* 25 (1974): 356.

Horwich, Richard. "Riddle and Dilemma in *The Merchant of Venice." SEL* 17 (1977): 191–200.

Hunt, Maurice. "Malvolio, Viola, and the Question of Instrumentality: Defining Providence in *Twelfth Night*." *Studies in Philology* 90 (1993): 277–97.

Jensen, Ejner J. *Shakespeare and the Ends of Comedy*. Bloomington: Indiana University Press, 1991.

Kafalenos, Emma. "Not (Yet) Knowing: Epistemological Effects of Deferred and Suppressed Information in Narrative." In *Narratologies*. Ed. David Herman. Columbus: Ohio State University Press, 1999: 33–65.

Kermode, Frank. *The Sense of an Ending.* New York: Oxford University Press, 1967.

Kerrigan, John. "Secrecy and Gossip in *Twelfth Night*." In *On Shakespeare and Early Modern Literature.* Oxford: Oxford University Press, 2001: 89–112.

Lewis, Cynthia. "Either/Or." *Charlotte Magazine* 11.6 (June 2006): 106–14 and 11.7 (July 2006): 100–107+.

——. *Particular Saints: Shakespeare's Four Antonios, Their Contexts, and Their Plays.* Newark: University of Delaware Press, 1997.

Lothian, J. M., and T. W. Craik, eds. *Twelfth Night.* Arden edn. London: Routledge, 1975.

Marks, Peter. "So Young, So Fragile, So Vexed about Sex." *New York Times* October 20, 1996: H13+.

Morse, Ruth. "What City, Friends, Is This?" In *Plotting Early Modern London: New Essays on Jacobean City Comedy.* Ed. Dieter Mehl, Angela Stock, and Anne-Julia Zwierlein. Burlington, VT: Ashgate, 2004: 177–91.

Osborne, Laurie E. "Antonio's Pardon." *Shakespeare Quarterly* 45 (1994): 108–14.

Rabinowitz, Peter J. *Before Reading: Narrative Conventions and the Politics of Interpretation.* Columbus: Ohio State University Press, 1987.

Scragg, Leah. "'Her C's, Her U's, and Her T's: Why That? A New Reply for Sir Andrew Aguecheek." *Review of English Studies* n.s. 42 (1991): 1–16.

Shakespeare, William. *The Norton Shakespeare.* Ed. Stephen Greenblatt et al. New York: Norton, 1997.

——. *All's Well That Ends Well.* In *The Riverside Shakespeare*. Ed. G. Blakemore Evans and J. M. M. Tobin. 2nd edn. Boston: Houghton, 1997: 538–78.

——. *As You Like It.* In *The Riverside Shakespeare*: 403–34.
——. *Julius Caesar.* In *The Riverside Shakespeare*: 1151–78.
——. *The Life of Henry V.* In *The Riverside Shakespeare*: 979–1020.
——. *Measure for Measure.* In *The Riverside Shakespeare*: 584–21.
——. *A Midsummer Night's Dream.* In *The Riverside Shakespeare*: 256–80.
——. *Much Ado About Nothing.* In *The Riverside Shakespeare*: 366–96.
——. *Twelfth Night.* In *The Riverside Shakespeare*: 442–74.
——. *The Winter's Tale.* In *The Riverside Shakespeare*: 1617–54.
Smidt, Kristian. *Unconformities in Shakespeare's Later Comedies.* New York: St. Martin's Press, 1993.
Smith, Peter J. "M.O.A.I. 'What Should That Alphabetical Position Portend?' An Answer to the Metamorphic Malvolio." *Renaissance Quarterly* 51 (1998): 1199–224.
Traub, Valerie. *Desire and Anxiety: Circulations of Sexuality in Shakespearean Drama.* New York: Routledge, 1992.
Van Dine, S. S. "Twenty Rules for Writing Detective Stories." In *The Art of the Mystery Story: A Collection of Critical Essays.* Ed. Howard Haycraft. New York: Brossett and Dunlap/Universal Library, 1947: 189–93.

Index

Page numbers referring to illustrations are in *italics*; chapters from this book are in **bold**.